Reinventing India

For the memory of our friend and mentor B. H. (Ben) Farmer, Reader in the Geography of South Asia, Fellow of St John's College, and long-time Director of the Centre of South Asian Studies in the University of Cambridge.

Reinventing India

Liberalization, Hindu Nationalism and Popular Democracy

Stuart Corbridge and John Harriss

Polity

First published in 2000 by Polity Press in association with Blackwell Publishers Ltd

Editorial office:
Polity Press
65 Bridge Street
Cambridge CB2 1UR, UK

Marketing and production:
Blackwell Publishers Ltd
108 Cowley Road
Oxford OX4 1JF, UK

Published in the USA by
Blackwell Publishers Inc.
Commerce Place
350 Main Street
Malden, MA 02148, USA

ISBN 0-7456-2076-0
ISBN 0-7456-2077-9 (pbk)

A catalogue record for this book is available from the British Library.

Library of Congress Cataloging-in-Publication Data
Corbridge, Stuart.
    Reinventing India: liberalization, Hindu nationalism and popular democracy / Stuart Corbridge and John Harriss.
        p. cm.
    Includes bibliographical references and index.
    ISBN 0-7456-2076-0—ISBN 0-7456-2077-9 (pbk.)
    1. India—Politics and government—1947- I. Harriss, John. II. Title.

    DS480.84.C783 2000
    954.04—dc21

                                                                00-039986

Typeset in 10 on 11.5 pt Times
by Kolam Information Services Pvt Ltd, Pondicherry, India
Printed and bound in Great Britain by Marston Book Services Limited, Oxford

This book is printed on acid-free paper.

Contents

Acknowledgements

Both of us have researched in and on India throughout our professional lives, and this book is in part our attempt to make sense of that experience, stepping far beyond the particular engagements of our 'field' researches in Tamil Nadu, Bihar, Orissa and West Bengal. In its conception, design and writing, the book has involved each of us in equal measure; we hope that readers will find no awkward seams in our text.

We are grateful to a number of friends and colleagues for sharing with us some of their own experiences as citizens or students of India, and for encouraging us in this venture: thank you, then, to Jim Bentall, Arvind Das, Haris Gazdar, Anil K. Gupta, Ronald Herring, Craig Jeffrey, Sarah Jewitt, Sudipta Kaviraj, Sanjay Kumar, Satish Kumar, James Manor, Emma Mawdsley, Saraswati Raju, V. K. Ramachandran, Sunil Sengupta, Manoj Srivastava and Rene Veron. We are also grateful to Alpa Shah and Glyn Williams for commenting on the drafts of some chapters, and, most especially, to Barbara Harriss-White in Oxford and Meghnad Desai and Chris Fuller at the LSE for their many detailed comments. In several places we have indicated where one or other of them cannot be entirely exonerated from responsibility for the interpretations that we offer, although for the rest we alone are responsible. We would also like to thank two anonymous referees for their helpful comments on a first draft of the book; P. Jacob, Deputy Editor of 'Frontline' (Chennai) for his courteous assistance; and Sandra Byatt, Sarah Dancy, Lynn Dunlop, David Held and Anna Oxbury for their editorial advice and support.

We are also grateful to the University of Chicago Press for permission to reproduce as Map 1 a version of a map prepared by Matthew Edney for his book *Mapping an Empire: The Geographical Construction of British India 1765–1843* (1997); and to Oxford University Press (India) for permission to quote from P. Chatterjee, *A Possible India: Essays in Political Criticism* (1997).

And for so many gifts that have nothing (much) to do with writing books a specially big 'thank you' to Joan and Joanne, and to Gundi, Mark, Kaveri and Elinor.

S. C. and J. H.
Miami and London

Abbreviations

AICC	All-India Congress Committee
AIDMK	All-India Anna Dravida Munnetra Karagham
ASG	Alternative Survey Group
BAMCEF	All India Backward and Minority Employees' Federation
BJP	Bharatiya Janata Party
BKD	Bharatiya Kranti Dal
BLD	Bharatiya Lok Dal
BSP	Bahujan Samaj Party
CACP	Commission on Agricultural Costs and Prices
CPI	Communist Party of India
CPI(M)/CPM	Communist Party of India (Marxist)
CPI(M-L)	Communist Party of India (Marxist-Leninist)
CSP	Congress Socialist Party
DMK	Dravida Munnetra Karagham
ICS	Indian Civil Service
INC	Indian National Congress
JD	Janata Dal
MCC	Maoist Coordination Centre
MLAs	Members of the Legislative Assemblies
NSSO	National Sample Survey Organization
NRIs	Non-Resident Indians
OBCs	Other Backward Classes
RPI	Republican Party of India
RSS	Rashtriya Swayamsevak Sangh
SC	Scheduled Caste
ST	Scheduled Tribe
UNCTAD	United Nations Conference on Trade and Development

UP	Uttar Pradesh
VHP	Vishwa Hindu Parishad

Glossary

adivasi – original people; preferred name for Scheduled Tribes

ahimsa – reverence for animate life; non-violence

Akhand Bharat – undivided India

akhara – gymnasium

Backward Castes – low (mainly Shudra) caste, but not including Scheduled Castes or Untouchables; see also Other Backward Classes (or Castes) (OBCs)

Backward Classes – the 'weaker sections', generally consisting of the Scheduled Castes, Scheduled Tribes and Other Backward Classes

bahujan samaj – the common people

bhadralok – 'respectable folk' (Bengal)

bhakti – Hindu spiritual tradition laying stress on devotion

Bharat – India

Bharat Mata – Mother India

brahmacharya – celibacy

bullock capitalist – yeoman farmer; middle peasant

chakravartin – world conqueror-ruler

dacoit – robber, criminal

dalal – broker

dalit – Marathi word for Untouchable; the oppressed

desh – country

dirigiste – state-directed or dominated (in context of economic development)

Ekatmatayajna – the 'All-India Sacrifice for Unity' (politico-religious pilgrimage organized by the Vishwa Hindu Parishad in 1983)

garibi hatao – an 'end to poverty' (slogan of Indira Gandhi)

Gau Mata – Mother Cow

gurudwara – Sikh place of worship

Harijans – 'children of God'; term used by Mahatma Gandhi for 'unclean' or 'Untouchable' castes

Hindutva – literally 'Hindu-ness'; the idea of Hinduism as India's true national faith

Hindu Rashtra – the Hindu nation or state

hul – rebellion; uprising

izzat – honour

jati – caste in the sense of named 'birth group'

kar sevak – a volunteer in the movement to build a Ram temple at Ayodhya

Kayastha – literate/scribal caste of north India; now seen as 'high caste'

Khilafat Movement – movement to restore the Caliph (after World War I)

kisan – peasant

kisan raj – peasant rule

kulaks – rural power-holders, usually from the rich peasantry

kumbabhisekham – temple renovation rituals (especially Tamil Nadu)

mandir – Hindu temple

masjid – mosque

Naxalites – rural insurgents; well organized in Bihar and Andhra Pradesh; originally from West Bengal

Other Backward Classes (or Castes) (OBCs) – socially and educationally deprived communities (not including the Scheduled Castes or Tribes) for whom remedial actions are authorized by the Constitution

panchayat – council; institution of local government

panchayati Raj – official system of local self-government

pracharaks – full-time RSS (Rashtriya Swayamsevak Sangh) organizers

raiyat – tenant, sometimes peasant cultivator

raiyatwari – system of tenure in which tenants paid rent directly to government

ramshila – the 'bricks of Lord Rama'

rashtra – nation

Ramjanmabhoomi – movement to build a Ram temple at the site of the Babari Masjid in Ayodhya, Uttar Pradesh (the reputed site of Ram's birth)

sadhu – Hindu holy man; renunciant

Sanatan Dharm – orthodox or traditional (Brahman-led) Hindu religion

Sangh parivar – the RSS 'family' of organizations

sant – saint; holy man

sanyasi – Hindu renunciant

sarkar – government

sati – ritual self-immolation of Hindu widows

satyagraha – truth force; Gandhian politics of truthfulness and non-violent resistance

Scheduled Castes (SCs) – in effect, the official term for Untouchable castes; those castes recognized by the Constitution as deserving special assistance in respect of education, employment and political representation (other than the OBCs)

Scheduled Tribes (STs) – in effect, the official term for India's 'tribal' or *adivasi* populations; those communities recognized by the Constitution as deserving special assistance in respect of education, employment and political representation (other than the SCs and OBCs)

shuddhi – purification and (re-)conversion to Hinduism

Sufism – devotional or mystical tradition within Islam

swaraj – self-rule or independence

swadeshi – self-provisioning; Indian manufacture and consumption

swayamsevak – RSS volunteer

thuggee – crimes committed by purported religious cult of thieves and murderers

trishul – trident; emblem of god Shiva

uttam – low caste

varna – the four categories (or 'colours') which traditionally define and divide Hindu society (Brahmans; Kshatriyas; Vaishyas; Shudras)

yatra – pilgrimage or religious procession

zamindar – revenue collector and landholder (under the British)

zamindari – system of land revenue administration under which the *zamindar* landlord collected rent from peasants for payment to the (colonial) government

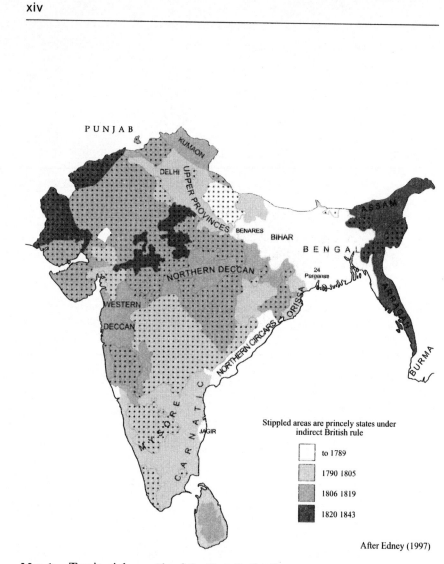

After Edney (1997)

Map 1:   Territorial growth of the East India Company, to 1843
Source: Adapted from Edney (1997), p. 20

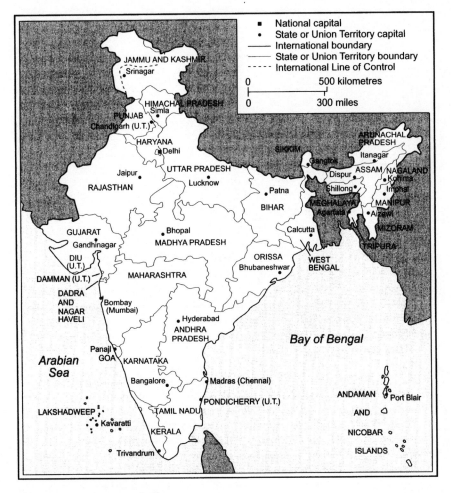

Map 2: Contemporary India

Preface

'The Bombs Exploded Underground But The Shockwaves Are Global'...
'Jubilant India Shrugs Off World Disapproval'... 'Explosion of Self-Esteem
. . .': these were some of the headlines in British newspapers after India's
triple nuclear test on 11 May 1998 at Pokhran in Rajasthan. This first test
was followed two days later by a further pair of explosions. The world was
outraged. Indians, mostly, were delighted. 'There is a tremendous feeling of
pride', said one of the country's leading industrialists. 'With a simmering
feeling that they have been pushed around too long, Indians are hopeful that
the tests will grant them the recognition that they have long craved', wrote
the local correspondents of London's *Financial Times*. Later in the year, in
its *Annual Country Report* on India, the same distinguished newspaper
declared that:

> By default and design in equal part, India's economic, political and strategic
> place in the world suddenly looks vastly different.... Who, for example, would
> have forecast that India's likely growth rate this year of 5 per cent of GDP
> would make the country one of Asia's best performers?... No-one, likewise,
> correctly forecast that the Bharatiya Janata Party, installed six months ago as
> the head of a fractious coalition government, would so suddenly and drama-
> tically alter India's global strategic relations, as it did by detonating five
> nuclear test blasts and claiming status as a 'nuclear weapons power'.[1]

The fact that no one forecast India's nuclear tests in May 1998 is both a
measure of the suddenness of the tests, as the correspondent of the *Financial
Times* surmised, and a reflection of the prevailing ignorance about the
country in the 1990s. The Bharatiya Janata Party (BJP) is widely known to
be associated with Hindu nationalism, or 'Hindu fundamentalism' as it is

sometimes described, and to have been closely involved with – if not actually responsible for – another critical event in India's recent history: the destruction by Hindu militants of an old mosque at Ayodhya, in the north Indian State of Uttar Pradesh, in December 1992. But a little more knowledge would have told that the ideological father of modern Hindu nationalism, Veer Savarkar, long ago raised the rallying cry that Indians should 'Hinduise all politics and militarise all Hindudom' (cited by McKean 1996: 71). Later, in an address, he exhorted high-school students to bring the 'secret and science of the atom bomb to India and to make it a mighty nation' (p. 89). India's nuclear tests were long foretold,[2] and the BJP, in spite of its electoral dissimulations, had never really made any secret of its militant intentions. Pokhran showed just how far the project of 'militarising Hindudom' has been taken, just as Ayodhya showed that Savarkar's call to 'Hinduise all politics' has not been ignored.

The story that we tell in this book is not just an account of 'the rise of the BJP', however, or of Hindu nationalism, though these both have an important place in our narrative. Our purpose is to tell the story of India's contemporary history so as to explain how and why it is that the country has changed so much. For we believe that the changes which the *Financial Times* referred to are not just of passing significance. While the world has hardly noticed, its attention usually focused elsewhere – on the dramas of the collapse of the Soviet system, and the conflicts which followed it; on the spectacles of economic growth and sometimes of spectacular collapse in East Asia and Latin America; or on the recurrent wars of Africa and of southwest Asia – Indian society and the Indian polity were changing. These changes, which have indeed been ones both of 'default' and sometimes of 'design', account for the different place that India is coming to hold in the world. But this is not a book about international relations or defence or foreign policy. Our concern is with the relations of state and society in India and with Indians' understandings of them, and of themselves, in a country whose importance can no longer be set aside. That this should be so is one sign, perhaps, of the success of the BJP. Certainly it is a marker of change.

Though all countries, all states and nations, are in a sense being imagined and re-imagined all the time,[3] India was the subject of a particular, very deliberate act of invention. In December 1946 a group of dominantly upper-caste Indians, many of whom had been educated in English, most of them men, met in the capital city of colonial India, New Delhi, to begin debating what sort of a country theirs was to be in the future. This was the Constituent Assembly, which drew up the Constitution of India that was promulgated in November 1949, over two years after the country had finally won its freedom from colonial rule. We begin, therefore, with an account both of the context in which this assembly met – the India that had been changed if not transformed by two centuries of British rule – and of the ideas and imaginings which influenced its work. The Constitution envisaged that India would have a modern, and therefore secular and democratic state, endowed with the task of bringing about 'development' in what was thought to be a poor and backward society. As we argue, the whole enterprise of 'development' as it took off in the post-war world owed a great deal to the arguments within the Indian nationalist movement and in the Constituent Assembly. Development was the *raison d'être* of the modern state and the source of its legitimacy. Much of the rhetoric was splendid, and to read the speeches of some of the brilliant and noble men who were members of the Assembly – the 'tall and inspiring men' of the nationalist elite, as Rajni Kothari describes them – is still a source of pleasure and of inspiration. But what we think of as the founding mythologies of 'modern India' – a version of 'socialism', secularism, federalism and democracy – reflected many compromises and gave rise to much confusion. The modernizing, developmental mission of the new state, too, was in an important sense one that was imposed by an elite which was not notably democratic in its own attitudes or actions, and which had a history of negating expressions of a popular will.

In the second part of the book we give an interpretive account of the shifting politics of India, and of the factors which have shaped these politics at different levels and sites in Indian society, as we narrate the history of India's developmental state. The story we tell culminates in vigorous attempts to re-imagine the country, its economy and society, in the 1990s. The reinvention which is taking place in contemporary India – which we analyse in greater detail in the third part of the book – is different from that which took place in the Constituent Assembly. It is not a considered process as the earlier invention was, but rather one of struggle and negotiation. Indeed it has come about partly by default, as a result of the failings of the modernizing mission of the Nehruvian state. These have created spaces for the reforming ambitions of certain economists and politicians, inspired by economic neoliberalism, and for the politics of Hindu nationalism. But there is 'design' there too. The arguments for economic reform had been nurtured for a long time by economists such as Jagdish Bhagwati and T. N. Srinivasan, who stood outside the centre-left mainstream of Indian economics, before a particular conjuncture in 1991 provided an opportunity for the implementation of their ideas. The 'design' of Hindu cultural nationalism – the establishment of a 'Hindu state' – has an even longer history, going back to certain of the reform movements of the nineteenth century. The Hindu nationalists played an important part in the struggle for freedom from colonial rule, but their place and their influence was denied during the ascendancy of the modernizing nationalist elite. Their erasure from the official history was reflected not only in their absence from a popular representation like Richard Attenborough's famous film *Gandhi*, but also in their neglect – until the last few years – by most academic social scientists. Their kind of politics did not fit well into the models and the theorizing of mainstream social science. But all the while the persistent activity of what should probably be described as the most effective 'grass-roots' organization to which India has given rise, the Rashtriya Swayamsevak Sangh, nurtured both the ideas and the organizational base for Hindu nationalism. The ideological gap which was left by the earlier nationalist elite's failure – or unwillingness – to engage with the mass of the people, except in a paternalistic or modernizing mode, was partly filled in the 1990s by the ideology of *Hindutva*, while the failures of India's bourgeois politicians left a vacuum into which Hindu nationalism has expanded. Now, at the beginning of the twenty-first century, the Bharatiya Janata Party, as the political wing of the Hindu nationalist 'family' of organizations (the *Sangh parivar*), holds pole position in India politics.

We describe both economic liberalization, and Hindu nationalism, with their sometimes contradictory but often surprisingly complementary agendas for the reinvention of India, as 'elite revolts'. Both reflect and are vehicles for the interests and aspirations especially of the middle class and higher-caste Indians. But we emphasize the plurality of these 'revolts', for though the problems of collective action amongst the elites may be less severe than those which affect the politics of subordinated classes, India's elites are heterogeneous, and there are important conflicts of interest and aspiration amongst them. And the reinvention of India by Hindu nationalism will finally be constrained, we believe, because its organic conception of the Hindu nation fails to convince the many in Indian society who have long been the objects of caste, class and gender oppression, and who have sometimes benefited from state-sponsored processes of secularization or economic development. The designs of the Hindu nationalists and of the economic reformers are opposed by a diversity of social and political movements which are part of another long history, that of resistance to the established order by those who have been the objects of oppression. Already in the 1870s in Maharashtra, a Non-Brahman leader, Jotirao Phule, had founded an organization, the Satyashodhak Samaj, which in 1889 published a paper proclaiming: 'We do not want the National Congress because it does not represent the interests of the people' (cited by O'Hanlon 1985: 284). Movements from below like Phule's were successfully silenced by the nationalist movement. But they did not go away, and they have been emboldened by the spaces for democratic politics which have opened up, slowly and unevenly, since the introduction of universal suffrage. In India now, in addition to the authoritarian, homogenizing aspirations of Hindutva, there are popular mobilizations with emancipatory objectives, and some others – notably those of the 'Backward Castes' – with designs on the state. The reinvention of India that is going on is a struggle, not a planned process, and we conclude by tracing out the lines of struggle and their relationship to the design for India mapped out in the Constituent Assembly.

This is not a 'theoretical' book, though we believe that it is sensibly informed by theory and part of our purpose has been to trace and understand ideas about Indian society and the state. We have no 'model', but we do follow Partha Chatterjee and Sudipta Kaviraj – the inspiration of whose words and writings we want particularly to acknowledge – in finding

Gramsci's idea of the 'passive revolution' provocative in regard to India's modern history. India experienced the establishment of parliamentary democracy under a universal franchise without having first gone through an industrial revolution; and the Indian bourgeoisie, though more strongly established than were the bourgeoisies of other former colonies, was far from exercising hegemony at the time of independence. There had been no bourgeois revolution. The bourgeoisie had to compromise politically, therefore, with rich peasants and with other members of India's 'intermediate classes'[4] – self-employed producers, traders and others employed in services (including some 'government servants', who are 'self-employed' *de facto*, as they procure bureaucratic rents) – and it was forced to rely on the bureaucracy for carrying forward India's development. In this way an expensive and technocratic 'passive revolution' was substituted for social transformation, and, partly in consequence, the Indian polity has come increasingly to be dominated by richer farmers and their associates within the growing rural-urban 'middle class'. The elite revolts of the 1990s and the reinvention of India which they entail – including the increasing importance of regionalism in Indian politics – have been prompted by India's changing engagements with the global political economy, and by external events, including – notably – the threats perceived in the rise of Islamic fundamentalism. But they are the outcomes, in large part, of struggles around the assertiveness of hitherto subordinated classes, and of struggles amongst these classes, often fought out on lines of caste and community, which have come about as a consequence of the progressive 'ruralization' of Indian politics.

Our analysis is unashamedly unfashionable. Though it is necessarily concerned with the politics of identity, it is founded nonetheless on a concern with class formation and the dynamics of accumulation; and in a context in which the economic ideology of neo-liberalism remains influential, and in which 'post-structuralist' and 'post-colonial' ideas are pervasive, our analysis may be unfashionable, too, in reaching the conclusion that the history of independent India continues to be written around the state and the 'state idea'.

PART I

The Invention of Modern India

1

The Light of Asia? India in 1947

In the mass of Asia, in Asia ravaged by war, we have here the one country that has been seeking to apply the principles of democracy. I have always felt myself that political India might be the light of Asia.

Clement Attlee, 1946[1]

Clement Attlee's remark about political India serving as the 'light of Asia' was probably well intentioned, and in some respects it marked a new beginning in the history of relations between imperial Britain and colonial India. By 1946 it was clear to most observers that India's independence was not far off, and not many months later a future President of the Republic of India, Dr Radhakrishnan, was quoting Attlee's remark in favourable terms in the Constituent Assembly. Post-colonial India would be a beacon of democracy and liberty in a world emerging from fascism, war, and Empire. Even so, the irony of Attlee's declaration would not have been lost on those members of the Constituent Assembly charged with inventing a new India in the years 1946–9. Most Congressmen took the view that Britain, by 1946–7, was bent on destroying the fabled unity in diversity of India, and had succumbed to and fostered the two nations theory put forward by Jinnah and the Muslim League. They were soon proved right. In addition, British rule in India could hardly be described as an experiment in democracy, either in representative or in participatory terms. The British ruled India with the help of local notables, but with little regard for the claims of political citizenship that grew to fullness in Great Britain between 1832 and 1928. India was pivotal to the Empire from which Britain benefited, yet few coherent efforts were made to improve the living conditions or education levels of the majority of India's households. For most such men and women the light of Asia shone very darkly, if it shone at all.

In chapter 2 we examine the Constituent Assembly's attempts to invent a post-colonial India which, rhetorically at least, would be everything that British India was not: a democratic, federal Republic of India committed to an ideology of development. Before embarking on this examination, however, it is important that we say something about the state of India in 1947, and that we briefly consider the political and economic legacies of British rule in India. We will also make some preliminary observations on the programmes of the nationalist elites who delivered India from Britain on 15 August 1947.

1.1   The Political Legacies of Empire

When the British left India they left behind them two countries – India and Pakistan – that had been shaped by more than 250 years of economic, political and cultural contact with the English East India Company and the Raj. This is not to say that Indian history during this period was made only by the British, or by Indians reacting to and resisting British definitions of modernity and community. The writings of nationalist, 'Cambridge school'[2] and subaltern historians alike have discredited this sort of imperial history. Nevertheless, the very geography of India in late 1947 pointed up the contradictory and contested legacies of European rule in South Asia. When Nehru was sworn in as the first Prime Minister of India he took charge of a country that was still being carved up by Cyril John Radcliffe, the mapmaker of Partition, and where ambitions for a unitary territory were disrupted by the remnants of French and Portuguese conquests in South Asia (as in Pondicherry and Goa) and the need to integrate 565 Princely States into the new Republic.[3] Meanwhile, in divided Bengal, the government had to face up to the tragic legacies of the famine of 1943–4 – a famine caused in no small part by the state's failure to provide an adequate system of relief to compensate for the lost entitlements of agricultural labourers and artisans.[4] To uncover these legacies in more detail, it is useful to review some key moments in the political construction of power in British India, from Company rule to the end-games of Empire by way of the age of high imperialism that peaked around 1914.

Company rule

The British were not the first European power to acquire a base in South Asia, but the English East India Company was more successful than its French, Dutch, Danish and Portugese rivals in moving inland from its footholds on India's eastern and western seaboards. Following the battles of Plassey in 1757 (where Clive defeated the French and their Indian allies after moving north from the Company's base in Madras), and Buxar in 1764 (where the British defeated the Nawabs of Awadh and Bengal, and after which the Mughal Emperor ceded the Diwani (the right to the revenues)), the Company was secure in its control of much of eastern India. This security derived in part from the strength of the Company's standing army, and from British seapower, but it derived even more so from the Company's success in winning the support of certain Indian social groups.[5] Many of these groups, including trading and banking houses, were free to transact with the British on the fringes of a Mughal empire that was slowly being unpicked. For their part, the British were content at first to clip into the uncertain and overlapping sovereignties of the Mughal Empire.[6] By the early nineteenth century, however, there were signs that the British would attempt to rule India in a more unitary fashion than had been attempted even by Moghul emperors like Akbar or Shah Jehan.[7] The growth of the Company's standing army was one sign of this intention; another was the growth of a civilian bureaucracy. Following Lord North's regulating act of 1773, the Governor-General and his council in Calcutta sought to rule British India with the assistance 'of about 400 covenanted civil servants' (Bose and Jalal 1998: 68), and with the consent of a Parliamentary board of control in London.[8]

In practice, British rule in India had depended from the outset upon the recruitment of Indian troops and Indian civil servants. These networks of rule became more extensive in the first half of the nineteenth century as the British moved to acquire Gujarat in 1803 (to ward off a Maratha threat in western India), as well as Punjab and Sind in the early 1840s. The British also entered into treaty arrangements with Indian rulers outside the areas of direct British rule, as in Hyderabad or Mysore. By the middle of the nineteenth century, these Princely States were under British indirect rule through the Residency system, and most had surrendered powers over foreign and defence policies to the British Paramountcy. Some States also surrendered their fiscal and monetary powers to the British, and herein lies one key to British rule in South Asia.[9] To finance their military campaigns in India, not to mention their trade with China, the British relied heavily upon their control of land revenues in the subcontinent.

The East India Company devised two main systems to guarantee a flow of tribute from rural India. In Bengal, Governor-General Cornwallis introduced the Permanent Settlement of 1793 in the forlorn hope of turning local revenue collectors (*zamindars*) into improving landlords. The *zamindars* of Bengal were expected to collect rents from the *raiyats* (peasants), and remit a fixed sum each year to their colonial masters. Many *zamindars* were unable to meet the regular demands placed upon them by the British, and many were bankrupted in their attempts to squeeze the peasantry for the benefit of the Company. Some *zamindars* found their rights to property and the revenue being transferred to other *zamindars*, or to bankers and traders in urban Bengal. The peasants, for their part, soon found that British rule required them to support a coercive and many-tiered system of tributary colonialism – a system that would make agricultural improvement difficult for more than 150 years.[10] Elsewhere, *raiyatwari* systems of land revenue administration were put in place that linked the colonial authorities directly to the *raiyat* (if not the actual tiller of the soil) by means of land revenues that could be periodically reassessed. The *raiyatwari* system took hold in about two-thirds of the Madras Presidency, and was reinvented with local variations in parts of the Bombay Presidency and Punjab.

British control of India's land revenues did not go uncontested, any more than did their attempts to introduce or impose European languages or laws. In the 1820s and 1830s there were revolts in Chota Nagpur and western India which pitted the Kols and the Bhils, respectively, against Company officials who sought, amongst other things, to increase revenues by converting forest lands into fields.[11] These local rebellions were followed in 1855–6 by the Santhal *Hul* (uprising) in Bihar, and in 1857–8 by the military mutiny or Revolt across northern India. In the wake of these rebellions, the British moved in 1858 to a system of direct (crown) rule in India. Henceforward, 'the ratio of Indian to European troops was [intended] never to be more than 2:1' (Bose and Jalal 1998: 96), and new steps were taken to bend India's economy to Britain's imperial purpose. In the fifty-year period leading up to World War I, the Indian economy was opened up to British manufactured exports, and most obviously textiles, even as peasants in the Indian countryside, along with some estates and plantations, were encouraged to grow cotton, tea, jute and indigo for sale abroad. The railroad system that took shape from the 1850s helped to speed the growth of Calcutta, Madras and Bombay as major port cities, and the British sailing and steamships that linked the sub-continent to Europe and China bolted together a system of payments that allowed Britain to finance its deficits with the rest of the world by running a substantial trade surplus with India.

Empire and reform

These economic arrangements inspired early Indian nationalists like Naoroji and Dutt to maintain that India's potential investible surplus was being lost to Britain. Instead of benefiting from British rule, India's wealth was being used to fund its own subjugation, and its industrial development was arrested by tariff and capital market policies which sought to make India safe for British manufactured goods.[12] As Bose and Jalal point out, it was partly to ameliorate '[s]uch charges of exploitation' that the British moved after 1858 to temper 'the rules of governance in India' (1998: 101). Some of these reforms had an obvious economic component, as for example did the Bengal Tenancy Act of 1885, or the Chota Nagpur Tenancy Act of 1908. These Acts sought to pacify rural eastern India by protecting peasants there from the 'unscrupulous' merchants, rent-collectors, moneylenders and landlords who preyed upon them.[13] Still other reforms were meant to address questions of political participation, and the legacies of these reforms continue to shape Indian politics in the post-Independence period.

Most aspects of the reform process in British India related to the problems that the colonizers faced in securing a measure of consent to their rule. Following the revolt of 1857–8 the British moved quickly to assure India's princes that their privileges would not be disturbed. The British also retreated from some of their policies for social and cultural reform, such as those previously embodied in Macauley's education minute of 1835, or the campaigns against *thuggee* and *sati*. Henceforward, the British would seek to rule India with some Indian support, but not by seeking the Europeanization of India. The British now sought to distance themselves from their Indian subjects. In the late Victorian period an unpleasant mixture of social Darwinism and racial theorizing encouraged the British to draw sharp lines between so-called European and Indian lifeworlds, a project that was exemplified in the clubs and military and civil architectures of the time.[14]

These competing ideologies of cooptation and exclusion were soon given a new twist in urban India. No matter how much the Raj relied on the fruits of rural India to balance its books worldwide, it also needed to secure a measure of political support from India's urban elites. From the time of the Indian Councils Act of 1861 the British sought to secure this consent by means of the slow and limited introduction of self-government. The act of 1861 provided for Provincial Councils to be set up in Bengal, Madras and Bombay that would be dominated by British officials but which would allow 'a few nominated non-official Indians [to be] consulted on legislative matters' (Bose and Jalal 1998: 104). This provision was extended by Lord Ripon in 1882 to municipal and local boards, and was taken rather further at the time of the Morley-Minto reforms in 1909. The Morley-Minto reforms continued the British policy of making self-government financially dependent upon the raising of local taxes, but they went beyond Ripon in their willingness to see elected or nominated Indians break out of the municipal circuit of politics to contribute at the Provincial level, or more rarely in the Legislative Council in Calcutta. This process of cooptation was developed further by the Montagu-Chelmsford reforms of 1919, and the Government of India Act of 1935, both of which extended the franchise among Indian communities (albeit only to men in 1919) even as they steered Indian politicians away from the Centre and towards the Provinces.[15] Here is one key to British rule in India in the first half of the twentieth century, and one of the Raj's enduring legacies in terms of the politics of post-colonial India. The Raj was constructed on the basis of a unitary conception of Indian territory and on the back of an unyielding commitment to political centralism. At the heart of the Raj was Calcutta, until 1912, and then Delhi or New Delhi. Even as Indian nominees and elected politicians were brought into the corridors of power in Patna or Lahore, they were kept away from those political responsibilities, notably defence and foreign policy, that were arrogated to the Centre. This remained true even after 1935, when the 1919 model of dyarchy (or separate lists of responsibilities for Indians and non-Indians at the Provincial level) was abolished in favour of the full participation of Indians in all departments of provincial government, and when the franchise was extended further. As most nationalists well knew, power in India rested with the Centre, and it was the capture of power at the Centre that came to define the political agendas of the Indian National Congress and the Muslim League.[16]

Number, divide and rule

In addition to opening up avenues of political participation within the Raj, the British sought to define the terms under which different groups of Indians could participate in the political process. Herein lies a darker legacy. Although we do not subscribe to the view that the British invented caste or religious community identities in India, it is clear that British policies of enumeration, and divide and rule, did much to harden these identities in the seventy or eighty years before Independence.[17] Part of the damage was done through the Census of India which the British introduced in 1872, and which was administered on a decennial basis from 1881. As Barney Cohn points out, 'what was entailed in the construction of the census operations was the creation of social categories by which India was ordered for administrative purposes' (Cohn 1996: 8), and by means of which supplicants could be recruited to the British cause. The blunt categories of caste and religion which feature in the Census of British India were not designed to respect the particularities of *jati*, and nor were they attentive to the possibility of forms of religious affiliation, like *bhakti* cults or *Sufism*, that cut across the boundaries between 'Hinduism' and 'Islam'. The colonial authorities then sought to build upon these brute categories by linking the (slow) evolution of representative government to the award of separate electorates and reserved seats for Muslims and Hindus. These awards were built into the reforms of 1909 and 1919, and were anticipated by Curzon's decision in 1905 to divide Bengal into 'Hindu' west Bengal and 'Muslim' east Bengal.[18] In the 1930s Britain sought to extend this courtship of Muslim landed interests by appealing in similar terms to lower caste Hindus; indeed, the aptly named communal award of 1932 saw British Prime Minister Ramsay MacDonald promise separate electorates for the (Hindu) Depressed Classes, much to the consternation of Mahatma Gandhi. In the event, Gandhi was able to secure the consent, finally, of B. R. Ambedkar, the leader of India's 'depressed classes', to a pact which refused the British offer of separate electorates, even as it accepted a larger number of reserved seats for the Depressed Classes in the Provincial councils.[19]

The Poona Pact found expression in the arrangements made for the 1937 elections to the Provincial Councils under the terms of the 1935 Government of India Act. But this was a minor concession by the British. As the Empire moved towards the endgame of 1946–7 it was clear that a negotiated transfer of power could not proceed without close regard for the power of the Centre in India's 'federal' set-up, or without recognizing the politicization of India's religious identities. In the end, British India was not able to hold together. By 1946 the Muslim League had regained much of the ground it had lost in the 1937 provincial elections, and its leader, Mohammed Ali Jinnah, refused to accept that a Congress party in control of a unitary India would safeguard the interests of the country's Muslims. Jinnah chose to throw in his lot with the landed interests of Muslim Punjab, and with some Muslim groups in Bengal, and he grudgingly agreed to Mountbatten's plan, in 1947, to create a new state of Pakistan from the western and eastern fringes of India.[20] For its part, the Congress came to power in August 1947 in a country beset by the horrors of Partition, and within whose major borders power had recently been shared with more than 500 Princes. In so far as the Congress had achieved its goals by electoral as well as non-electoral means, it had done so on the basis of a franchise that was restricted in the 1940s to less than 30 per cent of the adult population. Here was another legacy of British rule in India.

1.2   The Economic Legacies of Empire

The political landscapes of the Raj were shaped by Britain's commercial and strategic imperatives in the subcontinent. It is worth recalling that the English East India Company acquired territories in eastern India to secure a supply of goods for exports. Politics were ever driven by commerce in the days of John Company. But the economic dimensions of Empire remained strong even after the Company lost its trading monopoly with India in 1833, and long after the transfer of powers to the Crown in 1858. In the second half of the nineteenth century the rhythms of the Indian economy were dictated to an increasing extent by the rhythms of the European world economy. The Indian economy did well enough in the 1880s, but it suffered sharp downturns in the 1870s and 1890s, just as it would do again in the 1930s. India's manufacturing economy also had to contend with the Lancashire lobby in England. British cotton textile interests made it difficult for the Government of India to provide a measure of protection to the modern textile industry that emerged in the Bombay–Ahmedabad region in the late nineteenth century.

Limited structural transformation

It would be wrong to suggest that manufacturing industry failed to take root under the Raj. There were enclaves of industrial capitalism in India under British rule, and these were the more visible when compared with what was happening – or not happening – in colonial territories like Korea or Dutch Indonesia. The jute industry, centred in Calcutta, was dominated by British capital, but the cotton industry, based at first mainly in Bombay, 'was essentially Indian in origin, largely controlled by Indian investors, and increasingly administered by native managers and technicians' (Morris 1982: 572). India was the first country in Asia to have a modern cotton textile industry, preceding Japan by twenty years and China by forty (Maddison 1971: 56). By the First World War India had become, next to Britain, the world's greatest exporter of cotton yarn. By this time, too, the Parsi businessman, Jamshetji Tata, had opened the first Indian steelworks in Jamshedpur.

But if India was by 1947 the seventh largest industrial country by volume of output, it remained a predominantly agricultural country nonetheless. The national income accounts for 1950–1 show that agriculture accounted for 51.3 per cent of the total (in China, at about the same time, it made up an estimated 47 per cent of national product), while 'large-scale industry and mining' still accounted for only 6.5 per cent of GNP, and 'small-scale industry' for a further 9.5 per cent. In the labour force over 70 per cent of labourers were employed primarily in agriculture and less than 10 per cent in manufacturing (not counting household-based industrial production). Indian agriculture, meanwhile, was characterized by low levels of productivity when compared with other major Asian economies. Overall productivity (in relation to land) was almost twice as high in China, and in East Pakistan, as in India in the early 1950s; it was twice as high in Indonesia, more than three times as high in Malaya and five times as high in Japan.[21] Output of foodgrains per capita was estimated to be 269 kg in China, compared with only 194 kg in India (Byres and Nolan 1976: 14), while the reported figure for rice – the most important foodgrain in both countries – was 119 kg per capita for China as compared with only 66 kg in India.

The low productivity of agriculture in India was widely recognized at Independence. In its terse discussion of the independence of India and Pakistan, the *Economist* newspaper, in the issue for 16 August 1947, expressed the hope that 'the energy of the new governments will be concentrated without delay on the fundamental question of increasing agricultural production'. What it did not say, except perhaps by implication, was that the colonial state had failed to increase agricultural output, except in the case of some commercial crops. Indeed the output of foodgrains had tended to stagnate, and possibly to decline, in spite of increasing demand, in the period between the wars. The availability of foodgrains per capita – allowing for imports – declined during this period, and probably did not improve much in the 1950s.

An important reason for the low productivity of Indian agriculture was the low intensity of cultivation (given by the cropping index, which stood at 130.9 in China, for example, in 1952, as compared with only 94 in India in 1949–50),[22] and this in turn reflected the low level of irrigation. Water is the principal determinant of productivity in most Asian agricultural systems, and only 15 per cent of India's arable area in the late 1940s was irrigated. The colonial state invested very little in India's irrigation potential outside Punjab, and the country's larger irrigation systems were operated more to provide insurance against the failure of rainfall than to increase agricultural productivity.[23]

The failure to invest in irrigation can only be part of the reason for the dismal state of Indian agriculture, or, indeed, of rural society, at the time of Independence. There can be little doubt that the inequitable distribution of land ownership in India, and the continuing existence of landlordism (an estimated 35 per cent of cultivators were tenants at Independence, a high proportion of them sharecroppers (Byres 1974)), helped to create conditions in which the great majority of producers had neither incentive nor opportunity to invest in agriculture. This was especially the case in the *zamindari* areas of India, or in those areas where the British were keen to secure the consent of the landlord class regardless of the economic consequences. As Daniel Thorner, a perceptive observer of the Indian rural economy, wrote more than ten years after Independence:

> High rents, high rates of interest and low prices leave the mass of petty peasant producers with very little to invest in the development of the land, and keep them at the mercy of the more powerful people in the village. Thus, on the one hand, the grip of the larger holders serves to prevent the lesser folk from developing the land; on the other hand, the larger holders do far less than they might to modernise production on that part of their land that they farm directly with hired labourers. (Thorner and Thorner 1962: 3)

Structural transformation, in short, had not proceeded very far in India by the late 1940s or early 1950s. By 'structural transformation' we mean that major process of economic change in which there is a shift both in terms of the value of output, and of employment, from agriculture into the secondary and tertiary sectors of the economy. This follows from the fact that there are definite limits to the extent to which a purely agricultural economy can grow because of the limitations in the demand for agricultural products; economic growth entails increasing diversification and specialization of production. Tomlinson has suggested that 'an endemic demand constraint, notably for basic wage-goods including foodgrains has been both a symptom and a cause of much of India's recent record of underdevelopment' (1988: 131). He maintains that this pattern extends back into the colonial period, when, it seems reasonable to suppose, most rural households should be described as (net) 'consumers' rather than as 'firms' or 'production units', given that they did not have access to sufficient land to meet subsistence needs. Many were agricultural labourers paid at least partly in kind; some forms of tenancy, notably sharecropping, can be seen as scarcely disguised forms of wage labour. There were also types of indebtedness which resulted in a form of wage labour, 'especially for those dependent on loans in grain or money to sustain consumption while growing hypothecated produce' (p. 133). The scale of this sort of non-monetized transaction remained very extensive even after Independence. Estimates from the 1950s and 1960s suggest that between two-thirds and three-quarters of foodgrain output was not marketed directly for cash. Given that the majority of cultivators were dependent price-takers, it seems likely that the few, dominant, controllers of agricultural surplus were able all the time to depress real wages by shifting the rates of conversion between commercial crops and food crops.[24] Even many years later, in the late 1970s, it was found in one study that nominal wages paid to agricultural labourers tended to adjust to price changes so that their real wages remained more or less constant.[25]

Poverty

These were the circumstances in which living standards in India remained depressed. They were already a matter of controversy in the nineteenth century, and became the stuff of economic nationalism alongside the theory of the 'drain'. It seems likely that average per capita incomes were either stable or declining in the period between 1920 and 1947, having at best risen very slowly in the later nineteenth century. When the first authoritative estimates of the incidence of poverty were made, after Independence, it was suggested that in 1960–1 about 40 per cent of the rural population, and a little under 50 per cent of the urban population, were living in poverty.[26] It is difficult to be sure about comparisons at an earlier stage – they are problematical enough even for the present – but it is unlikely, even so, that India (c.1960) was exceptionally poor as compared with other major Asian countries. One estimate of the incidence of rural poverty in South Korea puts it as high as 41 per cent in 1965 (Castells 1998: 252), and one for rural Indonesia in the same year at 47 per cent.[27]

It must be stressed that India's poverty was not fundamentally the result of population pressures, or at least of population pressures acting independently of the forces of class, gender, community or imperialism. According to estimates made at the time, the population of India after the trauma of Partition and the creation of Pakistan was 338.7 million, or about one-third of the number estimated to be living in India in the year 2000.[28] By comparison with some other parts of Asia, India was not densely populated. In relation to the area of cultivated land, the number of people living in India c.1950 was less than half that of people living in China, or in East Pakistan (now Bangladesh), and not much more than half that of people living in Indonesia (even allowing for the then very sparse settlement of the so-called Outer Islands, which make up a large part of the country). Population density in India, in relation to cultivable land, was only about 15 per cent of that in Japan, and the imperial capital of India at Partition, Delhi, was still a small city – a city where those with the leisure to do so might visit its great historical sites by bicycle, following the guidebook written by the historian Percival Spear (1994).

Neither sheer numbers of people, nor population density figures, can explain the appalling poverty of many Indians after 200 years of British rule. The famines that hit India in the late 1890s and again in 1943–4 had more to do with the impact of imperial policies on the price of food and labour than with an average annual rate of growth of population during this period of about 1.8 per cent. Demographic pressures are equally unable to explain an average life expectancy of just 40 years in India in 1950, or a hideously uneven sex ratio (an estimated 1057 males for 1000 females in 1951), or the fact that less than 13 per cent of Indian women were classed as literate in 1961.[29] Nor should population pressures be blamed for the extra-ordinary differentials in income and wealth that marked out particular households, communities and regions in India before, during and after the period of British rule. British rule may have arrested the development of the Indian economy as a whole, but it did not check the fortunes and privileges of those families upon whom the British depended for support.

1.3 The Legacies of Indian Nationalism

The contradictory dynamics of British rule in India provided fertile and often confusing conditions for the emergence of Indian nationalism. Although the origins of the nationalist movement in India are conventionally traced back to 1885 and the founding of the Indian National Congress (INC), this is to define nationalism in India in a very particular way. The nationalism of the INC was a bourgeois, step-in-your-shoes sort of nationalism[30] until the time of Tilak and the 'extremist' tendency in the INC in the 1890s and 1900s, and only later did Gandhi convert it into a mass movement which reached out to rural India. But there were other forms of nationalism, or at any rate of anti-colonialism, that dogged the British throughout the days of Company Rule and the Pax Britannica: the revolts of the tribal periphery, for example, or of the Sepoys in 1857, or the Mundari *ulgulan* in the final years of the nineteenth century.[31] These local traditions of dissent, which were mirrored in countless labour disputes in both rural and urban areas, were given fresh impetus in the twentieth century by the mutiny amongst Indian naval forces which shook Bombay in 1946, and by the communist insurgencies which rocked Telengana and north Bengal in the 1940s (and which encouraged 'London . . . to get out of India as quickly as possible before anti-colonial politics became more radicalized than they already were' (Bose and Jalal 1998: 182)). We will return to these alternative or subaltern accounts of anti-colonialism later in the book; for the moment, let us put in place a more conventional narrative account of Indian nationalism.

The early nationalist movement

The foundation of the INC in 1885 followed on from a period of social reform and Hindu revivalism that was well represented in the activities of the Brahmo Samaj, which had encouraged a rather Christianized Hinduism earlier in the nineteenth century, and, after 1875, in those of the Arya Samaj. The Arya Samaj, in particular, which was strong in Punjab in the late nineteenth century, 'sought to include reformist postures on issues such as child marriage, widow remarriage, idolatry, travel overseas and caste – within a framework of the assertion of Hindu supremacy over other religious faiths' (Bose and Jalal 1998: 111). By advancing this sort of agenda, the reformist movements were at once able to contest European accounts of modernity (or the Christian, even secular, bias of the Raj), while also advancing a political standpoint that was modern in its own right. The tensions between religious and other forms of modern discourse in nationalist politics would later prove inauspicious. In the 1880s, however, it was common for members of Hindu India's urban elites to move in and out of reform politics and Congress politics, and to make common cause with Muslims in the INC's disputes with the Raj.[32]

In the 1880s and 1890s these disputes centred on the misuse of India's manpower and economic resources by the colonial state. Congress asked the British to make room for elected or nominated Indian politicians in its corridors of power, and it pushed for a greater induction of Indians into the Indian Civil Service (ICS). A particular concern of educated, urban Indians was that examinations for the senior ranks of the ICS were held in London and not in India, a state of affairs that continued until 1919. On the economic front, Congress complained that the development of Indian capitalism was being held back by an unwarranted 'drain' of India's wealth to Britain through the council bill system. Early Indian nationalists like Dadabhai Naoroji (who would later become the first Indian MP – for Finsbury – in England), and Romesh Chandra Dutt, suggested that 5 or 6 per cent of India's total resources were being remitted to Great Britain. They also disputed British claims that this was no more than a payment for services rendered, or a fair rate of return on inward investment.[33]

The drain of wealth theory would serve as a mainstay of nationalist rhetoric until 1947. It had the great virtue of tapping a chord and holding together a diverse political constituency. The idea that India was being exploited by the British was hardly far-fetched, and nationalists were able to invoke the drain theory to good effect whenever Indian fortunes were hit by downturns in the world economy. The nationalists could reasonably point out that India's economy had been restructured to serve the needs of its metropolitan masters, and that Indians financed both the costs of Empire (the Home Charges) and the military wherewithal which kept the Raj intact.[34] The drain theory appealed equally to Indian capitalists and Indian socialists, and even to some Gandhians.[35] No matter how much these competing groups differed in respect of the uses which they foresaw for India's vanishing funds, they could agree on the importance of contesting the drain itself.

Unity was much harder to come by on other fronts. The moderate Congress of the 1880s and 1890s found it hard to extract concessions from the

British, and the seeming failure of this first generation of Indian leaders encouraged the Maharashtrian, Tilak, to experiment in the mid-1890s with 'no revenue' campaigns and other forms of direct action. The famous split between 'moderates' and 'extremists' in the nationalist movement healed for a while after 1905, when Curzon announced the partition of Bengal. In 1905–6 Bengali leaders as diverse as Rabindranath Tagore (the poet-philosopher of the Bengali nation) and Surendranath Banerji (a first generation Congressman) joined in protest against this attempt to divide Bengal and to rule its eastern districts with the help of some Muslim landlords. With the support of many Muslim intellectuals and urban professionals, these and other leaders of Bengal began the *swadeshi* (self-provisioning) movement that would later be taken up elsewhere in India. But when the boycott of British cotton textiles threatened to get out of hand – that is, when it encouraged some revolutionary gangs to take up the bomb and the bullet, or when it provoked labour disputes – the moderate/extremist split opened up sufficiently for the British to exploit divisions with a characteristic mixture of repression and political reform (in this case the Morley-Minto reforms of 1909).

Gandhi and mass politics

The question of how best to deal with the British continued to be a problem for the Congress and its nationalist allies and rivals. To an extent this problem was 'solved' by the emergence, under Mohandas Karamchand Gandhi, of a mass nationalist movement that engaged men and women in rural areas of the subcontinent. After his return to India from South Africa in 1915, Gandhi sought to transform politics by pioneering new tactics of non-cooperation (which drew on *swadeshi* nationalism, of course) and non-violence. But any solution was bound to be temporary or provisional. The course of Indian nationalism was always caught up in a tensely dialectical relationship with British attempts to undo Gandhi's campaigns, or to unpick the threads that held the supporters of Indian nationalism together. It was also beset by competing accounts of what India 'was' or could be expected to be – what we might call competing imaginaries of 'India' or 'the Indian nation'.

Gandhi's own career as an Indian nationalist points up these tensions very well. In 1919 he set in motion an all-India campaign of non-cooperation that protested the inadequacy of the Montagu-Chelmsford reforms, that challenged the legality of the Rowlatt Act of 1919 (which allowed the British to hold Indians without trial even in peacetime), and that sought protection for the *Khilafat* in the wake of the defeat of Ottoman Turkey. In 1922 Gandhi called off this same non-cooperation movement. The trigger for his *volte-face* was an attack upon a police station in Gorakhpur District, United Provinces; Gandhi was concerned that the forces he had unleashed were becoming violent and in some cases revolutionary. Meanwhile, the British sought to disrupt the politics of anti-colonialism by providing fresh incentives for Indians to engage in constitutional politics at the Provincial level; they also stoked up Hindu–Muslim tensions by continuing to provide for separate electorates. Given these sorts of responses, which were always allied to the stick of repression and imprisonment, it is hardly surprising that Gandhi was faced with fresh dilemmas in the 1930s and 1940s. The basic questions remained: what was the proper balance between parliamentary and extra-parliamentary politics in the struggle for dominion or Independence, a problem posed with particular force at the time of the 1937 elections? what place might violence play in the politics of anti-colonialism? how might the nationalist community be held together in the face of the communalizing policies of the British? and what sort of India did this community – or communities – wish to see created?

Imagining India

In one sense, of course, we know the answers to these questions. The Congress was largely successful in the 1930s and 1940s in reworking a politics of civil disobedience and non-cooperation which culminated in the Quit India movements of the 1940s. The British were unable to persuade respected Indian leaders to agree to the sorts of power-sharing arrangements that kept elected Indians away from the imperial capital. The ledger books of Empire also worked in favour of the Quit India movements. By the end of 1945 London was in debt to Delhi and Washington, the power of the Raj on the ground was fading fast – as Sir Stafford Cripps conceded when he introduced the India Independence Bill in the House of Commons in 1947 – and the Labour Government of Clement Attlee was forced to negotiate Britain's withdrawal from India, something which the British had failed even to contemplate at the time of the 1935 reforms.[36] In the event, the end came sooner than London or the nationalists had anticipated, and withdrawal was accompanied by a Partition of India which revealed the failure of Gandhi's attempts to keep Hindus and Muslims together.

There are dangers, however, in closing a narrative account of Indian nationalism in such simple terms. For one thing, it implies that history was less messy than it really was. The Partition of India may well have been the product of Hindu–Muslim antagonisms, albeit manipulated by a colonial power desperate to buy time in its most prized possession, but as late as June 1946 Jinnah's All-India Muslim League was rejecting calls for a sovereign Pakistan and was exploring the 1946 Cabinet Mission plan for a three-tiered all-India federation where Hindus and Muslims would share power and seats according to a complex regional formula. We should also note that the Muslim League was unable to win the votes of a majority of India's Muslims until as late as the 1945–6 elections; its performance in the 1937 elections was quite abject, even in Muslim-majority areas. There never was a single Muslim identity or constituency in British India (any more than there was a singular Hindu or Indian identity). In addition, a remembrance of the nationalist struggle which is written around Gandhi, or even Gandhi and Jawaharlal Nehru, might remain faithful to many nationalist histories of the Freedom Movement, but it would not do justice to the range of individuals and groups who worked with, and sometimes against, these remembered heroes. This is not just a matter of finding room in our accounts of Indian nationalism for tribal revolts and *kisan* and labour struggles, although that is important enough. It is also a matter of recognizing, as many historians have not recognized until recently, the achievements and agendas of Vallabbhai Patel, Subhas Chandra Bose, B. R. Ambedkar and Vinayak (Veer) Savarkar, to name but four leaders of the anti-colonial struggle. These leaders outlined different agendas for dealing with the British (Bose preferring to raise and equip an Indian National Army to fight the British alongside the Japanese), and they developed very different perspectives on the possibilities and agendas for Indian nationhood and economic regeneration.

This last point matters to us because it highlights the uncertainty and conflicts that surrounded 'the invention of Independent India'. Although we will argue in chapter 2 that post-colonial India was invented in accordance with certain well-defined mythologies of rule (socialism, secularism, federalism and democracy), it is certainly not part of our purpose to suggest that 'Nehru's India' was the only India imagined by nationalist politicians, or that Nehru's vision was ever properly made flesh. Chapters 2 and 3 will offer commentaries on the ambitions of and inconsistencies in Nehru's design for a 'modern' India. As regards alternative visions of India (or *Bharat*), it is well known that Gandhi was opposed to the dirigiste and westernizing visions of Nehru. Gandhi (1997) made clear his views in *Hind Swaraj*, a book that he wrote in haste in 1908 but to which he remained true until his death in 1948. For Gandhi, the enemy was not only British imperialism, but the enemy within: the cancers of materialism and envy and excess which can take root in the minds of men and women, regardless of colour, caste or creed. True independence for India would have to attend to the body corporeal as well as the body politic. *Swaraj*, or self-rule, would be found, Gandhi argued, in a politics of truthfulness (*satyagraha*) that would deliver the body from false desires. (Gandhi's account of *swaraj* drew inspiration from most of the world's great religions. Although Gandhi was perceived by many Muslims to be the embodiment of a certain form of Hinduism – and by some 'Untouchables' too – it is not inconsistent to say that Gandhi's Hinduism was of a non-textual kind which found room for the more ascetic teachings associated with Christ and the Buddha, as well as Kabir and Mohammed.[37])

What is less well known is that Gandhi's remarks in *Hind Swaraj* were addressed rather more to Veer Savarkar, the ideological father of Hindu nationalism and the author of *Essentials of Hindutva* (Savarkar 1922), than to Bose, Patel or Nehru (three men not yet in Gandhi's compass).[38] Gandhi was assassinated in January 1948 by Nathuram Godse, an articulate Brahmin from Maharashtra and a lapsed member of the Hindu nationalist

Rashtriya Swayamsevak Sangh (RSS). At his trial, Godse declared that, 'I firmly believed that the teachings of absolute *ahimsa* [non-violence, or reverence for life] as advocated by Gandhiji would ultimately result in the emasculation of the Hindu Community and thus make the community incapable of resisting the aggression or inroads of other communities, especially the Muslims' (after van der Veer 1994: 96). The India that Godse wished to see built after Independence was a strongly masculine India, an India which would develop – as Savarkar argued it should – a military-industrial capability that would befit its status as a great power.

In the light of India's nuclear weapons tests of May 1998 it would be foolish to discount the relevance of Savarkar's views in contemporary India, and we will have cause to return to his life and teachings later in this book (chapter 8). For the moment, though, we will make the point that the story of Indian nationalism should not overlook the role played by 'political Hinduism'. The Hindu Mahasabha recruited a large number of men and women for some parts of the nationalist cause in the thirty years before Independence, and yet neither its personnel nor its Hindu nationalist outlook should be conflated with the Congress nationalism of Gandhi or Nehru.[39] Similar tales might be told of Bose and Patel. Both men advanced agendas for post-Independence India that were at odds with those of Gandhi and Nehru, and both had strong bases of support. Although events conspired to leave Nehru in charge of India from 1950, it was not clear in the mid-1940s that Nehru's sketches for a future India would survive either the 'leftist' politics of Bose and his allies (not to mention the communist insurgencies in Bengal and Telengana), or the conservative political instincts of Patel and his many supporters.

1.4   Conclusion

A lot remained to play for when the Constituent Assembly (1946–9) sat in New Delhi to discuss plans for what turned out to be the Republic of India. In this chapter we have provided some background on the legacies of British rule in India, and these legacies (of arrested development, political centralism and limited democracy) provided a context within which a newly Independent India was to be fashioned, and a template against which this new India could be imagined and counterposed. But the invention of India in the period from 1946 to 1956 didn't only have regard for the legacies of empire, and certainly not in a simple or direct sense. The invention of modern India was also fought out between several of the constituencies that had taken shape under the Raj – big business, various landed elites, organized political groupings – and was sternly contested within the ranks of what became the Congress Party. In chapter 2 we consider the invention of modern India during the critical years of the Constituent Assembly and the early 1950s. Although we highlight the role played by Nehru and the 'socialist' wing of the Congress party in the construction of Independent India, we also pay attention to the limitations of Nehru's rhetorics of change and transformation. Modern India was not invented by Nehru alone – no matter how tall he walked among the 'tall and inspiring men' who shaped a new Indian nation (see chapter 3) – nor was modern India forged entirely within India, or in disregard of the intellectual and geopolitical forces that helped to shape the deliberations of the Constituent Assembly. Although this is not our primary concern, we recognize that the history of India needs to be written with regard for South Asia's changing position in the post-war global political economy.

2

'Sovereign, Democratic, Federal, Socialist, Secular': The Invention of Modern India

There is some magic in this moment of transition from the old to the new.
Jawaharlal Nehru

WE, THE PEOPLE OF INDIA, having solemnly resolved to constitute India, into a SOVEREIGN DEMOCRATIC REPUBLIC and to secure all citizens:
JUSTICE, social, economic and political;
LIBERTY of thought, expression, belief, faith or worship;
EQUALITY of status and opportunity;
And to promote them all;
FRATERNITY assuring the dignity of the individual and the unity of the nation;
IN OUR CONSTITUENT ASSEMBLY this twenty-sixth day of November 1949, do HEREBY ADOPT, ENACT AND GIVE TO OURSELVES THIS CONSTITUTION.
The Preamble to the Constitution of India

'The first task of this Assembly is to free India through a new constitution, to feed the starving people, and to clothe the naked masses, and to give every Indian the fullest opportunity to develop himself according to his capacity.' So said Jawaharlal Nehru in the closing debate on 'The Resolution of Aims and Objects' (22 January 1947), one of his many addresses to the Constituent Assembly of India.[1] For Nehru, the *raison d'être* of government in modern India, independent India, was to liberate the minds and bodies of ordinary Indians by purposeful acts of economic and social transformation. The poverty of India, according to Nehru and his wing of the nationalist movement, was a result of British policies which left India weakly industrialized and agriculturally depressed. It was also a result of longstanding patterns of inequality which found expression in the power of India's Princes and landlords, and which were reproduced by the pre- or anti-modern ideologies of casteism and religion. It was the duty of government, Nehru thought, to propel India into the modern world by effecting the structural transformation of the Indian economy. Planning would be the handmaiden of government in this venture, and democracy and state-sponsored education would shine the light of reason where previously there existed only superstition or theology.

Many members of the Constituent Assembly which was formed in 1946 would have agreed with Nehru's account of the Assembly's 'first task'. In fact, some of Nehru's ideas were so widely shared that it seemed hardly necessary that the Constitution which they were drawing up for the new state should say that India would be 'democratic' or 'secular' or even 'socialist' (though this last term was more problematic, as we shall explain). In the event, the Constitution which they finally promulgated on 26 November 1949 did say that India was to be a 'sovereign democratic republic', but the words 'socialist' and 'secular' were only introduced into the preamble of the Constitution much later, as a result of a cynical amendment passed during the period of 'Emergency Rule' of Prime Minister Indira Gandhi (Nehru's daughter) between 1975 and 1977.[2] Why was this? Was it because socialism or secularism were contested terms in the late 1940s, or was it because they were taken for granted by the nationalist elites charged with the invention of modern India?

The answer lies somewhere in between. We begin this chapter with some observations on the make-up of the Constituent Assembly which sat in New Delhi either side of Independence in 1947. Although Nehru, with Ambedkar, took charge of the Assembly in key respects, and not least in regard to the drafting of the Constitution, the Assembly was not cast in the progressive garb that Nehru claimed for his wing of the Indian National Congress. The Assembly, like the INC itself, was dominated by well-to-do men from India's higher castes, and Nehru's dream of a socialist India, such as it was, had to be reined back in the face of conservative opposition to his proposals. We return to these observations on the character of the Constituent Assembly in the final part of the chapter, where we take up Barrington Moore's remarks on the paradox of democracy without bourgeois revolution in independent India. For all his power within the Congress Party, and within India at large, Nehru could not construct the sort of developmental state that emerged in South Korea or Taiwan after 1950, and Partha Chatterjee is not alone in arguing that Nehru had to resort to a passive revolution which substituted planning for political reform. (Chatterjee also questions whether Nehru's dream of modernity was shared by the men and women who lived in the countryside or in the regions, and who made up most of what passed for civil society in India). But these qualifications notwithstanding, it is still the case, or so we shall argue in the middle part of this chapter, that Nehru provided a template for the invention of a modern India, *and* that what we shall call the mythologies of rule in Nehru's India (ideas of democracy, socialism, secularism and federalism) have consistently affected the political and economic landscapes of India since 1947, even where they have been honoured more in the breach than in the observance. It is in this sense that we speak of the invention of India in the 1940s and 1950s. We are not claiming that Nehru invented India as a true *Light of Asia*, nor are we claiming that Nehru's prospectus for social change measured up to his own rhetorics of developmentalism, nation-building or democratization. We will argue in chapter 3 that many of the pathologies of misrule that became evident in the 1970s or 1980s emerged from decisions taken – or not taken – in the Nehru years. What we do claim is that an idea of India was put into play during this period which contributed to a new understanding of India 'abroad' (India as the world's largest democracy, India as a secular state, India as a developing country), and which contributed, slowly and imperfectly, to new understandings of what it meant to be an Indian within independent India. There was, to paraphrase Nehru, at least some magic in the moment of transition from the old to the new. We should not forget this.

2.1   The Constituent Assembly

The Constituent Assembly was set up as a result of a Cabinet Mission sent to India in March 1946 by the new Labour government in Britain. It had been in prospect for some time. The Plan produced by the Cabinet Mission directed that the Assembly should be elected by the legislatures of the Provinces of British India, which had themselves been elected into office in December 1945 on the basis of a franchise so restricted by tax, property and educational qualifications that it included only 28.5 per cent of the adult population. The members of the three communal categories, Muslims, Sikhs and a 'General' category (including Hindus and all others), were to elect separately a proportion of the provincial delegates in line with their share in the population of the province. The Princely States, which were not directly governed by Britain, were to have 93 delegates, partly elected and partly nominated. The Assembly elections were held, according to plan, by July 1946, but the first meeting of the Assembly did not take place until December of that year. In the interim, Wavell, the Viceroy, sought unsuccessfully to reconcile the two major parties – the Indian National Congress and the All-India Muslim League. The League, for some time the champion of the two-nation view of India's future, and by now supported by large numbers of Muslims, had decided upon a boycott of the Assembly almost immediately after the election, because of its fears of the Hindu domination of a body controlled by a large Congress majority. In the end the Muslim League delegates never did take up their seats, and after the Partition of British

India in August 1947 the Congress accounted for more than 80 per cent of the members of the Assembly.

The character of Congress

The Constituent Assembly was, therefore, in effect a one-party body. Some commentators have argued that it was representative of India, nonetheless, because of the character of the Congress, which was that of a movement which sought to be inclusive and encompassing rather than that of a political party. In keeping with this character the Congress pursued deliberate policies to ensure that so-called 'minorities', including Parsis, Anglo-Indians, Indian Christians and members of the Scheduled Castes and Scheduled Tribes, were represented in the Assembly under the 'General' category.[3] Indeed, the members of these minorities finally accounted for 37 per cent of the provincial membership. The Congress High Command also instructed that certain hand-picked individuals were to be elected in the different Provinces, including some who were not actually Congressmen but who had particular and valued expertise as lawyers or administrators. Amongst them was Dr B. R. Ambedkar, who has sometimes been described as the principal author of the Constitution, and who was from the Scheduled Castes – an Untouchable, or *Harijan* (the euphemism, meaning 'child of God', was given by Gandhi to name those who were 'outcastes' from the 'caste system'). It was another of these men, K. Santhanam, who said to Granville Austin, the author of a study of the framing of the Indian Constitution, that: 'There was hardly any shade of public opinion not represented in the Assembly' (Austin 1966: 13). Austin seems to agree. He argues that while there were no representatives in the Assembly from either the Communist Party or the Socialist Party, or from the Hindu Mahasabha, their views were well represented amongst Congress members.[4]

These comfortable conclusions about the representativeness of the Assembly may be challenged. The Congress was an organization dominated by a social elite, and it was not notably democratic in its own workings,[5] whilst the Constituent Assembly was made up quite disproportionately, in relation to their numbers in the population as a whole, by Brahmans and members of other high castes (like *Kayasthas*). The Indian National Congress had been founded as a pressure group for their own interests by middle-class, professional men, most of them from these high castes. They assumed that the educated were the 'natural leaders' of the people, and that the greater political rights which they sought were being demanded 'not for the whole population, but for such portion of it as has been qualified by education' – as Gokhale argued in his presidential address of 1905 (quoted by Sarkar 1983: 90; see also chapter 1.3). Although the Congress moved on from this position in the years which followed, and though, through the genius of Gandhi, the Congress became a mass movement in the 1920s and 1930s, it retained – even if not so blatantly – the elitist attitudes which

Gokhale expressed.[6] Many of the members of the Congress in the Constituent Assembly mistrusted party politics, and they were inclined, like the British, to set their conception of the state above those of any of its constituent members.[7]

This may seem an improbable claim in view of all that was said in the Constituent Assembly debates about the need for socio-economic revolution – and we will temper it shortly when we come to Nehru – but the conservative instincts of the Congress leadership can be seen in the ways in which it sought to manage popular movements in the decades leading up to Independence. Chatterjee argues that: 'While the nationalist leadership sought to mobilise the peasantry as an anti-colonial force in its project of establishing a nation-state, it was ever distrustful of the consequences of agitational politics among the peasants' (1993: 160). Pandey, too, maintains that the Congress leadership in Awadh in the 1920s, 'helped, by their refusal of continued support, to bring the peasant movement to its knees' (Pandey 1982: 189). True political nationalism was expressed, perhaps, not by the Congress movement, but rather by the social movements of the low castes, which challenged caste hierarchies and power relations in their struggles for education and religious equality. Aloysius quotes Ambedkar's definition of nationalism: 'a social feeling . . . a corporate sentiment of oneness which makes those who are charged with it feel they are with kith and kin' (1997: 153); and he argues, with Ambedkar, that 'the foundation of this sentiment of one-ness could only be provided by a destruction of caste hierarchies and elite exclusiveness' (as summarized by Omvedt 1997: 1966). This is a view which refuses to accept the identification which was made by the political elite in the Constituent Assembly between the 'state' which they were constructing, and the 'nation'.

2.2   Nehru and the Invention of Modern India

There are grounds for questioning, therefore, just how representative the Congress-dominated Constituent Assembly can possibly have been. Nehru, in moving the 'Resolution on Aims and Objects' in the first debate of the Assembly, on 12 December 1946, began by speaking of the Assembly itself as representing the will of the people: 'We have met here today because of the strength of the people behind us and we shall go as far as the people – not of any party or group but the people as a whole – shall wish us to go.' This fine rhetoric was, of course, a necessary fiction: it is part of the idea of the modern state in European thought, in which Nehru was deeply imbued, that it is both democratic and embodies the general interest and the 'will of the people'. But it is also a part of the idea of the modern state that it exists in the context of civil society, which is understood to be a sphere of voluntary, free association between people with its own autonomous existence, and which exists in a kind of creative tension with the state – both in opposition to it and sometimes supportive of it. India, arguably, had no such civil society at Independence. How, then, was Nehru to stamp his vision on India, even supposing that he had a clearly worked out vision in the first place? How, too, could he hope to escape the conservative biases of the Constituent Assembly?

Nehru in command

The paradox of the Nehru years can be explained in part by reference to the unusual position which Nehru came to occupy in Indian politics in the period from 1946 to 1951. We have noted already that the Indian National Congress which Nehru led with Gandhi and Patel was not an obvious vehicle for effecting radical social change. The Congress published resolutions on the importance of agrarian reform in the 1930s, but Congress governments in the Provinces rarely made this a priority at the time of British rule.[8] Patel, moreover, had close links with India's big business class, and looked to private capitalists to effect the industrial modernization of India.[9] Gandhi, for his part, looked to village self-government and rural 'development' as bases for the moral regeneration of India. But Gandhi was assassinated in January 1948, and he had in any case opted out of the process of government before the time of the transfer of power. When Patel died in December 1950 Nehru was left in pole position in the Government of India. By 1951 he was back in charge of the Congress party too. In 1950 Purushottamdas Tandon was elected as the President of Congress with the backing of Patel and his right-wing supporters. As Chatterjee notes: 'The conservative groups [fronted by Tandon and Patel]...were in favour of a much tougher policy towards Pakistan and sharply opposed to the proposals for new social legislation on the reform of personal laws and greater state control over the economy' (Chatterjee 1997a: 9). Nehru shot them down.

> In August 1951, Nehru resigned from the working committee [on party organ-
> ization], claiming that there were serious policy differences between him and
> the party leadership. The parliamentary party expressed its confidence in
> Nehru's leadership. Within a few weeks, Tandon was forced to resign and
> the AICC [All India Congress Committee] elected Nehru as Congress Presid-
> ent. For the moment at least, the superiority of the government wing of the
> party was established by creating a single unified leadership. (pp. 9–10)

Nehru's ability to transcend the conservative instincts of the party that he led again until 1954 (when his lieutenant, U. N. Dhebar, assumed the Presidency of the Congress) was enhanced further by the traumas of Parti-tion, which signalled the need for national unity and the dangers of religion intruding in party politics, or vice versa, and by the coincidental births of independent India, the Cold War and a new ideology of developmentalism. In the 1950s Nehru was able to exploit the rivalry of the USA and the USSR to secure massive aid funds for his programmes of industrial transformation (see chapter 3), and these programmes in turn had the blessing of the industrial powers and the Bretton Woods institutions. Nehru's way was the 'right way'; indeed, for some in the west, and in the Comintern, it was the only way. The development orthodoxies which took shape in the 1950s placed a particular emphasis on the economies of scale that economists associated with manufacturing industry, and they painted a grim picture of underemployment and low productivity in agriculture. The two-sector model of a developing economy which features in the work of Lewis and Rostow was mirrored in India by the Nehru-Mahalanobis strategy for industrial growth at the time of the Second and Third Five Year Plans (1956–66).[10]

But this is to jump ahead. Although events in India and the world economy ran kindly for Nehru in the 1950s, it remains the case that Nehru was already at the helm when the British left India in August 1947. It was Nehru who moved the 'Resolution on Aims and Objects' when the Constituent Assembly met on Friday 12 December 1946, and there are good reasons for believing that Nehru drafted this resolution. It is thus not unreasonable to suggest that Nehru – together with Ambedkar – was a principal author of India's constitution; nor is it unreasonable to suggest that it was Nehru, who, in the main, if not quite in circumstances of his choosing, gave voice to four broader mythologies of rule which sought to present 'modern India' to itself and to the rest of the world (Corbridge 1995). (By mythology we mean to suggest, following Barthes (1972), a code by which people are supposed to lead their lives and which remains for the most part unexamined.)

Democracy

When Nehru advertised India to the rest of the world as a democracy – the 'world's largest democracy' – he had in mind a country in which suffrage would be universal, in which elections to Parliament would be held at least every five years, and in which representatives would be accountable to their electors in and through particular constituencies. Like most members of the Constituent Assembly, Nehru's understandings of democracy and government had been shaped by the Raj and Westminster, and by the limited experiments in democracy that were signalled by the reforms of 1909, 1919 and 1935. An alternative understanding of what democracy might mean had been promoted by Gandhi and some of his followers, who sought a distinctively 'Indian' form of government. The alternative was founded on a view of the centrality of the village in Indian society, and on hostility to the idea of the modern state, partly because it was seen as a western concept. In essence, it was proposed that there should be directly elected village councils (or *panchayats*), with a hierarchy of indirectly elected bodies above them, up to a national *panchayat* which would handle only a minimum set of functions.

That India would have a centralized Parliamentary constitution was, however, nearly certain from the outset. Austin notes that not one person complained in the debate on the 'Resolution on Aims and Objects' that *panchayati* government was not on the agenda for discussion: 'Members spoke of democracy, socialism and the responsibilities of legislatures but not of the necessity for an "Indian" form of government' (Austin 1966: 33). In later debates, over the next two and a half years, the omission was sometimes noted, but in the end the inclusion as one of the Directive Principles of the Constitution of a clause about the establishment of village *panchayats* was admitted only grudgingly by the Congress leadership.[11] The realities of power, in the context of Partition and its consequences in terms of internal and external security, as well as of their whole experience of government, made Nehru and Patel and others resolutely hostile to *panchayati* democracy as to other Gandhian ideas. They also saw direct election as a pillar of the social revolution that had to be brought about. It was believed that with indirect elections the creation of a national consciousness would be virtually impossible. And, as Nehru had written in 1938, a directly elected Assembly would 'represent the people as a whole and [would] be far more interested in the economic and social problems of the masses than in the petty communal issues which affect small groups' (quoted in Austin 1966: 46). It would in itself be an instrument of change because it would give people an awareness of their collective strength. Finally, as Austin argues: 'The Assembly's adoption of a democratic, centralised, parliamentary constitution meant that members believed that to achieve the object of social revolution India must become a modern state' (p. 49).

Federalism

It would be easy to mock these sentiments given what we know about the workings of democracy in India over these past fifty or so years. Westminster-style representative democracy has not been incompatible with vote-banks in the Indian countryside,[12] and India's democracy was not given proper constitutional protection against executive rule through the appropriation of Emergency powers (as provided for by Article 352 of the Constitution).[13] But these criticisms can be pressed too far. Governments in India have been voted out of office with some – indeed, with increasing – regularity, and the idea of one person one vote is now lending encouragement to the political and economic ambitions of India's so-called Backward Classes (see chapter 9). India's free press may also have provided some protection against famine.[14] In any case, the idea of democratic rule in India is not confined to the Lok Sabha in New Delhi. The Constitution also sought to provide Indians with a set of legally enforceable Fundamental Rights which would guarantee their liberty and free speech and which would protect them against exploitation. These Rights are meant to bear upon the operation of the legal and judicial systems in India. In addition, the

Constitution provides for Indians to vote at different spatial scales. The myth of federalism finds expression in the Rajya Sabha (or Council of States) at the Centre, in a division of powers, responsibilities and resources between the Centre and the States, and in the direct election of Members to the lower houses of State parliaments (or Legislative Assemblies). Elections have also been provided for, since 1957, at the *panchayat* level.[15]

The federal principle in India is thus not entirely lacking in content. States are responsible for maintaining law and order locally, and for a range of 'nation-building' activities, including health, education, agriculture, forestry (in the main), power, roads (save for national highways) and urban development. To pay for these activities, States are given various grants in aid from the Centre and they can raise their own funds from sales taxes, liquor taxes, urban land taxes, and agricultural and rural land taxes. States also have their own High Courts. It remains the case, nonetheless, that the federal principle is only weakly entrenched in India. The Constituent Assembly, and Nehru and Patel perhaps most especially, worried that a more potent federalism in India would weaken feelings of national unity in the country and would make it harder for governments in the Centre to push ahead with the 'social revolution' that was needed to secure economic development. The powers of the States in Independent India were thus curtailed from the outset, very much as they were under the 1935 Government of India Act. States were made financially dependent on the Centre (in effect),[16] and the Centre was represented in the States in the person of the Governor and through the major All-India Services (the Indian Administrative Service, the Indian Police Service and the Indian Forestry Service). The Centre was given the power to create new States and to revise State boundaries (as it did at the time of the States Reorganization Act, 1956: see chapter 3). The Governor, who *de facto* is an appointee of the Prime Minister of India, has also been given the power to suspend State governments and their Chief Ministers according to certain very broad conditions laid down in the Constitution.

The myth of federalism in India has been tested on a number of occasions, both by governments in the Centre suspending elected governments in the States, and by States or significant groups of actors within States (as in Punjab and Kashmir) seeking to secede from India. (In 1963 the States lost their right to secede from the Union.) Whether the spirit of the federal principle was adhered to more in the time of Pandit Nehru than in the time of his daughter, Indira Gandhi, is something we will examine in part II. The point we wish to make here is that the centralizing logic of the Indian state was a very deliberate creation of the Constituent Assembly.[17] The Assembly was to some extent bound by convention, current practice and memory. The model for the Constitution of the Republic of India was the Government of India Act of 1935. At the same time, and this brings us back to Nehru, the stated purpose of India's constitutional changes was to 'feed the starving people, and to clothe the naked masses'. And this brings us, in turn, to ideas of socialism and secularism, or at the very least to an ideology of development and nation-building.

Socialism and secularism

It is as well to draw this distinction. Socialism, as we hinted earlier, has long been a controversial term when it comes to India's official descriptions of itself, let alone the descriptions made of it by others. It only became a part of the official language of state in the 1970s under Mrs Gandhi, and began rapidly to disappear from view as the country continued with the pro-market reforms which began in earnest in 1991. Nevertheless, a certain bias to a Fabian conception of socialism was apparent in the rhetoric and delibera-tions of the Constituent Assembly, and this rhetoric appeared to grow stronger in the 1950s when supporters and critics alike began to equate Indian planning with a 'socialist model of development'. When Nehru moved the Resolution of Aims and Objects in the Constituent Assembly he made clear his own commitment to socialism in the sense of economic democracy, even as he pulled back from declaring India to be a socialist state:

> We have given the content of democracy in this Resolution and not only the content of democracy but the content, if I may say so, of economic democracy in this Resolution. Others might take objection to this Resolution on the ground that we have not said it should be a Socialist State. Well, I stand for Socialism and, I hope, India will stand for Socialism and that India will go towards the construction of a Socialist State, and I do believe that the whole world will go that way. But the main thing is that in such a Resolution, if, in accordance with my own desire, I had put it in, that we want a Socialist State, we would have put in something which may be agreeable to many and may not be agreeable to some and we wanted this Resolution not to be controversial in regard to such matters.

It would be hard not to read this part of Nehru's speech as evidence of his unwillingness to rock the Congress boat, let alone to upset the applecarts of big business and landlordism. Ambedkar made this point to Nehru when he declared that: 'I should . . . have expected the Resolution to state in the most explicit terms that in order that there may be social and economic justice in the country, that there would be nationalisation of industry and nationalisa-tion of land.' The Resolution refused such a statement, and the nationaliza-tion of land has never seriously been considered in independent India. Nevertheless, it would be wrong to assume that Nehru's nods towards socialism were simply rhetorical. It would be more accurate to say that Nehru understood socialism in the broader sense of uplifting the poor – or in the modern sense of giving 'every Indian the fullest opportunity to develop himself according to [his or her] capacity' – and that he believed that such uplift could best be secured through a mixed economy in which the state would be responsible for building up heavy industry and the infrastructures (dams, electricity, transportation) necessary to support it. This in turn required a strong state: a well-funded state, a centralized state (Nehru expected his conservative opponents to acquire power in the regions), and a state imbued with the spirit of reason and progress. Nehru also believed that the uplift of the poor would be secured by the poor themselves, *once* they had been liberated from ignorance and prejudice by education and modern health-care systems. Here was the myth of secularism. For Nehru and his supporters, casteism was the enemy within, and it was as much the product of unreason as was the communalism that had brought about the Partition of India in 1947. Government should maintain a separation between the public and the private spheres, at least when it came to religion, and should provide modern citizens with the words and concepts that are needed to understand the private sphere in non-religious terms.[18]

Nehru, in short, was committed to the modernization of the Indian 'nation' and – notwithstanding his defence of the public/private divide – of Indian bodies. To the extent that the Constitution of India bears his impress, and it clearly does, we find this broad attachment to 'liberty, development and directed social change' in the tense relations between the Fundamental Rights guaranteed by the Constitution and the Directive Principles of State Policy which are 'the conscience of the Constitution' (Austin 1966: 50). The Fundamental Rights of the Constitution seek to guarantee a person's negative freedoms: freedom from arbitrary arrest, freedom of speech and so on. The Directive Principles 'aim at making the Indian masses free in the positive sense' (p. 51). It is here, among the Directive Principles, that we find references to the promise of social and economic justice. Under Article 39 the state is enjoined to

> direct its policy to securing (a) that the citizens, men and women equally, have the right to an adequate means of livelihood; (b) that the ownership and control of the resources of the community are so distributed as best to serve the common good; (c) that the operation of the economic system does not result in the concentration of wealth and means of production to the common detriment; (d) that there is equal pay for equal work for both men and women.

And, under article 43, it is required 'to secure . . . to all workers, agricultural, industrial or otherwise, work, a living wage, [and] conditions of work ensuring a decent standard of life'. Amongst the other Directive Principles there are provisions for what now would be called affirmative action on behalf of India's Scheduled Communities, and a commitment to the provision by the state 'within a period of ten years from the commencement of this Constitution, for free and compulsory education for all children until they complete the age of fourteen'.

The continuing failure of the Indian state to invest in the education of its children, or even to safeguard them from the worst forms of child labour, gives the lie to at least some of the developmental rhetoric that first surfaced in Nehru's India. But we should be wary of moving from acceptance of this point to the broader claim, now being made in some quarters, that democracy and development have never seriously been tried in India, or that they are foreign to Indian traditions or self-understandings. This is not how we see things. Nehru and the modernizing wing of the Congress Party were able to imagine, and to a lesser extent invent, a new India in the period between 1946 and 1956, and this 'imagining' was informed, centrally, by the four mythologies of rule that we have just discussed: democracy, federalism, socialism and secularism. We would further contend that these mythologies were given a measure of institutional form which lifted them, to some degree at least, above the pious platitudes that surrounded their invention and propagation. Underpinning Nehru's design for a new India were the All-India Services (notwithstanding that they followed a British model of governmentality), the Planning Commission, the Five Year Plans (particularly from 1956, with the Nehru-Mahalanobis model), regular elections, a Supreme Court, respect for a free press, an implicit agreement by major political parties to keep religion out of public politics, reserved jobs and constituencies for the Scheduled Castes and Tribes, an apparent commitment to agrarian reform, and so on (see chapters 3–5). We would also contend that the mythologies of governance associated with Nehru's India have struck deeper roots than some critics allow, and that they continue to inform public understandings of the rhetorics and responsibilities of government (see chapter 9). Nevertheless, we also recognize, with Ambedkar, that the development project which Nehru (and the Constituent Assembly) proclaimed on behalf of India could never hope to be realized in the absence of political and economic reforms at the local and regional levels. And these reforms were never likely to be secured – or in some cases even fought for – in a country where the bourgeoisie was as weak as it was in India in 1947.

2.3 Of Civil Societies and Passive Revolutions

It is time now to return to a remark we made earlier about the apparent absence of civil society in India. The so-called 'failure' of the Nehruvian project (development, individual liberty, nation-building) is read by some commentators as evidence of a broader 'Orientalism' which is built into India's experiments with modernism, and of India's 'natural' rejection of this attempt to impose social change from without. This point of view is most often associated with the Gandhian political psychologist, Ashis Nandy, but other versions of this argument have been advanced recently by Ronald Inden and T. N. Madan.[19] Inden contends that 'Development' in independent India has been established by courtesy of a concept of Reason – embodied in planning, the Planning Commission and in Nehru himself – which is every bit as transcendental as the religious progresses that endowed the medieval king of kings with the 'luminous will' of Vishnu (Inden 1995: 271). In each case, particular pilgrimages are sublimated into a grander idea of Progress or Modernity; a grander idea that turns its backs on the lives and wishes of a majority of Indians who are expected to heed their master's voice and respond dutifully. A parallel argument has been made by T. N. Madan in respect of Nehru's account of secularism. Nehruvian secularism, according to Madan, is an alien concept in India, and not one to which ordinary people can be expected to relate. The Constituent Assembly's prospectus for the transformation of India failed because it sought to invent a foreign India and could not, in the end, secure the support or the understanding of the non-English speaking masses.

These are challenging arguments, and we will review them at length later in the book. It is worth saying here that our own perspective on state–civil society relations in India stops short of these claims. We have problems with an account of Indian politics which seems so relentlessly to celebrate 'difference' or the 'fragment' and which ends up, perversely, reifying 'the Nehruvian project' and 'the essence of India' in the name of anti-essentialism.[20] We also have problems with points of view which suggest that all forms of 'westernization', or even modernity, are foreign to the life-worlds of ordinary Indians, or which assume that these same Indians are opposed to most aspects of development as it is ordinarily conceived and understood. People live more comfortably on the borders between rural and urban worlds, 'western' and 'eastern' worlds, modern and pre-modern worlds, than some prophets or critics of high modernism allow.[21]

What needs to be explained is why development in India – in the sense of an expansion of people's capabilities[22] – has faced the obstacles that it has done, both before and after 1947. The best way to judge post-Independence India is not, then, to condemn it for failing to measure up to an assumed Other Path or (pre-modern) Golden Age, but to examine in an insistent way the conditions of existence (class forces, institutional practices, discursive assumptions) of the mythologies of governance which were mapped out for India by the Constituent Assembly. To say this, of course, is to describe our task in parts II and III of this book. But it also inspires us to close part I with a review of the work of Barrington Moore. It is here, we contend, and in the 'Gramscian' works of Sudipta Kaviraj and Partha Chatterjee, that we find some more useful pointers to the state–civil society relationship in modern India.

The balance of class power

In his classic comparative study of the *Social Origins of Dictatorship and Democracy* in the modern world, Barrington Moore argues that the particular problems that India experiences follow from the paradox of the establishment of political democracy (the ideal form of the modern state) without there having been an industrial revolution (1966: 314ff). 'Democracy' we take to mean: government by the people; the form of government in which sovereign power resides in the people and is exercised either directly by them (participatory democracy) or by officers elected by them (representative democracy).

Clearly, this is a statement of an ideal, for it evades the real problems of collective action which arise from the fact that the goals held by individuals ('the people') rarely coincide absolutely. Approaching the ideal of democracy, therefore, depends upon the differentiation of the realm of politics from overall systems of inequality in a society – so that collective decisions are not made by particular individuals or groups of people because of the power derived from their economic or social status (Rueschemeyer et al. 1992: 41ff). In practice, democratic forms of government, involving the accountability of the executive to an assembly of representatives elected through free, open elections, in the context of freedom of expression and association, can never eliminate altogether the significance of differences of wealth, power and status in society. Thus it has been that Marxists have generally rejected representative democracy as a sham which conceals the exercise of power by the dominant class. The view which is expressed by Barrington Moore, however, and following him by Rueschemeyer and his associates, is that the ideal of democracy is approached more or less closely according to the balance of class power in a society, and the nature of the state system. The development of capitalism is, in some ways, actually conducive to the approaching of the democratic ideal because it weakens the power of landlords and strengthens subordinate classes, shifting them from the relatively unfavourable environment of peasant agriculture in which, as Marx argued in *The Eighteenth Brumaire*, they are 'like potatoes in a sack', divided from each other, lacking a sense of collective interest, and given their identity by the more self-conscious classes which make up the rest of society. The democratic ideal is approached more closely, too, if the state-system (the organization of the state) is relatively autonomous in relation to society. But there is a narrow gap between the Scylla of a state-system dominated by particular interests within society, be they landlords, industrial capitalists or financiers, and the Charybdis of a state-system which is absolutely autonomous and able to exercise dictatorship over society, over-riding the interests and aspirations of 'the people'. This is where 'civil society' enters the equation. The more developed the sphere of private, voluntary association, of civil society, the wider the gap between the Scylla and the Charybdis, and the greater the space for democracy, for it implies that different interests are organized within society and are able to hold the organizations in the state system to account (an argument derived from Rueschemeyer et al. 1992).

In India, towards the end of the colonial period certainly, the realm of politics was not at all clearly differentiated from overall systems of social inequality. This point was made with extraordinary lucidity by Ambedkar, speaking in the Constituent Assembly:

On the 26th January 1950, we are going to enter a life of contradictions. In politics we will have equality and in social and economic life we will have inequality. In politics we will be recognising the principle of one man, one vote, one value. In our social and economic life we shall, by reason of our social and economic structure, continue to deny the principle of one man, one value. How long shall we continue to live this life of contradictions? How long shall we continue to deny equality in our social and economic life? If we continue to deny it for long, we do so only by putting our political democracy in peril. (Quoted in Khilnani 1997: 35)

The same point was later made by Moore, who argued that the balance of class power in India at independence was hardly conducive to approaching the democratic ideal. According to Moore: 'The character of the upper classes and [the country's] political institutions have suggested some reasons why there was not in India the kind of economic and political movement towards capitalism and political democracy that parts of Europe displayed' (1966: 330). His argument is that the system of tax farming, on which the rulers of pre-British India depended, built in deep constraints on the expansion of productivity, and that with increasing exploitation it broke down, and with it the whole structure of government. It was in this context that Europeans established their territorial foothold in India during the eighteenth century. But the effects of the arrangements the British made in the nineteenth century for land tenure and raising taxation, and for governing the country, were such as to entrench parasitic landlordism.[23] And so, 'Despite poor cultivation [Moore writes of the poor quality of cultivation in India "which contrasts in the sharpest possible manner with the garden-like peasant agriculture in China and Japan"] the peasants did generate a substantial economic surplus...[but] the foreign conqueror, the landlord and the moneylender absorbed and dissipated this surplus. Hence economic stagnation continued throughout the British era and into the present day' (1966: 316). Moore continues the argument with such clarity that it is worth quoting his own summary of it at length:

> British authority rested heavily on the upper landed classes. The native bourgeoisie, especially the manufacturers, on the other hand felt cramped by British policies, particularly on free trade, and sought to exploit a protected Indian market. As the nationalist movement grew and looked for a mass base, Gandhi provided a link between powerful sections of the bourgeoisie and the peasantry through the doctrine of non-violence, trusteeship, and the glorification of the Indian village community. For this and other reasons, the nationalist movement did not take a revolutionary form, although civil disobedience forced the withdrawal of a weakened British empire. The outcome of these forces was indeed political democracy, but a democracy that has not done a great deal toward modernizing India's social structure. (p. 316)

The work of historians since Moore's time has qualified this analysis, which is informed by a Marxissant historiography no longer in favour, but has not radically altered its broad thrust. David Washbrook, in two major articles which review the subsequent historiography, draws attention (as Moore did not) to the economic power of South Asia before the nineteenth century, when it was 'responsible for a much larger share of world trade than any comparable zone and . . . may have possessed upwards of one quarter of the world's total manufacturing capacity' (1988: 60). And it seems that arguments resting on the proposition that India lacked the social and cultural institutions associated with the development of capitalism in Europe, or that pre-British systems of government created economic stagnation, or that pre-colonial India had a 'traditional' economy based on reciprocity and redistribution rather than on the market, have all been found wanting by historians. Washbrook argues that, rather than resulting from the 'breakdown' of governance in India in the eighteenth century, Europeans were drawn in by the logic of indigenous processes of change which 'enhanced the importance of cash, guns and the security of property in ways which gave the Europeans, and particularly the British, strategic advantages over Asians' (p. 72).

In the early nineteenth century, however, as Moore surmised, the effects of colonial rule were indeed to enhance the power of Indian owners of capital and land over producers and labourers, so that it can be argued 'they had never had it so good'. This also meant that India embarked on a process of capitalist development which more or less prevented its ' "normal" economic consequence in industrialization', and in which capital was accumulated 'almost exclusively by expropriating an ever larger share of resources from labour and the production system without having to take the risk of re-investing more than a tiny fraction of capital' (Washbrook 1988: 87). In the later nineteenth century there was growth in the agricultural economy, but the attitude of the colonial government towards the capitalist transformation of agriculture was distinctly ambiguous. One of the key contradictions of British rule was that after a certain point the economic interest of the colonial power might have been served by a more vigorous development of capitalism in India. But the prospects of an active Indian capitalism were politically threatening:

> the raj saw the agrarian problem much more in political than in immediately economic terms. Its policies of social conservation and peasant protection flowed from the fear that if competitive capitalist relations were allowed freedom to take over the countryside, the resulting conflict would destroy the raj's own institutions of government and political security. (Washbrook 1981: 685)

Moore probably overestimated the continuing power of large landholders in the later part of the colonial period, for by this time the substantial peasantry was the rural class which counted. But Washbrook's further argument, here, rather confirms the broad outline of Moore's thesis.

Similarity and difference

The ambiguities in the attitude of the colonial government towards the development of Indian capitalism were part of a wider ambiguity which ran throughout colonial policy, and which we touched upon in chapter 1. On the one hand, the British sought to modernize Indian society through rationalizing institutions and by attacking customs which were offensive to the European mind. An ideology of 'progress' was essential to the colonizers' own sense of the legitimacy of their rule – the way in which they justified the empire to themselves. But on the other hand, and at the same time, it seemed practically right, and could be conceived to be morally right, to respect Indian ways of doing things and to concede the legitimacy of difference. Thomas Metcalf, in his study of the *Ideologies of the Raj* (Metcalf 1995), argues that there was throughout an enduring tension in British attitudes between two ideals, one of 'similarity' and one of 'difference'. He believes that there never was a coherent set of ideas in terms of which the British thought about their rule and their relations with Indians, and that on balance the most powerful perspective was that which emphasized difference. Sudipta Kaviraj makes a related point. Even nationalist text-books, he points out, have argued that the British built 'rationalist institutions' – the common law, the bureaucracy and the judiciary: 'But the institutionalist instinct of British imperialism was hardly coherent. Spells of evangelical utilitarianism were tempered by an ingenuous regard for traditional eminence. Many of these colossal structures of colonial "rationalism" had feet of vernacular clay [and were by-words in petty corruption]' (Kaviraj 1984: 227).

Modern historians, therefore, have come to question Marx's judgement that British rule 'produced the greatest, and, to speak truth, the only social revolution ever heard of in Asia'.[24] The preference now is for Marx's conception of pre-British India as having had a cellular character: because of the influence of the caste system and of village organization – which created 'a huge mass of locally coordinated social cells' (Moore 1966: 340) – government imposed from the outside was not necessary to secure local order, in contrast with other societies (notably China). Satish Saberwal, more recently, has spoken of: 'The cellularity characterising Indian society [as having had] manifold implications for its historical experience' (1996: 39). Saberwal associates it with the ethical plurality which arises from the existence of segmented codes for conduct, related to different caste groups, and he argues that: 'Given this traditional autonomy of segmental codes, the idea of extensively binding normative orders [across society as a whole, and] effective down to particular persons has been relatively alien to India's historical experience' (p. 65). We will return to this argument – which recalls some aspects of Weber's views on the distinctiveness of Hindu society (Weber 1958) – and to its implications in part III. In the present context, it is important because it lends weight to Kaviraj's argument concerning the failure of the colonial state fully to implement its 'Enlightenment' project of establishing in Indian society the same rational-legal order characteristic of the West and a common set of values. Khilnani makes the point simply when he speaks of there having been 'no [we might say "little"] reshaping of common beliefs in the society at large' (1997).

The segmented, cellular character of Indian society, far from having been destroyed by colonial rule, as Marx perhaps thought would be the case, seems rather to have been accentuated by it. The arrangements which the British made regarding land tenure, taxation and local administration tended to enhance the power of village officers, to create or at least to exaggerate the integrity of villages as social units, and to weaken supra-village social organization.[25] Some historians and anthropologists further believe that British rule, by weakening or eliminating local kingship, both increased the power of the Brahmans, and made it appear that the caste system was organized around the centrality of religion, and a religiously ordained social hierarchy – whereas there is quite strong evidence, they believe, to suggest that kings or their local equivalents were the pivots of the social order (Dirks 1987; Raheja 1988). In sum, the British entrenched the divisions of Indians amongst themselves. This was, perhaps, not so much as part of a deliberate strategy of divide and rule (though see chapter 1.1), as because of a deeply rooted idea that civil society in India is 'naturally' divided (Washbrook 1997: 40).

The contradictions of colonial ideology, in the stretch between utilitarianism, rationalism, reformism and compromise with the 'difference' reflected in Indian society, are mirrored in those of Indian nationalism. Partha Chatterjee has argued that the nationalists were committed to the establishment of modern, western-style institutions in the public sphere, and their criticism of colonial rule was precisely that it restricted or even violated the principles of modern government in India. But, at the same time, their very sense of national identity was predicated upon belief in the existence of difference, and of distinctively Indian spiritual values, based in the family. In the private sphere, therefore, 'the domain of the national was defined as one that was different from the "Western". The new subjectivity that was constructed here was premised... on particularity and difference... the hegemonic movement of nationalism was not to promote but rather, in a quite fundamental sense, to resist the sway of... modern institutions' (Chatterjee 1993: 75). Among the implications of this argument is the view that the institutions of a modern state are not rooted, in India, in a civil society of freely associating individuals sharing a common set of beliefs and a common moral code. Herein, of course, lies a strong challenge to, and critique of, the modernizing agendas for India mapped out between 1946 and 1956.

2.4   Conclusions

The findings of recent scholarship have been to confirm and to extend Barrington Moore's suggestions: the balance of class power in India – given the weakness of the bourgeoisie and the persistence of the peasantry – was not at all conducive to participatory democracy at Independence, while at the same time civil society (in the European sense of this term) can hardly be said to have existed. So where does this leave us? Kaviraj and Chatterjee, in explaining the process of social change in modern India, have both referred to Gramsci's idea of 'passive revolution', and this helps us to go beyond Moore's conclusions in respect of the 'developmental state' in India. According to Chatterjee:

> in situations where an emergent bourgeoisie lacks the social conditions for establishing complete hegemony over the new nation, it resorts to a 'passive revolution', by attempting a 'molecular transformation' of the old dominant classes into partners in a new historical bloc and only a partial appropriation of the popular masses, in order first to create a state as the necessary precondition for the establishment of capitalism as the dominant mode of production. (1986: 30)

Kaviraj argues, more straightforwardly, that because of the weakness of the bourgeoisie in India, it comes necessarily to depend on a state-bureaucratic agency to bring about social transformation. Transformation, in short, does not come about as a result of a process from within society, but is sought to be achieved by administrative fiat. This was what was set in place in India, at first through the work of the Constituent Assembly, and later by the Planning Commission and by the Nehru-Mahalanobis plan for India's structural transformation.

There is a good deal to be said for this argument, and we will be using it as a starting point for much of our analysis in part II. Chatterjee and Kaviraj are right to draw attention to the lack of popular support for, and understanding of, some aspects of the Nehruvian project for the invention of 'modern India'. They are also on firm ground when they draw attention to the doubly *dirigiste* nature of Indian high modernism: to the fact that it was effected in the name of the people by an executive arm of the state, and that its success would depend upon the power of that executive to secure a sufficient degree of autonomy from India's propertied elites both to issue its administrative decrees and to see them carried out at the local level.

But the pessimism which is built into the accounts of Kaviraj and Chatterjee needs to be tempered in one crucial respect. Sunil Khilnani has described the Constitution of India as 'a baroque legal promissory note' (1997: 35), and so of course it is. But he also insists that it has exercised far-reaching influence over India's subsequent history, and we should not lose sight of this point. When Kaviraj speaks of a 'state of neighbourly incom-munication between the spheres of middle-class and subaltern-class dis-course' (1994: 53), he is pressing a compelling insight too far. We will argue in parts II and III of this book that these spheres of discourse have collided and fused more often than Kaviraj (or Chatterjee) allows. We need to develop an understanding of state–civil society relations in post-colonial India which suspends this too-fast opposition, and which begins to flesh out the changing contradictions of state policy and uneven development in India in a manner that calls to mind nothing so much as Kaviraj's account of the contradictory trajectories of the British Raj. To put it one last way – and to bring our discussion back to Nehru and the Constituent Assembly – we need to hold together three sets of observations on the state and politics in India: we need, first, to recognize the elite-dominated and frankly 'colonial' struc-tures of governmentality which emerged in some parts of post-colonial India and which imposed constraints on the Nehruvian project of structural transformation; we need, second, to acknowledge the intended and un-intended consequences of Nehru's attempt to provide four new mythologies of rule for independent India; and we need, third, to treat with a mixture of caution and regard those accounts of post-colonial India which suggest that 'European modernity' has no place – or no roots – in Europe's Other, in 'Bharat-India'.

PART II
Contested Modernities

3

The 'Tall Men' and the 'Third Way': Nehru, Patel and the Building of Modern India

---

The first generation of independent nationhood [was] dominated by tall and inspiring men.

Rajni Kothari (1970: 4)

There is a third way, which takes the best from all existing systems – the Russian, the American and others – and seeks to create something suited to one's own history and philosophy... what we are trying to do... is, planning under a democratic pattern of socialism.

Jawaharlal Nehru (Karanjia 1960)

The greatest of all amongst the 'tall men', those who had led the Freedom Struggle and who then dominated Indian politics into the 1960s was, of course, Jawaharlal Nehru. His position amongst the leaders of the Congress had long been a special one, because of his close relationship with Gandhi – whose successor he unquestionably was – and his popular standing. His role in the first generation of independence has been described – perhaps with a touch of irony – as that of a rationalist 'philosopher king' (Kaviraj 1991: 85). But great though Nehru's influence was, his commitments to the universalistic values inspired by the European Enlightenment, and – by the 1940s – to a Fabian version of social democracy, were contained by the absolute priority which he gave to the unity of India and, as a necessary condition of this, the unity also of the Congress party. Neither did these views of Nehru's on the directions that India should take command general or unquestioning support. Gandhi and Bose were not alone in offering alternative ideas about what 'India' should be, and amongst the 'tall men' there were many who were sympathetic in a way that Nehru never was to the ideas of the Hindu nationalists, as well as to the right-wing and more authoritarian directions represented by Patel.[1] By 1946, and in the years up to his death in December 1950 – in the time that has been described as that of the 'Duumvirate' – Sardar Patel exercised at least as much authority as Nehru, and arguably more, because of the control which he exercised over the organization of the Congress, which he sought to transform from a movement embracing diverse political views into a disciplined political party. It has often been argued – as by one of us elsewhere (J. Harriss 1989: 72) – that Patel's death, and the subsequent political manoeuvres through which Nehru wrested the Presidency of the Congress from Patel's man, Tandon, created circumstances in which Nehru was given room to impose the vision of India which we described in the last chapter. It is possible, however, that this view fails properly to recognize the length of the shadow which was cast by Patel's legacy, and in doing so overestimates the extent of both Nehru's authority in the 1950s, and the degree to which post-independence India was constructed as a nation-state in the image of its own modernist rhetorics.

The conventional historiography of the development of India after Independence has offered a narrative in which 'the Nehru years' are opposed as a kind of 'golden age' to what has happened subsequently. It is well summed up in Kohli's considered statement that: 'Over the past two decades [he is referring to the period from the later 1960s to the end of the 1980s], a legitimate and moderately stable state that was confident of its ability to lay out India's agenda for socio-economic change has evolved into a reactive state' (1990a: 8). The argument is presented most forcefully in Paul Brass's *The Politics of India Since Independence* (1990, 1994), which accents the significance of political leadership, and tends to present the change that Kohli describes as the outcome of the antinomies in the leadership of Nehru and of his daughter. The Rudolphs, too, in their *In Pursuit of Lakshmi* (1987), though they have less to say about the Nehru years than has Brass, present a picture of India's rise and fall and associate it with roles of the two Prime Ministers.

None of these political scientists explains the changes which have taken place so much in terms of contrasts in the personalities of Nehru and Mrs Gandhi as have some other writers, who have looked for explanation in Mrs Gandhi's personal sense of insecurity (e.g. Hart 1976; but see also Rudolph and Rudolph 1987: 137). And it would be perverse to try to write the history of these years without paying close attention to the aspirations, judgements and actions of the two great national leaders of India. Yet the imagery of 'rise and fall' can be misleading. It reflects a tendency to idealize Nehru's role and to overestimate his achievement. Of course it is reasonable to entertain the counterfactual, and to argue that but for the events of 1950–1, which abruptly resolved the tension between Nehru and Patel, it is doubtful whether India would, by the mid-1950s, have had a regime subscribing so unequivocally to universalist and secularist values. And there is still justification – even after the elapse of a decade – for Kaviraj's remark that 'modern India is still held together by a partially infringed frame which is the legacy of his period' (1988 [1997]: 63). Certainly the Nehruvian constructions (both of India as 'socialist, secular, democratic', and of the Congress as the guardian of this state) remain a fundamental point of reference in the discourses of Indian politics (see also chapter 10). But it is also important to recognize both the limits of his achievement – which were inherent in the contradictions of 'the third way' which he sought to establish – and the extent to which the political problems that engulfed the Nehruvian construction of Indian modernity in the 1970s and 1980s were the outcome of a system of rule which became established in 'the Nehru years' but which he did not fully control.[2] Indeed, the contradiction of the centralization of power at the Centre, alongside (and in dialectical tension with) the declining authority of the state, usually associated with Mrs Gandhi, seems to have developed initially during Nehru's long premiership. We look first, therefore, at the system of rule which became established in the early years of independence.

3.1   The Congress System and the Governance of India

'Congress becomes the Raj'

In its already long history before 1947 the Congress had embraced both the character of a revolutionary nationalist movement, and that of an opposition party with some experience of government at the Provincial level. By the 1940s the focus of political struggle had shifted to that of the form of government of the independent state and, it has been said, by this time 'the Congress was becoming the Raj', in the sense that the Congress leadership – drawing partly on the experience of office in the Provincial ministries – looked more and more to taking over the instruments of the colonial state. Patel, in particular, was concerned that the institutions of state power – the police, the army, and the civil service – should not be undermined, and there was continuity of personnel as well as of institutions and ideas even after the end of British rule. David Arnold has written of the Congress and the police that: 'Far from dismantling the repressive apparatus of the raj, the incoming Congressmen sought to strengthen and refurbish it to meet the current crisis and to guarantee the political succession' (1988b: 219). And: 'One of Patel's first steps [as Home Minister] was not only to assure the civil service that its position in the new government would remain the same . . . but to tell the politicians not to interfere with its functioning' (Kothari 1970: 111; see also Frankel 1978: 80–1). It has become plain, subsequently, that many, if not all, of the bureaucratic pathologies which have constrained economic development and progressive social change in India, have to do with the entrenchment of colonial practices – like the frequency of transfers – which were themselves the outcome of the ways in which the British ruled through Indian subordinates. The argument of Nehru's biographer, Gopal, that: 'The failure to dismantle the civil services and to replace them with a new machinery of administration suited to the objectives of free India set up unnecessary hurdles' (1984, vol. 3: 282) was put, no doubt, in partial defence of his hero. But his point of view has been widely shared.[3]

It seems that Patel turned the immense problems of holding the country together in the period immediately after Independence – the problems of dealing with the effects of Partition, of securing the integration of the former Princely States (including Jammu and Kashmir), and of dealing with armed resistance in Telengana – into the means of reinforcing the coercive capacity of the state at the Centre. At the same time, the supremacy of the Congress government over the Congress party was secured in the late 1940s – though not without a struggle, for Kripalani, the Congress President until his resignation over this issue in November 1947, had sought to make the pronouncements of the interim government subject to prior approval by the Congress President and the Working Committee. The continuities between the colonial and post-colonial states were reflected nowhere more clearly than in the Constitution itself, which took more than 250 of its clauses from the Government of India Act of 1935 – including 'the ones which Mrs Gandhi would use "constitutionally" to suspend the constitution and to revive a form of President/Viceroy's rule last seen in 1939' (Washbrook 1997: 37). The relegation of economic and social rights to the non-justiciable Directive Principles of the Constitution, while private property rights were enshrined amongst the Fundamental Rights, is a further important reflection of 1935. The inclusion of property rights amongst the Fundamental Rights came to exercise a very powerful constraint upon moves to bring about social transformation (see Austin 1966, ch. 4, on the differences between Nehru and Patel over these clauses; and Frankel on their long run implications – 1978: 439–42). Indeed, in spite of the formal separation of legislature and executive, rule by ordinance remained significant. In the first twenty years of independence 'more than 100 regulations, 100 presidential acts and 150 ordinances were enacted...[in a] riot of executive regulation' (Jalal 1995: 47).

But perhaps of as much importance for the development of post-colonial India as these institutional trends was the *coup de grâce* which Patel – with the support of Rajendra Prasad and C. Rajagopalachari – administered to the Congress socialists in 1948 when he won the approval of the All-India Congress Committee (AICC) for an amendment to the constitution of the party prohibiting the continuation of organized groups within the Congress. As a result of this decision the members of the Congress Socialist Party, which only ten years before had been extremely influential, voted to establish their own separate party, fragmenting in the process their already thin ranks. Their departure meant that 'Nehru's socialist support inside the Congress was sharply attenuated' (Frankel 1978: 72), and it was further weakened when several of the Congress progressives, including some of Nehru's close friends, left the party in the course of the struggle over the Presidency in 1951. The realignments that took place over this period represented a fundamental weakening of the reformists within the Congress, giving rise to a feeling amongst them, in spite of Nehru's apparent supremacy after 1951, of 'being encircled within their own party organisation' (Kaviraj 1988: 59). This had significant implications for their project of social transformation, including the tendency, increasingly, to rely on the bureaucracy as the instrument of change. This is a moment in our narrative at which to reflect a little more on the history of socialism in India.

Socialism and the Congress

Only a short while before the AICC passed the amendment to the party constitution which brought about the departure of the Congress socialists, its Committee on Objectives and Economic Programme had set out radical general principles concerning public ownership and the role of the state, including the statement that 'land, with its mineral resources and other means of production, as well as distribution and exchange, must belong to and be regulated by the community in its own interests' (cited by Frankel 1978: 68). Impeccably socialist sentiments. Yet, it seems, at the same time, the leadership was anxious to get rid of the avowedly socialist grouping within the party. This apparent contradiction in the statements and actions of the Congress leadership reflects a long history of tension within the movement over the relations between nationalist objectives and those of bringing about change in Indian society, which had to do, also, with ambiguities in the relationships of Gandhian and socialist thinking. Both his philosophical convictions and his experiences of movements of protest and resistance, in Champaran in 1917 and later in Kheda and Ahmedabad, led Gandhi and his followers to advocate a line of class-conciliation.[4] He believed that the 'Constructive Programme' in which he urged all Congressmen to participate – programmes of 'village uplift' directed at improving the livelihoods of the mass of poor people – would gradually bring about a major shift in power. As their lives and livelihoods became a little more secure, so the ties of dependence which bound the poor to the upper-caste village elites would be weakened, and in the end the upper-caste 'trustees' of society – responsible, according to Gandhi's theory of trusteeship, for using their wealth on behalf of the masses – would come to cede their power. Others, including Nehru, at least at some points through the 1930s, were not convinced and saw a need for class struggle – influenced, perhaps, by the rural struggles in which they sometimes became involved when these shifted from resistance to paying taxes to the colonial government to making demands against the prerogatives of landlords. Following the Resolution of the Karachi Session of the INC in 1931, which extended the definition of political freedom to include an 'end to the exploitation of the masses . . . and real economic freedom for the starving millions', ideas of class conciliation and of trusteeship were more openly attacked.

This was the context of the establishment, first, of the Congress Socialist Party (CSP) by Jayaprakash Narayan and Narendra Deva in 1934, and then of its endorsement of class struggle at its second conference in 1936. At the same time, individual communists – members of the still secret and banned Communist Party of India – were allowed to join the CSP, and through this means they sought to infiltrate the Congress. The success of the left in shifting the position of the Congress was marked by the adoption of radical proposals for agrarian reform in the Congress manifesto for the elections to the Provincial Legislatures in 1937, and then in the election in 1938 of Subhash Chandra Bose, who had committed himself to the CSP, as Congress President. But this, as events turned out, was the apogee of the influence of the CSP and of the left more generally within the Congress. In 1939 Gandhi – by now deeply alarmed at his waning influence in the nationalist movement – succeeded in engineering the resignation of Bose as President, and shortly afterwards the communists became increasingly isolated from the mainstream of the movement when, following Germany's attack on the Soviet Union, they dissented from the wartime Quit India Movement of 1942 and won the opprobrium of being seen as tools of the imperial power.

The apparently contradictory events of 1947 and 1948 have to be viewed against this background. Throughout, the leaders of the Congress – Gandhi, Patel and Nehru, too – gave absolute priority to the objective of securing freedom, and to the unity of the Congress movement in pursuit of that end. Nehru, in particular, seems throughout these years to have adopted contradictory positions. Pramit Chaudhuri has shown how in some of his writings before 1931 Nehru saw capitalism as being inseparable from imperialism:

> The one implied the other, political subjugation of the colonies feeding upon and in turn nurturing economic subjugation. This duality in turn evoked a dual response to end that subjugation, that of nationalism and socialism, the former striving towards political independence and the latter towards economic independence. The latter could not be achieved without the former, and the former was meaningless without the latter. (1988: 275)

Nehru also quite clearly recognized both the limits of his own party's commitment towards socialism, and that 'nationalism as such offers no solution to the basic economic problems of the country. The greatest problem today is the agrarian problem and nationalism has no real solution to it ... Socialism directly tackles all such problems' (cited by Chaudhuri 1988: 275). Yet in spite of these views, and many comparable public statements made at different times in the 1930s and into the 1950s, Nehru repeatedly drew back from translating these ideas into practice. And neither he, nor any other of the leaders of the Congress, nor indeed of the Communist Party of

India, had any truck at all with the alternative democratic tradition of low-caste, peasant-based protest articulated by Phule in the nineteenth century, and reflected in movements of resistance from below in the 1920s and 1930s (see chapter 2 note 6; see also chapter 9.2).[5] In practice Nehru always gave priority to the integrity of the Congress as the instrument of nationalism – expressed directly in his election slogan of 1952: 'The Congress is the country and the country is the Congress.' He seems implicitly to have accepted the Gandhian strategy of class conciliation combined with a gradual, indirect attack on the social foundations of exploitation, through the Constructive Programme: 'It is against the background of these assumptions that Nehru's preoccupation with avoiding premature polarisation around sensitive issues of economic reform [as we saw in the very first of the Constituent Assembly Debates, when he moved his Resolution on Aims and Objects], and his determination to maintain the Congress Party as a unifying force at the national level, even at the cost of short-term concessions to the propertied classes, become most convincing' (Frankel 1978: 111).

A less charitable interpretation of Nehru's stance is that he vacillated, or that his personal loyalty to Gandhi led him to compromise. Whatever the reason for his failure, finally, to stand by his intellectual position, the defeat of the Congress left in the late 1940s exercised an important influence on later events, as Frankel and Kaviraj have argued. Nehru's authority, though rarely disputed very openly – at least in the 1950s – was always constrained. The progressives were outnumbered by Patel-inspired conservatives in the Congress Working Committee, and 'from the mid-1950s onwards, the *modus operandi* of consensus proved to be propitious for the maintenance of the status quo' (S. Das 1994: 286). In this way, as well as through his institutional legacy, Patel left behind a long shadow – and the struggle for socialism in India was in large measure defeated before it was begun.

Centre and periphery in the 'Congress system'

Even while the Congress socialists sought, in the 1930s, to move the organization to the left, it was changing in ways which can now be seen to have sealed the fate of their project. The prospect that the Congress would form ministries under the provisions of the Government of India Act brought in many new members, attracted by the possibilities of government patronage; and it has been shown that 'almost half of all the Congressmen who joined in the 1930s were recruited from the prosperous proprietor castes, owning holdings between twenty-one and a hundred acres' (Frankel 1978: 73, citing work by Kochanek 1968). Many of these men were capable of being quite unscrupulous in their efforts to win control of the party at local levels, through stratagems such as the manipulation of membership lists.[6] The attractions of 'the loaves and the fishes of offices and jobs' (Ashok Mehta, cited by Hawthorn 1982: 210) began to pervade the political system, and these struggles for local control became even more intense after 1947.[7]

The English-educated urban intelligentsia who had supplied the great majority of the Gandhian and socialist workers were placed at a disadvantage in
local struggles for control over the party organizations, and: 'By 1949
conservative coalitions built by the dominant landowning castes in alliance
with urban businessmen had captured effective control of most District and
Pradesh Congress Committees' (Frankel 1978: 74).[8]

Here we should elaborate a little on the nature of local power, for it is a
theme to which we will necessarily return throughout this book. Local power
structures were illuminated by anthropological studies in the 1950s and the
early 1960s. These usually treated villages as basic units for analysis and,
influenced as they were by the functionalist social theories of the time,
represented them as ordered systems structured by caste and territory,[9]
and centred around the role of the locally 'dominant caste' – high ranking
in status terms, and controlling land and people.[10] In the context of modern
electoral politics members of these caste groups often came to function as
key intermediaries, operating in the area of their dominance, and brokering
the relations between state-level politicians and village people. A characteristic statement was that of F. G. Bailey: because of 'the fundamental fact of
the economic and social cleavage between the middle classes and the common people [the] politician cannot reach his electorate, the voters cannot
communicate with the politicians and administrators, [and] the gap is
bridged by the political broker and his network' (1963: 111). These 'brokers'
were local notables – landed, wealthy, in positions of power in the institutions of local government – who usually exercised authority, also, as members of a locally dominant caste. Such men came to form the organizational
base of the Congress-dominated political system.

By the early 1960s, as Myron Weiner showed in his study of the Congress
at that time, the party had built an organization, but one which was dependent on the authority which was exercised locally by 'big men' and oiled by
patronage – the exchange of offices, jobs and access to public resources for
the mobilization of electoral support – rather than being based on active
cadres (Weiner 1967). Rajni Kothari described this as a system: 'in which a
dispersed structure of power is brought together in terms of intermediate
"networks" which take the form of autonomous sub-systems in the larger
political system;' (1970: 91). Kohli's account is more graphic: 'That chain of
important individuals stretching from village to state, and eventually to the
national capital, welded by bonds of patronage, was one central feature of
Congress's success until the 1960s' (Kohli 1990a: 186).

But the result was that the leadership at the Centre, including even Nehru
– in spite of his enormous prestige – effectively became locked out of
influence at the State level and below, and was relatively powerless in
relation to State party organizations. These came to be led by a new generation of political leaders, drawn from amongst the local 'big men', rather
than from the professional, English-speaking intelligentsia.[11] They were
described at the time as 'coarser, less idealistic, less intellectual, more

caste-bound, more provincial' (Hanson 1966: 251) – but also as 'the only men, perhaps, who can and do tame the wild forces beneath them; they then lead them into the ways of the Plan and the all-India polity; they are the great intermediaries between the two styles of politics' (Morris-Jones, writing in 1961,[12] quoted by Hanson 1966: 251). Nehru might have been 'the arbiter of national policy', but his ability to push policies through to their implementation at local levels was tightly constrained by the dependence of the political system on the intermediation of the 'big men'. He and the progressives around him, dedicated to the task of modernizing and developing India, came to rely increasingly on the bureaucracy as the instrument of social transformation – though the bureaucracy, as we have argued, largely remained as it was when it was an agency of a colonial state, moulded by the tasks of maintaining order rather than by those of development and social change.[13] The dependence of the political system on the intermediation of a hierarchy of local notables is both reflection and cause of the seeming failure of the elite around Nehru to create, or to create quickly, 'a popular common sense about the political world, taking the new conceptual vocabulary of rights, institutions and impersonal power into the vernacular everyday discourses of rural or small town Indian society' (Kaviraj 1991: 90). The intermediaries on whom the system depended did not always translate the language and the values of the modernizing elite into a vernacular, or share in the creation of a common political language. They bridged different styles of politics, as Bailey and Morris-Jones both suggested, but in doing so they also kept these styles apart. Kothari seems to have meant something like this when he said of the 'intermediate networks' within the political system that they 'both aggregate local interests, and protect their identity and potency' (1970: 91). The result was that the whole project of modernization and development remained largely external and imposed, although, as we shall see later, important roots were being planted in 'Indian' soil even during this period.

Locality, region and nation

At the same time, however, the Congress political system was instrumental in maintaining the 'unity in diversity' which the leaders of the struggle for freedom had believed to be essentially characteristic of India. In spite of Nehru's fears – he warned that 'a boiling cauldron' was being stirred up – and the predictions of some political scientists, the language issue was not fatally divisive in the 1950s and 1960s.[14] The most dramatic statement was that of an American political scientist and journalist, Selig Harrison. In his book *India: The Most Dangerous Decades* (1960) Harrison argued that organized dominant castes, their boundaries fixed ultimately by those of language, were the force behind the agitation for linguistic States which began in 1953 when, after massive popular protests, the Telugu-speaking state of Andhra Pradesh was created. The Centre was forced to appoint the

States Reorganization Commission, and – much against the wishes of Nehru – finally to concede demands for the redrawing of other State boundaries on linguistic lines: in 1960 Bombay was divided into Maharashtra and Gujarat, and Punjab was divided into Punjab and (Hindi speaking) Haryana in 1966. Harrison's view was that the prospect of economic development was giving rise to intensified political-economic competition in Indian society, and that 'Caste...has provided a basis for the new economic and political competition, and the new caste competitors form ranks...according to native linguistic regional ties' (1960: 5). The creation of linguistic States would give rise to tremendous centrifugal strains, and he envisaged the breakdown of the regime, not perhaps for so long as the Congress maintained control in most States as well as in the Centre, 'But in the event of a divergence of parties in power at the centre and in a number of states...a Constitutional scheme that assumes a national competition between nationally responsible parties can only aggravate the competition between the states and New Delhi' (1960: 6). Elsewhere he wrote of the likelihood of 'a shambles of feuding regional ministries', perhaps to be followed by the establishment of a 'new authoritarian or quasi-authoritarian order' (quoted by Hanson 1966: 249).

Harrison's jeremiad was ill-founded. As Hanson, writing not long afterwards, argued meticulously and at length, events after 1960 did not seem to justify Harrison's fears about linguistic States, while: 'The sequence of dominant caste, linguistic state, and national disunity is too unilinear an explanation' (1966: 249). What about those major States in which dominance is contested between different caste groups? What about States in which caste played only a minor role in politics? Most importantly, perhaps, Harrison disregarded the powerful material interests of State politicians in the Union (which Hanson's book itself documents). Yet some of his points were well taken, even if his own constructions upon them were not. Subsequent events have shown that there is an inherent tension between the Centre and the States which has not led, and is not likely to lead to the disintegration of the Union, but which has contributed powerfully to the transformation of Indian politics (see, for example, Brass 1982; and chapters 4 and 5 below). His sense of the way in which caste was moving out into politics and of the agency of organized caste groups in collective competition was insightful,[15] while his remarks about popular 'pulp culture' – though expressed in a patronizing way – anticipate arguments concerning the gaps in understanding which have played an extremely important part in the progress of Indian modernization (see Kaviraj 1991, and the discussion above). Harrison wrote: 'Intellectual activity in each region will to a considerable extent be the pulp culture of popular writers who will address themselves to the swelling millions of new literates in the regional languages. The pulp culture will, by its very nature, be predominantly parochial in its horizons' (1960: 79). Popular 'pulp culture', sometimes in the form of screenplays, has surely contributed powerfully to the rise of regional political movements like the

Dravidian parties in Tamil Nadu, the Telugu Desam in Andhra or the Shiv Sena in Maharashtra – which have come to exercise a strong influence over Indian politics.[16]

It was considered by those writing in the 1950s and 1960s, however, that through the organization which we have described, the Congress was successful in holding together 'a nation which, without it, would rapidly degenerate into a mere assemblage of rival communities and regions' (Hanson 1966: 254, arriving, after all, at a conclusion not far away from Harrison's).[17]

The 'dominant party system'

The Congress, as an organized political movement, had been successful in holding together disparate elements in the struggle for political freedom, and it continued to do so as a political party after 1947. It was part of Nehru's organizational genius, in Kothari's view (1970: 157), to recognize that the Congress could and should combine the characters of movement and of party, and in doing so it came to occupy not only the centre ground of Indian politics but also much of the terrain both to the left and to the right. Throughout the 1950s and 1960s it was the only party with a national organization, built as we have seen of a network of political affiliations downward, and capable of assimilating divergent interests upward to the centre (see Kothari 1970: 154). Through it, the Congress was capable both of dividing the opposition, by responding to the fragmentation on the lines of caste and ethnicity within Indian society, and of winning wide support. And though it functioned in the context of what was (and remains) a 'Westminster-style', parliamentary democracy, the Congress remained hegemonic in the period up to the later 1960s. One of the leaders of the socialist opposition, Ashok Mehta, himself said that the role of the opposition parties was not so much to 'oppose', as to be constructively critical, and in this way to act as a 'corrective' to the ruling party (Kothari 1970: 158). The Congress contained within itself different, more or less organized interests, upon which opposition parties could hope to bring some pressure to bear. This was the political set-up described by Rajni Kothari and following him by Morris-Jones, as 'the dominant party system' (Kothari 1964; 1970, ch. 5): a system in which 'dominance coexisted with competition but without a trace of alternation [of parties]' (Morris-Jones, cited by Kothari 1970).

To begin with organized opposition came mainly from the left. The combined vote of the socialist parties and of the Communist Party of India (CPI) in the first general elections in 1952 amounted to almost 20 per cent of the total. But the socialists were already divided, as we have seen, and, as a result of the fragmentation of the Congress Socialist Party following its enforced independence, were rapidly losing the base of support in Bihar and Uttar Pradesh which had been created by the activities of young socialists during the Quit India Movement. The CPI had pursued the theoretical line of supporting bourgeois nationalism, and therefore of allying with the Congress. It had relatively strong support only in those parts of the country – Kerala, West Bengal and Andhra – where the Congress leadership of the nationalist movement had been weaker. In 1948, however, the Party – following a new political line set by the *Cominform* – denounced the Congress for its compromise with imperialism, and supported armed struggle (in Telengana, in particular). The failure of these tactics weakened the party, and though it succeeded in increasing its share of the vote by comparison with the socialist parties in 1957, and in becoming the largest single opposition party in 1962, it remained isolated in its particular regional redoubts.

On the right, in the 1952 general elections, the Congress confronted the newly formed Jana Sangh, started by S. P. Mookerji, a former President of the Hindu Mahasabha who had represented Hindu nationalist opinion as a member of the interim government in 1947. From the outset the Jana Sangh had an important, though never straightforward relationship with the Rashtriya Swayamsevak Sangh (RSS). With the advantage of the hindsight of nearly fifty years it is possible to discern in the RSS, even in the early years of independence, the most significant and innovative organization in India, alongside the Congress.[18] The roots of Hindu nationalism can be traced back (as for example by Jaffrelot and by McKean, both 1996) to the Hindu reform movement, the Arya Samaj, in the later nineteenth century, and then to the Hindu Mahasabha. Both articulated a sense of weakness in relation to the occidental and the Muslim 'Others', and a response to it both in the ideological assertion of difference, and in the creation of an organization comparable with a 'church' (which had largely been lacking within the diffuse traditions of Hinduism). The ideology of Hindu nationalism was codified, notably in Savarkar's concept of *Hindutva*, in the 1920s (see our discussion in chapter 8), and it was in this context that Keshav Balram Hedgewar founded the RSS in Nagpur in 1925, as 'a cultural organization concerned with national rejuvenation' (Madan 1997: 222). Its professed non-involvement in politics has been from the outset a political strategy – its objective being 'political domination through cultural homogenisation' (p. 225).

Emphasizing the importance of education and of character-building, partly through disciplined physical exercise, the RSS 'placed its mission within a familiar and prestigious indigenous framework' (Jaffrelot 1996: 71) – that of the *akhara* (gymnasium) and the model of the Hindu religious sect. Through these institutions the RSS quite rapidly built up an extensive network of dedicated volunteers (*swayamsevaks*) across north India. Banned for a time following the assassination of Gandhi by Godse, a former *swayamsevak*, when the organization came out from underground some activists believed that it would be wise for the RSS to be directly involved in party politics, and they became associated with the Jana

Sangh. Thereafter, the relations of the Jana Sangh as a political party, and of the RSS as a politico-religious sect were marked by ambiguities. It seems never to have been true to say that the Jana Sangh was simply a 'front' for the RSS, but equally the party was never entirely independent of 'the mother organization'. From quite an early stage, in the 1950s, the short-term political ambitions of the leaders of the Jana Sangh were tempered by the determination of the gurus of the RSS not to sacrifice the long-term objective of building *Hindu Rashtra* (the Hindu state). The line taken by the party oscillated, as a result, between an instrumentalist strategy of integration into the political mainstream, partly by pursuing the same sorts of strategies – exploiting particularism – that were used by other parties, and, on the other hand, more militant ethno-religious mobilization. In the process the Jana Sangh came to have a party structure which was distinctive in the Indian context, being dependent more on a network of activists than on clientelism.[19] But the significance of these developments only became apparent in the perspective of the 1990s. In the 1950s Nehru succeeded in isolating and marginalizing the Hindu nationalists, contesting their legitimacy, repressing their activities, and establishing secularism as the norm of the Indian political system. The Jana Sangh won some support amongst shopkeepers and businessmen, mainly from the upper castes, in the towns of north India, but it remained electorally weak. In the 1960s the principal opposition to the Congress from the right was mobilized by the Swatantra Party, founded in 1959, and representing the interests of big business and aristocratic landlords. It also took on positions associated with Hindu nationalism, and won endorsements from Hindu religious leaders.

In the three general elections of 1952, 1957 and 1962 the Congress won large majorities both in the Lok Sabha and, with some notable exceptions, in State assemblies, though without winning a majority of votes. Although it was hegemonic within the political system, therefore, its dominance depended upon the fragmentation of the opposition. The results of the first general elections in 1952 alarmed Nehru because they seemed to him to reflect the relative weakness of support across the country for the Congress, and they thus confirmed him in his commitment to a politics of conciliation – the style and way of working described by Frankel as 'accommodative'. The Congress Party may have been 'India's central integrating institution' (Manor 1988: 650), but while it was at this time an extraordinary amalgam of thorough-going opportunism and, at the level of the 'High Command', of great idealism, its organizational strength depended ultimately on the distribution of patronage. This machine was the instrument of India's modernization in the 1950s and 1960s, with which the national leadership sought to find a 'third way' to national economic development, combining directive planning and formally democratic politics.

3.2   The Indian Developmental State

The necessity of development

The state of newly independent India needed to secure the economic development of the country. The arguments of economic nationalism had come to dominate the critique of colonial rule and above all else the new government had to overcome the 'backwardness' and poverty which were seen as having been brought about by colonialism: 'a developmental ideology was [therefore] a constituent part of the self-definition of the post-colonial state' (Chatterjee 1993: 203). For all the very sharp differences of view amongst the 'tall men' about the most appropriate policies for realizing this objective – Patel, favouring free enterprise and resisting the creation of a Planning Commission, Nehru advocating, albeit inconsistently, 'socialist' approaches – there was a widely shared conviction that the state must necessarily play the leading role. The question was what the content of that role should be.

The Congress had established a National Planning Committee (NPC) in 1938, and though its work effectively ceased after about eighteen months, following the outbreak of war, it succeeded – Chatterjee has suggested – in establishing an idea of planning as a way of determining 'national' interests by 'experts' outside the domain of politics. It was in this forum that the ideological baggage of Gandhi's hostility to industrialization (and thus to 'development-as-economic-growth') was disposed of. Echoing the sentiments of a comment of Nehru's on the proceedings of the NPC, Chatterjee suggests that: 'The debate on the need for industrialisation, it might be said, was politically resolved by successfully constituting planning as a domain outside "the squabbles and conflicts of politics" ' (1993: 202). Then, before the end of British rule, the colonial government itself began to lay out policies very like those which were advocated by nationalists, and these last gasp efforts of the colonial government stimulated Indians to try to do better.

The most celebrated of their essays was the so-called 'Bombay' plan of 1944, drawn up by a group of leading industrialists, which – unsurprisingly – emphasized industrialization, but also argued that 'cooperative farming appears to present less difficulties than any other method', and envisaged that 'practically every aspect of economic life will have to be so rigorously controlled by government that individual liberty and freedom of enterprise will suffer a temporary eclipse' (quoted by Hanson 1966: 41). The 'People's plan' produced by the communist M. N. Roy and the Indian Federation of Labour argued, meanwhile, for the expansion of the public sector of the economy and anticipated the 'socialist pattern' which was formally adopted in the resolution of the Avadi meeting of the Congress in 1955; while S. N. Agarwal's Gandhian Plan – 'essentially no plan at all, but an essay in economic morality' (Hanson 1966: 43) – presupposed the acquisition by government of private assets. Amidst all the differences of emphasis and ideology, therefore, there was a general acceptance of the centrality of the role of the state which was part of, and probably helped to form, a much wider consensus. When what came to be known as 'development theory' took off, in the 1950s, it was concerned centrally with the issue of how to bring about growth in the colonies or former colonies which were becoming 'new nations': 'The goal of development was growth [requiring industrialization]: the agent of development was the state and the means of development were [national economic planning in the context of the macroeconomic policy instruments established at Bretton Woods]. These were taken-for-granted presumptions of "development theory" as it evolved from the 1950s onwards' (Leys 1995: 7).

India came on occasions to represent a paradigmatic case of the application of the positivistic orthodoxy of this sort of development theory, which took little or no account of history and presumed to offer law-like propositions about how development-as-growth could be brought about. As Ronald Inden has summed it up: 'The foremost of the congeries of practices that came under the heading of development in Nehru's India was planning, a utopian practice [at the time the advocates of planning would have said "scientific"] that would make India a modern nation' (1995: 248). Much of Nehru's own activity, in his frequent travels up and down the country, reinforced the symbolic significance of development projects and the concrete (often literally so) achievements of planning.[20] Planned development was a crucial part of the legitimating ideology of the Congress in power; and 'planning', as a domain constructed as being outside politics, became an essential instrument *of* politics.

Ideology and theory

Studies over the last decade or so of the historically extraordinarily rapid rates of economic growth in the major East Asian countries have given distinctive content to the idea of 'the developmental state' (though it actually has a much longer history, going back at least to List, writing in the nineteenth century). There has been a lot of debate as to just how important state intervention has been in accounting for the rapid growth of the 'Asian Tigers', but there is a good measure of agreement about the characteristics of their states.[21] They have, or have had, authoritarian regimes, in which, *de facto* or *de jure*, one party has held power, and has successfully mixed repression (notably of labour) and legitimacy (achieved by means of social redistribution). They are regimes with powerful elites in which the political leadership and the top echelons of the bureaucracy are intimately linked and united by determined national developmental objectives; and they have had competent economic bureaucracies, insulated from politics, and with the authority to direct and manage economic and social development in the pursuit of national interests as these have been defined by the political elite.[22] It is interesting to reflect that, in the 1950s, India seems to have shared most of these characteristics – and, probably not incidentally, that India enjoyed sustainedly high rates of economic growth at this time.

The Congress party, as we have seen, was hegemonic and Congress governments were perfectly capable of acting in an authoritarian manner, as for example in interventions in States which were run by other parties – notably Kerala, after the Communist Party had taken power there in the 1957 elections. There was a powerful elite – the 'tall and inspiring men' of Kothari's figurative statement – and there were close links between top bureaucrats and the political leadership. They came, after all, from amongst the same social groups, and they were united – as we have argued here – by a commitment to national economic development. In the 1950s the Planning Commission, established at last in 1950, did constitute a 'competent economic bureaucracy' with real power to direct the economy – though this was derived significantly from Nehru's personal authority in the national arena, and it was felt, at the time, that the 'experts' were perhaps too dependent on the clout of the ministerial members of the Commission (see Hanson 1966, ch. 3). In the Second Five Year Plan, in particular, India's economy was developed within the framework of a rigorously conceived plan.

But the Congress regime of the Nehruvian period differed in two respects, at least, from the kind of regime which is depicted in the contemporary model of the 'developmental state'. First, as we have explained at length in earlier parts of this chapter, the power of the Congress depended upon networks of intermediation and of clientelism – 'irrational politics' as Chatterjee puts it (1993, ch. 10) – which all the time, and increasingly, involved compromise and accommodation, so that the power of the leadership at the Centre to implement the policies which it espoused was limited. This was reflected in the steadily increasing power of the National Development Council (NDC), which brought together the Chief Ministers of the States of India, as against the authority of the Planning Commission. The deliberations of the NDC involved a lot of horse-trading over the distribution of resources from the Centre, and it has been said that: 'Politicians' interest in "socialism" had less to do with acceptance of the Laskian or Nehruvian vision of social democracy than with a desire to get their hands on new resources for the spoils game by extending the state sector' (Manor 1982: 100; see also Hanson 1966). In the 'Tiger' regimes, by contrast, the historically dominant social classes were all in disarray, in the context – variously – of military defeat and the outcomes of armed revolutionary struggles, so that their ruling elites did not need to compromise with local power in the way that was characteristic of the Congress regime in India. Then, later, in the cases of Japan, Taiwan and South Korea, they were shored up by US military power – under the umbrella of which successful redistributivist land reforms were carried through, completing the demise of the landed classes (those who were becoming if anything more powerful in India at the same time). Second, and relatedly, though there was a shared commitment amongst the Indian ruling elites to national economic development, there was no unanimity at all about the ways in which development should be achieved. There was a common view of the centrality of the role of the state, but – as we have put it – no agreement at all about what the content of that role should be. Robert Wade has commented in his seminal study of the developmental state in Taiwan that what distinguished that regime was not the particular policies which were chosen but rather: 'a consistent and coordinated attentiveness to the problems and opportunities of particular industries, in the context of a long-term perspective on the economy's evolution, and a state which is hard enough not only to produce sizable effects on the economy but also to control the direction of the effects, which is a more demanding achievement' (1990: 343). Neither the Nehruvian regime, nor any of its successors in India, has had these capacities.[23] Their lack is reflected very clearly in the compromised and compromising nature of key policy statements made by the Congress party and by the government.

In 1948 the government published an Industrial Policy Resolution in which it asserted exclusive rights to start new enterprises in key areas of the economy but offered reassurances to the private sector against the possibility of nationalization of existing enterprises, and to foreign firms. In the following year, however, the party served notice to India's propertied classes in the Report of the Congress Agrarian Reforms Committee, which proposed radical social reform and favoured a pattern of village-based cooperative farming. Yet the Draft Outline of the First Five Year Plan in 1951 suggested that the planning effort would involve reliance on private sector initiatives and, in agriculture, on technological improvements rather than on institutional reform. But the final version of the Plan (which was for the period 1951–6), published in December 1952, had a more radical tone, endorsing the main recommendations of the 1949 Report of the Agrarian Reforms Committee, whilst still stopping short of the generalized attack on private ownership rights in land contained in that report. The Industries (Development and Regulation) Act of 1951, meanwhile – the Act which, more than any other, established the so-called 'Licence-Permit Raj' which is now believed to have constrained India's economic growth[24] – had envisaged an expanded role for the private sector of industry even whilst legislating that no new units, or substantial expansion to existing ones, should take place without licence from the state. Subsequent statements, made in the Lok Sabha in 1954, and in the resolution of the Avadi Congress of 1955, of commitment to bringing about a 'socialist pattern of society' notwithstanding, the new Industrial Policy Resolution of 1956 continued to offer reassurance to the private sector. What emerged from all these, at times flatly contradictory statements, might very fairly be described as an attempt to define a 'third way', drawn between the extremes of a market-driven, private enterprise economy and a centrally planned state-led economy. But, as has often been the case with such attempts, there was also a lot of muddle, resulting from the conflicts and compromises between different, underlying interests, which the regime all the time sought to accommodate. It is hard to avoid the conclusion of Sukhamoy Chakravarty, an outstanding economist who was also actively involved in Indian planning, that: 'It is a reasonable conjecture that the compulsions of building up a post-colonial state based on consensus led Nehru to compromise to a much greater extent with vested interests than was necessary' (Chakravarty 1987: ch. 2, note 11).

The most coherent and theoretically considered framework for the planned development of the Indian economy was that established for the Second Five Year Plan (1956–61) under the direction of P. C. Mahala-nobis – a physicist who was also a distinguished statistician, who advised the Cabinet from 1955, and was a Member of the Planning Commission from 1959. The Plan reflected Mahalanobis's view of the need to build up capital goods production ahead of demand, and following from this what has generally been described in terms of an 'Import Substitution Strategy' of industrialization (ISI) that differed in the Indian case from what was being done elsewhere in the world in the same period – notably in Latin America – where the focus was rather on the production of consumer goods. But in general the Mahalanobis Plan rested on propositions which were supported in the economic theory of the time, and it can fairly be seen, as Chakravarty has argued (1987, ch. 2), as a variant of the classic growth model developed by (Sir) Arthur Lewis.[25] It focused on the supply side of the economy, identifying as the principal causes of economic backwardness shortages of material capital and a low capacity to save. 'The argument that domestic demand could possibly be a constraint on the growth process was not even mentioned as a hypothesis that needed to be rejected' (Chakravarty 1987: 11); and while unequal distribution of income was believed to be undesirable, 'a precipitate transformation of the ownership of productive assets was held to be detrimental to the maximisation of production and savings' (p. 10).

The key elements of the Plan were then to build up, alongside private agriculture, modern capital-intensive industry in the state sector, leaving the production of consumer goods to a (supposedly) more labour-intensive private industrial sector, with both protected by tariff barriers and import controls. Increased public investment was expected to give rise to large profits, including profits in the private sector. But these would be taxed for reinvestment. Chakravarty's argument (widely shared) is that this strategy for achieving economic development was not analytically shallow, but that it involved two crucial flaws. First, it rested on extremely optimistic and, as it proved, wholly unjustified assumptions about the possibility of bringing about rapid agricultural growth through institutional changes requiring little investment of resources (it treated agriculture as a kind of 'bargain base-ment'). This optimism was encouraged by the good foodgrains harvest of 1954–5. Second, it made extremely simplistic assumptions about the political process of planning, which came about, perhaps, because of that construc-tion of planning as an 'expert' realm which we described earlier. Specifically:

'insufficient attention (was) paid to the problem of how to obtain resources for public investment purposes while encouraging the growth of income in private hands' (1987: 18). These were the two causes of what became known at the time as 'the crisis of Indian planning' in the mid-1960s, around and just after the time of the death of Nehru in 1964.[26] The immediate cause of this crisis was the downturn in public sector investment, which followed from the failure to mobilize resources through direct taxation, together with several conjunctural factors: notably the droughts which caused serious shortfalls in agricultural production in 1965–7, and the effects of India's traumatic defeat by China in the war over the north-eastern border, in 1962. These two crucial 'flaws' in Indian planning derived, ultimately, from the attempt to combine directive planning with conciliatory, consensus politics – which was Nehru's 'third way'.

Practice and achievement

Deeply flawed though it was, it is important also to recognize the achievements of Indian planning under Nehru. It did, after all, constitute a very major and systematic attempt to bring about the kind of social and economic revolution which the members of the Constituent Assembly had wanted to be achieved. The 1950s and early 1960s saw rates of industrial growth of around 7 per cent per annum – not just relatively but absolutely high rates of growth. The autonomous and rapid development of Indian capitalism at this time was the result, largely, of public development expenditure under the plans; and the industrial structure changed very significantly (as Balasubramanyam (1984: 112) argues).

The government spearheaded investment in crucial and high-risk sectors 'while making finance available to the private sector to take advantage of opportunities as a consequence of its own investment and its protectionist policy' (Patnaik 1979: 6). Yet, because the framework rested in practice on the idea of a mixed economy with incentives to private investment, public investment could not be financed by a heavy reliance on direct taxation of property incomes. The resources for public sector investment came from deficit financing, indirect taxation (including excise duties, sales taxes and commercial taxes) and foreign aid. Foreign aid and deficit financing – narrowly defined as borrowing from the Reserve Bank of India only – together accounted for 43 per cent and 42 per cent respectively of the total public sector plan outlays in the Second and Third Plans; and in the end the Second Five Year Plan, according to Hanson (1966), was bailed out by American aid (including food aid transfers under Public Law 480). The additional tax revenue mobilized in the Second and the Third Plans came largely from indirect taxes, the share of which in total tax revenue increased from 62 per cent in 1955–6 to 71 per cent in 1965–6. Patnaik argues that: 'Since the impact of indirect taxes and deficit financing tends to be a regressive one, markets for mass consumption goods did not increase to any substantial extent...And this tended to reinforce the reliance upon protection and public investment as stimuli for industrialisation' (1979: 6).

This reliance then helps to account for the inefficiency of Indian industry, shown in generally high levels of underutilization of capacity, high costs and low levels of factor productivity, both in the private and in the public sector. But whereas most public sector industries failed to make profits – they became 'as much hospital as commanding height' (Herring 1998: 10; and see Chaudhuri 1979: 155–63) – there is no reason for doubting that the period of planning, from 1951 to 1966, was one in which the industrial interests of big business generally prospered, in spite of the hostility of the dominant political culture to them (as Kochanek explained: 1974). At the end of the Third Plan in 1966 the private sector contribution to the output of organized industry was still around 80 per cent of the total. And in spite of the powers which government had to control industrial growth it is clear that not only did the government fail to check the development of powerful monopolies, but also that the licensing regulations actually accentuated them: 'Over the years, the share of total approved investment allocated to the four largest business houses – the Birlas, Tatas, J. K. and Shri Ram – actually increased' (Frankel 1978: 335). The Indian economy in the Nehruvian period of planning became locked into socially inefficient but privately profitable capitalist development. It was a pattern of development, too, which failed to generate very much additional employment, and there was little change in the overall structure of the labour force.

The agrarian question

Rates of growth of output in agriculture were less impressive than in the rest of the economy. Total agricultural production between 1952–3 and 1964–5 grew by 3.42 per cent per annum, non-foodgrains (including especially sugar cane and oilseeds) at 4.79 per cent per annum and foodgrains (cereals and pulses) at 2.75 per cent. These rates of growth are not low either historically or comparatively (Chaudhuri 1979: 58), and they represented a definite shift after a long period of stagnation and decline. But still, given that the population was growing at more than 2 per cent per annum, it is clear that agricultural production in general, and food production in particular, barely kept pace with increasing numbers. When Dandekar and Rath measured the incidence of poverty in 1960–1 they found that nearly 50 per cent of the population were living below a very modestly set poverty line (see chapter 1.2). India was clearly a long way indeed from that objective which Nehru had put before the Constituent Assembly in 1946, of 'giving every Indian the fullest opportunity to develop himself according to his capacity' (see chapter 2). Both Nehru and Mahalanobis unquestionably were concerned with distributional issues, and plan documents emphasized the values of growth with equity. But, as Chakravarty argued: 'The model failed as a distributive device because the initial distribution of income-yielding assets such [*a fortiori*] as land was very unequal and the state had very few instruments of control to siphon off rising private incomes into additional public savings' (1987: 30). The failure to tackle the agrarian question in the early years of Independence was, we believe, the prime cause of the failure of Indian planning (in relation to the high aims which were set for it), and it has exercised the most profound influence upon the subsequent social and political development of the country.

What do we mean by 'the agrarian question'? Even if we do not – with Jawaharlal Nehru – believe that development is synonymous with economic growth, economic development is necessary to the realization of the object-ive of giving people 'the fullest opportunity to develop themselves according to their capacities'. Economic development entails structural transformation (as we argued in chapter 1), and in this process, in the case of an initially primarily agricultural economy like that of India, the central problem is that of how to develop agriculture, to provide food and raw materials, whilst also transferring resources from agriculture to the rest of the economy. This is 'the agrarian question'. It has been resolved, or sought to be resolved, historically, in various ways. One approach is that of forced appropriation and transfer of resources from agriculture, though this is likely to be counter-productive because it quickly leads to decline in agricultural output. Some-thing rather like this was attempted in a number of countries in sub-Saharan Africa in the 1960s and 1970s, when governments tried to fund a process of accumulation by taxing export agriculture, through the operations of state marketing boards, which – in combination with some other factors – resulted in declining agricultural output and economic crisis (see Bates 1981). Per-haps the most successful recent experience, on the other hand, has been that of Taiwan, where, building on a history of Japanese colonial investment in agricultural research and infrastructure, and in the wake of redistributive land reform, the Kuomintang government in the 1950s succeeded both in raising agricultural output and incomes and in bringing about a net transfer of resources from agriculture for investment elsewhere in the economy (see Amsden 1979). In this case investment in raising productivity in agriculture created a surplus which was tapped through government intervention in the terms of trade between agriculture and non-agriculture (specifically, between fertilizer and rice). The range of possible approaches is potentially wide, depending on the type of landholding structure and the choice of policies affecting the relationships between agriculture and non-agriculture – between 'town and country'. Varshney concludes his considered review of the agrarian question by arguing, however, that a route like that taken in Taiwan – 'make agriculture productive (via technological investments) but transfer resources through taxation or the terms of trade' – is best for most low-income countries (1995, ch. 1).

In India in the 1950s and early 1960s the approach that was taken was one which aimed to improve agricultural performance 'on the cheap', so to speak, through institutional reforms rather than through investment in improved technology and infrastructure,[27] in the context of policies regarding the allocation of public sector investments and perhaps of the intersectoral terms of trade (this is much more contestable) which were 'urban-biased'.[28] In fact, the structural problems of the Indian agricultural economy were such as to justify the case for institutional reform, but the principal reforms that were needed, which would have brought about radical change in the structure of land ownership and the organization of agricultural production, though often mooted, were never implemented. And in practice both the way land reforms were implemented, and the other institutional innovations which were put into effect – community development programmes, the expansion of agricultural cooperatives, and the establishment of institutions of local government (*panchayati Raj*) – tended rather to deepen than to resolve the existing structural problems, and to entrench the local power of rich peasants. This meant that when, after Nehru's death, the approach of 'making agriculture more productive through technological investments and price incentives' was taken up (in the 'New Agricultural Strategy' associated particularly with C. Subramaniam), the option also of transferring 'resources through taxation or the terms of trade' was politically impossible, for the power of the richer landholders was too great. Indeed some estimates suggest that – 'urban bias' arguments notwithstanding – there was probably a net transfer of resources into agriculture in the 1950s and 1960s, and perhaps in the 1970s as well, so that: 'Agriculture may not have contributed a significant amount of savings to the industrial sector. It may also partly explain India's slow industrial growth rate until the late 1970s' (Varshney 1995: 20). The failure to resolve the 'agrarian question' was comprehensive.

There were many, 'experts' and politicians, who recognized and advocated the case for radical land reform. Given the agrarian structure which we described earlier (see chapter 1.2), the concentration of land ownership (5 per cent of households, in the early 1950s, owned 41 per cent of the land, while the bottom 61 per cent of households owned only 8 per cent) and the dependence, associated with their 'compulsive involvement in the market',[29] of the mass of small producers on landowners, moneylenders and traders (roles sometime combined by the same individuals), Indian agriculture suffered from what Daniel Thorner described as 'the depressor' (1956: 16). With this term he referred to agrarian production relations which made it paying for landlords and other rural 'big men' to live by appropriating rents, usurious interest and speculative trading profits from the impoverished mass of the peasantry – and thereby limited the possibilities of productivity raising investment. Redistribution of land might have cut through this crucial problem, but it did not take place – and scholars have continued to identify the existence of 'the depressor' (amongst others, see J. Harriss 1982). The Congress Agrarian Reforms Committee advocated land reform and the cooperative organization of agricultural production in its report of 1949;

and much the same arguments were put again in the 1950s, partly inspired by the example of China, visited by expert missions in the middle of the decade. Finally the 'Resolution on Agricultural Organisational Pattern' for the Nagpur Congress of 1959 proposed the implementation of these ideas. But it met with such a barrage of criticism (and not least from Charan Singh, later a prime minister of India, and then a leading Congressman from western Uttar Pradesh, where he had an important following amongst dominant caste Jats) that Nehru rapidly back-tracked, saying in the Lok Sabha in February 1959, very shortly after the Nagpur meeting, that: 'There is no question of coercion' (in order to form village-based cooperatives). The whole initiative of Nagpur rapidly dissolved, and the cause of radical land reform, nationally, was finally lost. The Nagpur Resolution departed from the principles of conciliation and accommodation on which the political system that we described earlier was based, and it made Nehru more vulnerable to attack than ever before (see Frankel 1978, ch. 5).

But while probably desirable changes in the agrarian structure of the country did not take place, neither was there much support at this time for a strategy based on price incentives and profit maximization. And yet with the failure of land reforms to affect the power of the larger landholders, the other institutional innovations championed by Nehru – community development, cooperatives and *panchayati Raj* – mainly fell under their control, served their interests (as Daniel Thorner's many 'rural rides' showed: e.g. Thorner 1964; see also Etienne 1968) and failed to realize significant improvements in agricultural performance. Again, the 'third way' – neither socialist, nor one which made for efficient capitalist development – which was dictated by the requirements of the political system, served India badly in the longer run. (In the short run, somewhat paradoxically, Nehru's pursuit of a 'third way' on the global stage – positioning India as a leader of the non-aligned movement – allowed India to access foreign aid from the USA as well as from the Soviet Union and its allies. Grain transfers under Public Law 480, together with an increase in the area under cultivation, ensured that India would not reap the grim rewards of its agricultural strategy until the middle part of the 1960s.)

3.3   Conclusion: The 'Strangulating Embrace' and the 'Fall' of Nehru

The effects, therefore, of the policies which were followed in the pursuit of planned development in the context of a political system which depended on conciliation, were to enhance the power of those who were the most important holders of property rights – in the first place, the industrial and commercial bourgeoisie and the rich peasantry – and of the bureaucratic office holders whose discretionary powers were increased with the greatly expanded role of the bureaucracy as a whole. The power of the bourgeoisie and of the rich peasantry also mapped on to the relations between the central government and State governments, for the bourgeoisie was influential at the centre – in spite of an adverse political culture there – and the rich peasantry, increasingly, was powerful in State governments. They were, therefore – in a telling phrase – locked in a kind of 'strangulating embrace', each depending on the other, but also in conflict with the other.[30] The relationships between these three 'proprietary classes' have been analysed subsequently, in his influential model of the political economy of Indian development, by Pranab Bardhan (1984), which we discuss in the next chapter.

As we have argued here, the strangulating embrace of the bourgeoisie and the rich peasantry created a political context in which it became impossible for the regime at the centre to continue to implement the Nehru-Mahalanobis planning model because it could no longer mobilize the public investment resources to do so. Frankel sums up: 'Plan policies for agrarian reform and reorganisation were at the heart of the economic framework for increasing foodgrains production, raising the level of savings, and mobilising surpluses essential to financing large-scale industrial development schemes, As concessions to the propertied castes slowed down the tempo of institutional change, the government's capacity to raise additional rural resources for development programs declined' (Frankel 1978: 202). The government's capacity to raise tax revenues from the urban, industrial propertied classes was no greater. The faltering of the planning effort reflected heightened struggles for the resources and the distribution of patronage on which the political system depended – 'growing demands on static resources led to bitter internal disputes inside the Congress party' (p. 202; and see also Kohli's account of the role of struggles at the local level over resources controlled by the state in accounting for the decline of Congress organization; 1990a: 196ff). It became increasingly difficult to accommodate opposition. There was a sequence of events towards the end of Nehru's life – the defeat of the Nagpur resolution and the mobilization of right-wing opposition in the Swatantra Party, which it was difficult to accommodate within the ruling consensus; and perhaps even more significantly the 'exodus of farmer support from the Congress and the formation of regional farmers' groupings' (Kaviraj 1988 [1997]: 67),[31] India's defeat in the border war with China and the loss of his principal radical supporters in the cabinet, and electoral reverses in 1962, when, partly as a result of party in-fighting, 49 Congress ministers were defeated – which showed up the extent to which the Nehruvian project was fading before his death in May 1964. It was fading, in a sense, into the shadows left by the legacy of Sardar Patel.

4

Jealous Populism, Crises and Instability: Indira's India

India is Indira, Indira is India.

D. K. Barooah (Congress President)

In India, the 'kulak' has marched boldly through the door of politics.

T. J. Byres (1981)

Only a little more than five years after Nehru's death the Nehruvian design of modern India seemed to lie in ruins. The Congress party, Nehru's instrument for the modernization of India, and the unity of which he had seen as being more or less synonymous with the unity of the country, was shattered in 1969 as a result of the struggles for power between his daughter, Indira Gandhi, and the old leadership of the party. Before that time, the Planning Commission, that body of 'experts' capable of interpreting and implementing 'the interests of the nation' outside the domain of politics, had been reduced to a mere advisory committee, and the whole enterprise of planning had been placed into question with the postponement of the Fourth Five Year Plan. In the countryside the gradual transformation which he had sought to bring about through community development was being displaced by the 'green revolution' and the agrarian capitalism of which it was the vehicle. The Ministry of Community Development had ceased to have an

---

The expression 'jealous populism' was used to describe the Indira Congress at the time of the Emergency by the English writer, David Selbourne (1977). It is quoted by Partha Chatterjee, who comments further that it was 'utterly intolerant of rival populist mobilizations, and hence violently repressive' (1997a: 25). Put into the plural, the phrase seems to us to describe very well the contending regimes in India since the demise of the Nehruvian design (if not all of its ideas) at the end of the 1960s.

independent existence. What was described officially as 'agrarian tension' was quite widespread. The country had suffered the humiliation of bowing down before the powers of the United States and the Bretton Woods institutions, and had devalued the rupee, in the effort of trying to secure the continued flows of foreign aid on which the economic transformation of India had so clearly come to depend. The policy of non-alignment had become a sham. Domestically, the way of conciliation, compromise and consensus had given way to confrontation, and casteism, communalism and violence were on the increase.

It is extremely doubtful whether Nehru's short-lived successor, Lal Bahadur Shastri – Prime Minister only from the time of Nehru's death in May 1964 until his own, in January 1966 – or his daughter Indira intended to dismantle the design for India which he had sought inconsistently but still tenaciously to put into place. That they did so was because of the pressures which resulted from the political situation within the country, and those which came from without, and both sets of pressures were the result, largely, of the contradictions generated by the Nehruvian 'third way' which we discussed in the last chapter. The 'standard' historiography, representing the Nehru period as one in which there was 'a legitimate and moderately stable state that was confident of its ability to lay out India's agenda for socio-economic change' (Kohli 1990: 8), and the period afterwards, dominated (even after her death) by Mrs Gandhi, as one in which that state declined in its capacity to bring about change, even whilst it became more authoritarian, is not wrong. But, as we have argued, it is misleading in so far as it seems to overestimate the capacities of Nehru's regime actually to implement the agenda which it set out, and to underestimate the political contradictions to which it gave rise, and which resulted in its own demise. Not least, the Congress party was no longer able to accommodate different interests in the way that it had before, and it was already internally divided and riven by conflict before Nehru died. Over the next quarter-century, there came a succession of governments which together presided over the decline of the state-as-organization and which allowed the growing challenge of *Hindutva* to the modern state idea.[1]

4.1   From the 'Congress System' to the 'Indira System' of Authoritarian Democracy

Nehru refused to nominate a successor, arguing that it was for the people to choose, but in fact he seems to have done all that he could to ensure that the champion of the right, Morarji Desai, would not be the choice of the Congress leadership. The 'Kamaraj Plan' of 1963, under which a number of senior Congressmen were induced to resign from office to devote themselves to the renewal of the Congress organization, played its part in this; and Nehru and the State leaders of the party seem tacitly to have helped each other to ensure that Shastri would take over. Shastri was a moderate and a conciliator, and it was felt that he was 'one who could be safely entrusted with the office of Prime Minister by a group of state leaders intent on establishing a consensus style of government under the new pattern of collective leadership' (Frankel 1978: 242). It was against this style of leadership that Mrs Gandhi contended at the end of the decade, finally splitting the party in the process.

Changing gear: the 'New Agricultural Strategy'

Shastri's brief premiership initiated a number of changes which had profound implications for the future. By the time that he came into office the Third Five Year Plan was already running into trouble. Failures in agriculture were leading to increasing prices and inflationary pressures; shortages of raw materials and low demand constrained rates of industrial growth; and the limitations on the mobilization of resources domestically which we explored in the last chapter were bringing about both pressures on the balance of payments and increased reliance on indirect financing and especially on foreign aid. This dependency meant in turn that India started to become subject to pressures to change policies from the World Bank and from the United States such as had not existed before. In 1965 the Bank initiated a major study of India's economic policy, which finally reached the conclusion that the public sector plans were too ambitious, that the role of domestic and foreign private capital should be increased, and that greater priority should be given to agriculture – and in agriculture to incentives for agricultural modernization (such as had been advocated earlier, in 1959, in what is generally thought to have been an influential report of the Ford Foundation).

These conclusions were presented to the Government of India as conditions for substantial new inflows of aid. The United States government, under Johnson, tied the continuation of Public Law 480 food aid, on which India – because of the weakness of agricultural growth – had come increasingly to rely, to much the same set of policy changes. But these external influences coincided with internal pressures for change, to which Shastri himself seems to have been somewhat sympathetic, and it is simply not true to argue, as some have done, that the policy changes which came about at this time were the result of 'American' or 'World Bank' intervention. Key players in the 'home team' had shown their hands before the push for change came from the outside, and the Nehruvian model had so far lost impetus as to have made it very difficult for its remaining champions in the Planning Commission to keep up the fight.[2] Shastri quietly reduced the influence of the Planning Commission and enhanced the powers both of the Cabinet and of the ministries, partly by establishing a new secretariat attached to the Prime Minister's office. This was headed by L. K. Jha, a senior civil servant with strong inclinations towards policy shifts like those that were, subsequently, advocated by the World Bank. The powers of the State Chief Ministers, through the National Development Council, to recommend policy were increased. Shastri also appointed C. Subramaniam as Minister of Agriculture, and Subramaniam led the decisive move away from the institutional approach to agricultural development preferred under Nehru to what he himself referred to as the 'New Agricultural Strategy'. This emphasized technological change and price incentives to induce farmers to invest much more heavily in modern inputs, notably chemical fertilizers, even if this did mean making concessions to the private sector. It was at this time that new higher-yielding varieties (HYVs) of wheat – the successful cultivation of which required heavier applications of fertilizers – were introduced into the country, and what soon came to be called the 'green revolution' began. We discuss these important trends later in this chapter. Here we emphasize their significance in marking a departure from the Nehruvian model, and from the social goals that had been established in the Constituent Assembly, and their implications for the whole planning process. Subramaniam's strategy for agriculture called for the allocation of a greater share of public sector resources, particularly for increasing fertilizer supplies. This brought about a major tussle over plan financing between the Finance Ministry and the Planning Commission, and the Ministry of Agriculture – in which the leverage of the latter was increased by the effects of the disastrous droughts of 1965–6 and 1966–7 – and this contributed both to the delaying of the start of the Fourth Five Year Plan and to the events which led the Government of India, finally, to give in to pressures for the devaluation of the rupee, in June 1966, and to introduce a more liberal import policy. Aid from the United States was resumed almost immediately.

The breaking of the 'dominant party'

By that time, however, a so-called 'Syndicate' group of State leaders of the Congress, headed by Kamaraj from Madras and including also Atulya Ghosh from West Bengal, S. Nijalingappa from Karnataka, Sanjiva Reddy from Andhra and S. K. Patil from Bombay, had secured the appointment of Indira Gandhi as Shastri's successor, expecting that she would be acquiescent to their collective leadership and to the decision-making by consensus which had by now become established. Mrs Gandhi thus came into office without a power base of her own, to confront a situation which was both economically and politically extremely difficult, in an atmosphere of pervasive violence in the country, with the drama of devaluation already unfolding, and the Congress party in disarray, fractured by factional disputes. Devaluation gave ground to the opposition on both the right and the left, so that by the time of the 1967 general elections opposition parties for the first time openly attacked the basic principles established under Nehru's leadership, the left calling for constitutional changes in order to implement socialist policies and the right rejecting most of the programme of social transformation. The Congress offered little by way of a programme in reply and in the event suffered dramatic defeats, mainly to the benefit of Swatantra and the Jana Sangh – though, as Frankel put it, it was 'almost impossible to read the choice of an ideology' (1978: 360) in the electors' verdict. Rather, '[t]he Congress as the government party was the object of a great deal of censure and of electoral reprisal' (Kothari 1970: 203). Its majority in the Lok Sabha was reduced to twenty-five, and the party failed to win majorities in eight States. Amidst the carnage were some spectacular losses, which included Kamaraj, S. K. Patil and Atulya Ghosh. Commentators at the time described 'the end of Congress dominance'; and the elections were followed by an extraordinary phase of defections and counter-defections as different coalitions struggled for power in State governments ('between March 1967 and March 1970, defections in the states reached the astounding figure of 1,827, compared to the total number of seats in all assemblies of 3,487': Frankel 1978: 365). This led to violations of parliamentary and constitutional norms. President's Rule was imposed in five States in 1967 and 1968. The 'Congress System' of conciliation and accommodation, with a strong Centre and strong governments in the States, was no longer functioning, and there was from this time a developing bifurcation between national level and State level politics, which was subsequently established institutionally by Indira's tactical decision to delink national and State assembly elections in 1971. Bifurcation culminated in the power of State-level political parties in national politics in the 1990s, when they held the balance of power between the Congress, the Bharatiya Janata Party and congeries of opposition to them both. As the Rudolphs argued: 'Congress party leaders [henceforward] confronted a more complex and less manageable political world than that of the Nehru era and the Shastri interregnum, when policy issues and factional struggles at the center and in the states could be settled within the Congress fold' (1987: 201). Selig Harrison (see chapter 3) must have felt that his gloomy prognosis about the future of India, as a shambles of feuding States and ministries, was being fulfilled.

Meanwhile, the earlier failure of the Nehruvian regime to realize its social goals and the drift in policy through the 1960s away from their attainment meant that inequality grew,[3] and popular discontent began to be translated into political action by different factions of the left. Both communist parties – the CPI had split in 1964, and the CPI (Marxist) thereafter favoured a more radical political line in closer sympathy with that of the Chinese Communist Party – organized 'land grab' campaigns in several States to take over land from the larger landholders who had successfully evaded efforts at land redistribution. An armed struggle developed from early 1967 in the Naxalbari area of West Bengal, in the narrow strip of Indian territory between Nepal and (the then) East Pakistan, involving tribal, low-caste and Muslim peasant communities in conflict with landlords, and this was instrumental in giving rise to the formation on May Day 1969, of the CPI (Marxist-Leninist), committed to the Maoist line of people's war. The

Ministry of Home Affairs, in 1969, published a report on *The Causes of the Present Agrarian Tension*, which identified as underlying causes of these and other movements and events (such as the appalling slaughter at the hands of high-caste landlords of Scheduled Caste labourers in an incident at Kilven-mani in Tamil Nadu, also in 1969), the failure of land reforms, and as proximate factors the consequences of the new strategy in agriculture, which were thought to be enhancing inequalities. It seemed that the 'green revolution' in India was turning red (a refrain then picked up by researchers and writers in India and beyond).[4] But the factional and coalitional in-fighting in State governments made them incapable of addressing the prob-lems to which the report referred.

The struggle between Mrs Gandhi and her 'makers' in the Syndicate unfolded in this context of political disorder, increasing social conflict, and of the continuing 'crisis of planning' which had been marked first by the postponement of the Fourth Five Year Plan[5] and which was now showing up in the relative stagnation of the industrial economy as well as in agricul-ture. It seems that – in common with others in the Congress – Mrs Gandhi, no matter what her own political or economic philosophies (which are now rather difficult to discern in the trail of her political career), began to perceive the need to return to 'economic leftism' in order to win back popular support. Her turn away from the growth-oriented policies which had become so influential was accompanied by a turn away from the United States and towards the USSR, moves which were supported by the left wingers in the Congress who were now organized in the Congress Forum for Socialist Action.[6] They included communists like Mohan Kumaraman-galam who were pursuing a strategy of renewing the Congress as a party of socialist transformation by reorganizing it to reach down to the grass roots. The Forum activists saw in Mrs Gandhi a leader who seemed to share their aims and principles and she saw them, evidently, as allies against the Syndicate.

The struggle for control of the Congress developed over a Ten-Point Programme which was actually initiated by the Syndicate (it was proposed by Atulya Ghosh) as part of a response to the defeats which the party had suffered in the 1967 elections. This programme 'to accelerate the attainment of a socialist society', though it was in fact little more than a re-statement of long-standing principles of the Congress, became the focus of a sharp ideological debate which etched out the divisions and the disarray in the Congress leadership. It included proposals 'to implement social control of banking institutions' and 'to curb monopolies and the concentration of economic power' as well as to take 'a positive step towards the provision of minimum needs to the entire community'. But it also included a new proposal to remove privileges 'other than the privy purses' which had been granted to the ex-princely rulers as part of the accommodation which Sardar Patel had reached with them when they entered the Union. The radicals in the Forum argued that there was no reason to stop at social control of the banks, which should be nationalized outright. And they saw no reason why the Princes should retain their purses. Over the next two years the struggle in the party was turned into an ideological confrontation, over these issues in particular, and Mrs Gandhi came to represent herself as standing for the social change to which the party had been committed in the past, against a reactionary old guard in which Morarji Desai was by now the dominant figure. When the split in the party finally came about, ostensibly over the question of who should be the candidate for the Presidency of India, it was constructed by Mrs Gandhi in a letter to the members of the All-India Congress Committee as being, not a 'fight for power', but a conflict between 'those who are for Socialism, for change and the fullest internal democracy and debate in the organisation on the one hand, and those who are for the status quo, for conformism and for less than full discussion inside the Congress'.[7]

Given that there was no longer any possibility of returning to the old Congress politics of accommodation, it might seem that Mrs Gandhi should have been able to lead the government and the country emphatically towards the radical social transformation about which she spoke in her letter, and to which the party had really only ever paid lip-service (as in some of the points in the Ten-Point Programme). But of course her political position, at the end of 1969, remained weak, and, when it came down to it, she rejected the politics of class struggle represented by the Marxist opposition. Her own fraction of the party, the Congress-(R), was as much in disarray as was the Congress-(O).[8] The Congress-(R) 'had lost about forty per cent of its organisational strength compared to that of the undivided party', and that support was very unevenly divided between States (Frankel 1978: 429–30). In the years which followed, leading up to the declaration of the Emergency in 1975, in her continuing efforts to secure her power Mrs Gandhi sought to steer a path between the right and the left, and in the process she was 'pushed into the continuing use of populist appeals that promised radical social changes' (p. 435) whilst doing nothing – rather the reverse – to build a system of governance which would facilitate those changes. Her positions involved, in many respects, a reprise of those which had been taken by Jawaharlal Nehru. But the social context was very different as, partly because of the failures of the planning process, social polarities and conflicts had become more intense, and the legitimacy of the whole regime much more fragile. As Chatterjee puts it: 'the new state [in 1950] represented the only legitimate form of the exercise of power because it was a necessary condition for the development of the nation' (1993: 203). Then, as the 'development of the nation' faltered, so the legitimacy of the exercise of power was called increasingly into question. At the same time the organizational capacities of the ruling party and of the government were diminished. In these circumstances Indira's populism made for a dangerous game, raising expectations which could not be fulfilled. Her response, then, to opposition, was to resort to frankly authoritarian rule, in the Emergency of 1975–7, using those powers of the colonial state which had survived in the Constitution of 1950.

The new pattern of Indian politics: the 'decline of dominance'

Yet, not long after the split in the Congress, Mrs Gandhi achieved a position of paramountcy such as her father had never held. She called for fresh general elections early, in 1971, and in a contest which is quite well summed up in the slogans of *garibi hatao* (get rid of poverty) – which Mrs Gandhi proposed to the electorate that she would achieve by peaceful parliamentary means – versus *Indira hatao*, 'get rid of Indira', which is what (loosely) united the opposition parties, the Congress-(O), Swatantra, Jana Sangh and the Samyukta Socialist Party, she achieved a crushing victory. Not only was the Congress-(O) routed and the Swatantra Party nearly finished as a significant political force (its effective demise came after the State elections in the following year, delinked from national elections for the first time), but Mrs Gandhi also secured her ascendancy over her own supporters in the CPI (and those who had entered the Congress from the CPI who were activists in the Congress Forum for Socialist Action). They now depended on her, rather than the reverse. This was quite contrary to what most political commentators at the time had expected, and that they were so deceived supplies a clue to what underlay the transformation of the Indian political system from that time. As they wrote – after the event of the March elections of 1971 – Mrs Gandhi succeeded in reaching the voters over the heads of the intermediaries, the party bosses, local faction leaders and political brokers, whose role had been so well described by Bailey and by Kothari (see chapter 3, above), and who had previously mobilized the vote. The commentators did not expect the Congress-(R) to do well because: 'The limitations of organising electoral support through vertical patterns of peasant mobilisation – evident as early as 1962 – appeared much more severe in the wake of the split, when large numbers of local notables who had served the Congress as "link men" in the constituencies [had] defected to the Congress-(O)' (Frankel 1978: 429). But she mobilized direct popular support for herself as a symbol of commitment to reform, neither needing nor deriving support from the hierarchy of State and local party bosses who had sustained the old 'Congress System'. Mrs Gandhi, in particular, 'succeeded on a large scale in breaching the strategic position of the local factional leaders and intermediate elites as the political mobilisers of the poor peasantry. In a significant sense, it can be said that large numbers of the peasantry participated in the national political process for the first time' (Frankel 1978: 458). Indian politics were changed irrevocably.

   The transformation that took place in the operations of local power in the 1970s has been illuminated by another anthropologist, Marguerite Robinson, who studied local politics in a village and a taluk in Medak District in Andhra Pradesh over a twenty-five year period (see also our more extended discussion of Robinson's work in chapter 9). Here, it seems from Robinson's account, the kind of change which is recognized as having taken place over much of the country in the 1971 elections, occurred a little later:

> the pattern of local politics which underlay the elections in Narsipur taluk between 1957 and 1972 depended upon the delivery of vote banks to candidates by village leaders . . . [but] . . . the 1977 elections were structured differently. The components themselves were undergoing change (in varying degrees): land-owners were both losing land and competing for labour, the moneylenders had to compete with government credit sources; the Harijans no longer supplied force on demand. In addition, the new sarpanch, an agricultural labourer of middle caste rank, represented for the first time in the political arena the 'other' two-thirds of the taluk's population: those who are not landowners, Komatis or Harijans. Under these circumstances, the village vote bank collapsed and people voted – or did not vote – as individuals (or as households or in other small groups). (Robinson 1988: 248)

This analysis reflects the contradictory changes that were taking place in the rural economy and society of India. Partly as a result of state interventions which, partial and limited though they were (as we explain later in this chapter), still succeeded in building up the countervailing power of those who had for so long been subordinated in the hierarchical social system and the oppressive class structure of India, and partly because of the language of democracy diffused in the rhetoric of politicians, dominance (as we described it in the last chapter), increasingly, was challenged. The story of 'the decline of dominance' is a complicated and rather a contradictory one. Certainly this idea should not be understood as implying that local holders of economic power (and of course political power has been converted to economic power, perhaps as much as the reverse) are under immediate threat from subaltern classes. But traditional authority is no longer generally accepted. Jan Breman, who has studied a region of south Gujarat over more than thirty years, has written that in spite of the pervasive oppression of labouring people which he has so richly documented: 'in a fundamental way the ideology of inequality, presumably the hallmark of Hindu civilisation, to a large extent seems to have lost social legitimacy. I consider this observation to be the most significant recapitulation of my research findings.' And, he notes, 'there is a definite shift from a more vertical towards a more horizontal orientation in the principles of social organisation' (1996: 262).[9] This is a theme to which we will return in chapter 9. Its significance in the present context is in relation to the changes which took place in the 1970s in the political system. The 'decline of dominance', which – we should emphasize – was not brought about by Mrs Gandhi, meant that any other political leader, too, would have found it extremely difficult to continue to operate the old 'Congress system' in the 1970s (see Kohli 1990a: 190ff).

The 'deinstitutionalization' of politics

There was also a paradox in Mrs Gandhi's overwhelming victory in 1971 – which was enhanced by victory in the war with Pakistan later in the year that gave birth to the new state of Bangladesh, and by her success in the State legislative assembly elections of 1972. The paradox is that electoral supremacy and political power at the centre do not always translate into effective authority to govern, and it remains one of the essential aspects of Indian politics. It is tied up, too, with the fragility – in a sense, the ephemerality – of political power in India. Indira's triumph was a personal victory. It had not depended upon the party or its organization. Rather was she an indispensable symbol to the Congress. Because the development of a party organization had proved unnecessary to her securing of political power, and indeed might come to establish alternative leaders with strong, independent bases of power of their own, Mrs Gandhi did nothing to bring it about. Frankel suggests that she had 'neither the ideological conviction nor the organisational capacity for attempting the creative tasks of party reform that were necessary to redeem promises of socialist change through peaceful means' (1978: 462). As time went on Indira Gandhi found it less and less in her interests to rebuild the party organization. Certainly she was less and less able to do it, entangled as she was in the personal system of rule that she created.

What most observers have concurred in describing as the 'deinstitutionalization' of Indian politics[10] (which still persists) goes back primarily to the split in the Congress and the elections of 1971, even if its roots do lie in the failures of the Nehruvian model. The general lack, subsequently, of party organization linking centre and periphery, and extending into localities – such as had obtained in the particular forms of the old Congress – has both (further) weakened the ability of rulers to put policies into effect and (partly in consequence, of course) made them vulnerable to what have been described as 'wave' effects,[11] when the electorate is swung in different directions in successive elections by particular factors having to do with personalities or events, or simply by disaffection from a ruling party which has not delivered on its promises. These phenomena, and the consequent volatility of Indian politics, were associated with a general 'decline of ideology'. Political conflict came to be less and less about ideological and programmatic differences, and more and more about personalities (until these trends were checked by the political changes of the 1990s which we analyse in later chapters). What was generally offered to the electorate both nationally and at State level was one populist package or another, intended to appeal to voters across the diversity of interests by means of such slogans as 'One kilo of rice, one rupee', and without a coherent programme for the realization of the goals which have been proclaimed. In these circumstances elections became more and more like populist referenda, or plebiscites on the performance of particular leaders. And lacking local organization, come election time, politicians had (and still have) recourse, often, to 'black money' derived from the informal and illegal economies in order to fund their campaigns. This, in turn, contributed to the criminalization of politics – on a scale and of a kind unlike that of the graft and patronage of the old Congress machine – so that politics has become more and more a cynical game in which political capital is turned into private wealth and vice versa. The outstandingly successful political parties of the last quarter-century – the DMK in Tamil Nadu,[12] the CPI(M) in West Bengal and Kerala and the Jana Sangh/BJP in parts of north India – while they have certainly not been above the game of corruption, have also been distinguished by their relatively strong organizations.

Rather than rebuilding her party as an organization after 1971, Indira Gandhi sought to establish control by centralizing power into her own hands, in what Stanley Kochanek described as 'Mrs Gandhi's Pyramid'. He wrote:

> The elections of 1971 and 1972 in India marked the restoration of Congress dominance at the centre and in the states, a return to strong central leadership, and the apparent emergence of a more broadly based, ideologically coherent party. On the surface the 'Indira wave' appeared to have restored the pattern of one-party dominance that characterised the Nehru era. Yet a closer analysis reveals a distinctly different pattern of dominance. (Kochanek 1976: 93)

The long struggle of 1966 to 1972 had taught Mrs Gandhi 'a bitter lesson that led her to consolidate her power so that no potential challenger could emerge' (p. 104). Intra-party democracy ceased to function from this time, and has never been fully restored. Mrs Gandhi used her influence over the appointments of members of the Working Committee, the Parliamentary Board and the Central Election Committee to ensure the appointment also of compliant party Presidents with no power base of their own, and to intervene directly in the affairs of the State parties. Already by the time of the State legislative assembly elections in 1972 the party was even less capable of popular mobilization than it had been before, and Mrs Gandhi removed four State bosses just before those elections. This was the beginning of the long game of musical chairs which went on until the Congress had finally lost power in a majority of States, in which a string of those whom Kaviraj nicely describes as 'unspeakable nonentities' (1988 [1997]: 72) were thrust into office in the States by the Prime Minister, to be thrown out just as easily – since they were men who lacked organizational power. The game was ultimately counterproductive. It opened up new possibilities for factional in-fighting, and the more Mrs Gandhi sought to pull the strings from the Centre the less authority she came to exercise over State affairs, and over time power slipped away from the Congress to different parties with a regional base of support, or to coalitions of such political groupings.[13]

These were the circumstances which created India's authoritarian democracy – in which, as Vanaik says, 'both adjective and noun are important' (1990: 109) – and what has struck many outsiders, in particular, as the extraordinary tenacity of electoral democracy in India in spite of the apparent inadequacies of the country's whole system of governance. The contradictory character of India's politics was brought into sharp relief by the Emergency. Before we turn to it, however, we want to look more closely at what was happening in the economy at this time.

4.2   The Political Economy of Indian Development

'Structural retrogression' after the mid-1960s and compromised class power

As we have seen, the crisis of planning, with stagnation in agriculture, shortages of power and essential raw materials, increasing prices and – crucially – yawning budgetary deficits, led to pressures for reductions in plan outlays and for greater reliance on the private sector. In the initial period of what was called the 'plan holiday' between 1966 and 1969 outlays were reduced, in the context of the devaluation crisis. From this time the performance of the Indian economy as a whole (and especially of manufacturing industry), right through to the early 1980s, was generally unsatisfactory. Growth was slower than it had been before, and it was subject to sharp fluctuations from year to year. As compared with a 7 per cent growth rate in industrial production between 1951 and 1965, the period 1965–70 saw a mere 3.3 per cent growth rate and that between 1970 and 1982 4.3 per cent per annum – only a little above the average for twenty-three low-income countries listed in the World Bank's *World Development Report* for 1984 (see I. J. Ahluwalia: 1985).

There have been, broadly, three different explanations for the relative stagnation of industrial growth after the mid-1960s.[14] One view of India's economic policies, which anticipated the neo-liberal critiques of state intervention which came to dominate thinking about economic development in the 1980s, was in the work of Bhagwati and Desai (1970) and Bhagwati and Srinivasan (1975, 1984), and somewhat later in that of Isher Ahluwalia (1985). They argued that the wide range of controls on economic development in general, and especially on industry, including the extensive role assigned to the public sector, created inefficiency. Left-wing economists, on the other hand, emphasized the importance of demand-side constraints (as did Chakravarty, to whose study of planning (1987) we referred in the last chapter); while a third view associated industrial decline with the downturn in public sector investment and infrastructural bottlenecks. All three lines of thought can be justified, and it seems to us that each contributes to explanation. All three are brought together, however, in an analysis of the political economy of Indian development which shows how class structure influenced these outcomes. This analysis recalls Barrington Moore's argument, explaining India's politics and development as the results of the installation of political democracy in advance of a bourgeois revolution (see chapter 2).

S. L. Shetty argued that in the decade after the end of the Third Five Year Plan India experienced what he described as 'structural retrogression', referring to the facts that services had grown faster than commodity-producing sectors; that the growth of basic and capital goods industries had been even slower than the meagre average growth in industrial output; and that production of mass consumption goods had lagged behind that of elite-oriented consumer goods (1978). The demand side of the economy, neglected in the Nehru-Mahalanobis model, had struck back. At the same time there was evidence of a large amount of underutilized capacity; there had been virtually no growth in organized sector employment; and the real wages of industrial labour had declined. None of these features of the economy changed much in the 1980s. Shetty attributed the retrogression that he described to 'the decline of planning' which had, he argued, given rise to distortions in production and investment patterns in the private sector and serious financial mismanagement in the public sector, shown both in the frittering away of outlays in non-development expenditure, and in the distorted system of resource mobilization. The disproportionate growth, after the period of the first three Plans, of non-developmental expenditure was accounted for by subsidies, especially those for export promotion, which were shown to have been singularly inefficient, and for the public procurement and distribution of foodgrains, and by transfers to State governments for purposes other than development and capital formation, which involved political patronage extended to a few States in particular. Meanwhile, partly accounting for the persistent needs of some States for such special assistance from the centre, state agencies like the State Electricity Boards and Irrigation Departments had made huge losses for want of prompt recovery of dues, especially from rich farmers. Shetty portrayed enormous wastage of financial resources and, alongside it, a system of resource mobilization that was distorted by the government's inability or unwillingness to tax agricultural incomes, by reductions in the marginal tax rates on personal incomes and wealth in the non-farm sector, by the continued reliance on indirect taxation, and the resort to deficit spending. At the same time the declining trend of investment in the public sector had repercussions on the rate of capital formation in the private sector. The cut-backs in public sector investment in the 1960s had immediate effects on a range of basic and capital goods industries, many of which continued to experience demand constraints, so that they showed scant increases in output and high levels of underutilization of capacity.[15] There was more than ever evidence of the social inefficiency of Indian capitalism in the growth of monopoly powers on the part of some of the big business houses (in spite of the passage of the Monopolies and Restrictive Trade Practices Act in 1969),[16] while public financial institutions provided the major part of the investible funds deployed in the private manufacturing sector after the mid-1960s. Shetty believed that the easy availability (to some firms, at least) of investible funds at relatively low cost, and the low personal stakes of the promoters, induced higher capital intensity, as well as a siphoning-off of funds and a general lack of cost consciousness.

This analysis of the 'crisis of planning' and of its consequences showed that the same constraints which had started to become apparent even in Nehru's lifetime persisted and were even intensified by the relaxation of attempts to control and to plan the economy through the 1970s: the inability of the state to raise resources domestically; the failure of agrarian reform; and the demand-side constraints which were exacerbated still further by regressive taxation and associated with top-heavy industrialization. The principal beneficiaries appear to have been the larger business houses and the rich farmers who benefited from the 'new agricultural strategy' whilst paying very little indeed to the state through direct taxation (or, on balance, in the longer run, according to Varshney's (1995) analysis, through the mechanism of the terms of trade). These observations provide support for, and are explained in Bardhan's model of the political economy of India, as reflecting the outcomes of conflicts and compromises between three dominant propertied classes: the industrial capitalists, the 'rich farmers', and the class of white-collar workers and public sector professionals. None individually is substantially more powerful than the others and they are locked together in relationships of competitive interdependence. And: 'Although the autonomous power of the state can clearly increase if none of the classes constraining state action dominates the others, and although social cleavages make compromise difficult and multiply the stresses and strains on the polity, the Indian experience suggests that the very nature of class balance and heterogeneity may make the proprietary classes more interested in the maintenance of democratic processes' (Bardhan 1988: 216) – as was seen, finally, in the resolution of the Emergency in the middle 1970s (as Chatterjee argued, 1977 [1997]). The other concomitant of the compromised nature of class power in India is that: 'The Indian public economy has become an elaborate network of patronage and subsidies. The heterogeneous proprietary classes fight and bargain for their share of the spoils of the system . . .' (Bardhan 1988: 219), so that, as a result, the bulk of public resources have been frittered away in the manner that Shetty described.

The march of the 'kulaks'

A particularly important expression of conflict between the urban industrial and professional classes (and, over this issue, certainly, their allies amongst urban workers) and the dominant agricultural interests is observed in the struggles over farm prices and input costs, which became a recurrent feature of Indian politics after the inception of the New Agricultural Strategy. Technological change in agriculture and the intensification of production through the use of the 'green revolution' inputs of new, higher-yielding (basically because more fertilizer-responsive) varieties of the main cereal crops, fertilizers and plant protection chemicals[17] – the successful use of which has usually required investments also in irrigation in the context of India's agro-climatic conditions – have of course also required much higher levels of investment of cash on the farmers' part. As Subramaniam and his advisers very clearly recognized when they made the great gamble of introducing the higher-yielding varieties from 1966, farmers needed incentives if they were to invest in these modern means of raising agricultural productivity.[18] Technical studies have shown that intensification has often depended significantly on the ratio of the prices that farmers have had to pay for nitrogenous fertilizer, in particular, to output prices. Ever since the inception of the green revolution, agricultural prices and the costs of inputs have therefore been a major political question (see Varshney 1995). When a reforming Finance Minister, Manmohan Singh, sought to slash fertilizer subsidies in 1991 – they were by that time a major drain on the exchequer – he very rapidly had to backtrack in the face of the opposition of the agricultural lobby. Struggles over prices and subsidies (not only for fertilizers, but also for irrigation and electricity, required in particular to power the small irrigation pumps which have been instrumental in bringing the green revolution to many parts of India)[19] gave rise from the later 1970s to the so-called New Farmers' Movements, which were successful in mobilizing large numbers of people across large tracts of rural India in making demands upon the state – for higher output prices and lower input costs, or the cancellation of agricultural debts or irrigation charges (see our discussion of these movements in chapter 5; see also T. Brass 1995; Nadkarni 1987).

Those who have been most centrally involved in the politics of agricultural prices have been those whom Byres describes as 'kulaks' (1981: 58) – the Russian term, meaning 'fist', used to describe rural power-holders, usually with economic interests extending over agricultural production and trade, transport and other investments.[20] They are predominantly, if not exclusively, from amongst the rich peasantry which, as we described in the last chapter, had already established itself by the mid-1960s: 'By far the greatest beneficiaries [of the changes which took place in the 1950s] were the rich peasants. Their class-for-itself action became increasingly effective. They were stabilised as independent proprietors, and were on the way to becoming, in many areas of India, the new dominant class in the emerging agrarian structure' (Byres 1981: 49). As the new agricultural technology became available it was steered particularly towards the parts of the country in which the rich peasantry was powerful, and towards them in particular. It was said at the time that: 'If the Ford Foundation had not brought the green revolution to India [this was a slight embellishment of the truth], then the rich peasants of Punjab would have done so on their own' (H. Sharma 1973), and the policy of 'betting on the strong' of this period was as much response to as cause of their increasing power. Although the technology of the green revolution is technically 'scale neutral' – meaning that it can, in principle, realize more or less constant returns to different sizes of the 'package' of water, fertilizer and seeds – it is not, as Rao put it, 'resource-neutral' (1975: 44). Richer producers were at an advantage, certainly in the early days of the green revolution, because they were better informed, better able to carry the risk of increased investment, able to raise money capital more cheaply than poorer peasants, more likely to have access to fertilizers when they were in short supply, more likely to have access to irrigation, and more likely to command the labour required at times of peak demand. Poorer peasants did adopt the new technology, but with a lag, and not always to their benefit.[21] So the advent of the green revolution tended to lock the rich peasantry, of some parts of India in particular – to begin with especially Punjab, Haryana and western Uttar Pradesh – into a positive spiral of increasing wealth and political power. But it also – as they became a commodity producing peasantry[22] – locked them into the politics of agricultural prices and subsidies.

There were already clear indications from the middle of the 1960s of the increasing political power of the rich peasantry, and of their capacities to mobilize support across rural classes because of the connections of kinship, caste and patronage. Crucially, for the political future of India as a whole, their increasing local power in important parts of north India was tied up also with the horizontal mobilization of Backward Classes, eroding the hold of the historically dominant high-caste local elites and, in the process, that of the Congress Party. Charan Singh, long-time Congress leader in the Meerut District of Uttar Pradesh, first brought about the collapse of the Congress government in that State in 1967 by leading his supporters out of the party; subsequently, for the mid-term polls in 1969, he formed the Bharatiya Kranti Dal (BKD, or Indian Revolutionary Party), which emerged as the second largest party in the State. Singh's popularity was based on his record of championing cultivators' interests, including those of the lower ranking Backward Classes. The BKD appealed directly to the common economic interests of the members of these low-ranking castes against the existing political leadership, which was dominated almost exclusively by elite Brahmans and Thakurs. The results of the 1969 elections in UP 'signalled the first signs of changing patterns of peasant participation toward new forms of horizontal alignments, as customary ties between upper-caste landlords and low-status peasant cultivators and landless groups began to erode. The long-term viability of vertical patterns of political mobilisation was called into question within the Hindi-speaking heartland itself' (Frankel 1978: 387). Not long afterwards, of course, Charan Singh became a key figure in the opposition to Mrs Gandhi, and one of the leaders of the Janata Party, the coalition party which governed after the end of the Emergency in 1977. The story of that government, and of all subsequent governments of India, has depended to a significant extent upon the politics of the Backward Classes across north India, and of the rich peasant lobby. The local power which they exercise has been instrumental, too, in locking the state out of local control and in creating in some cases 'shadow state' structures (see Harriss-White 1997; and our discussion in chapter 7).

We believe, as we have sought to show here and in the last chapter, that the rise of the rich peasantry – 'the march of the kulaks' – has exercised a decisive influence over the development of India since independence.[23] The Rudolphs (1987), in their analysis of India's political economy, seem to agree in some ways and document the rise of the 'demand group' (as they describe it) of agrarian producers in great detail. But their construction upon it differs radically from ours. In their view this 'demand group' consists of those whom they describe as 'bullock capitalists', owning between two-and-a-half and fifteen acres of land, and whom they see as being like 'yeoman farmers' who are both numerically dominant and control more land than any other group in the Indian countryside. The dominance of this group accounts very substantially, in their view, for what they regard as the prevailing 'centrism' of Indian politics and the general weakness of class politics in the conventional sense. But this whole analysis flies in the face of an abundance of evidence from survey research and village ethnography which shows the power of a small number of landholders whose mode of operation of their lands is, however, that of 'rich peasants' or of capitalist farmers rather than of 'landlords' leasing out lands to serf-like tenant cultivators. What has perhaps confused the Rudolphs is that the evidence from India over the last fifty years of the process of proletarianization of poor peasant producers, and their reduction to the ranks of the agricultural wage labourers without lands of their own – as in the classical model of the 'differentiation of the peasantry' deriving, notably, from Lenin's analysis of agrarian change in nineteenth-century Russia – is very weak. What has happened is rather a process of partial proletarianization, in which there is a pervasive dependence upon wage incomes, but without complete loss of control over their small plots on the part of the poor peasantry.[24] In this context the rich peasants are often successful, as the history of the New Farmers' Movements shows, in mobilizing political support across rural classes, over issues of prices and subsidies; but to recognize this does not mean conceding to the idea that the Indian rural economy is characterized by sturdy 'yeoman farmers'.

Kulaks and Indian poverty

The economic dominance – *pace* the Rudolphs' analysis – of the numerically small class of rich peasants which controls a large share of the land, is quite fundamentally bound up with the reproduction of the pervasive poverty which is overwhelmingly characteristic of India. It is not just that the rich peasants exercise a very significant level of oppressive control over the lives of the poor peasants and the landless, to the point, sometimes of quite systematically denying them the means of livelihood (richly documented by Breman (1974; 1985a; 1996) for south Gujarat; and see Lerche (1995) on rural Uttar Pradesh), but also that, structurally, the counterpoint of their power is the vulnerability of the poor. The dependence of the poor is acute, so that they are frequently 'compulsively involved' in markets, in circumstances of 'forced commerce' – selling their produce at unfavourable prices even though they have no net surplus, and having subsequently to borrow at usurious rates in order to meet household and production needs, or selling their labour power even at rates below the 'market' wage.[25] Tomlinson has shown (1988), as we noted in chapter 1, how these conditions extended from the colonial period into the period of planning (as Bharadwaj demonstrated: 1974). The price-taking dependence of the mass of the rural people – who are now dependent more upon uncertain and usually irregular casual wage employment than on their own production – is instrumental in the reproduction of their own vulnerability and poverty, and at the same time, of the wealth and power of the rich peasant-kulaks. This structural inequality, partly because it results in such limited demand for non-agricultural goods and services, also constrains the development of rural non-agricultural activity, such as would help to tighten rural labour markets, improve wages and thus be instrumental in raising living standards (so that, contrary to the expectations and arguments of economists who have supported an 'agriculture-first' strategy of development, higher rates of growth of agricultural production have not had very strong linkages into growth, and the creation of productive employment, in the non-agricultural economy).[26]

The green revolution did not, in fact, have a dramatic effect on the rates of growth of agricultural output in India as a whole: 'the overall rate of agricultural growth has not shown any tendency to accelerate. At best, the rate of growth can be said to have remained constant' (Vaidyanathan 1988: 77). But it had positive effects on poverty, nonetheless, mainly because it made foodgrains relatively cheaper than they would have been otherwise, and at least for a time increased both employment and labour productivity in agriculture in those parts of India in which it became established, so that the capacities of poor people to purchase food were improved.[27] These effects were not in evidence, however, in the early 1970s. In the period after the 'crisis of planning' – in spite of, or perhaps because of, the New Agricultural Strategy[28] – it is rather likely that poverty levels increased. Rohini Nayyar's research shows, for example, that rural poverty increased quite dramatically – nearly doubling – between 1961–2 and 1970–1, and that it fell only very slightly thereafter, up to 1977–8 (Nayyar 1991, table 3.4, p. 47; but note that different studies reach different conclusions: see Chaudhuri 1979, ch. 8). Real wages were probably declining at this time both in agriculture and outside it (though this, too, has been disputed: see Lal 1976), even while people were becoming more dependent upon wage employment.

The problem of poverty began to be become even more important than it had been hitherto, as an object of specialist enquiry, from this time (stimulated by the publication of Dandekar and Rath's articles on 'Poverty in India' in 1971). Indian planners once again anticipated and helped to form an international consensus in the 1970s – as they had done in the very early days of planning – this time about the nature of poverty and what should be done about it. It was recognized that neither agricultural nor industrial growth would be sufficient to generate productive employment enough to do any more than contain the problems of unemployment and underemployment, and so special programmes were introduced into the Fourth Five Year Plan in 1970 to provide for what amounted to 'redistribution with growth' (later the slogan of the approach to poverty alleviation favoured by the World Bank).[29] These included projects for 'small farmers' (under the Small Farmer Development Agencies which were set up), and schemes for Marginal Farmers and Agricultural Labourers, all of which involved subsidized loans for the provision of productive assets, and later an experimental Crash Scheme for Rural Employment and a Drought-Prone Areas Programme. The principles of these programmes – against 'welfare payments' and in favour of helping poor people to employ their labour more productively – became part of the international consensus about poverty alleviation in the 1970s. 'Rural Development', as a programme for poverty alleviation (as was proposed in the World Bank Sector Paper on this subject of 1975), was influenced very strongly by these Indian precedents. The programmes continue, though they have been modified and developed in the Integrated Rural Development Programme, to the present, and they are considered to have had some positive effects. Equally, there is a lot of evidence about 'leakage upwards' of resources from them to richer rural people (see Guhan 1980 for an early assessment) – in much the same way, in fact, that had been true of community development programmes in the 1950s.

These grim trends in livelihoods were indicative of the deteriorating economic circumstances in which the political drama of the early 1970s unfolded.

4.3 The Emergency and the 'Janata Phase'

Approaching crisis

In spite of Mrs Gandhi's landslide victories in the 1971 and 1972 elections her party was almost immobilized by ideological cleavages, and the credibility both of the party and of her leadership declined remarkably rapidly. One important focus of dispute was over amendments to the Constitution that were intended, broadly speaking, to give priority to some of the Directive Principles over the Fundamental Rights, and so threatened the ideas of the supremacy of the Constitution and of the rule of law over parliament. They also promised the kind of radical social transformation that was looked for by Kumaramangalam – who argued that the proposed amendments reflected a new constitutional doctrine of the 'sovereignty of the people' – and by others on the left of the Congress, and in the CPI. But though Indira Gandhi seems genuinely to have been committed to bringing about the social changes that she promised in 1971 – 'it seems unfair to reduce her populism to political opportunism' (Church 1984: 236) – she also sought to redeem her promises through peaceful means, and in doing so to head off the threat from the Marxists. She tried, apparently, to take the path of accommodation and conciliation that Nehru had adopted, but without having the political means to do so. The result was that her support for the left was never consistent. Fearing that it had become a parallel organization within the Congress, she began to move against the Congress Forum for Socialist Action in 1972, and it was dissolved in the following year. But the principle of the supremacy of the Constitution became an issue around which opposition organized: and Mrs Gandhi became a prisoner of her own radical rhetoric of seeking to achieve social transformation by moderate parliamentary means. Her populism and the general weakness of political organization also meant that, because other channels were not available, and as demands increased in a worsening economic situation with steeply rising prices, opposition was expressed increasingly on the streets, provoking a repressive response (as in the way in which the government dealt with the railwaymen's strike in 1974, which involved 'the unprecedented use of extraordinary powers': after Frankel, 1978). It was joked that '*garibi hatao*' meant not a 'war on poverty' but rather 'poor *hatao*' – the abolition of the poor. There was a loss of confidence in the parliamentary system, reflected most strongly in an uprising in Gujarat in early 1974 against the State government, which was forcefully put down and which led to President's Rule being imposed in the State. By that time J. P. Narayan, the veteran socialist leader of the Congress, who had quit party politics twenty years before, and whose reputation for selflessness and integrity was unquestioned, had emerged as the unlikely leader of opposition; and the breakdown of the legitimacy of Mrs Gandhi's regime, and the final breakdown of consensus politics in India, crystallized in her open confrontation with 'JP' and the Movement of student followers which sprang up around him in Bihar. By the end of 1974 virtually the entire opposition (with the exception of the communist parties) had formed a National Coordinating Committee. The divisions in the Congress themselves hardened. Then, in 1975, Mrs Gandhi's position was weakened when she gave in to Morarji Desai's hunger strike calling for fresh elections in Gujarat. It was more or less at this point that the High Court in Allahabad reached its verdict, on 12 June 1975, in a case brought against Mrs Gandhi on grounds of electoral malpractice by her defeated opponent in the general elections of 1971. The Court ruled that she was indeed guilty of offences which, though very minor in themselves, required her to give up her seat in the Lok Sabha, and thus to relinquish the premiership. At exactly the same moment the results of the Gujarat elections, in which the Janata Front had ousted the Congress from power, came in. The situation remained charged and uncertain for two weeks. But in the early hours of the morning of 26 June opposition leaders and Congress dissidents alike were arrested, and at 7.00 a.m. the President, Mrs Gandhi's man, Fakruddin Ali Ahmed, proclaimed a State of Emergency. The show of force and the rigorous censorship that followed caused the 'JP Movement', deprived of leadership and lacking grass-roots organization, to melt away. It was at this time that D. K. Barooah came out with the awful aphorism 'India is Indira, Indira is India', with which we started this chapter. The contrast with Nehru's slogan, 'India is the Congress, the Congress is India' (see chapter 3), sums up the change which had come about in Indian politics.

'Emergency' rule

Mrs Gandhi presented the Emergency, both to the Indian people and to the world (where she won a good deal of support, as amongst senior members of the Labour Party in Britain), as being necessary for the social changes which India needed. They were represented in the Twenty-Point Programme, which was announced within five days of the President's declaration, and which included pledges in regard to the implementation of land reforms, the abolition of bonded labour, liquidation of rural debt, increased agricultural wages, lower prices, and the prevention of tax evasion. The irony of it all was that even with the sweeping powers that she had taken into her hands Mrs Gandhi could not bring about the changes that the Programme promised, without local organization. They became, as Francine Frankel puts it: 'quixotic commands for putting in place a grass-roots organization for popular mobilization by fiat from above' (1978: 551), and they foundered on those same rocks, in the basic structure of the rural political economy that we described earlier on in this chapter, on which earlier efforts at bringing about radical socio-economic change had also crashed. The rich peasant-kulak class was no more under the control of this authoritarian form of rule than it had been under formal democracy. Quite a lot was made at the time of the supposedly positive economic effects of Emergency rule, and indeed there was evidence showing that both the profits and the assets of big business went up (Chatterjee 1997a [1977]: 64; Rudolph and Rudolph 1987: 240). But with the advantage of hindsight it seems that they derived more from the repression of labour than from any real improvements in productivity, and that the growth performance of the economy was no higher than under the democratic regimes which followed the Emergency. Industrial capitalists, initially sympathetic, were rapidly disaffected by the uncertainties caused by the disruption of the rule of law, and by the evidence of cronyism deriving from the coterie around the Prime Minister and from which some were, of course, excluded. The dominant agricultural interests clearly had reason to be alarmed about the Emergency regime: 'in a systemic sense...the basic class alliance between the bourgeoisie and the landed gentry was jeopardised by the regime of the Emergency' (Chatterjee 1997a [1977]: 65). It was, however, the bureaucratic excesses, in north India, of urban resettlement programmes, and of family planning – associated especially with Mrs Gandhi's son, Sanjay – which seem to have been very largely responsible for the massive upset in the elections which Mrs Gandhi called, rather surprisingly, for March 1977. Her reasons for calling the elections were never made clear, but it seems that she expected to win, and that this misapprehension reflected her increasing isolation, and lack of information, behind the screen of sycophantic loyalists with which she had surrounded herself. In the event she was defeated resoundingly by 'the Janata wave', which swept all before it across the north of the country, but which only trickled into the south where the Congress survived to fight again from bases in Andhra and Karnataka. It brought at last, at the age of 81, Morarji Desai, that long-time adversary both of Nehru and of Mrs Gandhi, into the office of Prime Minister.

The politics of the period leading up to the Emergency showed the limitations of Indian democracy in the 1970s and set the scene for those which appeared in the 1980s. In the absence of democratic institutions – political parties organized democratically, and functioning institutions of democratic government at local levels – elections became the substance of democracy. Political leaders remained trapped within the populist rhetoric that they deployed in order to get themselves elected, raising the expectations of the electorate as they did so, and then being able to do little to meet them. As Kohli argues: 'Without an organizational base it is unlikely that an electoral mandate can be carried out, with centralization and powerlessness becoming simultaneous tendencies' (1990a: 189). Populism, as he said, is inherently destabilizing (p. 190); and there have been tendencies, in these circumstances, to resort to authoritarian means for maintaining control. But the Emergency itself showed up the limitations of authoritarian rule from the centre, when it extended only to control over State-level politicians, and had not the means to coerce the kulaks in particular.

The significance of the Janata

The success of the Janata Party established a non-Congress government at the Centre for the first time, and, given that support for the Congress-I had held up in the south and west, it seemed to some commentators that India had at last established a competitive two-party system. But the Janata Party did not last long. The leaders of the new government were a gerontocratic triumvirate: Morarji Desai, Charan Singh and Jagjivan Ram – a longstanding Scheduled Caste leader within the Congress and until the election campaign still a minister in Mrs Gandhi's cabinet. Ram's quitting of the Congress to throw in his lot, as the leader of a breakaway formation that he called 'Congress for Democracy', with the Janata, exercised some influence over the outcome of the elections. Reluctantly, Singh and Ram agreed to J. P. Narayan's nomination of Desai as Prime Minister. But the relationships between them were always uneasy, and Singh started actively to campaign against Desai only a year after the Janata triumph, using the misdemeanours of Desai's son, Kanti, as a lever for calling the Prime Minister's authority into question. The old men were, between them, single-mindedly self-destructive, and, as the Rudophs put it: 'Ambition, pride, hypocrisy and folly were spectacularly on display for three years' (1987: 165).

The Janata Party was indeed an unlikely combination of political forces, brought together in a single party only in their hostility to Mrs Gandhi; and the 'Janata wave' was clearly more a defeat for Mrs Gandhi than a victory for a new leadership and a new ideology. In fact the Jana Sangh was the largest group (with 31 per cent of the seats), and the Jana Sangh leader Atul Behari Vajpayee became the (generally respected) Foreign Secretary in the new government. It was followed by Charan Singh's Bharatiya Lok Dal (which he had formed in 1974 when the radical socialists of Bihar and Uttar Pradesh, and what was left of the Swatantra Party, came into the BKD) with 19 per cent. The BLD brought larger numbers of farmers into the Lok Sabha than had ever been there before, and it was the struggle for ascendancy between this peasant party and the rest which was the cause of the destruction of the centrist coalition of the Janata Party, as much, or more than the personal squabbles between the old men (see Chatterjee 1997a [1978]; and Vanaik 1990: 96–7). The other groups were the Congress-(O) (with 15 per cent), the Socialist Party (17 per cent), Congress for Democracy (10 per cent) and a group of dissident Congress members (led by Chandrasekhar, who had been detained during the Emergency). Of all these groups the Jana Sangh, with its associations with the RSS, was the best organized, and the fact that the Janata did not establish any kind of intra-party democracy reflected to some extent fears on the part of the leaders of the other groups that the Jana Sangh would be able to take over.

Rather remarkably, perhaps, the Janata was able to agree on policy directions – described as 'the path of Gandhian socialism based on political and economic decentralisation' – and it has been argued that its policy performance was quite satisfactory, even though it was not in power long enough to go far with implementation (Rudolph and Rudolph 1987: 172). The attempt to implement a neo-Gandhian policy reflected the sense that the leaders had that their legitimacy derived significantly from the moral authority of J. P. Narayan and his stature as a Gandhian (a sense which was reflected, too, in the decision of the Jana Sangh leaders, after the break-up of the Janata, to rename their party the Bharatiya Janata Party, thereby emphasizing the continuity of its associations with 'Gandhian socialism'). But it also, clearly, represented a means whereby right wingers from the old Congress, erstwhile Congress 'radicals', Hindu nationalists and north Indian peasants, could come together on ground which was also distinct from that on which Mrs Gandhi had stood. All could agree on a programme that involved decentralization, some shift of public sector resources to rural development, and encouragement for small-scale producers and 'independent cultivators'. The emphasis which began to be placed on 'appropriate technology' which would be employment intensive left a lasting mark in policy thinking, even if not in the practices of development in India.[30] Another lasting mark followed from the work of the committee which the Janata established on *panchayati Raj* institutions. The party did not remain in office long enough to implement its recommendations nationally, but they were influential in some states. Karnataka, notably, introduced a new system of democratic decentralization in 1983, which followed the recommendations of the Janata's committee, and they have remained a point of reference in Indian development discourses (P. Brass 1990: 119–20).

The message of Charan Singh's politics

But it did not last. Charan Singh's manoeuvres against Desai were instrumental in the break-up of the party in 1979, and when a politically resurgent Indira Gandhi withdrew her support from him, Singh remained only as a caretaker prime minister before the general elections of January 1980 restored that lady to office. With the advantage of hindsight, however, it seems that the deeper significance of the brief Janata phase is obscured by the petty squabbles of the old men. In an essay of remarkable insight, published in Bengali in 1978 and only recently reproduced in English, Partha Chatterjee expressed his sense of the danger for secular, socialist, democratic India in 'the message of Charan Singh's politics' (Chatterjee 1997a [1978]). The arrival into power of the BKD, amongst the political groupings which constituted the Janata, and Charan Singh's advocacy of 'rural bias' – in a way that this had never been done before – were reflections of the expanding political power of the rich peasantry, and not only in north India where Singh's own power base lay. The end of the Emergency had created the space, as Gail Omvedt has noted, for a new phase of rural agitations. In 1977–8 the Tamil Nadu Vivasayagal Sangam (Tamil Nadu Agriculturalists' Association), led by C. Narayanasamy Naidu, launched a campaign over the issues of writing off loans and the reduction of electricity rates: 'Roads were blocked, bridges destroyed, goods of farmers confiscated by cooperative societies were taken back; the chief minister labelled it a "naxalite pattern of agitation", and there were at least six killed in police firing' (Omvedt 1993: 111). Similar struggles were reported from different parts of north India, and in December 1978, on the occasion of his birthday, Charan Singh organized a two-million strong rally in Delhi, which was 'described by an observer as the occasion in which the "peasant is standing up as a class"' (Omvedt 1993: 111). As Chatterjee recognized at the time, it was becoming increasingly difficult to accommodate rich peasant power within the ruling power bloc (within 'the strangulating embrace'). Singh advocated policy positions which promised to tilt the terms of trade and resource allocations in a way which was found threatening by industrial interests. At the same time the rich peasantry devolved power away from the central executive to State and local levels. It was these threats that created uncertainty over the future of the Janata party; and Chatterjee observed the increasing opposition to Charan Singh from the owners of large-scale industry and commerce. He went on (prophetically, as it turned out):

> In view of the experience of the Emergency, all that these interests will demand is that central executive command be strong, but that it avoid the arbitrariness of the Emergency regime... The search is now on for a leader and a political organisation that have the ability to reorganise the structure of power along these lines. Needless to say, this provides the greatest opportunity for the return of Indira Gandhi. (1997a [1978]: 71)

At the same time, none of the left parties was succeeding in putting forward a credible alternative programme: 'Nearly all of the parties which call themselves communist are identifying enemies and seeking friends from within the existing structure of organised power... there is no vision here of pursuing any long-range political objectives' (p. 72). And (the crux of his argument):

> What is dangerous is that, in the meantime, a clear message is being sent out to a vast mass of labouring people in India – the message of Charan Singh's politics. From rich farmers to subsistence peasants, owners of agricultural land are being told: make your demands to the government for grants, for subsidies, for appropriate laws, and the labour that you have put into your lands from time immemorial will at last be justly rewarded; soon everyone will get rich. In the present state of the economy and of the class structure, this politics poses a grave danger. If this appeal succeeds in finding a stable home in peasant consciousness... [and if, at the same time]... the principles of an alternative structure of agrarian economy are not enunciated... through the political and economic programmes of the Left, the large bulk of the landowning peasantry will never again be brought around to the cause of socialism. Not only that, peasants could then easily come under the sway of some agrarian populist peddling dreams of kisan raj. (p. 72)

Events were soon to show that the Left did not succeed in enunciating an alternative programme, as we will explain in the next chapter, but rather scrambled behind the Farmers' Movements which 'really exploded' (Omvedt 1993: 111) in 1980. The dreams of *kisan raj* did indeed come to replace the aspirations which had been reflected in the agrarian movements of only a decade before – the 'agrarian tension' studied by the Ministry of Home Affairs in 1969. Omvedt sums up: 'the decade of the 1970s can be seen as one in which most activists of the Marxist left threw themselves into an effort to organise agricultural labour and poor peasant struggles and – while these struggles and their organisations stagnated or even fizzled out – a very differently focussed "agrarian revolution" was gathering strength...based on issues of market-dependent, bureaucratically oppressed peasantry' (1993: 105–8). Chatterjee was perceptive enough to have recognized this trend, and its wider significance, in the context of the wrangles that took place in the Janata phase.

4.4   Conclusion

In retrospect, therefore, we believe that the Janata phase concluded the second major period in India's history after Independence. The first was that of the Nehruvian regime, and in that time the attempt was made to realize those founding myths of India as a modern state and nation: democratic, socialist, federal, secular. By the time of Nehru's death, as we have argued in this chapter, the contradictions that were inherent in the political system which he had contributed to creating, and in the whole attempt at bringing about social transformation by bureaucratic means, in the context of a parliamentary democracy established in a state in which there had been no bourgeois revolution, had already become apparent. Nehru's successors were left with the task of coping with the contradictions, and the period that we have described here, of instability and crisis, and of increasingly and at last explicitly authoritarian rule, ensued. Yet the experience of the Emergency served if anything to reinforce commitment to the founding myths – or certainly those of democracy, federalism and of secularism – amongst the political elite of the country. The period can be seen as having culminated in an attempt, in the Janata phase, to re-establish the centre, and around a recasting of some of the themes of the foundation. The Janata period also marked both the decline of the radical left at the national level, pushed aside by the march of the kulaks through the door of politics, and the 'arrival' of the Hindu nationalist right (at least in the limited sense that it participated in government for the first time). But in this second period as a whole, in spite of the experience of the Emergency, the founding myths were not seriously called into question – though the battle over the Constitution in the 1970s did etch out the unresolved tensions in the Constitution between the ideas and principles which are reflected in the Fundamental Rights and those of the Directive Principles.[31] What distinguishes the 1980s, in our view, and in spite of the many continuities to which we have drawn attention in this chapter, is that the founding myths of India as a modern state did start to be called into question. In India's modern history January 1980 was not just the start of a new decade.

5

Drifting Towards Catastrophe: The Powerlessness of the Congress-(I)

India became increasingly democratic and increasingly difficult to govern.
Manor 1988: 72[1]

That then is the writing on the wall. The ruling classes in India no longer have a viable organisation of class rule. And they have very few options left. This is why indecision and immobility on the part of the Left becomes still more significant.
Chatterjee 1997a[2]

There is a theory which holds that all systems are flexible, but within certain limits. When the limits are stretched a 'catastrophe' may occur, and the system undergoes a fundamental transformation as a result. Using this idea as a metaphor rather than as a precise theoretical concept, the Indian polity can be seen as having moved close to, if not actually to have undergone catastrophe in the 1980s. Myron Weiner, a longstanding observer of Indian politics, argued in the early 1980s that 'with the disintegration of the Janata, Indian politics returned to normal' (1989 [1982]: 250). Indeed it seemed that Congress dominance had been restored:

In 1980 the Congress won 351 parliamentary seats with almost 43 per cent of the popular vote, as compared with 352 seats and nearly 44 per cent of the popular vote in 1971. In both instances the electoral coalition was similar. The Congress won the support of the very rich and the very poor, from Brahmins to ex-untouchables, from well-to-do businessmen and government bureaucrats to tribal agricultural labourers and Muslim weavers . . . a centrist programme won for Mrs Gandhi and her party not the support of the centre, that is, the middle classes and the middle peasantry who were either divided or opposed to the Congress, but rather the extremes of the class structure. (p. 242)[3]

The Congress remained the only truly national party.

Yet Weiner was far too perceptive an observer not to have qualified his own arguments about continuities. Given the weakness of its local organization, the Congress had never before been so dependent upon a single leader to sustain its political support, and so: 'The reinstating elections of 1980 produced an even more fragile system of authority than was produced by the elections of 1971 and 1972' (p. 258). In the years which followed the Congress drifted, unchecked because of the incoherence and fractiousness of the opposition, in which most parties – with the marked exception of the BJP and the communists – were split and split again by the ambitions of their inept and increasingly corrupt leaders. Having promised 'government which works', Mrs Gandhi failed to offer or to implement a coherent programme; and Rajiv, too, failed to take advantage of the opportunity which was presented by the most massive electoral victory that the Congress ever achieved, in December 1984, following his mother's assassination, to bring about change either in the party or in government. They were both leaders with attitudes rather than policies, with points of view rather than a coherent ideology (paraphrasing Weiner 1982: 253); leaders who responded to events rather than defining a course. The party they led was no longer, as Chatterjee recognized, an effective instrument of class rule.[4] But neither was there, yet, a real alternative. As a result – not because of any systematic rethinking of fundamentals – the foundations of the modern Indian state were progressively eroded and systemic 'catastrophe' approached.

The commitment of the political leadership to the 'socialist' objectives reflected in the Directive Principles of the Constitution had previously been genuine enough, even if it lacked analytically and in programmatic content. In the 1970s and (more so) the 1980s that commitment was reduced to mere lip-service in the pursuit of electoral majority, and it was largely for these reasons that India was not set more definitely on to a new path of development by means of economic liberalization, which put aside even the pretence of redistribution. Advertising companies were not the only ones to discover the size and clout of the Indian middle class; and this middle class of 'India' stood opposed to the village people of 'Bharat', according to the distinction made by the Maharashtrian farmers' leader, Sharad Joshi. Indian federalism, already strained in the 1970s by Indira Gandhi's attempts to centralize power, entered into crisis, notably because of the civil war which escalated in Punjab, as a result – at least in some measure – of the actions of the Prime Minister. Beside this tragedy, and the conflicts in Assam and (later) Kashmir, the actions of Mrs Gandhi's satraps in making and breaking State governments made for a theatre of farce. Indian secularism, too, came increasingly to be called into question by the actions both of Indira and Rajiv, and in the ugly communal conflicts between Hindus and Muslims, and Hindus and Sikhs, which recurred over much – if not quite all – of the country. Militant Hindu nationalist organizations staged unprecedentedly bold demonstrations. Before the end of the decade some of India's leading intellectuals had begun to argue that the idea of secularism for which Nehru, in particular, had stood, and which was reflected in the Constitution, was inappropriate for India, and misconceived (see, notably, Madan 1987).

As well as communal violence there were violent conflicts also between castes, on a wider scale than in the past. Partha Chatterjee observed in September 1980 that one of the manifestations of the increasing local power of the rich peasantry was the proliferation of guns:

> A recent estimate shows that...in Moradabad [UP] alone there are some eighty thousand firearms. By comparison, all of Great Britain has a total of 75,000 licensed guns. There are reasons to suspect that in several districts in Bihar or Punjab, there are even larger quantities of arms in the hands of locally powerful groups. Many observers have been astonished by the extensive use of firearms in the recent communal riots in Uttar Pradesh. If we keep in mind some of the changes in the political process in the north Indian countryside in the last decade and a half, there should be less cause for surprise. (Chatterjee 1997a: 77–8)

And as violence became more widespread and more intense so the power of the police grew,[5] and government became both less democratic in its functioning (if not constitution) and more corrupt. Paul Brass wrote of these trends that:

> The police are not in fact maintaining order in either the urban or rural areas of India, but are themselves amongst the most dangerous and disorderly forces in the country.... At the local level, protection from police victimisation and the use of the police to harass one's rivals have become crucial elements in the powers of local politicians. Politicians in the districts of India who wish to build a stable political base for themselves, must not only be able to distribute money and patronage but must also be able to control the police. (1990: 56)

By the end of the 1980s, therefore, the Indian state-system was, palpably, not working in many areas, and the modern state idea – with its elements of socialism, secularism, federalism and democracy – no longer commanded general support amongst the political elite or the intelligentsia in the way that it had before. The idea of India that was projected in the resolutions of the Constituent Assembly had both faded and started to be washed over by new designs.

5.1   Dominance without Authority: The Congress in the Eighties

Continuity and change in Indian politics

Indian politics in the 1980s featured many of the same actors as had appeared in the previous decade, together with new faces. Not least amongst the latter was the film-star hero N. T. Rama Rao who took power in Andhra Pradesh with his new Telugu Desam party, and who became a central figure of the opposition; but the most important of them all were Rajiv Gandhi, Mrs Gandhi's elder son, who became heir apparent after the death in a flying accident in 1980 of his younger brother Sanjay, and V. P. Singh, who came to prominence first as Rajiv's Finance Minister, and who by the end of the decade had taken over the leadership of India as head of the country's second non-Congress government. The plot of politics stayed much the same. The increasingly unstable balance of power between the industrial bourgeoisie and the rich peasantry, and between both of these and the bureaucratic-professional class, continued to create the political space for what came to be described as a 'weak-strong state', and for the simultaneous tendencies of increasing centralization and powerlessness.[6] What was new emerged from the tense relations between these tendencies and coalitions: what Atul Kohli called India's 'growing crisis of governability' (Kohli, 1990a).

Mrs Gandhi's recovery from her electoral defeat by the Janata in March 1977 was remarkably rapid, and was based on an offensive to regain the support of the minorities and the poor. 'This became clear in October 1977 when Mrs Gandhi, emerging triumphantly from the Janata government's first attempt to jail her, made a tour of south Gujarat and devoted her attention almost exclusively to the scheduled castes and tribes. Decrying Janata "anti-poor" policies, she lunched with Harijan families...[and]... spoke everywhere to large crowds' (Wood 1984: 209–10). The Congress-(R) – as it still was – split again in January 1978, over Mrs Gandhi's continued leadership, between what (later) became the Congress-(U), led by Devaraj Urs, the Chief Minister of Karnataka, and the Congress-(I) – which then performed well in State elections in February 1978 in Andhra Pradesh, Karnataka (where it won majorities) and in Maharashtra. Mrs Gandhi herself returned to parliament in November 1978, after winning a by-election from Chikmagalur (Karnataka), and within a year she had completed the toppling of the Janata government which had been so effectively begun by Charan Singh himself.[7]

The Janata eventually split into three: the Jana Sangh, which soon afterwards (in April 1980) became the Bharatiya Janata Party, Charan Singh's Lok Dal, and the rump Janata led by Chandrasekhar. The opposition degenerated after the 1980 elections into an alphabet soup of squabbling fractions.[8] The Lok Dal would split four times by the end of 1982. The Congress-(U) – which became the Congress-(S) when Sharad Pawar became president in October 1981 – also split. The Janata held together for a time, but without making much of a showing in elections, and it too was factionally divided. Throughout the early 1980s, in the period of Mrs Gandhi's government, the BJP remained the strongest non-Communist opposition party, and it was argued by one observer that 'an opposition that does not include the BJP will be unlikely to displace Indira Gandhi' (Hardgrave 1984:

215). The opposition alliances that at last formed in 1983 were themselves unstable as fresh general elections approached towards the end of 1984. Partha Chatterjee wrote, shortly after Charan Singh had reneged on a prospective merger between the Lok Dal and the Janata Party, and only a matter of days before the assassination of Mrs Gandhi, that: 'It is not true, as Mrs Gandhi so frequently alleges, that the opposition has only a one-point programme – that of removing her from power. If it did, the opposition would have been united long ago' (1997a [1984]: 94).

The base of support for the Congress-(I) had changed meanwhile, from that on which the Congress had relied in the Nehru era. Then the Congress had depended on the votes of the Hindi heartland of the north, which accounted for 42 per cent of the seats in the Lok Sabha, and within the heartland, it was generally reckoned, on strong support from the disadvantaged minorities – Muslims, tribals and members of the Scheduled Castes. This base of support started to decline from the 1962 general elections, and the trend of decline was only partially reversed in 1971 and again in 1980. From the 1970s, the south (Andhra Pradesh and Karnataka) and the west – above all Maharashtra – became the most reliable regional bases of support; and, in so far as the Congress had enjoyed a special electoral relationship with its Reserved constituencies, it was, according to the Rudolphs (1987: ch. 6), broken after 1977. From that time, they argue, minority voting went with regional and national trends.

The rise of the 'lower castes' and the mounting tide of regionalism

Electoral outcomes in the early 1980s were influenced more by the voting behaviour of those described as the 'lower castes', who generally made up about one-third of the population.[9] This is not, of course, a clear-cut category. If Brahmins, Kshatriyas and Banias are described as 'upper castes', then the principal farming castes across India – Jats, Yadavs and Kurmis in large parts of the north, or Marathas and Patidars in the west – may be called 'middle castes'. This leaves a diverse group of castes, and people who are marginal farmers, share-croppers and agricultural labourers, as well as those from traditional service and artisinal castes, sandwiched between the 'middle castes' and the Scheduled Castes and Tribes. It seems that by the 1960s it was very often these 'lower castes' who were most excluded, and that thereafter political trends in the States were influenced significantly by the ways in which these groups became mobilized politically. The success of the Congress in establishing its strongholds in Maharashtra and Karnataka in 1977 was significantly due to the support which it won from the lower castes (see Lele 1984; and Manor 1984); and in the 1980 State Assembly elections in Gujarat the Congress-(I) built a winning coalition with the so-called KHAM strategy, a deliberate attempt to bring together rather numerous but low-ranking Kshatriyas – an important fraction of the lower castes there – with harijans, *adivasis* (tribals) and Muslims in different parts of the State (see Wood 1984). In Uttar Pradesh, Paul Brass suggested: 'In the struggle among the landed castes [the middle castes and some from the upper castes in our terms], the Congress and the BKD/Lok Dal have been fairly evenly divided, which means that the low castes hold the balance electorally' (1984: 47); in Bihar the lower castes continued to be excluded; while in West Bengal and Kerala the Congress lost the support of the lower castes to the CPI(M).

The demands of the lower castes for a stronger political role gave rise to resistance or efforts at cooptation which underlay or were involved in the social struggles of the 1980s:

> Not surprisingly, dominant groups have tried to resist, redirect and exploit this potential shift in political power. This is evident in new levels of violence and corruption, in populist appeals to 'the poor', in calls for law and order, in the emergence of regionalism, in struggles over reservation for the 'backward classes', and in the efforts of political parties to recruit representatives from the lower castes. (Church 1984: 231)

The particular patterns of castes and classes in different States gave rise increasingly to specific patterns of politics.[10] National and regional politics became more and more differentiated from the time of the 1967 elections, as we observed in the last chapter, and the Congress share of the vote declined substantially in the 'delinked' State Assembly elections which took place after the 1980 and 1984 elections, as it had also for the Janata party after those of 1977. The regional parties, such as the Akali Dal in Punjab, the DMK in Tamil Nadu, the Telugu Desam in Andhra Pradesh, or the CPI(M) – which functioned in many ways just like a regional party in West Bengal – became increasingly important. In Bombay, the Shiv Sena, which had begun as a nativist or 'sons of the soil' movement in the 1960s, was successfully mobilizing the aggression of unemployed young men against Muslims, as well as against immigrant communities in the city. By the Rajiv era, the Rudolphs observed, 'regional parties operating within the federal system appear to be as important as centrist national parties in providing leadership and policy alternatives' (1987: 179). A decade later, in the mid-1990s, the regional parties held the balance of power nationally.

The new government formed by Mrs Gandhi in 1980, like her party, depended above all on personal allegiance to her and to her son Sanjay, whose coterie of hangers-on included adventurers like himself and some extremely shady characters. The criminalization of Indian politics, certainly in the particular sense of the election to parliament of a significant number of men, and some women, with criminal records, gathered pace from this time. 'It was a hasty coalition of hard-core loyalists of the past and a large number of new joiners of the bandwagon' (Das Gupta 1981: 148). The new Indira government proved remarkably inept in its first year in office, failing to offer any positive programme and allowing prices to rise alarmingly. The 'law and order' situation, which had figured prominently in Mrs Gandhi's election propaganda, deteriorated. Already in her first year in office the agitation against 'foreigners' – Bengalis/Bangladeshis – in Assam turned violent, presaging a litany of violent conflicts. They arose, at least in part, because of a lack of political organization at a remove from New Delhi. The State units of the ruling party were soon riddled by factional infighting as weak Chief Ministers, appointed by Mrs Gandhi, struggled against dissident groups. The climax came in Andhra Pradesh in 1982 when there were three changes of Chief Minister. It was in this context that N. T. Rama Rao formed a new regional party, the Telugu Desam, which won 46 per cent of the popular vote in State Assembly elections in January 1983. In that year, too, Mrs Gandhi lost her other southern bastion when the Janata Party, led by Ramakrishna Hegde, with the support of independents and of the BJP, came to power in Karnataka, replacing Gundu Rao's bungling and corrupt Congress-(I) regime (see Manor 1984 for more on this story). No moves were made towards rebuilding party democracy: 'Indeed, few state units took the necessary first step of enrolling party members. Chief Ministers, who lack popular followings, displayed little enthusiasm for what would likely be competitive power centres' (Andersen 1982: 123).

Indian politics were, therefore, confused and messy, on the sides both of the governing party, which enjoyed dominance but had little authority or capacity to change either economy or society, and of the opposition, which was unable to mount a combined assault. There was a complete lack of any sense of political direction when, on 31 October 1984, Mrs Gandhi was assassinated by two of her Sikh guards – the consequence of the war in Punjab that she had been instrumental in creating (as we explain later in this chapter). Her surviving son, Rajiv, whom she had brought into politics apparently against his own wishes following Sanjay's death in 1980, succeeded Indira in a manner which reflected the recognition within the Congress-(I) that the success of the party depended above all on the charisma of its leader. The elections that had already been called for December 1984 went ahead, and Rajiv, as we noted, won the largest victory that the Congress had ever achieved. He won against a disunited opposition and on the strength of a massive sympathy vote, to be sure, but Rajiv also campaigned effectively on a 'national unity' platform (and with all manner of attacks upon the opposition as 'anti-national').[11] Rajiv Gandhi also presented himself as a new broom; as someone capable of sweeping out the Augean stables and making a fresh start.

The 'system' prevails: Rajiv's failure

Rajiv did have an extraordinary opportunity in 1985 to bring about positive changes, and he set about his task energetically, proclaiming his intention of reforming the economy, of bringing about peaceful settlements in Punjab and Assam, and of rebuilding a Congress Party which was, more than ever, 'an organisational disaster' (Kohli 1990a: 340).[12] And in 1985, observers considered, he had a good year. The Indian political scientist Iqbal Narain saw in Rajiv at this time a leader much more in the mould of Jawaharlal Nehru than Indira had ever been. Narain believed that Rajiv's Presidential Address to the Centenary Congress in 1985 recalled Nehru's great speech about India's 'tryst with destiny' made on the night of India's freedom from imperial rule, and he thought that 'the vision that [Rajiv] cherishes is a case of change in continuity' (Narain 1986: 254). A year later the same writer had started to express his concerns about the gap between Rajiv's promise and his performance, both in government and in relation to the party. Others noted that Rajiv already, even at the Centenary Congress, had failed to carry the party with him. Only 5,000 out of 50,000 delegates were present at the concluding session of the Centenary Congress.

Rajiv's failure to rebuild the party ultimately made it impossible for him to deliver the other parts of his programme.[13] His power lay in his ability to win the popular vote, and as soon as he began to seem electorally vulnerable his command of the party faltered. He intervened in the allocation of 'tickets' (nominations) for the State assembly elections in 1985 in order to introduce a new 'clean' generation of politicians; he secured the passage of an anti-defection law to check that institutional malaise in Indian politics; and he encouraged Chief Ministers to act more independently. But at the same time, Manor observed, some people with unsavoury reputations were retained, including some of Sanjay's more notorious cronies (1988: 95–6). The decline in support for the Congress that was already in evidence in the State elections of 1985 led to some expressions of dissatisfaction by party functionaries.[14] Then, in December 1985, the party lost the elections in Assam rather badly. Chatterjee observed that: 'It is now being said quite openly in Congress-(I) circles that the new PM's clean-cut modern management style of functioning is not proving to be an effective vote-catching strategy among the larger electorate' (1997a [1985–6]: 124). Rajiv's own confidence in his ability to use his power to change the party organization began to weaken, and in 1986 his plans to implement organizational changes in the party were put off. The point was that these elections were found threatening by almost all who were connected with the Congress: those who held positions naturally favoured the status quo and feared that elections would lead to their being unseated, while those who were excluded had no reason to believe that the incumbents would not be able to manipulate the electoral process. The issue of bogus party membership lists created a furore in 1986, and the opposition of old 'Indira loyalists' was mobilized behind Kamalapathi Tripathi, whose position as the titular head of the party had recently been taken away from him. Rajiv equivocated, making concessions and 'postponing' the elections, supposedly until such time as the irregularities in the party lists had been corrected, and dropping ambitious plans to train party workers so as to inculcate the party ideology and build commitment. At the same time he purged senior leaders from the party.

Thereafter, in 1987, Rajiv was engulfed by corruption scandals, by the effects of the ouster from the government of V. P. Singh, who had started to command authority by his upright and 'saintly' behaviour, and by the loss of the State Assembly elections in Haryana in June – and all his plans for the reorganization of the party were shelved for good. Always inclined to rely on old school friends and whizz-kid technocrats or managers, and disparaging of the Lok Sabha, Rajiv retreated in the last two years of his premiership into a style of political management which was 'more Indira than Indira's'. It was summed up in raids which were made in 1987 on the offices of the English language daily *The Indian Express*, after that paper's exposure of the government over the Bofors affair,[15] and then in the efforts which were made to pass the Defamation Bill through Parliament in September 1988, which threatened the freedom of the press (see Chatterjee 1997a: 173–5). That state power was used as far as possible to suppress dissent was an eloquent testimony to the failure of Rajiv's initiatives in the face of familiar political pressures.

V. P. Singh, meanwhile, took over Rajiv's mantle as 'Mr Clean', and launched his Jan Morcha (people's platform) movement in October 1987. His own victory in a Lok Sabha by-election in Allahabad in 1988 marked his emergence as the leader of the opposition, and the opposition parties did well in by-elections in June of that year, in part because of seat adjustments between them. In August 1988 a National Front of seven parties was formed, the most important of them being the Janata, Lok Dal and the Jan Morcha. By October a formal unity party, called the Janata Dal, had been formed, and though it still appeared to be a fractious coalition – one writer said at this time: 'Why a workable coalition of opposition parties cannot be found is one of the most perplexing questions of Indian politics' (Wariavwalla 1989: 192) – the evidence of drift and decline of the Congress-(I) was quite as marked. In 1989, despite Chandrasekhar's hostility towards V. P. Singh's leadership, the Janata Dal (JD) contrived to hold together, and the JD and the BJP were able to agree on a large number of seat adjustments: 'The mainstream opposition finally set aside the secularist principles which its leader V. P. Singh stood for in order to benefit from – or at least not be harmed by – the strength of the BJP' (Jaffrelot 1996: 381). In the event, although the Congress-(I) still won over 40 per cent of the popular vote throughout the country, and 37 per cent of the seats (197 in total) in the Lok Sabha, the Janata Dal (141 seats) was able to form a minority government with the outside support of the BJP (86 seats) and of the communist parties (52 seats). India entered into a new phase of parliamentary politics at the cusp of the 1990s.

The Congress-(I) had governed India for almost ten years by this point, but ineffectually. The political system which Indira Gandhi did so much to create in the 1970s made it hard to initiate reforms in the 1980s. Tendencies towards, or actual authoritarianism, in this context, was not the means of creating a 'developmental state' – as it had seemed to be in the 'Newly

Industrializing Countries' of East Asia (see chapters 2 and 3 above) – but rather the response of an ideologically and politically bankrupt ruling elite which was entangled in its own populist rhetoric.[16]

5.2 Fumbling with Reform: The Political Economy of Development in India in the 1980s

It was not only India's political elite that was bankrupt by the late 1980s. The country, too, was fast approaching bankruptcy after several years of good growth, and an impending fiscal crisis deepened significantly under the National Front government (1989–91).

What had gone wrong in India's economic development? In his Radhakrishnan Memorial Lectures at Oxford University, Jagdish Bhagwati argued that India's 'weak growth performance reflect[ed], not a disappointing savings performance, but rather a disappointing productivity performance' (1993: 40).[17] Bhagwati blamed this poor productivity performance on 'extensive bureaucratic controls over production, investment, and trade; inward-looking trade and foreign investment policies; and a substantial public sector, going well beyond the conventional confines of public utilities and infrastructure' (p. 46). He also maintained that growth in India had been set back by an economic model which presumed that 'central planners would . . . be able to secure the information and knowledge that micro-level decision-makers alone would have' (p. 51), and that this led to 'inherently arbitrary decisions . . . [because] . . . one activity would be chosen over another simply because the administering bureaucrats were so empowered, and indeed obligated, to choose' (p. 50). Bhagwati argued, then, not just that Indian planning was bound to promote an inefficient, bureaucratized, over-licensed and often corrupt economic system, but that it would also take on a nightmarish, even Kafkaesque quality; the Indian model of planning was 'The Model That Couldn't' (1993, ch. 1).

An attempt was made early in the life of Rajiv Gandhi's government to act on ideas like these. The Budget of 1985 reduced income, corporate and wealth taxes, cut import duties on capital goods, provided tax breaks to exporters and largely eliminated licensing restrictions on investments in twenty-five industries. It reflected 'an attempt to change at least some of the conditions that the theoretical debate has pointed to as causes of slow industrialisation' (Rubin 1985: 948). The left-wing economist Prabhat Patnaik concurred to an extent with this view, when he argued that the declaration of the 'new economic policy' came about more because of internal pressures – the outcome of the 'crisis in public investment' which we described in the last chapter – than as a response to external influences (1994). A fraction of Indian capital had an interest in liberalization, in order both to enter the international arena and to expand into domestic channels for investment which had hitherto been closed. But while there were powerful groups with interests in effective liberalization, others were threatened either by the possible removal of the system of controls from which they had benefited because of their ability to manipulate them, or by direct or indirect competition from imports. Atul Kohli concluded from his research in the later 1980s that: 'Business groups have, on balance, decided that they are not ready to deal [with that part of the liberalization agenda which concerns] any major international opening of the economy' (1990a: 328).

Moves toward the liberalization of the economy soon slowed down after the initiatives of 1985–6. The government failed to carry the rank and file of the Congress party with it, and 'there is reason to believe [wrote Kohli] that the new economic policies hurt Congress politically among two numerically significant rural groups: the "middle peasants" and the scheduled castes' (1990a: 335). Thus: 'The "logic of efficiency" came into conflict with the "logic of democracy"' (Kohli 1988: 329), and the attempt under Rajiv 'to reassert the autonomy of high politics' (Rubin 1985), and to redirect the trajectory of development according to liberal ideas, was short-lived. In practice the underlying tendencies of the Indian economy – towards increasing public expenditure, increasing imbalance in taxation, and increasing resort to commercial borrowing – were intensified. India found it increasingly difficult to balance its books in its limited trading relations with other countries. Nor was it helped by a climate of what Joshi and Little call 'aid weariness' (1994: 162). In the period from 1981 to 1983 India was obliged to finance its current account deficits principally by borrowing from the IMF and from other non-concessional borrowing sources, and these borrowings duly added to its external debt totals. In 1982 India's total external public debt stood at 7.94 billion dollars, or 11.4 per cent of GNP. By 1990 India's total external debt had shot up to 70.12 billion dollars and the debt : GNP ratio stood then at 27.6 per cent.

The persistence of these underlying tendencies in the economy is explained in Pranab Bardhan's analysis of India's political economy in terms of the compromises which are made as the 'dominant proprietary classes' negotiate a balance of power – the model which we referred to in the last chapter. In his own Radhakrishnan Memorial Lectures, delivered a decade before Bhagwati's, Bardhan argued that it was not so much the model of planning that was at fault, but rather the failure of the Indian political system to provide an institutional context in which an efficient and equitable planning regime could be made to work (1984). It is Bardhan's contention – as it has been ours – that the autonomy which the government might have enjoyed in the 1950s, when the Planning Commission was more obviously in command, was lost by the 1960s in the face of opposition to agrarian reform by richer farmers and continuing campaigns by the industrial bourgeoisie against policies that would encourage competition. The state in India took on the form of a regulatory and not a developmental state, and it was unable to move against the rent-seeking activities of the proprietary classes which kept governments (and especially the Congress Party) in power. The Indian people paid the price of this inaction in continuing high levels of rural and urban poverty – although public spending did make some impact on rural poverty in the 1980s: see chapter 7.1 – and in low levels of job creation (not least in the 'formal' or 'organized sector' of the economy, where employment declined in the 1980s in spite of higher rates of growth).

The power of Bharat

Bardhan's account of the slow and inequitable nature of development in India (post Nehru) highlights political determinations in a way that Bhagwati's analysis does not. But it sometimes lacks the purchase that we find in Chatterjee's (or Kaviraj's) adaptation of Gramsci's model of the 'passive revolution' (see our comments in chapter 2). At the heart of this understanding is a view of the transformation of rural India through the 1970s and 1980s. Chatterjee notes that India's public finances, at both Centre and State levels, took a turn for the worse from the late 1970s – from the time of Janata rule and in response to the ruralization of political life in India. Joshi and Little also report an 'explosion of government expenditure' from 1978 to 1979 (1994: 164), mainly in current expenditure and largely on subsidies for food, fertilizer and exports. They concur that:

> The growth of the first two is clearly related to the strength of the farm lobby combined with the desire of politicians to prevent unrest in cities. Food subsidies doubled in the year 1976–77 and doubled again by 1984–85. The large increase in fertiliser subsidies can be quite precisely dated to the period of the Janata government. Fertiliser subsidies increased by Rs 60 crores to Rs 600 crores from 1976–77 to 1979–80; they continued at that level until 1982–83 after which there was another large rise to Rs 1800 crores over the next two years. (p. xxx)[18]

The hike in the fertilizer subsidy which took place in the years from 1982–3 to 1984–5 happened under a Congress government, and confirmed that by this time no government in India could afford to ignore the power of the rural lobby – a lobby which was keen to present the merits and claims of '*Bharat*' (the countryside) against those of 'India' (the city).[19] This lobby gained significantly in power through the second half of the 1980s, and although it was never quite united it was able to maintain, as Sharad Joshi told Jim Bentall in 1992, that: 'our farmers' movement is a movement for a second independence.... The British tried to squeeze this country for the benefit of the Empire. The "Black British" are doing the same for the benefit of "India" at the expense of "Bharat"' (quoted in Bentall and Corbridge 1996: 30–1). The organization which Joshi led, Shetkari Sanghatana, enjoyed some success in the 1980s in its attempts to organize crop-specific campaigns to increase farm output prices (for cotton as well as for some grains and vegetables), and to seek a minimum wage for agricultural labourers. Joshi was also appointed to the Commission on Agricultural Costs and Prices (CACP), after the Agricultural Prices Commission was reformed and renamed in 1985. Joshi was unsuccessful, however, in his attempts to forge an alliance with Mahendra Singh Tikait, the Jat farmer who succeeded Charan Singh as the leader of north India's richer farmers. The Bharatiya Kisan Union, which Tikait led to some local successes in the late 1980s and early 1990s, enjoyed support mainly in western Uttar Pradesh and Haryana, where it was more active in campaigns for lower input prices (cheaper water, electricity, fertilizers and pesticides) than for higher farm output prices.

These movements, which are often described in the literature as 'new farmers' movements' (see chapter 4.2), and which are organized in parts of Karnataka, Tamil Nadu, Punjab and Gujarat as well as in Maharashtra, Uttar Pradesh and Haryana, have been sociologically and politically very significant. Some have described them as being amongst the so-called 'new social movements', issue-based, standing outside regular party politics, capable of mobilizing large numbers of people, and organized to resist and to make demands upon the state rather than to take it over. They point to the apparent success of the farmers' movements in mobilizing people from across different rural 'classes' and argue that this demonstrates the redundancy of the conventional Marxian class sociology. Others, to whose views we are ourselves inclined, argue that these movements are vehicles and expressions of the interests of the richer and most commercially dependent cultivators, and that the participation by – for example – poor peasants and landless labourers in actions taken by the farmers' movements, has frequently depended upon coercion and upon the ways in which they have organized around ties of caste and kinship. Moreover, if the agrarian populism of the farmers' movements was effective in displacing class categories, it may also have enhanced the communalization of political discourse by highlighting 'political symbols and forms which generate and reinforce undifferentiated notions of a community of commodity producers' (Z. Hasan 1998: 109). Ironically, across north India, the farmers' movements helped to create conditions which were conducive to the communal and anti-Mandal upsurge of the 1990s (which we analyse in chapters 6 and 8), and so have assisted in their own subsumption, as a political force, in the growth of *Hindutva* politics.

The successes and significance of the new agrarianism of the 1980s are to be found in its attempts to colonize the CACP and in its capacity to put pressure on Central and State governments to increase the subsidies flowing into commercialized agriculture, even as food consumers (rural as well as urban) were afforded the protection of subsidized grain. But the scale of these input and output subsidies could not be sustained, as was brought home to India at the time of the Janata Dal-led National Front government of 1989–91. These subsidies, along with various export subsidies, were partially instrumental in keeping the Indian economy afloat in the 1980s, and may even have been linked to the relatively strong performance of Indian manufacturing industry during this decade (see chapter 7.1). But the subsidies were paid for, in the main, by massive borrowings from Indian householders, together with borrowings from abroad and from the accounts of Non-Resident Indians (NRIs); they were not financed by taxes upon the newly rich farmers of north and west India who gained most from the government's unwillingness to challenge the power of *Bharat*. When the National Front government came to power in 1989 – and when V. P. Singh moved to write off the debts of small (and not so small) farmers – the writing was on the wall. India's fiscal deficit had doubled over the previous decade, and the economic crisis of 1991 was waiting to happen.

Chatterjee's account of the passive revolution in India shows how the deepening of Indian democracy, and the ruralization of Indian politics, paved the way for a more extensive capitalist transformation of the Indian countryside than many thought likely or even possible, and this transformation changed the map of Indian politics at all spatial scales. The relative success of agriculture in the 1980s – and of the new farmers' movements – came with a political price tag which left the Congress Party (and to a lesser extent Central Government) in no man's land. Unable to dictate the terms of the political game, the Congress-(I) was forced to respond to the demands of the very people whom its policies had enriched but who still positioned the Congress as 'their' (*Bharat*'s) principal enemy. Political power slowly drained to the States and the Districts, where it followed (and precipitated) rounds of fiscal transfers. The bankrupting of the Congress Party in the 1980s may not have been looked for, but it was assuredly no accident.

5.3 Centre–State Relations and the Crisis of Indian Federalism

Developing tensions between Centre and States

The drift of monies and power to rural India – or at least to some rural communities and their representatives – had implications too for the management of Centre–State relations in the federal Republic, and this also changed the political landscapes in which the Congress was bound to operate. In the period from 1950 to 1967 the Congress Party lost power in the States only once, to the Communist Party of India (CPI) in Kerala. Yet between 1967 and 1991 the Congress Party won only 45 of the 98 elections held in the 15 major States of India, and it has continued to fare badly since 1991. The Congress has failed to win power in Tamil Nadu since 1967 and in West Bengal since 1977. Its hold on Bihar was weakened in the 1990s, first by Laloo Yadav's Janata Dal (or, latterly, Rashtriya Janata Dal) and, rather later, and not least in the Jharkhand-(Vananchal) region, by the BJP. In Uttar Pradesh, as we have seen, the Congress Party has been eclipsed by communal and casteist parties.

These setbacks can be linked to the rise of regional bourgeoisies in India, as well as to the ruralization of politics. Achin Vanaik maintains that 'centre-state conflicts and inter-state tensions are now primarily focused on economic and political, not cultural issues. The single most important class force behind these conflicts is the agrarian bourgeoisie, supported by the rural petty bourgeoisie, of the states in question' (1990: 124). But these conflicts have been exacerbated by what Ayesha Jalal has described as the emerging tensions between the 'inherent pluralism of India and the centralising structures of government' – tensions mediated by what she calls 'the expanding sphere of democratic politics and the withering away of the Congress's organizational and electoral bases of support' (1995: 169) – and in the long run these conflicts will only be resolved by 'a better balance of political and economic power between the centre and the states' (p. 183). This prospect failed to materialize in the 1970s or 1980s, notwithstanding talk of a second round of States reorganization or the existence of strong regionalist movements. Whereas the Congress Party in the 1950s, under Nehru, was prepared in practice (if not consistently) to grant a measure of political and fiscal independence to the States, and to work behind the scenes for a resolution of day-to-day conflicts, in the 1970s and 1980s the relative weakness of the Congress Party encouraged its leaders (and most obviously Mrs Gandhi) to rule the country by strategies of cooptation, deceit, division, and straightforward repression. In seeking to protect one version of Indian federalism, the Congress Party undermined the democratic foundations of modern India, and revealed its latent authoritarianism.

It is possible, of course, to overstate the contrast between the management styles of Nehru and his daughter in this context, as in others (see our remarks in chapter 3). There is certainly merit in Paul Brass's claim that Nehru sought to manage Centre–State relations according to four rules: that central government would not recognize groups making secessionist demands; that central government would not accommodate regional demands based upon religious differences; that demands for the creation of separate linguistic states would not be conceded capriciously; and that central government would not agree to the reorganization of a province if the demand was made by only one of the important language groups concerned (1994: 172–3). But we should also recall that President's Rule was imposed on eleven occasions in the period from 1950 to 1967, and that the Congress Party used the 1955 Report of the States Reorganization Commission to quash a longstanding demand for the formation of a Jharkhand State. Nehru was also skilled in the cooptation of State-level politicians, as he proved in 1963 when he helped to engineer the defection of the leader of the Jharkhand Party, Jaipal Singh, to the ranks of the Congress Party in Bihar. It was Nehru, too, who first rebuffed demands from Kashmiri nationalists, led by Sheikh Abdullah, for a plebiscite on the status of Kashmir, despite intimations to that effect prior to the time of Kashmir's (limited) accession into independent India.[20] And it was Nehru who ordered the suppression of

Naga separatists in the 1950s. As we remarked in chapter 3, Nehru's first and abiding objective was to secure the territorial integrity of independent India.

It remains the case, even so, that the dynamics of Centre–State relations in India have changed significantly in the post-Nehru era. In the period from 1967 to 1991 President's Rule was imposed on 78 occasions, and the average tenure of a Chief Minister shortened to 2.6 years for a Congress politician (from 3.9 years in the period from 1950 to 1967 – even as it rose from 2.0 to 2.6 years for non-Congress politicians).[21] In addition, while it remains true that 'New Delhi has an impressive track record of making larger per capita plan outlays to the less developed states' (Jalal 1995: 169), the governments of Indira and Rajiv Gandhi became skilled in using grants-in-aid from the Centre to reward their allies in the regions.[22] Such attempts to manipulate the map of fiscal federalism backfired on occasion, even so, and sometimes had to be backed up with payments to the leaders of local oppositional movements. In West Bengal, the charge that Congress and/or New Delhi has dealt less than fairly with the CPM has deepened hostility to the Congress in some parts of the State. In Bihar, too, successive regimes, including some Congress governments, have sought to blame the problems of that benighted State on New Delhi.

Federalism contested by violence: Assam, Punjab and Kashmir

If some of the eastern States have suffered at the hands of New Delhi, it is at the periphery of the country that India's 'centralized federalism' has been most seriously tested, and it is here too – in Assam, Punjab and Kashmir – that the machinations of Congress politicians have worked both to damage the integrity of India and to erode the effectiveness of the Congress Party itself.

In Assam in the 1980s the Congress Party found itself under fire from a regional autonomy movement which protested the State's 'unnatural' dependence on central transfers. These transfers accounted for more than 50 per cent of total spending from State resources under the Fifth Five Year Plan (after Jalal 1995: 173). Assamese students and urban professionals claimed that New Delhi treated the State like an 'internal colony', and had narrowed the range of economic opportunities that were due to Assam on account of its rich resource base of oil, tea, coal and timber. They also complained about Assam's lack of representation in the Lok Sabha (where it had just thirteen seats), and condemned New Delhi, again, for not protecting the 'sons of the soil' (the 'native' Assamese) from the locally dominant Bengali Hindus or from an influx of Bengali Muslims from Bangladesh.

The violence that rocked Assam in the early 1980s was contained for a while by an accord that Rajiv Gandhi reached in 1985 with some Assamese militants (an accord which promised protection against 'foreign intruders'), as well as by New Delhi's continuing policies of cooptation and divide and rule. But these same policies were to prove less effective in Punjab, where the regionalist movement which blossomed in the 1970s under the leadership of the Akali Dal, also took shape, at first, around a strongly 'economic' agenda. Although the 1973 Anandpur Sahib Resolution of the Akali Dal called 'for a general devolution of power from the central government to the states, and Indira Gandhi treated it as secessionist document . . . [n]owhere in it was a separate Sikh state mentioned' (Mahmood 1996: 117). The Jat Sikh farmers who pressed this resolution wanted New Delhi to rethink its policy for the division of waters between Punjab, Haryana, Rajasthan and Delhi. They were also keen to secure a State capital for Punjab (as opposed to one for Punjab and Haryana), as well as higher farm output prices and lower farm input prices (the classic politics of the commodity producing peasantry), and greater inward investment in support of non-farm employment opportunities (and not least at a time when changes to army recruitment practices were blocking off a traditional employment route for the sons of Sikh farmers).[23] None of this is meant to imply that the Akalis, or local *gurudwara* committees, were not also concerned to protect Sikh identities in a State (Punjab) where they were only just in a majority, but it is possible that New Delhi might have reduced pro-Khalistan sentiments in the late 1970s and 1980s had it attended more closely to the economic grievances of the Jat Sikhs.[24] But this it failed to do. Mrs Gandhi chose instead to 'view the Anandpur Sahib resolution as a subterfuge for eventual secession from the union' (Jalal 1995: 172), and sought to combat the Akali Dal by promoting Jarnail Singh Bhindranwale, the leader in the 1970s of a more militant and fundamentalist Sikh faction.[25]

This policy of divide and rule worked to the advantage of the Congress Party for a brief while. The Akali Dal did badly in the 1980 elections, and Bhindranwale agreed to campaign on behalf of the Congress. In the longer run, however, Mrs Gandhi's failure to read the map of Punjabi politics – her refusal to take advice from well-placed advisors, her reliance on Zail Singh – proved disastrous. Not only did the Congress Party, under Mrs Gandhi, fight religious fire with religious fire, thereby breaching one of her father's rules for the management of Centre–State relations, it also created a leader/ monster (Bhindranwale) who refused to do the bidding of his mistress/ Frankenstein. In the early 1980s Bhindranwale campaigned in favour of a separate Sikh State, and his followers began to attack Hindus in and around his centre of operations at the Golden Temple in Amritsar. Mrs Gandhi's errors were then compounded by her refusal to negotiate with either Bhindranwale or the moderate Akali leadership. Instead, she chose in June 1984 to deal with the growing terror and violence in Punjab by authorizing an army assault on the Golden Temple, the centre of the Sikh religion. Operation Bluestar secured the deaths of Bhindranwale and many of his supporters, but at a terrible price. Mrs Gandhi was herself killed in October 1984 as part of a Sikh backlash against the Congress Party and New Delhi, if not, indeed, against the idea of 'India' itself.

It was left to Rajiv Gandhi, once again, to pick up the pieces. In the first instance, he chose the path of conciliation and reform. An accord was reached with the Akali leadership in September 1985, and provisions were made for the transfer of Chandigarh to Punjab within one year and for the referral of other issues to commissions and courts. Large parts of the accord were never acted upon, however, and the Akali Dal government that took power in Punjab in September 1985 was hit by a fresh wave of militant activity, including a successful assault on the life of the moderate Sikh leader, Longowal. At this point the Congress government in New Delhi resorted to repression as its principal means of dealing with the crisis in Punjab. By the mid-1990s an estimated 25,000–30,000 Punjabis had lost their lives in the conflict, with many of them falling victim (in what was often reported as 'cross-fire') to the security forces.[26] The absurdity of India's democratic pretensions in this State was further underlined by the elections of 1992, which returned the Congress Party to power in Punjab in the face of a well-organized boycott by most factions of the Akali Dal. It was following this election that the Congress governments of Narasimha Rao (in New Delhi) and Beant Singh (in Punjab) moved to crush the Khalistan movement by means of police operations directed by Kanwar Pal Singh Gill.

The government of India has defended its record in Punjab in terms of a threat to national security which is said to emanate from Pakistan. And, doubtless, there is truth in the government's claim that Pakistani security officers have helped to train and equip Sikh militants, just as there is truth in the claim that Sikhs in London, Leicester, Toronto and Vancouver have provided funds for the Khalistan movement. But the wider message of the crisis in Punjab – or of the civil war that began in Kashmir in 1989, involving contending groups of militants struggling for a secular independent state, or an Islamic state, drawn quickly into conflict with Indian forces – is not a message of national security, at least not in the terms of what we might call the 'official discourse' of the Indian state. The civil wars in Punjab and Kashmir remind us that Indian federalism has not been working. Unable to recognize, and far less face up to the pressures that are promoting uneven development and cultural and regional pluralism, the Congress Party in the 1980s sought to clamp down on parties and movements that it coded as a threat to 'national unity' or to the hegemony of the ruling party.

In some cases, and for some periods of time, the policies of cooptation and divide and rule pursued by the Congress Party had their desired effects, as in Jharkhand or even Assam. In still other cases, the centralizing instincts of the Congress Party brought forward an equal and opposite politics of reaction and decentralization, as in many parts of south India or in West Bengal. The Congress Party has been flushed from power there, and is poorly placed to recover its position. And in two regions in particular, in Punjab and Kashmir, the seemingly illogical actions of the Congress Party worked to undermine the dream of consensual national unity to which it claimed to be committed; they also rode roughshod over regional and religious traditions that contested what Ashis Nandy has called 'the mytho-logy of an omnipresent, omnipotent central authority in modern India' (1990).

In these two regions, of course, the inflexions of political regionalism have been stiffened by religious identities from outside the Hindu mainstream, a point that is not always recognized in those narratives of crisis – at least in Punjab – which focus on the paranoia of Mrs Gandhi or the deinstitutional-ization of the Congress Party. Achin Vanaik makes an important point when he remarks that: 'Where regional territorial spaces were marked out as a consequence of linguistic pressures, local movements have largely stopped short of flirting seriously with secessionism. In contrast, the more tenuous incorporation of Kashmir, Punjab, Mizoram and Nagaland has had not a little to do with the fact that the cultural unity of the local groups in question had more to do with religious than with linguistic coherence' (Vanaik 1990: 163). In such places, too, the state in India has shown its determination to police the external borders of the 'nation-state', and its continuing desire to forge a convergence between the 'state' and the 'nation' in the body of modern India. What began to change in the 1980s was the terrain – religious and otherwise – around which these determinations and desires would be linked and fought out.

5.4   The Communalization of Indian Politics and the Challenge to Secularism

The rise of the Vishwa Hindu Parishad and the Ramjanmabhoomi Movement

With the advantage of hindsight we can see that the 1980s are remarkable for the rise not so much of the Bharatiya Janata Party as of the wider array of forces of Hindu communalism. Certainly it would have been difficult to predict in 1980 that the BJP would position itself as the leading opposition party, and 'the party of the future' in India, by the end of the decade. As we pointed out earlier (see chapter 3, note 18), it is remarkable that several major studies of Indian politics, published in 1990, made little reference to the BJP or to Hindu nationalism. In the period between 1980 and 1984, following its experience – in its Jana Sangh avatar – as part of the Janata coalition, the BJP tried to present itself as a moderate, centrist political party, and it then did disastrously in the 1984 general elections (taking just two seats in the Lok Sabha). At the beginning of the 1980s the Rashtriya Swayamsevak Sangh (RSS), too, though it still had a very strong cadre base across north India, had lost a lot of its dynamism. Yet, as Achin Vanaik has put it, by the beginning of the 1990s: 'In a context of deepening uncertainty and flux the BJP and the Sangh combine were the one collective force that had the organisational means, the ideological clarity and the inclination to pursue the politics of mass mobilisation' (1997: 313). And amongst the organizations within what Vanaik refers to as 'the Sangh combine', and others as 'the *Sangh parivar*' – that is the cluster or 'family' of organizations around the RSS, which includes the BJP and the Vishwa Hindu Parishad (VHP, the World Hindu Council) – it was above all the VHP that was instrumental in bringing about the transformations of the 1980s. As Thomas Blom Hansen has argued, what was new in the 1980s 'was not so much the employment of the idiom of communalism per se, but rather the ingenuity and the scale with which this idiom was differentiated and disseminated through an array of new technologies of mass mobilization' (Hansen 1999: 159). The VHP took the lead in this extraordinary campaign.

The VHP had been set up in 1964, the outcome of a meeting in Bombay of 150 religious leaders, which was probably convened at the behest of the RSS guru Golwalkar, and seems to have been stimulated by the earlier decision of the Pope to hold an International Eucharistic Congress in Bombay later in that same year. The meeting, which had long-run effects in forming linkages between the RSS and *sants, sanyasis, sadhus* and other Hindu religious leaders, established the VHP in order to 'revitalize Hindu society', and it took from the outset a distinctly defensive stance. Its aims were to mobilize Hindus – defined as 'all people who believe in, respect or follow the eternal values of life that have evolved in *Bharat*' – against the threats presented as being posed to them by Christianity, Islam and Communism. This defensiveness became transformed in the 1980s into an aggressive, anti-Muslim cultural nationalism. The unity of 'all Hindus', which the VHP claimed and sought to build, depended upon the identification of a threatening Other, found in the 'alien' Muslim. In spite of its association with Hindu spiritual leaders the VHP is not at all a scripturalist organization, or so van der Veer argues (1995), but rather it articulates a 'modern Hinduism' as the national religion of India, appealing in particular to an urban, middle-class constituency. This brings it into conflict with the principles of secularism laid down in the Constitution, for by the VHP's definition Muslims and Christians are not part of the Hindu nation. As the VHP gained in strength and influence in the 1980s, Indian secularism was called increasingly into question by voices of the street perhaps more significantly than by the discriminating arguments of scholars like Madan and Nandy.

It was not until the much-publicized incident of the conversion of Untouchables (although many of them were in fact Christians) to Islam at Meenakshipuram in Tamil Nadu in 1981, however, that the VHP really took off as an organization. It was able to respond to the sense of Hindu vulnerability that it was partially instrumental in arousing in response to the conversions, and thereafter its campaign for 'the defence of Hinduism' rapidly gained strength. Propaganda about the 'Islamic threat' led to the organization in 1983 of its 'sacrifice for unity', the *Ekatmatayajna* – a politico-cum-religious pilgrimage which sought to map out the mythological unity of Hindudom from the Himalayas to Kanyakumari and from the

Indus to the Seas (the Bay of Bengal) in which an estimated 60 million people took part (and see our discussion in chapter 8). It was successful especially in areas of inter-communal tensions where Hindus felt (or came to feel) threatened. There were many such areas by this time, for the incidence of communal riots had started to grow, as a result of diverse combinations of conflicts of material interest, and of local politics, and partly providing fuel for, partly responding to the ideological project of the Sangh combine. The *Ekatmatayajna* was the first of what became a continuing series of organized manifestations of religious community, claiming the public space and imagined national space for Hindus. The VHP itself 'was reorganised and expanded in the course of these campaigns [and a] permanent local infrastructure ... was established in large parts of the country' (Hansen, 1999: 154). For the first time the Hindu nationalist movement began to organize in the south, while it reached out, as well, to the large and prosperous Indian emigrant communities in North America, Europe, Africa and the Caribbean. The VHP had become a transnational organization.

In 1984, most significantly for the future history of India, the VHP began a movement for 'liberating' Hindu sites which it represented as having been taken over by Muslims. The most important of these sites was Ayodhya, in Uttar Pradesh, where there was a sixteenth-century mosque, the Babri Masjid, built according to local history, on a site where there had previously been a temple to the god Rama – the hero of the epic poem the Ramayana – on the site of his mythical birth. In 1949 an image of Ram was placed in the mosque by people then unknown and it was rumoured that Ram had come to claim his temple. There were riots and in the aftermath the Babri Masjid was locked up. In 1984 the VHP demanded that the lock on Lord Ram's birthplace be opened. Thus began the *Ramjanmabhoomi* Movement (for the 'liberation' of the birthplace of Lord Ram) which came to be the most effective mobilizational means of extending the ideas of Hindu nationalism, and it was mainly because of this that the VHP 'grew spectacularly in power and strength in the 1980s and developed an authority of its own, separate from the RSS' (Vanaik 1997: 312). The subsequent electoral successes of the BJP, too, cannot be explained without reference to the effects of *Ramjanmabhoomi* (see also our discussion in chapters 6 and 8). The Babri Masjid was transformed into a potent symbol of the way in which the Hindu majority was 'threatened' by the Muslim 'Other'. As Hansen points out, it came to stand for the violated rights of the Hindu majority within the paradigm of 'equal rights of communities' laid down within the Constitution, while making Ram 'into a metaphor of the essential Hinduness of Indian culture' (1999: 174).

The movement was perhaps assisted by the adaptation of the Ramayana which was watched by many millions on Indian public television in 1987 and 1988 – an adaptation which once more highlighted the significance of

Ayodhya within Hindu cosmology, and which, to the delight of the BJP, served up a more martial vision of Hinduism than many Indians, and many more non-Indians, had grown accustomed to. Then, in September 1989, the VHP organized, in villages across north India, the manufacture and the worship of bricks (the 'bricks of Lord Rama' – *ramshila*), and processions to bring them to Ayodhya to build a new temple for Ram, giving rise to another wave of communal violence. The worst of this was in the town of Bhagalpur in Bihar, where the Muslim population was largely wiped out. It was in the context of the demand for the 'liberation' of the temple at Ayodhya, too, that the VHP formed its youth wing, the Bajrang Dal, which subsequently played an important part in the demolition of the Babri Masjid, and later, in 1998–9, in turning communal aggression against Christians. It is 'known to recruit untrained, volatile, semi-lumpen elements in contrast to the hand-picked and throughly-coached RSS cadres' (Basu et al. 1993: 68). In the late 1980s the VHP also started a militant organization for young women, the Durga Vahini.

In February 1986 a judge of Faizabad decided that the disputed site at Ayodhya should be opened again to the public,[27] a decision which led to communal violence and protracted disputes between Muslim and Hindu bodies (notably the Babri Masjid Action Committee and the VHP). But the symbolism of Ayodhya was such that Rajiv Gandhi insisted at an election rally there in 1989 that he supported the VHP case – one of the more public of the many concessions which the Congress government made to communalism, and which helped to expand the space for it. The Congress-(I) indeed, by its actions and its inactions, effectively connived in the 'communalization' of Indian politics through the 1980s.

Congress capitulation to communalism

An early sign that the Congress Party would fail to support the 'myth of secularism' came in the wake of the assassination of Mrs Gandhi on 31 October 1984. Stanley Tambiah has referred to the anti-Sikh programmes which followed upon her death as a form of 'organized bloodletting', and he has reviewed evidence which shows that Congress workers played a key role in commandeering buses in Delhi to take enraged Hindus and their supplies of paraffin and weaponry to the residences and businesses of Sikh families (1990). Salman Rushdie has also not shied away from identifying the attackers; those 'angry Hindu mobs – among whom party workers of Mrs Gandhi's Congress-I were everywhere observed – [who] decided to hold all Sikhs responsible for the deeds of the assassins' (1991: 30), and who were responsible for the brutal killings of between 2,307 and 3,879 persons.[28] 'Almost three years after the massacres', Rushdie declared, 'not one person has been charged with murdering a Sikh in those fearsome days. The Congress-I, Rajiv Gandhi's party, increasingly relies on the Hindu vote, and is reluctant to alienate it' (p. 31).

There is some truth in this claim. We have noted previously that Rajiv Gandhi's landslide victory in the 1984 elections was won on the basis of an appeal to Hindu Indians, as well as on the back of a sympathy vote. The Congress-(I) played the communal card openly, effectively and shamefully. But the twists and turns of Congress politics in the second half of the 1980s do not quite make sense in terms of the party's appeal to the Hindu vote, as Rushdie perhaps implies. The growing powerlessness of the Congress, which we identified in the first part of this chapter, is rather to be explained in terms of its willingness to open up a political space for Hindu (and Sikh) nationalism, even as it pulled back from riding what Rushdie calls 'the tiger of Hindu fundamentalism' (1991: 31). The Congress Party in the 1980s was unsure as to what stance it should take in relation to the politics of communalism or religious nationalism. At times, and quite opportunistically, it continued to play the secular card: it sought to appeal to its traditional support bases among the rural and urban elites and among the Scheduled Communities. At other times, as in Assam, it sought to court the Hindu vote by moving against 'alien Muslims', a tactic that it favoured, too, in its clumsy attempts to play the anti-Pakistan card in Punjab.

Shah Bano and the threat in Indian secularism

On still another occasion, as in 1987, crucially, the Congress felt obliged to court its traditional support base among India's Muslims in specifically 'Muslim' (or religious) terms. In that year Rajiv Gandhi ensured the passage of the Muslim Women (Protection of Rights on Divorce) Bill through Parliament. This bill emerged in the wake of the Shah Bano affair and was a sop to conservative (not to say male) Muslim thinking on the family and divorce. Shah Bano *begum* had sued her husband for alimony from the time that he divorced her in 1978 – and successfully so in India's civil courts – but the 1987 Bill 'literally adopted the provisions of the shariat into the secular law' (P. Brass 1994: 233). In order to secure the support of influential Muslim power-brokers across north India, Rajiv Gandhi disregarded the secular foundations of the state that had been fought for by his grandfather, and trampled on a political philosophy that had, according to conventional wisdom, afforded Muslims a measure of freedom and protection in a country dominated by non-Muslims.

It is still not clear why Rajiv Gandhi endorsed the Muslim Women Bill in 1987, a bill that he had opposed in 1985 and 1986. Short-term electoral advantage is surely part of the answer (the Congress was facing important elections in 1987 in Haryana, Jammu and Kashmir, and Kerala), but it is by no means the whole story. Another part of the answer lies in the changing 'identity politics' of India's religious communities in the 1980s. The Congress Party in the second half of the 1980s had to react to certain changes within a (diverse) Muslim community that was itself reacting to the rise of Hindu nationalism in India, and which was registering various battles and debates around Islamic identity that were raging elsewhere in South and West Asia.[29] Whatever the reasons for the Congress *volte-face*, one of its major effects was further to encourage the rise of Hindu nationalism. The Bharatiya Janata Party was able to use the passage of the Muslim Women Bill to support its claim that a 'pseudo-secularism' in India had worked to the disadvantage of the majority Hindu community; that it was, in fact, a form of minoritarianism which required the reform of Hinduism even as it reinforced the most anti-modern practices of India's leading minority religion, Islam.

This claim, as we have seen, goes back to the time of the Hindu Mahasabha (see chapter 2, and also chapter 8). It was a consistent, if usually muffled claim within Indian politics through the 1950s and 1960s. In the 1980s, however, the critique of secularism that was sustained through the 1970s by the Jana Sangh – a critique that complained about special treatment for Muslims, and which campaigned for a politics of equal 'religious' privilege – was repackaged by its successor organization, the Bharatiya Janata Party (BJP), as a more forceful affirmation of the claims of the Hindu majority. More so than the leadership of the Jana Sangh, the leadership of the BJP in the 1980s aimed to recover an ideology of *Hindutva* from the works of Veer Savarkar and others, and to present these ideas forcefully, imaginatively and without apology to the Indian public. Lal Krishna Advani, in particular – after the party shifted from its attempt in the early 1980s to present a centrist image – was keen to press home the argument that India was labouring under a doctrine of 'pseudo-secularism' which had been imposed on the country by Nehru and the modernizing wing of the Congress Party. 'True secularism', he argued, would recognize the essential 'Hinduness' of India in cultural terms; it would also call into question, as Jalal so felicitously remarks, 'the Nehruvian conception of state secularism as not only coterminous with the polity but also representative of Indian nationalism' (Jalal 1995: 241).

Having done so much in the 1980s to open the door to the communalization of Indian politics, the Congress Party now feigned to watch in horror as the BJP reaped the rewards of Congress opportunism and vacillation. The more serious minded amongst the Congress ranks, to the extent that any remained, were forced to recognize that the political map of India had been decisively reworked in the 1980s, in ideological as well as in party political terms. The bankrupting of the Congress Party went hand in glove with a weakening of the (state)-secular principle in India. In so far as any political party offered a coherent vision for India at the start of the 1990s it was not Congress; it was, rather, the BJP with its ideology of *Hindutva*, or the claim that the unity of India is to be found in the Hindu culture which defines it and gives it meaning.

5.5 Conclusion: The Failure of the Left

The electoral successes of the BJP in the late 1980s and 1990s were remarkable, and they speak to profound changes in the nature of party organization and identity politics in India at this time. But not all BJP supporters voted for the party's *Hindutva* ideology. A goodly proportion were more concerned with law and order or reservations issues, or wanted to register their disenchantment with the Congress. And nor was the rise to power of the BJP uncontested, either at the national level (by the Congress and the National Front) or at the State and District levels. It says a lot about Indian politics during this period, however, that a right-wing political party, the BJP, was more often brought up short by casteist political groupings than by an organized Left opposition. Why should this have been so, when India has a powerful radical intelligentsia, a long history of communist activism, and three States (West Bengal, Kerala and Tripura) in which communist parties have held office for long periods? The question seems even more to call for an answer when we consider the circumstances of the early 1970s, when communists were organizing actively in many parts of the country and leftists (actual or former communists) were sufficiently influential in government at the Centre as to have been able to have pushed through amendments to the Constitution in pursuit of social transformation (see chapter 4).

Part of the answer to this question lies in the history of communist politics in India. The leadership of the mainstream communist parties has been largely upper caste and middle class, which may have played some part in explaining their fixation, encouraged initially by the Comintern, with identifying the 'progressive' and left-oriented leaders of the Congress as the party of the national bourgeoisie, and with 'latching on to them in a bid to provide a "leftist" thrust to the policies of the Indian state' (Chatterjee 1997a [1985–6]: 162; and see Gail Omvedt's account of the history of the Communist Party of India – 1993: chs 1 and 2). In addition, it seems that in the 1970s the success of some communists in imparting just such a leftist thrust to government policies backfired upon them when Mrs Gandhi stole their clothes and then succeeded in sidelining them. The Congress – as under the leadership of Devaraj Urs in Karnataka in the 1970s, or in Gujarat in the early 1980s – was quite often successful in mobilizing poorer people politically. Elsewhere, other parties – like the DMK in Tamil Nadu – were effective in projecting themselves as the representatives of the poor and working people who might have been expected to, and in some other parts of the country actually did support communist parties. Regional parties such as the DMK and the Akali Dal, and later the Telugu Desam, were successful in winning support on the basis of an identity which cut across class differences. The numerical and organizational weakness of the Indian working class – including the political divisions in the union movement deriving from the affiliations of the major unions with political parties – has always been a limitation in conventional left-wing politics.

But the success of a party like the DMK hints at something else besides: the importance of non-Brahmanism (in this case), or more generally of caste affiliations in the prosecution of the political agendas of various oppressed and/or upwardly mobile (and mainly rural) communities. Partha Chatterjee closes the essay from which we have already quoted by declaring that: 'the crucial political task is to educate the people that an unstable structure of central power is proof that the ruling classes are unable to rule India, and that instead of this being a cause for fear and anxiety, it offers wholly new opportunities for popular mobilization and radical transformation' (1997a [1984]: 106). This may be so, but it is possible that Chatterjee's invitation to a more imaginative Left politics failed to anticipate the ways in which the landscapes of 'elite' *and* 'non-elite' Indian politics would be changed in the 1990s. We will explore this issue further in chapter 6 and in chapters 8 and 9.

6

'Elite Revolts': Reforming and Reinventing India in the 1990s

The new elite that has emerged and follows those in command in the global framework no longer tries to keep up the socialist rhetoric but is following the capitalist path. They, in fact, bluntly say that those millions of people who are left out are in fact a drag.

Rajni Kothari (1988: 2591)

We have reached rock-bottom in world stature, economically, in every way. If the BJP is an alternative to a better end then so be it.

An Indian businessman (quoted in *India Today*, 15 May 1991)

It is a great sorrow to me that this transition from the old order towards an emerging India... had to occur accompanied by violence. But it is without doubt a transition from the old to the new.

Jaswant Singh (quoted by Jaffrelot 1996: 475)

There was a mood of cautious optimism in India at the beginning of the 1990s, so Partha Chatterjee wrote at the time (1997a [1989]: 200). The aura both of competence and of integrity surrounding Vishwanath Pratap Singh promised much after the disappointments of Rajiv Gandhi's period in office. Yet, as Chatterjee also wrote, the auguries were disquieting. Internally fractious and in a parliamentary minority, the government which Singh headed only by virtue of a ruse, in which Devi Lal, now the Deputy Prime Minister, had ceded the highest office to him in order to defeat a challenge from Chandrasekhar,[1] depended upon the non-opposition (or 'support from outside') of the Left parties and of the BJP. Public finances were a shambles, after 'the mindless spending spree in which Rajiv Gandhi and his men had

---

The idea of a 'revolt of the elite' is taken from Sudipta Kaviraj (1997: 19)

indulged' (Chatterjee 1997a [1989]: 201), and the public debt-to-GNP ratio was almost double what it had been in 1980. The kidnapping in Srinagar of the daughter of the new Union Home Minister, Mufti Mohammed Sayeed, showed the extent of animosity which was felt in Kashmir towards what militants there described as 'Indian rule' and ushered in a new challenge to Indian federalism. And only shortly after the formation of the government, the VHP relaunched the Ramjanmabhoomi movement with its mission of 'liberating' the Ram temple at Ayodhya and – in the process – of changing the Indian conception of 'secularism'.

As it turned out the short-lived government led by V. P. Singh played the overture to a decade in which India has been transformed. Singh had seemed to promise the restoration of at least some of the principles and values of the Nehruvian state. Instead, the economic reforms of the 1990s, the 'democratic upsurge' that has occurred alongside them, and above all the rise of the Bharatiya Janata Party, have embodied the reinvention of India's mythologies of rule. This is what is implied in Jaswant Singh's reference – in a distant echo of Nehru speaking in the Constituent Assembly – to 'a transition from old to new'. The idea of an 'elite revolt', which we use with reference to the first and the third of these movements of change, is certainly tendentious, but the image seems appropriate because of the manner of their deliberate assertions or re-assertions of power against modern India's mythologies of rule (explicitly against socialism and federalism and secularism), and against the popular forces that those mythologies have encouraged (and hence, less explicitly, against democracy).

It is always dangerous to venture judgements on the significance of contemporary events, but there is a strong case for believing that the economy of India was reshaped – if not entirely reinvented – by the programme of economic reforms that was put into place by V. P. Singh's successor as Prime Minister, Narasimha Rao, and by his Finance Minister Manmohan Singh. The Congress Party which Rao led had not promised reform in its election manifesto of 1991, but it came to power at a moment of economic crisis, and was quickly persuaded by the international financial institutions, and economic liberals in the Indian establishment, to treat a crisis of liquidity as if it was a crisis of solvency (or even of development).[2] The immediate conjuncture which made for this opportunity was the situation created by the Gulf War earlier that year, which had both increased the prices that India had to pay for oil and reduced remittances from Indians working in the Gulf region, in a context in which the country's international credit rating had been downgraded by the two leading credit rating agencies. This decision, which was taken as a consequence of the political instability created by the fall of the government of V. P. Singh, both reflected and gave rise to increased difficulty in the field of commercial borrowings, and also to capital flight as Non-Resident Indian investors withdrew their local deposits. External reserves fell in early to mid-1991 to a level equivalent to only two weeks' worth of imports. These immediate circumstances were underlain by the ballooning fiscal deficit, and growing external indebtedness, which followed from the way in which Rajiv Gandhi's 'dash for growth' had been financed in the later 1980s (the 'mindless spending spree' of Chatterjee's account: see above).

The new government immediately sought a stand-by loan from the International Monetary Fund and devalued the rupee. These actions were followed by Manmohan Singh's first budget, which laid out what was in the Indian context a radical strategy for stabilizing the economy and reducing the budget deficit, and by policies which promised structural adjustment. 'The bitter pill of devaluation, expenditure cutting and inflation', Chatterjee wrote, was to be given 'the sugar coating of export-led growth and foreign investments' (1997a: 220). We will describe the reforms, their implementation and implications, and the debates surrounding them in the next chapter. But we note here that a collapse in India's balance of payments in 1991 did not

> reflect any major adversities in the real economy: agricultural and industrial output remained normal, and inflation was not abnormally high for the period. The fact that this primarily financial crisis was seen ... as so all-pervasive in the economy is an indication of the much greater significance by this time of finance capital, both domestic and international, in changing the course of the Indian economy and economic policies. (Ghosh 1998: 324)

We also note that the reforms of the 1990s have worked to the advantage of India's business and financial (and even agricultural) elites – those elites who have been in revolt against some aspects of the state-managed capitalism that served their interests previously – and have not yet empowered the majority of Indians. Whether the reforms have been gradual and rather erratic in practice, or quite deep-seated (because implemented by 'stealth': see our discussion of Rob Jenkins's work in the next chapter), it is evident, as Jayati Ghosh argues, that: 'The [new] growth pattern is one which is based on the market created by (at most) the upper one-third of the population. This not only has distributive and welfare implications but also means that the market remains narrower than its potential' (1998: 326). And, ideologically, the reforms have justified the pursuit of individual wealth as never before. Rajni Kothari had seen the signs already in the 1980s: there was an inclination to view the poor as responsible for their own fates, and as a drag on the rest, in a way which was quite new.[3]

It is possible that this 'bias against the poor' will be tempered by the 'second round' of reforms promised by the new BJP-led government in November 1999 – reforms which might yet improve the country's stocks of infrastructure and human capital. This would reflect pressures on the BJP to behave as a national party – one that can appeal beyond its support base amongst the 'Forward Castes' and urban middle classes – as was apparently recognized in the so-called 'Chennai declaration' of the BJP's National Executive and National Council, in December 1999. The declaration sought delicately to reposition the party, and to provide a theoretical framework for moving it from being 'an ideology-driven outfit to an aggregative party'[4] – capable, indeed, of occupying the space in Indian politics left by the decline of the Congress.

But none of this is assured. In this chapter we examine in particular the rise to power of the BJP, and we consider the role played by 'political Hinduism' (or Hindu nationalism) in meeting the challenge of India's rural and Backward Class communities. For here, we believe, are two further and more certain moments in the reinvention of India in the 1990s: the Mandal-ization of politics (following the decision, in August 1990, of V. P. Singh to act on some of the recommendations of the report of the Second Backward Classes Commission), and the politics of the *mandir* (symbolized most aggressively in the destruction of the Babari Masjid in Ayodhya in December 1992). These moments of transformation are in turn related to the emergence of a middle class in the countryside as well as in the city, and to what Yogendra Yadav has called a 'second democratic upsurge' in independent India.

The reinventions of India which have taken shape since the 1980s are very different from the more concerted and singular act of invention that marked the period from 1946 to 1956. If India was being reinvented at the end of the twentieth century – and in one sense, course, it is always being reinvented – it was not being invented in line with some 'revealed truth' (or plan), as once was the case. In his essay 'Waiting for a Text', Geoffrey Hawthorn maintains 'that politics everywhere, and *a fortiori* in the Third World, is a matter of local invention as much as international imitation' (1991: 42). In the dialectics of Indian politics in the 1990s elite assertions on one side (some parts of which were imitative) and subaltern mobilizations on the other intersected with the politics of caste, community and spatiality.

6.1 Social Change and the Politics of the 1990s

We have argued that from well before the final decade of the twentieth century the BJP, with its often problematic but always significant connections with the cadre-based organization of the RSS, and its links with the other organizations of the *Sangh parivar*,[5] has been – with the exception of the CPI(M), at least in West Bengal – the most coherent and the best organized force in Indian politics. It has also been the only party – again with the exception of the CPI(M) – with a definite design for India, and which has apparently not been entirely in thrall to those whom Chatterjee describes as 'self-seeking and unprincipled political speculators', for whom 'politics is . . . a business, like speculating in share markets . . . a risky business where you can go bust all of a sudden, but where you can also make a fortune if things go all right' (1997a: 213–14). As the BJP has held office in various States (since February 1990) it has been subject to the pressures of 'normal politics' in the Indian context, and its record in government has not generally been impressive. Its unity is indeed 'partly an illusion', as Sudipta Kaviraj argued (1997: 14), which could be maintained only so long as it did not hold office and therefore could afford the luxury of having only a single plank in its policy platform. But still, its leaders have appeared to have a purpose which is higher than that of the pursuit of individual power for private gain,[6] and they have held together in a way that has distinguished them both from the old men who led the Janata in the 1970s, who lost the initiative because of their personal squabbles, and from the leaders of the National Front in the 1990s. And there is a collegiality in the BJP leadership which marks the party out from the Congress, the dependence of which upon the almost monarchical charisma of the 'ruling' (Nehru-Gandhi) family was marked again in 1998 when the party turned to Sonia Gandhi, Rajiv's widow, for leadership.

The rise of the 'middle class'

Given these arguments about the distinctiveness of the BJP one might ask why it had to wait so long in the wings. While there is no doubt that the BJP has constructed the constituency for Hindu nationalist politics, aided enormously by the campaigns of the VHP in the 1980s and 1990s (as well as having been, at times, threatened by them), and by the constant presence of the RSS, it has also found more fertile ground and an expanding base of support as a result of changes which have taken place in Indian society. These include the growth in numbers and in influence of a middle class that straddles city, town and countryside, and the weakening of 'traditional authority' which has both liberated the power of youth and built up a sense of a threatened social order for which the BJP seems now to provide the main defence.

The category 'middle class' is a problematical one, perhaps especially so in the Indian context. It has become fashionable, not least in the popular imagination, and is generally defined by income and its correlates, mainly a variety of branded private consumer goods. It includes what has always been described as the 'petty bourgeoisie' – small industrialists, businessmen and traders – as well as employees in the corporate sector, and the middle ranks of the professions and the civil service. But it also now includes large numbers of rich peasants or farmers.[7] By the 1980s, indeed, rural society over much of India was more diversified than it had been before. Though there had not been by then (nor has there been subsequently) over very much of the country the kind of rapid growth of productive, value-adding, but also employment-intensive rural non-agricultural activities which have characterized the successful East Asian economies (see, for example, Saith 1991), there has been growth in non-agricultural employment and, in the more dynamic rural regions of India, of diversifying investments outside agriculture. It has been remarked that a class of 'ruppys' – 'rural upwardly mobile persons' – has arisen,[8] and some of them, as well as members of historically dominant castes, have made the kinds of business and consumption investments observed by Rutten (1995) amongst Patidars in south Gujarat, and those described by Jeffrey from western UP, where 'richer Jat farmers have been largely successful in converting agricultural wealth, flowing from capital intensive sugar cane and wheat agriculture, into social links and cultural capital' (1998: 3)

The development of the Indian middle class in the countryside and in small towns, as much as in big cities, was perhaps initially of interest mainly to the marketing profession, and its growth in the 1980s was marked by the rapid expansion in numbers of television sets (which rose from about 2 million to 30 million in the 1980s), by increases in the production of cars (which grew nearly five times in the 1980s), refrigerators (nearly four times) and of motor scooters (which grew over eleven times).[9] *India Today* wrote in 1985 that the members of the 'middle class' who were the purchasers of these kinds of consumer goods were: 'Rajiv Gandhi's people, at home in a new political climate, happy with the new political jargon, relieved that the Government no longer tries to tax everyone to distraction in the name of the poor, enamoured of a prime minister who understands the importance of colour TV' (quoted by Dubey 1992: 138). Various estimates have been made of the number of these people. One such, based on surveys carried out in 1989–90, arrived at a figure of 176 million, including 13 per cent of rural and 42 per cent of urban households. Amongst the latter, it has been said: 'There has been a 90 per cent increase in average family incomes . . . during the 1983–88 period (alone).'[10] It is on the basis of estimates like these that India is sometimes said to be the most important potential market anywhere in the world, which clearly gives international big business a strong interest in the liberalization of trade and investment.

The wide base of support for the BJP in the vacuum left by the Congress-(I)

The members of the middle class may have been keen supporters of Rajiv Gandhi in the mid-1980s, but by the 1990s it was clear that many of them were switching their allegiance to the BJP. As Christophe Jaffrelot has written: 'The BJP attracted support by default because the Congress-(I) was deeply unpopular. Moreover the BJP probably won over former Congress-(I) supporters all the more easily because it appeared to be the sole proponent of a political project – the building of a strong India – which had been established and assiduously promoted by Indira Gandhi' (1996: 433).[11] By the 1990s the Congress had lost this mantle because of its perceived corruption and inefficiency, and its factionalism. It was for this reason –

amongst others, perhaps – that the BJP also began to win support not only from its traditional base in the trading castes but also from prominent executives, ex-servicemen and former top administrators. The National Front/Janata Dal, meanwhile, lost support amongst the middle classes, who are predominantly from higher and middle-ranking castes, both because of its advocacy of the policy of reservations for members of the Other Backward Classes, and because of the mayhem which was brought about in 1990 by that policy (see below).[12]

How far religious feeling has been an important consideration for the 'new' middle class is a matter of debate. Jaffrelot argues that on the whole the middle classes did not play a large part in the mobilization around Ramjanmabhoomi in 1990 and that: 'For such people religious factors apparently played a minor role compared to their opposition to the reservations policy and commitment to a more disciplined (or even authoritarian) form of politics and the clean image of the BJP' (1996: 433). On the other hand, a survey conducted in Delhi and western Uttar Pradesh shortly after the demolition of the Babri Masjid showed that 60 per cent of white-collar professionals and 62 per cent of traders approved of the assault, while amongst workers support fell to 28 per cent. And there is evidence that amongst the significant number of middle-class people who 'have acquired economic status but not corresponding social status' there is an anxiety 'to bring the two into consonance' partly through religious observance and congregational activities (see Dubey 1992: 157). Christopher Fuller has observed in Tamil Nadu the development of an active programme for the training of Brahman temple priests in the Sanskrit scriptures, and that 'With official approval and partly aided by the [Chief Minister's Temple Renovation and Maintenance Fund], there was in the early 1990s a rapid rise in the number of temple renovation rituals (*kumbabhisekham*), which are the most dramatic expression of the wave of temple-focussed Hindu revivalism running through the state' (1998: 7).[13] The employers of priests for the recitation of Sanskrit verses which they do not actually understand – and which most devotees do not understand – include, prominently, members of the growing middle class. Jaffrelot is perhaps too quick to dismiss the significance of religion in accounting for their support for Hindu nationalism.

Other critical elements in the support base of the BJP are the middling and higher castes. Youths who participated in the Ramjanmabhoomi agitation in 1990 often belonged to the upper castes, and their apparent over-representation among the 'martyrs' who were killed or wounded in the confrontation with the security forces which took place at Ayodhya on 30 October 1990 has to be understood in the context of protests over the Mandal Commission report and the issue of reservations. More generally there is reason to suppose that the weakening of 'traditional authority' has evoked a defensive response from the upper castes. The wider context is that described by Atul Kohli in these terms:

The picture that emerges [from his research in the 1980s] is that of an increasing authority vacuum. The organizational ability of the Congress party has declined, and popular new parties have failed to fill the organizational vacuum. In addition, traditional authority patterns in the social structure have been weakened; the capacity of the dominant castes and of other 'big men' to influence the political behaviour of those below them in the social hierarchy has diminished. (1990a: 384)

Kohli failed, of course, to anticipate the way in which the BJP was to move into the 'authority vacuum' in the 1990s, and the appeal of the party on these grounds.[14] But the circumstances which he describes help to account for the way in which the ideology and practices of the BJP resonate amongst members of the upper castes – as well as for the increasingly overt violence in the relations between upper and lower castes in the 1990s, as those who used to exercise authority have resorted increasingly to the use of brute force in trying to maintain their power, sometimes claiming as they have done so what Susan Bayly has described as a 'mandate of righteousness'.[15]

Members of the upper castes predominate, still, amongst the higher echelons of the leadership of the BJP, although electoral considerations have pushed the party into recruiting individuals from the Backward Classes into prominent positions, in what has been described as a programme of 'social engineering'. This programme was indeed acted upon, in Maharashtra (Hansen 1996a), in Madhya Pradesh (Jaffrelot 1998), and in Uttar Pradesh, where the BJP government led by Kalyan Singh (himself from a 'backward' community) at the end of the decade clearly tilted towards the backward classes. The conflict which then developed between Kalyan Singh and the central leadership of the BJP in 1999, and which led, first, to his (forced) resignation as Chief Minister, and then to his resignation from the party, was widely held to have checked this social engineering, at least in UP.[16]

The diversity of support which the BJP has been successful in mobilizing also presents problems for it, however, for the interests of many of its upper/middle-caste and middle-class supporters are primarily in authority, stability and order, and in the affirmation of Indian nationalism and of the status of the country as a great power in the context of a globalizing world order. These modernist and modernizing claims come into conflict with the demands of other supporters of Hindu nationalism whose intentions are in some senses distinctly anti-modernist, and some of whose actions have, at times, caused disorder (see also Jaffrelot 1996: 435). The problems thus posed for the BJP are reflected, for example, in the tensions which became evident late in 1999 over the electoral commitment – which Prime Minister Vajpayee was forced to reiterate in December of that year – not to pursue the construction of the Ram temple at Ayodhya, or other key issues of the campaign for *Hindutva*, as part of the agenda of the National Democratic Alliance.

But this is to jump ahead. It is time, now, to tell the story of the rise of the BJP through the 1990s, and thus of the second of the 'elite revolts' which is reconstructing India.

6.2 'Mandal' and *Mandir* and the Rise of the BJP

The strains in the ruling coalition of the National Front headed by V. P. Singh, both within and among parties, and with its 'outside supporters', were immediately apparent early in 1990. The BJP, in particular, sought a harder line on Kashmir. The State elections in February confirmed the results of the 1989 general election, with the National Front and the BJP emerging victorious in the north, while the Congress-(I) held on to Maharashtra. The BJP took office in Madhya Pradesh and in Himachal Pradesh and entered into coalitions with the Janata Dal (JD) in Gujarat and Rajasthan, while the JD won in Orissa, and in Bihar, which was the only state in the Hindi belt where the BJP did not make much of a showing (reflecting the political mobilization there of the OBCs). The efforts of the government at the centre, meanwhile, to develop economic policies in the pursuit of greater liberalization of trade and investment, already constrained by the need to accommodate the demands for subsidies of the richer farmers represented by Deputy Prime Minister Devi Lal, had hardly been announced when they were swept aside in the turmoil caused in the middle of the year by a struggle for power between Lal and V. P. Singh. Lal was finally dismissed by Singh on 1 August. A few days later, on 7 August, the government announced a 27 per cent reservation of jobs in the central government services and public undertakings for socially and educationally Backward Classes, other than the Scheduled Castes and Tribes (who already had a 22.5 per cent reservation), which was in line with the recommendations of the Second Backward Classes Commission (the Mandal Commission). This decision was justified by reference to the claims of social justice, though at the same time it clearly was intended to build support for the JD amongst the OBCs against the disaffection of the Jats in northern India (supporters of Devi Lal), and, by working on the caste divisions within the Hindu community, against the threat from the BJP. And indeed the BJP was placed in a quandary, torn between its traditional support among upper castes who would be badly affected by the new policy, and the numbers of the OBCs in the electorate. It therefore expressed support for the principle of reservations, but based on economic criteria, and threw its weight behind the VHP campaign over the temple at Ayodhya – which enabled the party to distance itself from the government, and in the end successfully to weaken the political unity of the OBCs (Z. Hasan 1998: 219).

Mandal and the issue of reservations

The fury unleashed by various high-caste communities, mainly across north India,[17] in the wake of Singh's decision was quite predictable, not least in view of that which had already been wreaked in several States in the 1980s by anti-reservation movements (Mitra 1987). Public-sector jobs in India are much sought after and are regarded by many high-caste men (and some women) as a bulwark against the uncertainties of life in the country's private sector. As one respondent told the anthropologist Jonathan Parry when he was working at the public-sector steel plant in Bhilai, Madhya Pradesh, there was 'no mother or father like it' (1996). And now this parental support was being removed, or so it seemed, along with unchallenged access to India's elite universities and medical and engineering schools.

The Mandal decision led to furious debate, too, amongst Indian intellectuals as to the merits and demerits of positive discrimination through the reservations policy. Some, like the anthropologist A. M. Shah, opposed the equation which was made by Mandal, and in some legal judgements, between the idea of the existence of a 'class' (meaning 'category') of people who are 'socially and educationally backward' and particular castes, arguing that this is sociologically misconceived (Shah 1996a; Sivaramayya 1996). Critics held, like some of the members of the first Backward Classes Commission indeed, nearly forty years before, that the policy of reservation on caste lines served only to enhance the significance of caste categories, and so to exacerbate or to create conflicts; they argued that the policy was discriminatory and incompatible with that efficiency which, in public services, is in the longer-run interests especially of poorer people in Indian society (a case which was put very cogently by Shah, 1996b); and they held that the policy, anyway, mainly benefits those who are better-off amongst the lower castes, not the truly disadvantaged, whether from higher or lower castes. Some, therefore, including the BJP, made the case for positive discrimination on economic grounds alone. On the other side were those like Radhakrishnan, who argued that 'the justification for reservation is self-evident' (1996: 204), given the strong historical association between membership in particular caste communities and social exclusion. The arguments of the critics of Mandal and the advocates of the criterion of 'merit' would only stand up if there were to be equalization of educational opportunities. Chatterjee put this case vigorously, recognizing that the system of reservation of jobs will have only limited economic impact, benefiting mainly the 'creamy layers' of the backward classes, but supporting the system nonetheless, because it promises to take away at least some institutional power from the higher castes. Not surprisingly, therefore, the reaction of some members of the upper castes to the Mandal decision was ferocious (an 'elite revolt' indeed): 'there are few things more ugly than the flaunting of the cultural superiority of dominant minorities' (Chatterjee 1997a: 210).

The mandir

In the face of Congress vacillation on the reservations issue, many high-caste Indians, particularly in urban north India, turned to the BJP to protect their interests, and though the party refused to set its stall against 'reservations' – it dared not because of the electoral calculus – its antipathy to some aspects of Mandal was well known. This was the context in which L. K. Advani launched his Rath Yatra ('chariot procession'), when he travelled 10,000 kilometres across eight States in a vehicle designed to represent an epic chariot, decorated with the symbols of the BJP, and planned to reach Ayodhya on 30 October 1990 to inaugurate the Kar Seva (the 'building of the temple'). Intended to strengthen Hindu solidarity, the Rath Yatra proved an effective strategy, intensifying the Ayodhya movement, and helping the Hindu nationalists to penetrate villages more effectively than ever before. The Congress compromised; V. P. Singh tried to negotiate, but having failed in this sought to take tough action, authorizing the Janata Dal Chief Minister of Bihar (and OBC leader), Laloo Prasad Yadav, to arrest Advani on 23 October. As a result of this action the BJP withdrew its support (from the outside) for the Singh government, and not long afterwards V. P. Singh, further weakened by a split in his party, was replaced as Prime Minister by Chandrasekhar, at the head of a minority government which relied on Congress support (and which was to last only for the few months up to March 1991).

The agitation over the construction of the temple at Ayodhya, meanwhile, became increasingly violent. The Kar Seva movement continued despite the preventive orders issued by the Janata Dal government of Uttar Pradesh (led by Mulayam Singh Yadav, another OBC leader), and there was a confrontation between *kar sevaks* (volunteers) and the security forces on 30 October, when some of the former were shot. Support for the BJP grew in the aftermath of the firings, and was cultivated and mediated through the networks of the *Sangh parivar*. A cult of martyrs was born, and assiduously fostered through the production by J. K. Jain Studios of what came to be a very widely distributed video depicting police repression. The sense of vulnerability felt by many Hindus, Jaffrelot argues, 'was transformed into exasperation against the political authorities... [while]... anger was channelled against Muslims' (1996: 422); and Z. Hasan writes that: 'Opposition to the secular state and the necessity of Hindu unity to rewrite the agenda of the state... became central to middle class perceptions' (1998: 211).

The controversies over both Mandal and the *mandir* remained unresolved, while communal violence continued through the political uncertainty of the early months of 1991, and the election campaign which followed, when the BJP sought to derive as much benefit as possible from Ayodhya. In the event the party succeeded in winning 120 seats and 20 per cent of the valid votes cast, establishing itself as the second party nationally. It might have done even better than this had it not been for the sympathy vote for the Congress in the second phase of the election, following Rajiv Gandhi's assassination on 21 May 1991. The BJP remained, however, as Harold Gould put it, more a 'mega-regional party' than a truly national party, restricted to the Hindi belt. Its success elsewhere, notably in Karnataka, was attributed by commentators to local factors rather than to the appeal of Hindu nationalism.[18]

According to Christophe Jaffrelot's interpretation of events, by this stage the BJP, having become the second largest party in the Lok Sabha, and having formed a government in Uttar Pradesh, faced the dilemma to which we referred earlier in general terms. It was now anxious not to be seen as a single-issue party, sought to reduce its dependence upon ethno-religious mobilization and – recognizing the reasons why many members of the middle classes supported it – wanted to be seen as fulfilling its commitments to discipline and order. The VHP and the Bajrang Dal, however, still insisted on the construction of the temple at Ayodhya. The BJP faltered and the Congress was able to regain the initiative. Against the odds, Narasimha Rao consolidated his position at the head of a minority Congress government – bolstered both by the reluctance of politicians from all parties to contemplate fresh elections, and by the concern of other parties to keep the BJP out – and for a time political debate became focused on economic reform. Then, in October 1992, the VHP – rather to the discomfiture of the BJP government in Uttar Pradesh, which was caught in a contradictory position, between its ideological commitments and its concern to act as a responsible party of government – announced that the construction of the temple at Ayodhya would start again on 6 December. Events moved rapidly, and swung beyond the control of the BJP. By 5 December 1992, it is estimated, 150,000 *kar sevaks* were assembled in UP. The following day, against the wishes of the Hindu nationalist leadership – or so they have always claimed – at about 11.00 a.m., the *kar sevaks* broke through a cordon of RSS volunteers, and, equipped with ropes, pick-axes, shovels and hammers, set about the demolition of the Babri Masjid. It was complete before 5.00 pm. The forces of the state, this time, were suspiciously absent. That the demolition was planned hardly seems in doubt. Who was involved in the planning is less clear. The BJP and the RSS have always claimed not to have been; in any case, the events of 6 December 'demonstrated that the Hindu nationalist movement was largely dominated by the VHP activists, sadhus, Bajrang Dalis and other kar sevaks ... these actors were recognised as having more weight in the RSS-VHP-BJP combination than had generally been thought to be the case' (Jaffrelot 1996: 458). The other crucial element was the way in which the Congress had persistently compromised with communalism, by now over a long period, providing the *Sangh parivar* with opportunities to push the boundaries of what was possible outwards.

The demolition was followed by appalling communal violence, especially in Bombay, where rioting continued into January 1993. The struggle rapidly became one between Muslims and the police, revealing the depth of communal bias amongst the 'law-keepers', and 'shattering the myth of the state' (Hansen 1998a; but see also chapter 9.5). The second worst affected city was Surat, in south Gujarat, and, in the Hindi belt, Bhopal. It is not an exaggeration to say that relationships between Muslims and Hindus throughout India have been quite fundamentally changed by these events.[19] Part of the reason for this is that distinctive norms of behaviour which had evolved in Indian Muslim society, and which had excluded fundamentalist concerns, have been weakened. Fundamentalist leaders have found space for the assertion of a new Muslim identity, and aim to attain greater unity among Muslims as a political entity.[20] These trends were reflected, for example, in the development of communal violence in the south Indian city of Coimbatore where later, during the 1998 election campaign, a bomb was set off by a militant Muslim organization at the site of a meeting at which L. K. Advani was due to speak.[21]

In the short term the Hindu nationalist movement probably gained from the demolition of the Babri Masjid. As we noted earlier there is some evidence to show that it was not strongly opposed by the middle classes in north Indian cities, and in practice the Congress government of Narasimha Rao, though in the immediate aftermath it arrested BJP leaders, banned the RSS, VHP and Bajrang Dal, and dismissed the BJP-led State governments in Madhya Pradesh, Rajasthan and Himachal, was, as ever, ambiguous in its statements and hesitant in its actions. But the longer-run consequences for Hindu nationalism were not clear-cut: 'While the demolition was in one sense the logical culmination of the Ayodhya movement, it deprived the RSS-VHP-BJP combination of a powerful symbol. As the results of the 1993 [State] elections... show, it was easier to mobilise Hindus *against* the Babri Masjid than *for* anything else' (Jaffrelot 1996: 458, emphasis in the original).

The new pattern of Indian politics and the uncertain march forward of the BJP[22]

The upshot of the five State elections of 1993 was not particularly good for the BJP. It suffered as the incumbent party, and lost power in Madhya Pradesh and in Himachal Pradesh, and although it emerged as the largest single party in Uttar Pradesh it was kept out of office by a coalition of hostile parties headed by Mulayam Singh Yadav. Only in Rajasthan did the party somewhat strengthen its position, while it also won a majority and formed a government for the first time in Delhi. A commentator remarked at the time that 'the Hindutva wave had waned for the BJP, but the Congress had benefited only marginally' (M. N. Roy 1994); and this judgement was confirmed over the following two years. The BJP now pursued a more cautious line, combining a new interest in the OBC vote – a leading spokeswoman, Uma Bharati, said 'Kanshi Ram [the Dalit leader of the Bahujan Samaj Party, powerful in UP: see chapter 9 below] has woken us up' (cited by Jaffrelot 1996: 534) – with the populist-nationalism of its economic policy and attacks on the economic reforms. (In its Economic Policy statement of 1992, the BJP, following work done earlier by the RSS, announced that the future for India lay not with unbridled capitalist growth, but in 'self-confidence and capability in consonance with our cultural mores and ethos', and in a 'Swadeshi of a self-confident, hard-working modern nation that can deal with the world on terms of equality' (as summarized by Hansen 1998b: 302).)[23] The Congress of Narasimha Rao, meanwhile, though it secured a parliamentary majority for the first time in 1994, became mired in corruption scandals – in which the Prime Minister himself was increasingly implicated – and factional infighting. It did poorly in four State elections in November 1994, and then lost both Gujarat and Maharashtra to the BJP (in Maharashtra in coalition with the Shiv Sena) early in 1995. Laloo Prasad Yadav, meanwhile, kept out both parties in Bihar, returning to power with an increased majority.[24]

In his analysis of these State assembly elections between 1993 and 1995 Yogendra Yadav argued that they seemed to mark the beginning of a third phase in the history of India's party system. The first was that of Congress dominance; the second, from the 1970s, 'saw the emergence of genuine competition to the Congress, both at the state and at the national level, often aided by electoral waves... This phase [he suggests calling it the 'Congress-Opposition System'] saw the emergence of bipolar consolidation in various states without yielding a bipolarity at the national level' (1996: 99). The third phase, initiated by the State elections of 1993–5, and confirmed emphatically in the general election of 1999, marks 'a move towards a competitive multi-party system which can no longer be defined with reference to Congress' (p. 99). This, he thought – presciently, as subsequent events have shown – would probably give rise to a vacuum in the party system at the national level. The 'democratic upsurge' which was reflected in the State assembly elections was driven by 'the enfranchisement of the backward castes' – 'the acceleration of the delayed but inevitable rise of the OBCs to political power in north India' (p. 102) – but participation in a democratic process does not by itself lead to participatory democracy. The new multi-party system, he observed, included a number of exclusivist formations with sectional agendas – like that of the Bahujan Samaj Party in Uttar Pradesh, and: 'Ironically, most of these political formations which serve as instruments of the democratisation of society in favour of hitherto disenfranchised sections, are themselves completely undemocratic in their organisational set-up as well as style of functioning' (p. 100). A serious erosion had in fact taken place, he argued, of parties as organized vehicles of politics. They had come to be identified almost entirely with elections, and the 'democratic upsurge' was inherently associated with a loss of trust in the other institutions of politics. (This may be an overly pessimistic assessment, in the light of later events – notably the return to office in 1998 of a reforming Congress Chief Minister, Digvijay Singh, in Madhya Pradesh, and then of Chandrababu Naidu, of the Telugu Desam, the dynamic 'Chief Executive' of Andhra Pradesh in 1999. Their successes gave some reason to hope at the end of the decade that the development of regional parties and distinct regional patterns of politics would mean the establishment of more responsible and responsive governments.)[25]

In spite of its parliamentary majority in 1994–5, and the seeming success, at that moment, of its economic reforms (at least from the perspective of the middle classes), the decline of the Congress, Yadav observed, appeared to be inexorable. But the rise of the BJP was uncertain, and support for it seemed to be confined to the Hindi belt. The social constituency for a 'third force' which would be an alternative to both, had clearly expanded, but it remained fractured and divided between diverse regional and sectional parties. Its leading party, the Janata Dal, was strong indeed only where it functioned – in Uttar Pradesh and Bihar, Karnataka and Orissa – like a regional or casteist party.

This analysis has been borne out by the subsequent developments in Indian politics. The 1996 general elections saw the BJP emerge for the first time as the largest single party, though without significantly expanding the basis of its support numerically, socially or geographically, over 1991. Its success, indeed, depended very heavily on the fact that opposition to it was divided in UP, where it won 52 of its 161 seats. The party did not command a majority, and Atal Behari Vajpayee formed a government which clearly could not survive. It lasted for thirteen days, to be replaced by a thirteen-party 'United Front' government, combining the Left and the National Front, and formed from those parties which Yadav had described as constituting the 'third force'. This kept going under two Prime Ministers – first H. D. Deve Gowda, and later I. K. Gujral – for eighteen months with the outside support of the Congress. When that support was withdrawn fresh general elections (the Twelfth Lok Sabha elections) were called, for February–March 1998. This time the BJP made somewhat more progress than in 1996, securing a few more seats (179 as against 161) and, more significantly, a larger share of the popular vote, in spite of the fact that it lost support in States such as Maharashtra and Rajasthan. Gains came from east and south India where support for the BJP previously had been almost non-existent. But this breakthrough 'was made possible only because of the new alliances that the BJP . . . made [unconstrained by any considerations of principle] with the regional parties in these states' (Hansen and Jaffrelot 1998: 323), and by the splits within and the decline of the Janata Dal. The rise of the BJP, therefore, during the 1998 elections was 'real but modest' (p. 323), and in forming a government it relied heavily on its successful regional allies. As commentators noted: 'For all its public pronouncements that it is a party whose time has come, the BJP is, electorally speaking, a strong but peculiarly vulnerable party' (Ramachandran and Rawal in *Frontline*, June 1998). When, a little over one year later, the most unpredictable of its allies, Jayalalitha's All-India Anna DMK, withdrew its support – for transparently self-interested reasons – Vajpayee's second, longer-lived BJP government fell, in April 1999.

The pattern that Yadav discerned in 1995 was broadly confirmed again by the Thirteenth Lok Sabha elections of October 1999, when the BJP was returned to office in New Delhi as the leading party in a majority coalition. At first glance, and on one level, the supremacy of the BJP appears to have been confirmed. With the support of its twenty-three allies in the National Democratic Alliance it at last commanded a convincing majority in the Lok Sabha. It was widely expected that the party would succeed in retaining office for a long period, and possibly even for a full parliamentary term. It was no longer vulnerable, as it had been, to the defection of any one of its alliance partners. The Congress-(I), meanwhile, secured fewer seats than in any previous election. Yet the party increased its share of the popular vote (to 28.5 per cent), whilst – in spite of Vajpayee's popularity with the electorate – the vote share of the BJP fell by almost 2 per cent (to 23.7 per cent). The BJP's claim to power was determined by its success in forming a rainbow of alliances, and by the particular permutations of votes in different States (its large number of victories in Maharashtra, for example, being due to the split in the Congress vote in that State), not because of any sweeping mandate for its programmes or ideology. The authority of the Congress in State governments, too, was much greater than that of the BJP, following its victories in Karnataka and Arunachal Pradesh, and (in an unholy alliance with Sharad Pawar's National Congress Party) in Maharashtra. It is fair to conclude, with Yadav and Kumar (1999: 120), that: 'The BJP's almost unstoppable upward march has come to a halt' – in spite of the fact that it has clearly established itself as a national party. The BJP now largely determines the agenda of Indian politics; but it is still not supported by the majority of voters, who are, however, divided in their affection for other parties.

6.3   The BJP in Power

An advertisement published widely in India in May 1999, carrying a picture of Vajpayee, made several claims on behalf of the recently defeated BJP government. The first of these was that Vajpayee had 'established India's self-respect by conducting the Pokhran blasts', referring to the explosion of five nuclear devices at that test-site in May 1998. And this single action clearly was the most outstanding taken during the thirteen-month period in office of Vajpayee's first government. In relation to our narrative the significance of this event lies particularly in what it suggests about the nature of the BJP; and in this regard scarcely less important was the shift in Hindu communal aggression also towards Christians, and the responses of the government to a series of horrific attacks upon them in 1998–99. Less dramatic but also significant were the packing of the Indian Council for

Historical Research and the Indian Council for Social Science Research with *Hindutva* sympathizers of doubtful academic standing, and later moves to change the curriculum in schools so as to highlight Hindu nationalist themes. The concessions which were made, however, in spite of the earlier *swadeshi* rhetoric of the party, to international capital were striking. Towards the end of its time in office, for example, the government pushed a bill to allow foreign equity into insurance in India, ironically with support from Congress, and against the opposition of the RSS and of many in its own ranks. This followed the passage of an amendment to the Patents Act which brought Indian legislation into line with the requirements of the World Trade Organization. The Budget of 1999 was well received by big business in India and outside, and confirmed the orientation of the BJP, in practice, towards finance capital. This orientation was further underlined when the new BJP-led government that took office following the 1999 general elections announced its commitment to a 'second round' of economic reforms.

The nuclear tests, though dramatic, were not really surprising.[26] The BJP had promised in its election manifesto that it would resume nuclear testing, and as Prakash Karat (a CPI(M) Politburo member) wrote: 'The bomb was the mascot of the RSS long before the Ram temple acquired religious-political overtones for it in the 1980s' (quoted in *Frontline*, 21 May 1999). Savarkar, the first ideologue of Hindutva, and Golwalkar, the successor to Hedgewar, the founder of the RSS, had both strongly urged that the Hindu Rashtra should have 'nuclear teeth'. And it is believed that the first three men to know about the tests in May 1999 were Vajpayee, Advani and Professor Rajendra Singh, supremo of the RSS. India's Finance and Defence Ministers, it is said, were informed after the event. These reports seem entirely plausible, and reflect the continuing close links between the BJP and the RSS.

The immediate reaction in India to the blasts was generally positive to the point of being ecstatic. The press in New Delhi wrote glowingly of India's 'Great Power' status. There was a widespread sense that 'We'd shown them', and that the action was a mark of self-confident assertion which must win the country respect. The BJP won a huge surge of support, according to opinion polls, and this must have been a significant part of the calculation of an insecure government. These feelings were even enhanced when Pakistan responded, predictably, with its own series of tests. But only a little later it became clear to many in India as well as outside just how serious a miscalculation the tests had been. Not only were they counterproductive in regard to India's international relations, heightening tensions in the region and exposing Indians (as they began to realize) to the dangers of nuclear war, but they also had the effect – far from enhancing India's power – of subjecting the country to greater pressure from the United States. India was not admitted, as some in government had perhaps thought likely, to the 'nuclear club' and the Vajpayee government was forced rather 'to engage in a protracted non-transparent negotiation with the United States over what India's nuclear weapons status can be allowed to be'. Only a week after the tests the Cabinet 'quickly pushed through Central Government counter-guarantees for four fast-track power projects in different states', as the government sought to assuage the fears and accommodate the interests of international capital; and though it was claimed at the time that the US-led economic sanctions which were imposed would be ineffective, it became clear later that they did have negative effects on the flow of foreign capital. Both portfolio investment into India and foreign direct investment were sharply reduced in 1998–9, in spite of the concessions which were made by the BJP to international capital.[27] Meanwhile, the voters of Delhi, Madhya Pradesh and Rajasthan – all long-standing bastions of the BJP – showed in State assembly elections in November 1998, when the party suffered major reverses, that popular enthusiasm for the bomb had been very short-lived.

The nuclear tests reflected the continuing pursuit by the BJP in office, of the agenda of long-run social and cultural change (of *Hindutva*) laid down by the RSS, the 'moderate and acceptable face' of Mr A. B. Vajpayee notwithstanding. The same conclusion may be drawn from the response of the government to the series of atrocities against Christians that came to international attention in January 1999 when an Australian missionary and his two sons were burnt alive in a village in Orissa. In the year which began with the assumption of office by Vajpayee there were well over 100 incidents of attack on Christians, their places of worship and their religious literature, whereas, 'It is estimated that over a period of 32 years, from 1964 to 1996, there were only 38 incidents of violence against Christians'.[28] Part of the reason was that, following the demolition of the Babri Masjid, Christians had been prominent in public discussions of communalism and in taking initiatives to promote secularism. They, with Muslims, became identified as enemies of the nation, and the object of a campaign of intimidation embarked upon by the VHP and the Bajrang Dal, purportedly to stop conversions to Christianity. Together with the events themselves, which reflected the new virulence of a politics of hate in the country, what was so striking was the response of the government:

> At every opportunity that has presented itself since the graph of violence against Christians began rising, in both rhetoric and deed, leaders of the ruling coalition have failed to exercise their authority in the cause of sanity and order. Prime Minister A B Vajpayee visited the riot-torn district of Dangs in Gujarat but chose not to censure the administration that had been derelict or condemn the Hindutva cabal that had wrecked a tradition of amity and social solidarity. He mildly admonished the miscreants for taking the law into their own hands and tacitly held the victims responsible for their suffering, by calling for a 'national debate' on religious conversion. (Muralidharan and Ramakrishnan, in *Frontline*, 12 February 1999)

The compulsions of office, like the 'compulsions of politics' (a phrase used by Thomas Hansen's BJP informants in Maharashtra – 1996a: 198), cause many a twist and turn, and there have been many moments when it has seemed that the BJP leadership is quite cynical in its willingness to do whatever is necessary to win and secure political office. Yet, despite the exigencies of the day-to-day politics in which the BJP is necessarily involved, there is no reason to believe that it is not still committed to the project of creating the Hindu *rashtra* in the longer run.[29]

6.4 Conclusion: Elite Revolts and Vernacular Voices

We remarked at the beginning of this chapter that discerning the trends in contemporary history is fraught with difficulty. We are confident, however, that the last decade of the twentieth century will be seen by future historians as having been marked by the rise of the BJP and by India's hesitant experiments with economic liberalism. Assessing the implications of these trends is much more controversial, and that is the task of part III of this book where we will develop the case which we have sketched in this and the preceding three chapters – that the invention of India reflected in the Constitution is being fundamentally reworked. But we have argued here that these great trends of the 1990s are in some senses to be understood as 'elite revolts', reflecting the assertions especially of upper castes and middle classes.

No less important than these 'headline' tendencies are the less strikingly evident social and political processes which are associated with what we have referred to as 'the deepening of democracy'. In this case no definite breaks are to be discerned, and this historical trend cannot be associated either with specific events which seem to constitute transformative moments, like the demolition of the Babri Masjid or the passage of Manmohan Singh's first budget in 1991. Indeed, in many ways Church's summary of social and political struggles, written in 1984, which we quoted in chapter 5, and which refers to 'new levels of violence and corruption', to populism, to 'the emergence of regionalism', to calls for law and order, to struggles over reservations and to 'the efforts of political parties to recruit representatives from the lower castes', seems no less apt fifteen years later. But the trends and processes that he described have intensified. As Yogendra Yadav, Zoya Hasan and others have observed, the vacuum created by the progressive self-destruction of the Congress Party has been filled in different ways in different parts of the country, though invariably by parties which have depended upon mobilizations of 'lower castes'. This has further deepened the regionalism which has always been a feature of Indian politics (think of Selig Harrison's writings in the 1950s: see chapter 3) – but which now perhaps has more positive connotations than it was previously held to have (as we noted with reference to the governments of Digvijay Singh and Chandrababu Naidu).

It is also associated, however, or so Pranab Bardhan has argued, with pervasive corruption, the erosion of the state – in the sense of the undermining of the practices of Weberian bureaucracy – and the further criminalization of politics. For Bardhan, then:

> Along with political power drifting from the Centre to the regions, there is [evidence of] an associated drift towards the backward and lower castes. This is clearly a sign of democratic progress in an unequal society... What is disturbing, however, is that the diminishing hold of elite control and the unfolding of populist democracy... have been associated with a loosening of the earlier administrative protocols and a steady erosion of the institutional insulation of the decision-making process in public administration and economic management. (1998: 132–3)

Other writers have described the 'fuzziness' of the boundaries between state and society and the development (oxymoron though it may be) of an 'informal state' to parallel the 'informal economy', and we consider some of their arguments further in the next chapter.[30] Bardhan goes on, however, to argue the much stronger point, with which we agree only in part, that:

> There is a certain nonchalance in the rampant corruption among politicians in the newly emergent groups. Lower caste leaders, when they come to power, are sometimes quite unapologetic about being corrupt. They say that the upper castes in control of the state have been corrupt for decades, and now it is their turn. Corruption is thus seen as a collective entitlement in an amoral game of group equity. (p. 133)[31]

It is possible that politics in the sense that Nehru would have understood the word *has* largely been abolished in India. In its place – and in place of Congress hegemony – there is a bewildering landscape of struggles, which embrace but cannot be resolved into conflicts between classes, and which refuse to answer to the Fabian conception of politics and governance that was once mapped out for India, and which is presumed still in many of the arguments of international development agencies, including the emperor of them all, the World Bank. Their prescriptions so often seem to presume a form of the state, as an instrument of rationality, and of political processes, which are not at all realistic representations of Indian realities.

But if the trajectories of social and political change in contemporary India cannot easily be placed in the grand narratives of modernity, they have been profoundly influenced by them. The high ideology of liberal democracy which guided the members of the Constituent Assembly and so largely formed the Constitution of India is being *reshaped* by popular beliefs and ideas: 'The subaltern acceptance of the democratic invitation inevitably means a reshaping of the political agenda in accordance with their tastes, convictions and expectations' (Yadav 1996: 103). We do not entirely agree, therefore, with Sudipta Kaviraj's assessment of what he calls the 'cultural consequences' of uneven capitalist development in India:

Over the long term, the strategy of development in India, precisely through its relative successes, has tended to reopen the deep division of discourse in Indian society, between a homogenising elite, speaking English, the esperanto of the upper orders, and a vast lower-order population, looking and speaking with intense vernacular hostility against some of the consequences of this form of capitalist development. (1991: 87)

There is a deep division of discourse in Indian society – as polling data showing the lack of knowledge or understanding amongst the mass of rural people in India about 'economic liberalization' richly testifies. But it seems to us that the language of Hindu nationalism, and the way in which the mobilizations around it interact with the subaltern movements that Yadav refers to, has created a new and distinctive relationship between elites and masses. As we will attempt to establish in part III, the worlds of the English-speaking and vernacular orders are not closed to one another in quite the way that Kaviraj suggests.

Part III

The Reinvention of India

7

The Dialectics of Reform:
The State and Economic
Liberalization

The energy, talents, and worldly ambitions of India's many millions...need merely an appropriate policy framework to produce the economic magic that Jawaharlal Nehru wished for his compatriots but which, like many well-meaning intellectuals of his time, he mistakenly sought in now discredited economic doctrines. We finally have this elusive policy framework within our grasp.
Jagdish Bhagwati (1993: 98)

Calls for the radical privatization of the state ignore the effective radical privatization, informalization and now mafianization that South Asian states have been undergoing for much longer than the era of liberalization of the 1990s.
Barbara Harriss-White (1997: 19)

Just a few months after delivering his reform budget of 1991 the Finance Minister of India, Manmohan Singh, was under pressure to account for India's 'new' reliance upon the Bretton Woods institutions and to explain why this would not lead to a form of dependent development that would exclude or even impoverish the mass of India's labouring poor. In an interview with *The Economic Times* (of India) in March 1992 Singh maintained that his reforms could hardly make India more dependent upon foreign powers or foreign capital. After reminding his readers that 'When Panditji wrote the opening chapter of the Third Plan he never talked about self-reliance in the autarchic sense, that we will never use foreign brands', Singh argued that Nehru's aim was to ensure that India had 'the capacity to finance our import needs through our own export earnings [and] without artificial props of concessional aid' (vital though these might be in the short run). Over the years this objective had been perverted, and 'the economic affairs secretary of the government of India [had been forced] to go to Paris' to beg for aid. In Paris this same secretary would be told 'this is right, this is wrong' and the criticisms of the western powers would 'enter into [his] policies'. Now, by contrast, or so Singh maintained, the economic secretary could do business with western capitalists on equal terms and could look 'every investor straight in the eye'. It was thus 'utter hypocrisy to say that all these years we were self-reliant and suddenly Dr Manmohan Singh and Mr Narasimha Rao have surrendered the country's sovereignty'.

It is hard not to sympathize with some aspects of Singh's complaint, overstated though it surely is. In the 1950s and early 1960s Nehru was able to treat the Indian countryside as a 'bargain basement' only because he was able to count on cheap flows of foodgrains from the United States under Public Law 480 (see our discussion in chapter 3). Plans for the structural transformation of the Indian economy likewise took advantage of sizeable flows of concessional finance and technical assistance from countries on each side of the Cold War divide: from the United Kingdom and West Germany, as well as from the USSR and Czechoslavakia. In the 1970s these dependencies were continued, and in the 1980s they were added to by a sizeable loan from the IMF and a significant increase in borrowing from abroad, including from members of the Indian diaspora. These loans came to substitute for the foreign capital that was forgone, for example, when Mrs Gandhi drove IBM and Coca Cola from the country in the 1970s.

With the benefit of hindsight we can see that the reforms which Singh initiated in 1991, and which continued unevenly through the 1990s, did begin to change India's relationship with the global market-place, and did so without surrendering some intact and mythical notion of sovereignty that had been handed down from Gandhi or Nehru. The reforms also secured some much needed changes in India's industrial, trading and financial regimes. India's experiments with 'socialist' planning may have laid the foundations of balanced economic growth (in both spatial and sectoral terms), but they did little to fulfil the country's economic growth potential, and it would take a good deal of special pleading to argue that *dirigiste* development empowered the poor (except indirectly as a result of revised government spending policies in the 1970s and 1980s: see below) as opposed to those who could negotiate access to the License and Permit Raj. By the late 1990s there was cross-party support for a second round of reforms that would speed the integration of India into the global economy, and which would seek to exploit India's capacity to supply cheap 'knowledge-based' goods (including software) to the world market.

With hindsight, too, we can see that the liberalization of the Indian economy in the 1990s met with less resistance than some commentators had judged likely, and – more contentiously – that it may have increased the country's long-term trend rate of growth. Advocates of liberalization have been keen to argue that the reforms have attracted foreign capital to India, and have ushered in new working practices and technologies that are improving rates of productivity growth in the country's manufacturing and service economies. The new India is thus not only a land of BMWs and Daewoos, or of Star TV and Sahara Airlines (where once there were only Ambassadors, Dordoorshan and Indian Airlines), but a country where there 'has been a sea change in *ideas* about the role of the state and the role of markets in India's economy' (Parikh 1999: 1; emphasis in the original). The main worry of neoliberals is that it might take a second fiscal crisis to push the government into a fresh wave of reform, including the liberalization of agriculture and India's labour markets. Some neoliberals also worry that the government is not doing enough to support the reforms with investment in education, health and the public infrastructure.

The neoliberal account of the process of economic reform in India has much to commend it, but an insistent preference for 'markets' over 'states' can blind its adherents to the politics of economic liberalization (save for the view that politics – in the form of vested interests – is an impediment to reform), both in terms of the mainsprings of reform and of its social and spatial consequences. In this chapter we develop the argument (first made in chapter 6) that the reforms in India have been prosecuted by or on behalf of social elites which have been in revolt against an earlier model of state-directed economic development. The fact that some of these reforms have been desirable, or that they have been prosecuted successfully on occasions, and even for the greater good, does not gainsay this argument. Nor is our broader argument upset by the challenges which have been raised against this reform agenda by some of India's more recently established elites, and most especially by those new masters of the countryside who came to power in the wake of the green revolution. The failure to 'reform' India's agriculture in the 1990s reflects the power of this elite to shape the course of India's 'liberalization' every bit as much as the reforms in India's industrial and trading economies reflect the desires and ambitions of the country's business classes. Our contention, simply, is that 'liberalization' in India has not yet run counter to the (varied) interests of the country's most powerful social groups, at least not in any sustained way, nor has it run in favour of the country's social majorities.

We also maintain that the dynamics of reform must internalize and reproduce a set of contradictions in the process of accumulation which reflect these consistent and yet contending patterns of bias. These contradictions account in part for India's continuing fiscal deficits, and they are evident, for example, in the willingness of some State governments to provide cheap or even free electricity to farmers even as spending on primary education continues to fall short of the levels needed to empower the poor or to improve India's stock of 'human capital'. Above all, these contradictions account for the *partiality* and *instability* of the reforms process in India. They help to explain the gap which we observe between the neoliberal dream of reform (unlocking the 'energy, talents, and worldly ambitions of . . . millions', as Bhagwati puts it) and the particularities of the reform process in India (where many of those with assets have been set free, but where a lack of investment spending – or even market regulation – continues to lock poor women and men into badly paid, vulnerable and even dangerous jobs).

To make this argument we first review the 'pre-history' of the reforms in India. We draw attention to the positive and empowering effects of government spending policies in the 1980s (in terms of poverty reduction), and we challenge the view that the reforms of the 1990s were a necessary and inevitable response to the fiscal crisis of 1989–91, deep though that crisis was. The crisis of 1989–91 offered a window of opportunity for those amongst India's business and financial elites who wanted to renegotiate the state's relationships to private capital and the process of accumulation. In the succeeding parts of the chapter we review the main elements of the reform programmes that were put in place in the 1990s, before turning to an evaluation of the reforms in terms of their effects upon growth, stability and social justice. Although we take seriously the claims of the pro-reform lobby, and indeed of those – like Rob Jenkins – who argue that the momentum for reform has come from government officers in New Delhi and the States, rather than from particular social classes, we maintain that an agenda for reform in India has emerged (whether by stealth or by grand design) in which the country's business and trading regimes are consistently given priority over its 'social investment' regime. This ordering of priorities erodes the capacity of the reforms to deliver sustainable economic growth or development. We also contend that a measure of reform in India's formal economy has been pursued in tandem with a 'deregulation' of some of the country's much larger informal economies, and that this threatens the labouring poor with new depredations and renewed exploitation.[1] A new dialectic of centralization and decentralization in the country is allowing New Delhi and the States to regulate in favour of capital in the formal economies of India (often to good effect), even as an ideology of deregulation is encouraging certain 'intermediate classes' to seize command of an 'informal state' at the local level, there to enforce a form of 'actually existing Indian capitalism' that is based on 'primitive accumulation' or 'accumulative cruelty' (after Harriss-White 1997: 12–14). Fully to understand what the reforms might mean to different constituencies in India – and to anticipate what directions they might take in the years ahead – it is necessary to interrogate this new dialectic and review the competing social forces that are reshaping the economic spaces of modern India.

7.1   A Pre-history of Reform: The Indian Economy in the 1980s

There is a natural tendency to understand the past – including the recent past – in terms of the concerns of the present, and with the benefit of hindsight. Proponents of economic reform in India maintain that the Indian economy was building to crisis through the 1980s and that stern corrective actions had to be taken in the 1990s to ward off a threat of bankruptcy. We reviewed part of this argument in chapters 5 and 6, and we will return to it in greater depth later in this chapter. It needs to be said here, however, that hindsight can play tricks with the memory. Although there was a body of opinion in the 1980s that was critical of India's planned development – we think of the *Economist* newspaper as much as academics like Jagdish Bhagwati and T. N. Srinivasan – the contemporary literature on the Indian economy in the 1980s was more bullish than pessimistic. This optimism related to three developments in the 1980s: patterns of government spending that helped to promote agricultural growth and reduce rural poverty; the strong performance of India's manufacturing economy and some export sectors; and the economic reforms introduced at various points in this period by the Congress and National Front governments. It is useful to review these developments before turning to the crisis years of 1990–1 and the advent of the 'reforms proper', as they are generally called.

Poverty

We touched briefly on the question of poverty levels in chapter 5. The estimation of poverty levels or trends is always difficult, even in a country like India which is blessed with good data sets from the National Sample Survey. In the post-1991 period, as we shall see, heated debates have raged between those who think that the process of economic liberalization in India has had no significant short-term effects on rural or urban poverty, and those who blame the reforms for a significant increase in distress or destitution. These debates hinge on the price deflators chosen, on the reliability of the data collected on wage rates (where wages are often paid in cash and kind), on the base and end years used for purposes of comparison, and on questions of seasonality, gender and spatial coverage. Even allowing for these considerations, however, there is a fair degree of consensus on the changing maps of rural and urban poverty in India prior to the reforms – between 1977 and 1990 – and on the reasons for these (positive) changes. According to official estimates, rural poverty declined from 51.2 per cent of all rural households in 1977–8 to just 20.6 per cent in 1990–1, with the absolute number of the rural poor also decreasing over the same period from 252.9 million to 128.6 million (notwithstanding population growth). A similar decline has been charted for urban India. A second method also reveals a decline in the percentage incidence of poverty in this period, but less markedly. According to the National Sample Survey Organization (NSSO) method of poverty estimation pioneered by Bagicha Singh Minas, the percentage of rural households in poverty in India fell from 57.3 per cent in 1970–1 to around 33.7 per cent – 35.0 per cent in 1989–91. Significantly, the rate of decline of urban poverty charted in this model is less than in the countryside.[2]

Whether one trusts the official or the Minas poverty estimates (and we have difficulties with the official figures), it is clear that the percentage incidence of rural (and possibly urban) poverty diminished significantly in the late 1970s and 1980s, even if – as Gupta's (1995) careful analysis confirms – the sheer number of people in poverty continued to rise.[3] Given that the stated aim of planned economic development in India is the alleviation of poverty, it might be thought that the shifting maps of poverty in India through this period would be read as signs of (relative) government success rather than of failure. Gupta is too astute to jump to this conclusion, but he does accept that a decline in the incidence of rural poverty in India in the 1980s was prompted by a switch in government spending policies that dates back to the mid-1960s and the green revolution. As Gupta points out, the rural poor in India are mainly the labouring poor, which is to say marginal farming households and landless labourers. The rural poor gain entitlements to food from the number of days that they work per season or year, and from the wages that they collect per contract (per day, week, season or whatever). Their principal concerns are thus with the price of cereals and other foods, the availability of work, and local wage rates. Gupta suggests – quite plausibly – that rural labour markets tightened in most of India's States through the 1980s. In some cases this tightening was effected by strong labour movements, as in parts of Kerala and (possibly) West Bengal. More usually, rural households benefited from the spread of irrigation technologies and double-cropping, and from the growth of non-agricultural employment opportunities in the rural economy. (This was especially marked in areas like the Bombay–Bangalore corridor, or along the Bombay–Delhi highway: see Abhijit Sen 1996, 2463). Some households also benefited from government-directed rural credit or employment guarantee schemes. A number of these schemes were initiated and largely funded by the Centre, including the Integrated Rural Development Programme (IRDP), the National Rural Employment Programme (NREP), the Rural Landless Employment Guarantee Programme (RLEGP), Jawahar Rozgar Yojana (JRY), the Employment Assurance Scheme (EAS) and a programme for the Development of Women and Children in Rural Areas (DWCRA).[4] The Tamil Nadu Noon Meal Scheme and Maharashtra's Employment Guarantee Scheme would count among the best-known State-level poverty relief schemes, albeit for different reasons.[5]

Opinion varies on the cost-effectiveness of these schemes. Critics report high administrative costs and poor loan recovery rates in some cases, and ineffective targeting of beneficiaries and simple corruption in others.[6] The schemes also took shape within a framework of increased government financial support for the Indian countryside through the Commission on Agricultural Costs and Prices, and from rising subsidies for water, electricity and fertilizers. It is not unreasonable, then, to make some cautionary remarks about the stability – or sustainability – of this pattern of financial support for *Bharat*, or to draw the conclusion, with Abhijit Sen, that what is striking about the experience of the 1980s is that despite the declining dependence of non-agricultural sectors on the performance of agriculture [see below], the prices of agricultural goods rose faster than the general price level. This meant a reversal of the earlier terms of trade movement against agriculture, and this also went against the international trend of a worldwide movement of terms of trade against agriculture. (1996: 2462)

We will come back to this conclusion later. By the same token, it would not be unreasonable to conclude, *as well*, that government spending policies in the 1970s and early 1980s were effective in helping to reduce levels of rural poverty. Critics of planned development in India too often assume that all government spending is bad, or that government deficits emerge only from the rent-seeking behaviour of political elites. In fact, deficits emerge when governments fail to finance current spending from taxes and other receipts, or when the rate of return on borrowed monies fails to match the price charged on the loan.

Manufacturing

Rural India was not the only 'success story' in the 1980s. Sen makes the important point that parts of India's manufacturing economy made great strides in this decade, in the process lessening the dependence of the urban 'formal' economy upon the performance of India's foodgrain economy. This lessening of dependence was a mixed blessing and may not augur well for the future. The major growth areas in India's 'formal sector' economy in the 1980s – chemicals, consumer durables and high-technology services – created little in the way of employment opportunities for rural workers, skilled or otherwise. Such workers continued to depend on employment opportunities in the countryside or in the urban informal sector. At the same time, however, the organized sectors of the urban economy learned in the 1980s how to ride out the price changes associated with 'periods of relative stagnation in agricultural output [such as 1983–7]' (Sen 1996: 2461, and compare with our later remarks on the economic slowdown of 1997–8 in chapter 7.4). Just as the spread of new irrigation technologies in the 1980s meant that Indian agriculture was less 'a gamble on the rains' than it once was, so too was Indian industry slowly liberated in the 1980s from its dependence on changing patterns of agricultural output. India's manufacturing economy grew at an average annual rate in excess of 8.0 per cent in the 1980s, which is considerably above the rates of growth recorded in the 1960s and 1970s, or even in the 1950s. This rate of growth was achieved in a decade that was sometimes unfavourable for poor or middle-income countries: a decade which began with a crippling global recession, and which is associated above all with the developing countries' debt crisis. According to John Adams: 'Output in India's peer countries grew at only 1.7 per cent in the 1980s (excluding China from the comparison because of the doubtful validity of its numbers). Thus, during the 1980s India grew almost twice as fast as the average rich industrial country and about three times as fast as the typical poor developing country' (1990: 79–80; referring to overall economic growth).

It is important that we underline this point. Although Adams proceeds to discuss various 'troubles... in financial areas' in 1988 and 1989 – 'a huge fiscal deficit, excessive monetary growth, rising inflation centered on key market-based commodities, a large balance-of-payments deficit, and a rapid loss of international reserves' (p. 91) – the dominant tone of his review of the Indian economy in the 1980s is positive and at times celebratory. And in this judgement he was not alone.[7] As he points out:

> the 1980s were identified [by others] as the decade of India's 'take-off' during which the country sustained savings and growth rates that crossed and remained above crucial thresholds. Estimates of total output growth in each of the four post-independence decades clearly demonstrate this transformation: in the 1950s, output was up by 37 percent; in the 1960s, up by another 37 percent; in the 1970s, up by 33 percent; and, in the 1980s, up by 60 percent. With population growth averaging 2.2 percent a year after 1950, the rate of expansion of per capita income had been barely over 1.0 percent per year from 1950 to 1979. Then, with annual growth in national output averaging 5.1 percent through the 1980s, per capita income growth more than doubled the earlier pace, cutting in half the time it takes to add another Rs 100 to the average Indian's material well-being. (1990: 79)

The 'Rajiv effect'

Adams attributes this 'take-off' into sustained growth to a combination of five 'possible causes': a change in India's policy regime, improvements in capital efficiency, technological developments, increased expenditure-demand flows (from consumer spending, migrant remittances and government disbursements) and the possible coming of age of India's long-term public sector projects (pp. 80–1). We have already examined the role of increased spending in boosting economic growth in the 1980s, and we agree that growth was boosted by migrant remittances and some improvements in capital efficiency (in the public and private sectors). What is significant about this expanded list of 'possible causes' of growth, however, is that it begins with changes in India's policy regime. According to Adams: 'The explanation [for improved growth in the 1980s] most commonly given in the expert establishment is that after about 1978 a liberalization of economic policy allegedly unlocked the government's long-binding shackles on the private entrepreneurial sector (p. 80).

There is some truth in this suggestion, and it is worth noting that the reforms of the 1990s did have some antecedents in the late 1970s (when the Janata government introduced an Open General License category in respect of import policy),[8] and through the 1980s. Rajiv Gandhi used his government's first budget in 1985 to proclaim his faith in a new India that would seek to 'do a Korea', as he so memorably and ungrammatically put it. His government reduced corporation and personal income taxes in order to give incentives to the private sector (see our discussion in chapter 5), and it shortened the list of items reserved for 'small-scale industry'. The cement market was also deregulated and greater competition was introduced into the telecommunications industry, amongst several others (after Adams). But these innovations hardly changed the course of India's accumulation model, and Adams is right to conclude that 'the scant degree of reform that was achieved can hardly have been sufficient to have caused a doubling of the rate of per capita economic growth in an economy as large and diverse as India's' (p. 81). The so-called 'Rajiv effect', if it existed at all, was mainly confined to a feeling that the government was looking on the private sector in more kindly terms than hitherto; it did not add up to a conclusive and irreversible shift in official economic thinking.[9]

7.2   Crisis and Reform

A shift in government policy was finally brought about in 1991. But why did it occur at all? The usual answer to this question is that the reforms of the 1990s were a necessary response to the economic – and especially fiscal – excesses of the 1980s. We have already suggested the need for some caution in accepting this view, and the model of government spending that it seems to entail. In particular, it discounts the successes of the 1980s, and it ignores the role played by some of India's business leaders in arguing for reforms that served their private or corporate interests. It cannot be denied, however, that the Indian economy overheated in the late 1980s and that a significant gap opened up between what we might call the real economy and the financial economy. Increases in rural wage rates in the 1980s were not financed in full – or by more than 50 per cent according to one estimate (Abhijit Sen 1996: 2461) – by increases in productivity, and increased government spending on defence, loan waivers and subsidies went unmatched by increases in government tax or other receipts (indeed, Rajiv's reforms decreased the tax burden on middle-class households).[10] As we reported in chapter 5, the government of India chose in the 1980s – and especially in the late 1980s under Rajiv Gandhi and V. P. Singh (and not least, by the former, in the name of 'liberalization') – to finance its deficits by borrowing from captive financial institutions at home and from commercial banks abroad. Although domestic savings in India continued to be high through the 1980s, they were 'pulled down by increased dissaving by the public sector, comprising the union government, the state governments, and the public sector enterprises' (Khatkhate 1992: 49). By 1990–1 India's fiscal deficit stood at nearly 9 per cent of GDP – up from 6.4 per cent in 1980–1 – and inflation was moving above the 10 per cent mark. The fiscal deficit in turn impacted on India's balance of payments in the late 1980s, notwithstanding an exchange-rate policy that was deemed appropriate by most economists. As India's debts mounted abroad, so too did its reserves of foreign currency dwindle at home. By the early summer of 1991, as we remarked in chapter 6, India had sufficient reserves to pay for barely two weeks' worth of imports, and its international credit rating had been downgraded by Moody's and Standard and Poor. It was at this point, too, following the failure of the Chandrashekhar government to get its Union budget passed in February 1991, that Manmohan Singh, a respected economist and ex-Governor of the Reserve Bank of India, was appointed as Finance Minister in the incoming Congress government of Narasimha Rao; to Singh fell the task of restoring a measure of credibility to India's fading reputation for economic competence.

The reforms

The beginnings of the reform process in India are most often dated to June–July 1991 and to such iconic events as the presentation of Manmohan Singh's first (Union) budget to the Lok Sabha. Singh's budget speech followed hard on the heels of a devaluation of the rupee by about 18–20 per cent against leading currencies. The budget aimed to stabilize the Indian economy and bring down the fiscal deficit from 8.9 per cent of GDP in 1990–1 to 6.5 per cent in the 1991–2 tax year. Singh proposed to cut the deficit in part by increasing government revenues, but rather more so (perhaps two-thirds of the net fiscal effect) by cutting defence spending from 3.1 to 2.8 per cent of GDP and by cutting subsidies for exports, sugar and fertilizers.

The stabilization of the Indian economy was a priority in the summer of 1991. Notwithstanding Singh's gestures in the direction of 'competitiveness' and 'good management practices', however, the Budget of that year was timid when it came to questions of structural adjustment, and not unexpectedly so. Some observers said the budget was in the long tradition of reformist talk exceeding practical actions; others complained that the figures didn't add up, or that it was a budget for 'disinflation'. Still others (see chapter 7.4) suggested there was no reason for stabilization to entail structural adjustment. But the reforming instincts of the Rao-Singh government were demonstrated soon enough, and not least in the programmes for investment and trade policy reform that were announced in July 1991. These programmes at first promised more significant changes in the Indian industrial economy than did a set of linked proposals for the reform of India's financial and agricultural sectors, but in these sectors too there were significant reform initiatives throughout the 1990s, as the following summary makes clear:

India's investment regime   The process of industrial reform began with what Rob Jenkins calls 'a big bang' (1997: 20). By 1992 the system of industrial licensing that had taken shape over the previous forty years had been dismantled in all but 18 designated industries (including drugs and pharmaceuticals, cars and sugar), and for all locations save for twenty-three 'millionaire' cities where licenses were still required for new ventures or project expansion within twenty-five kilometres of the central business district. The government also took steps to encourage foreign equity investment in the Indian economy (allowing automatic clearance of imported capital goods in delicensed projects where the foreign exchange was provided by inward investment); it substantially relaxed the provisions of the Monopolies and Restrictive Trade Practices Act (a new Act in October 1991 focused on unfair practices and consumer protection); it provided further incentives for foreign equity investment of up to 51 per cent in high-priority industries; it encouraged foreign technical collaboration in these same industries; it allowed private sector companies to trade in industries that had once been arrogated to state-owned enterprises; and – under an amendment from October 1991 – it gave permission for non-resident Indians to 'have 100 per cent equity in existing or new companies operating in India' (Khatkhate 1992: 58). Although the World Bank has expressed disappointment that fewer than fifty non-departmental Central public enterprises were faced with privatization in the 1990s (World Bank 1998: 12), it did also note in 1997 that: 'In manufacturing, [private sector] Indian firms have restructured and upgraded their industrial basis, often through alliances with foreign firms' (1997b: 6). The automobile industry is often mentioned in this regard, although many of the joint ventures in this sector date from the early or mid-1980s.

Trade policy reform   Rapid progress was also made in 1991 and 1992 in the field of trade policy reform. Nominal tariff rates in India prior to the reforms were among the highest in the world, and foreign trade was further hindered by a vast range of discretionary and quantitative restrictions. To improve India's trading regime, and to ensure a measure of complementarity with India's new investment regime, the Rao government removed cash compensatory support, replaced replenishment licenses for exporters with an Exim scrip (a certificate issued as evidence of exports) with a uniform replenishment rate, and eliminated 'several categories of discretionary licenses previously used for importing intermediate goods and components' (Khatkathe 1992: 59). These early reforms were strengthened by a depreciation in the 'real effective exchange rate' of the rupee that lasted from 1991 until 1995 (but which was reversed in the second half of the 1990s). Although import taxes accounted for about 17 per cent of the total revenues of central government in 1991–2, average tariffs and non-tariff barriers were also reduced significantly by the Rao-Singh government, and further reductions have been promised by the BJP-led government which took power in October 1999. By 1996 the average tariff in India was 25–6 per cent, as against 87 per cent in 1990 (or a nominal tariff rate of 117 per cent according to one non-government source).[11] The budget of 1997–8 further 'reduced maximum tariffs to 40 per cent from 50 per cent (from over 200 per cent in 1990–1) and the import weighted average tariff to 20.3 per cent' (World Bank 1997b: 7). This achievement, however, was partly undone by the government's decision to raise tariffs on all non-oil products by three percentage points in September 1997, and it remained the case, in 1998, that 'despite the reforms, about 63% of import lines were covered by non-tariff barriers of one kind or another, according to UNCTAD, higher than almost all comparable countries' (World Bank 1998: 17).

Financial reforms   The reform of India's banking sector was slow to gather pace, but significant changes were introduced in the second half of the 1990s. The sector had been nationalized in 1969 with the aim of making funds available to government more cheaply than hitherto. Commercial banks were required 'to hold 38.5 per cent of their incremental deposits (the "statutory liquidity ratio" or SLR) in low-yielding government securities and deposit 25 per cent with the Reserve Bank of India as reserve requirement (the "cash reserve requirement", or CRR)' (Varshney 1996: 12). India's banks thus served a social role and were only indirectly required to make lending decisions on the basis of commercial considerations. The reforms have changed the context in which India's banks have to work. Staffing levels have not yet been greatly altered, and nor have domestic banks been faced with a rigorous programme of privatization. But new private banks have been allowed to emerge (including a significant number of foreign banks), and they have been allowed to raise funds in the capital markets. The government–bank nexus is still intact (very much so: see our comments in section 7.4 on India's 'internal' debt crisis), but the CRR was reduced to around 10 per cent in 1997–8, at which time, too, the SLR stood at 25 per cent. The new credit policy of April 1998 continued these reforms by allowing banks to set their own rates on loans under Rs 200,000, up to a maximum equal to the prime lending rate; it also 'raised the maximum rate on NRI foreign currency deposits over one year by 0.5 percentage points and lowered the rate on shorter deposits by 0.25 percentage points' (World Bank 1998: 14). By mid-1998, private banks accounted for about 17 per cent of bank assets, up from 11.5 per cent in 1991–2 (p. 14), and pressures mounted at the end of the 1990s for further reforms in the non-bank financial sector (including the insurance sector).

Other reforms   The reform process has been less even or extensive away from the chosen areas of investment, trade and finance. As we have noted already, the offer of public firms for sale remains something for the future in many States, although a measure of 'privatization' has been effected by new policies which have allowed the entry of private firms into once nationalized sectors. Set against this, a robust (or formal) exit policy for 'sick firms' has yet to take shape at the national level, and proposals for the reform of the agricultural sector – proposals for its greater export orientation, for the possible abolition of the Food Corporation of India, for greater 'targeting' in the operations of the Public Distribution System – have often foundered between plan and implementation.[12] There were signs, however, at the end of the 1990s, that this might be changing. Although liberalization has thus far most affected the working lives and public perceptions of India's urban populations, it is likely that future reforms will press hard for the phasing out of controls on domestic trade in agricultural products (including movement and storage controls: see World Bank 1998: 25) and for the de-reservation of agro-industries which are presently on the small-scale industry reservation list. Some of these reforms will be welcomed by the new class of rich farmers or *kulaks* who have come to power in the country-side, but it is possible that resistance to the reforms will also grow if these same farmers are exposed to competition from foreign seed suppliers or agro-chemical corporations (as per the Dunkel Draft: on this, see Panini 1999). It also remains to be seen how the government will seek to remove – or phase out – the fertilizer, water and power subsidies which these rich farmers have long taken for granted, and which they protected through the 1990s.

7.3   Committed to Change: Neoliberal Orthodoxies and the Pluralist Critique

Within two years of Manmohan Singh's first budget in the Lok Sabha, the Finance Minister had commissioned a review of his reforms by Jagdish Bhagwati and T. N. Srinivasan, two economists who had worked on India's Third Five Year Plan in the 1960s and who had made reputations for themselves in the 1970s and 1980s as critics of *'dirigiste* development'. Bhagwati and Srinivasan commended the reforms, and celebrated the role played by Manmohan Singh in pushing them through in the face of vested interests and academic orthodoxies. But Bhagwati and Srinivasan also warned, as Singh no doubt expected them to warn, that much remained to be done, and they recommended a programme of privatization as a way of generating funds to pay off India's 'substantial accumulated government debt' (Bhagwati and Srinivasan 1993: iii). They also pressed for reforms of India's taxation and financial systems in line with the recommendations of the reports of the Chelliah and Narasimhan Committees.[13]

The neoliberal assessment

In striking this note, Bhagwati and Srinivasan confirmed that the process of economic reform in India had just started and they proposed, in effect, that any evaluation of the reforms would have to decide if the changes introduced in the years 1991–3 amounted to a glass half empty or a glass half full. For the most part, at least until the late 1990s, the neoliberal camp has been prepared to accept that the reforms are ongoing (many of Singh's initiatives were continued by Chidambaram in the Deve Gowda government, and a 'second round of reforms' was promised in October 1999 by the new BJP-led government) and necessary, and they have been keen to associate evidence which points to improvements in the Indian economy, or Indian economic performance, with the process of structural adjustment introduced by Manmohan Singh. Thus the World Bank declared, in a report dated 30 May 1997, that:

> The reforms of the past six years brought about an unprecedentedly strong economic performance. For the third year in a row, GDP growth is estimated to have grown by about 7 percent in the fiscal year 1996–97, placing India among the world's best performing economies. Unlike similar episodes in the past, this expansion has been driven by private investment (which reached the historically high level of 18 percent of GDP out of a total investment of 26 percent in the last two years), and has not put pressure on the balance of payments. In spite of the persistent poor performance of public savings, national savings have risen (from 23 percent of GDP in 1991–92 to 26 percent in 1996–97). The country's external position is strong. The current account deficit was 1.1 percent of GDP in 1996–97; the country's US$94 billion external debt declined to 27 percent of GDP in 1996–97 from 34 percent in 1991–92, and the debt service to 24 percent of current account receipts from 29 percent. ...[All in all] the liberalization of the economy has reduced distortions and increased external and internal competition. (1997b: i)

Manufacturing growth, trade and foreign direct investment

There can be little doubt that the reform process in India has been more successful in terms of some of the performance indicators used by the World Bank than critics have cared to acknowledge. The stabilization programme that was put in place in 1991, and which won financial support from the World Bank and the IMF, led to a recession in India's industrial economy in 1991–2 but failed to reduce India's total GDP at factor cost (the growth rate that year was 0.8 per cent). Thereafter the economy rebounded quickly and quite forcefully, both in comparison with past rates of growth in India (or so the World Bank argues) and in relation to some other developing economies. In 1992–3 the rate of growth of GDP at factor cost was 5.3 per cent, in 1993–4 it was 6.0 per cent, and in 1994–5 it was 7.2 per cent. Still more encouraging was the performance of India's manufacturing economy. Manufacturing bore the brunt of the near-recession of 1991–2, but it recovered to record annual rates of growth of 10 per cent or more in the middle part of the 1990s. At least some of this growth was made possible by productivity gains (Majumdar 1996).

The success of India's manufacturing sector did not translate into a sustained improvement in the country's trading position – although the deficit on the trading account (exports minus imports) was reduced from $9.4 billion in 1990–1 to $2.8 billion in 1991–2, mainly by cutting merchandise imports, it opened again to $8.9 billion in 1995–6 – but funds from non-resident Indians (NRIs) helped to bridge the gap in terms of the current account as a whole. By financial year 1994–5 India had enough foreign exchange reserves to finance 21 weeks of imported goods, and by the end of March 1998 the World Bank was able to report non-gold reserves 'equivalent to more than 6 months of goods imports (including gold, over 7 months of goods imports)' (World Bank 1998: 4).

In addition, and perhaps more significantly, the government could claim some success in attracting foreign direct investment into India. Although foreign firms were not missing from India prior to the reforms, they were scarce on the ground, and in 1991–2 foreign direct investment totalled just Rs 158 crores (or 13.5 per cent of a total approval figure of Rs 1160 crores). By 1994–6 this position had improved to the respective figures of Rs 4132 crores, Rs 9973 crores and 41.4 per cent, and in 1995–6 actual foreign direct investment rose to Rs 6750 crores.[14] The main beneficiaries of this inward investment were Maharashtra, Tamil Nadu, Delhi, Karnataka, Gujarat and West Bengal: about 45 per cent of India's FDI proposals were received by these six States or Union Territories in the period from August 1991 to May 1996. The United States was the principal contributor of approved funds on a year-by-year basis, followed by Germany, Japan, the UK, South Korea and the Netherlands, and the funds found their way into a wide range of industrial sectors, including, most notably, chemicals, engineering, electronics, pharmaceuticals and finance.

The pace of reform

By the mid-1990s India could reasonably be described as an emerging market, and the *Economist* newspaper was moved to acclaim the reforms as 'nothing less than a repudiation of India's distinctive approach to development – a repudiation, that is, of Nehru's vision of socialist self-reliance' (*Survey of India*, February 1997). If the neoliberal camp had any doubts about the reforms they related to the pace and depth of the changes that central government had induced. T. N. Srinivasan had early on complained that: 'The credibility of the reform package and the probability of its successful implementation would be enhanced if it is implemented within a short time span' (1991: 2145), and in this judgement he later received support from Jeffrey Sachs, the Harvard economist and guru of rapid economic reform (much to the annoyance of Padma Desai).[15] For the most part, though, neoliberals have been content to accept 'that the initial speed and scope of reforms in India were just about right' (Bhagwati 1998: 37), and most have chosen to campaign for a second round of reforms that would foster growth and thereby deal with the substantial fiscal deficits that emerged in the second half of the 1990s. Deepak Lal, for example, has argued that the very scale of the central government deficit in the late 1990s – 'about 6 per cent of GDP, one of the world's largest' according to the World Bank (1998: xiii) – must encourage the government to make reforms which recognize that 'globalization is an irreversible process' (Lal

1999: 46). Jagdish Bhagwati, meanwhile, has called upon the government to enact new policies in the

> two areas where reforms are necessary and crucial if the outward orientation [of the economy] is to produce growth rates of 9–10 per cent rather than of 6 per cent and if we are truly to reproduce the East Asian miracle (rather than a pale and anaemic copy thereof) a quarter century behind schedule; [namely] (i) the public sector which cries out to be privatized now (but where the ability to deal with the entrenched unions is a major obstacle) and (ii) the ability of firms to extract greater efficiency from the labour force, including the application of changed laws that permit workers to be laid off as necessary, though with appropriate safeguards. (1998: 38)

The pluralist critique: competition States and the management of economic reform

It is still not clear when or how the government in New Delhi will get to grips with these questions, but the unwillingness of the government of India to embrace the 'shock therapy' that was in fashion for a while in the ex-Soviet Union or parts of Latin America does not mean that a second round of reforms has not already been tried in some of India's States, or has not gained the active support of some of the politicians who are accused of going slow on reform for fear of vested interests. It is one of the virtues of Rob Jenkins's recent work to have shown that liberalization has been more radical and continuous than some of its critics (or boosters) allow, and that it has been so, not least, because of the rise of 'competition States' within India's federal democracy. The competition waged by the governments of Tamil Nadu and Maharashtra to host a Fiesta (Ford Motor Company) assembly plant is just one instance of the changing context for economic policy in India. (The battle, incidentally, was won by Tamil Nadu in 1996.)

Jenkins has further argued that complaints about the powers of organized labour are often misplaced, and that:

> despite laws forbidding firms from dismissing workers, many chronically loss-making companies have simply locked their factory gates as elected state governments looked the other way, preferring to let this practice proceed quietly.... Union leaders argue that while they have shown flexibility by toning down labour stridency, 'management militancy' has been on the rise, abetted by state governments. This is borne out by the statistics: while the number of person-days lost because of strikes decreased by almost half, from 12.43 million in 1991 to 6.6 million in 1994, the number lost due to management lockouts has actually increased over the same period. (1997: 162)

The willingness of the government of Rajasthan to develop a new mining policy in 1994, or of the communist government of West Bengal to court

foreign multinationals (even as it denounced Manmohan Singh's surrender
to the IMF), or of the government of Orissa to break-up the State electricity
board, are also treated by Jenkins as evidence that the reforms in India,
which began with a big bang in New Delhi, are being 'increasingly implemented in the form of successive micro-reforms in different states, at different times, and under different political circumstances' (p. 160).[16] It is a
mistake to suppose that the reforms in India have stalled, or that they are
still a glass half empty.

Perhaps more significantly, it is Jenkins's wider argument that the reforms
in India have been pushed through as quickly and consistently as they have
been because they have been guided by politicians who are experienced in
building coalitions, and who have worked behind the scenes in India's
democratic polity 'to blunt the edge of opposition [to reform]' (p. 160).
Jenkins thus has no truck with those proponents of 'democracy-in-general'
or 'good governance' who seem to think that democracy is only (or
mainly) about open and competitive politics, accountability and transpar-
ency, and who constantly bemoan the meddling of politicians in
matters 'economic'.[17] He notes instead that 'governing elites at many levels
of the Indian polity were attracted by the potential of liberalization to
provide new sources of patronage to substitute for some of those forfeited
by the shrinkage of the state's regulatory role' (p. 6), and he suggests that
the more skilled and accomplished of these politicians – a group that ranges
from Narasimha Rao and Deve Gowda to Sharad Pawar and Biju Patnaik –
have sought to capture many of the benefits of liberalization for
themselves and their supporters by means of 'obfuscatory and manipulative
tactics' which seek to neutralize opponents or less deserving followers. In
addition, then, to 'outright pilfering', these power brokers make use of
the following tactics: 'shifting unpleasant responsibilities and blame to
political opponents, surreptitiously compensating selected interests,
concealing intentions, reassuring and then abusing the trust of long-time
political allies, and obscuring policy change by emphasising essential
continuity' (p. 9). In Jenkins's view, the reform-initiating state in India is
at once a democratic state and a dirty state, and this is why it has been so
effective.

7.4   An Elite Revolt? The Partiality of the Reforms

The pluralist view of politics in India that informs Jenkins's work stands as a
welcome contrast to the more anodyne accounts of the state and politics that
are to be found in some neoliberal writings on liberalization. His work also
chimes with that of Ashutosh Varshney, who has sought to argue that the
Rao-Singh government was able to exploit a fear of the BJP in the early
1990s to garner support for – or acquiescence to – some of its pro-market
reforms.[18] Varshney and Jenkins credit politicians in India with building

support for policies that were expected to be more divisive than they have sometimes proved to be.

But Jenkins also contends, more controversially, that the reforms in India have been pushed through by government (or governments) in abeyance of particular class interests and without regard for an ideology of economic change. Jenkins maintains that, 'Contrary to the conventional wisdom, the projection of an economic "vision" for India played virtually no part in [the] process [of] sustaining adjustment or liberal reforms' (1997: 8), and he takes strong exception to the views of those 'structuralists' (including Pranab Bardhan) who fail to understand that: 'nothing so grand as a "social contract" [a vision of reform put to the people openly by the government] is necessarily required, or even desirable, if government proclaims intentions that are more modest than "a project of national economic transformation"' (p. 40). In Jenkins's view, this sort of 'wooden Marxist political economy'[19] is unable to grasp the essential messiness and government-directed nature of the reforms, or the fact that: 'The Indian reform programme has succeeded largely because it proceeded by stealth' (p. 40).[20]

The bias of the reforms

There is something to be said for this argument. Jenkins demonstrates with great clarity how an understanding of the speed and scope of the reforms in India cannot usefully be developed except in relation to an account of the workings of government, and with proper regard for government's ability to win a measure of independence from the powerful constituencies which press upon it. His work means that we must tread carefully when describing the reforms in India as an 'elite revolt'. If some of India's urban, industrial and financial elites have been in revolt against an earlier model of economic development which served some of their interests very well, as we believe they have been, we need to recognize that this revolt was being staged in part against a model that had run its course and which needed to be reformed. We should also acknowledge that the sequencing of the reforms process in India has been dictated by political considerations as much as by economic imperatives, with the result that structural adjustment has not always corresponded to the desires of particular class groupings or business elites.

But while all this is true, we believe that Jenkins fails sufficiently to acknowledge the partiality of the reforms process that he has done so much to uncover – a partiality which lends support to our argument that the reforms in India, whether or not they have been driven by a singular 'vision', have been phrased so as consistently to address the concerns of India's urban and industrial (and even agricultural or political) elites, with little regard, as yet, for the impact of structural adjustment upon the poor or upon the sustainability of the reforms themselves. When Jenkins writes of the 'skill with which Indian politicians have practiced reform by stealth [in] the coal sector', he is, after all, writing about a policy that intended 'a quiet start . . . towards deregulation' in that industry (1997: 216). And when he writes about 'a deft display of political legerdemain [that] . . . transferred a substantial portion of the [foodgrain support] subsidy from consumers to farmers', he recognizes that 'the government has [thereby] made essential commodities more expensive for the poorest of the poor' (p. 207). Moreover, when Jenkins describes the local level workings of the reform process in Maharashtra or Rajasthan he provides us with chapter and verse on policies that have consistently favoured some class groupings over others. Whether it is management lockouts in Mumbai, or reforms to the Public Distribution System which favour richer farmers, or privatization policies that create new opportunities for corruption for bureaucrats or politicians, or new policies which legitimize land thefts or land consolidation, Jenkins is describing a political project which is broadly consistent with certain class interests and not with others. (Only the most wooden of Marxists would look for greater consistency.) Indeed, when Jenkins writes of land grabbing by politicians in collusion with criminal gangs, he writes that: 'the ethos of liberalization – and its attendant rhetoric of necessity – has created the climate in which such actions have become politically justifiable, even if their subversion for private profit remains at least nominally obscured' (p. 125).

This is not just a matter of semantics. When Jenkins uses the words 'of necessity' in this passage he is putting his finger on two things that we consider to be central to a more rounded understanding of the liberalization project in India (one that moves beyond the issues of trade or investment reform): namely, its one-sidedness, and its disposition towards and legitimation of violence around the processes of accumulation and regulation. By one-sidedness we have in mind, first, the ways in which the reforms in India have encouraged a new regime of private capital accumulation which is increasing levels of dependency and volatility in the Indian economy; secondly, we have in mind the continuing failure of the Indian state (despite much rhetoric to the contrary) to invest in educational, health or infrastructural projects that would improve the capabilities of the poor and which would, crucially, upgrade the stock of India's social and human capital (to borrow from current World Bank jargon).

Sustaining the reforms

Although the World Bank has been a strong supporter of the reforms in India, it was recently obliged to acknowledge that the slowdown of the Indian economy in 1997–8 was caused in large part by a decline in agricultural growth in the preceding year. The World Bank went on to draw the conclusion, predictably enough, that a '[S]ubstantial reduction of the government deficit . . . [and] broader, deeper, faster deregulation of external and internal markets to encourage efficiency improvements and higher private investment' (1998: xiii) would be required to prevent the reform process from running out of steam (including a reform of India's agricultural markets).[21]

What it chose not to acknowledge was that India's agricultural successes in the 1980s and 1990s depended heavily on just that government spending which it now decried, or that, more generally, the reforms in India might have succeeded rather more in their own terms had they attended to the strengths as well as the weaknesses of the pre-reform system of economic accumulation and management.

This last point, of course, has been raised by many liberal and Left critics of the reforms in India, including Amit Bhaduri and Deepak Nayyar, who have contended not only that 'The bravado about free market efficiency and a minimalist State is historically illiterate', but also that, 'The restructuring of economies, if it is to be a success, must not only introduce correctives to eliminate weaknesses but also plan consolidation to build on strengths that emerge from past development experience' (1996: 46). Bhaduri and Nayyar draw on this insight to maintain that, 'the origins of the crisis in the [Indian] economy at the beginning of the 1990s lie essentially in the cavalier macro-management of the economy during the 1980s and not in a misplaced strategy of development since the mid-1950s' (p. 47).[22] It then follows, or so they suggest, that the crisis of 1991 should have been treated as a temporary crisis of liquidity (for which a programme of economic stabiliza-tion alone would be required) and not as a full-blown crisis of solvency or economic development (which would necessitate a much broader package of structural adjustment). The fact that these two moments were conflated is evidence, in their view, that the government of India allowed its vision of economic reform in the 1990s to be driven by the concerns of crisis manage-ment pure and simple; so much so, indeed, that 'the government . . . turned the necessity of going to the IMF into a virtue' (p. 50).

It is possible that this view of the reforms is not sufficiently attentive to the depth of the fiscal crisis of 1989–91, and it might be argued that Bhaduri and Nayyar pay too much attention to the roles played by economic theory and theoreticians in the supposed reinvention of India as a market-oriented economy post-1991. Vested interests also played their part, including those private capitalists in India, and NRIs abroad, who used the crisis years of 1989–91 to mount a strong case for structural adjustment. Even so, there is some truth in their suggestion that India's economic reforms have been dictated by a 'theoretical fundamentalism in policy formulation which comes to be dominated by outside [textbook] thinking' (1996: 52), and not by 'a natural transition in the strategy of development [that] emerges from experience and learning within countries' (p. 51). This fundamentalism is apparent in the way in which reformers have read the history of Indian economic development since the mid-1950s (as a failure or an opportunity lost), and in the way in which the crisis of 1991 was blamed on high levels of public spending in the 1980s. Bhaduri and Nayyar point out that public spending in itself is neither a vice nor a virtue; what matters is the uses to which such public spending is put and the social rate of return that it earns. Many reformers were unprepared to make this distinction, and they were even less disposed to recognize that government spending in the early 1980s had encouraged growth in the Indian economy or secured a measure of poverty reduction in the countryside (see the first part of this chapter).

A further lack of realism was apparent in the reformers' attitudes to India's balance of payments difficulties and its trading imbalance. Bhaduri and Nayyar suggest that the IMF and the Government of India have been in tow to an economic model which looks for adjustment exclusively through the price mechanism, and which finds no place for the multiplier effect of government spending cuts (which they estimate at 'three times the original reduction in the government deficit' (p. 59)). They also worry about the longer-term effects upon India's industrial base of a policy designed to reduce demand for imports by cutting incomes and purchasing power. While it is true that India's manufacturing economy performed well enough in the first five years of the reform era, fears have been voiced about the substitution of foreign for domestic capital in India's industrial economy, and about the short-sightedness of removing government support from India's infant industries.[23] These fears translate into concerns about the balance and stability of India's economy post-reform. In its report on the fiscal year 1996–7, the Alternative Survey Group (ASG) suggests that: 'one of the problems of recent trade policy is the increased focus on the export of primary products, which implies both reduced value addition and susceptibility to worsening terms of trade for primary products. On the import side, the Indian manufacturing process is also getting to be more import intensive' (ASG 1997: 34). The ASG notes that while India's trading deficit was indeed reduced from $9.4 billion in 1990–1 to $2.8 billion in 1991–2, it increased steadily to $8.9 billion in 1995–6 as manufactured imports flooded the country. This trading imbalance requires India to bridge its shortfall on the current account with money derived from Non-Resident Indians working abroad and from foreign investment (as we noted previously). In the period from 1991–2 to 1995–6, foreign direct investment in India totalled $3.4 billion and foreign portfolio investments totalled $14.0 billion. Remittances from Indians working abroad, meanwhile, increased from $2.8 billion in 1992–3 to $7.5 billion in 1995–6 (ASG 1997: 35). These funds were attracted to India by high rates of interest and a promise that such deposits would be 'designated and repayable in foreign exchange (except for a small part on non-rupee repatriable rupee deposits)' (p. 36). As the ASG points out, the remittances earned from Indians working abroad covered India's accumulated trade deficit of $23.5 billion in the period from 1991–2 to 1995–6. India's profit and interest remittance obligations over this period were also covered – in effect – by foreign borrowings, inward investment and net external assistance. Without such funds India would be in a mess.

Neoliberals might see nothing wrong with this state of affairs; at any rate, they would welcome private capital inflows as a means of bridging India's deficits until such time that those deficits can be brought under control by public spending cuts or further trade liberalization.[24] But critics of the reforms in India see a country drifting dangerously towards a state of indebtedness and economic dependency in an uncertain world economy. In their view (and in ours) there are lessons to be learned from East Asia, but these are not the lessons which Bhagwati draws. The real lessons of East Asia are the lessons of development economics: that inclusionary and sustainable patterns of development are most likely where states take measures to redistribute assets on an egalitarian (albeit private property) basis, and where states provide effective support for their infant industries before removing that support in a transparent and consistent manner. At the heart of this prospectus there is the realization that 'development states' have to intervene consistently in 'market' relationships, and must provide assured financial support for those sectors and institutions (including infrastructure, education and health care) which ensure the conditions of existence for long-run economic growth and development.[25] *Contra* Srinivasan, what matters here is precisely the question of sequencing, or of what comes first. Any attempt to open up a country to foreign capital or markets before the seeds of growth are truly sown will create the conditions for what Lipietz calls 'exclusionary growth', or the unequal and volatile growth trajectories that we have seen in Mexico or Brazil since the early 1980s (and which we might be seeing now in parts of South-East Asia).[26] Exclusionary growth strategies allow private affluence to coexist with public and environmental squalor, and they make a virtue out of a country's poverty or low wage costs. In the longer run they ensure that a country is revisited by balance of payments crises, and may push it into an unhealthy dependence on flows of mobile capital.

It is too early to say whether India is another Mexico in the making, although some warning signs are clearly there (and not least in terms of sluggish export growth and a growing dependence on foreign portfolio capital to balance the country's books). It is clear, however, that the trade policy reforms of the 1990s have occasioned debate and some discontent within India's industrial bourgeoisie (notably within the Bombay Club, which has voiced concern about the intrusions of foreign capital, and among those business leaders who have confessed to a lack of confidence about the global competitiveness of Indian industry); the reforms have also been associated with a decline in development spending on the capital account which even Bhagwati and Srinivasan thought too steep when they reported to Manmohan Singh in 1993.[27] Notwithstanding claims that government spending is being or will be switched from public sector units to infrastructure and human capital projects, the reforms in India have done very little to lay the foundations of sustainable economic growth or to look after the interests of the country's poor and poorest (see below).

This brings us to a second criticism of the neoliberal assessment. We do not agree with Michel Chossudovsky's suggestion that India has been placed under the indirect rule of the IMF, but he makes an important point when he suggests that structural adjustment might encourage a damaging switch from the production of foodgrains to crops for export (1993). There is already evidence of well-to-do farmers in the Punjab switching from wheat to sugar cultivation in the post-reform period, and if food prices have remained more or less affordable in India since 1991 it is because – as the World Bank recently acknowledged – the post-reform years coincided with a run of good monsoons.[28] Chossudovsky is also on firm ground when he points to the anti-poor thrust of the Indian reforms, at least in their first phase (1991–3). Notwithstanding the claims of some neoliberals about the uplifting effects of the reforms upon the poor, the evidence points firmly in the opposite direction. In an important review of that evidence, Abhijit Sen maintains that a 'massive increase in rural poverty, by over 60 million people, in the first 18 months of reform was to a very large extent a direct result of the stabilization-cum-structural adjustment policies' (1996: 2468). Sen also contends that an apparent moderation in poverty levels in the years up to 1993–4 was caused very largely by a restoration of cuts in public spending to support rural employment growth.[29] Finally, Sen notes that the sequencing of the reforms in India has been handled in such a way that support for its rhetoric, and perhaps even for some of its policies, might now be forthcoming from parts of rural India as well as from the country's towns and cities. Just as some of India's urban elites have gained from the spiralling land prices to which liberalization has given rise, so also are India's richer farmers beginning to gain from a new agricultural policy which aims to increase output mainly as a response to 'the increased price of agricultural goods, notably food, relative to all other prices in the economy' (p. 2470).

As Sen points out, this policy can empower the poor 'only if the prices of goods and services they sell rises in line with the rise in [the] price of food which makes up most of their consumption basket' (p. 2470). On current trends this is unlikely. Projected cutbacks in government spending on employment guarantee schemes, together with rising unemployment and more brutal conditions in the non-agricultural markets in which the rural poor participate so heavily, are just as likely to ensure a rise in rural poverty levels as a fall. Away from the textbook worlds of economic theory, the reforms in India seem to be making life harder for the poor, and they are making Indian society more unequal. Recent patterns of education spending and provision make this point all too clearly. In many rural Districts of Bihar education for the poor exists on paper only, and the State government is unable (or unwilling) to find the money it needs to fund a proper system of schools inspection. Many teachers draw their salary whether they visit 'their' village or not. Meanwhile, in most of India's towns and cities a new wave of private schools is emerging which allows India's middle classes to top up their stocks of cultural capital.[30] Spending on education in India is on the increase, and markedly so, but it is leaving the poor behind. While it may not be accurate to speak of the reforms in India as being 'anti-poor' in some crass or intentional sense, it would not be inaccurate to describe their effects thus far as being 'pro-rich'; nor would it be wrong to suggest that the reforms have promoted a further concentration of incomes and assets in a country that is riven by social and economic inequalities.

Public spending choices: education, health and infrastructure

But what of the future? Many proponents of economic reform would agree that increased government spending on education, health and infrastructure is a *sine qua non* of long-term economic growth and development, but would insist, too, that governments must first earn the money to pay for these investments on a sustainable basis. This seems to be the position of Jagdish Bhagwati, and in some respects it is unremarkable, but we are less sanguine than Bhagwati that a switch in public spending will soon occur in India.[31] We take the view, with Jean Drèze and Amartya Sen (1995) amongst others, that funds could and should have been found for such projects through the 1990s, possibly on the basis of increased taxation – not least from the agricultural sector – or from cuts in the many transfers which are still made over to India's middle classes.[32]

We make this judgement on the basis of the government's spending record thus far, and on the basis of our claims about the partiality of the reforms. In terms of revenue spending, it is fair to point out, the percentage of funds allocated by central or State governments to social services (including education, health, social security and the welfare of scheduled communities) remained more or less constant at 29.5 per cent from 1990–1 to 1996–7, even as defence spending (revenue and capital) fell from 14.85 per cent of total government revenue receipts to 12.17 per cent over the same period. It needs to be borne in mind, however, that central government spending on social services only just exceeds that on the fertilizer subsidy in rupee terms, and that State expenditures on social services (which far exceed those of central government) fell as a percentage of total State revenue expenditures from 38.98 per cent in 1990–1 to 36.79 per cent in 1996–7).[33] The budget for primary health care was also cut in the early 1990s in favour of other areas of health expenditure.

When it comes to the capital account, moreover, and more importantly, it is clear that spending has been switched away from the social sector since 1990, a point conceded by the World Bank in its *India: 1998 Macroeconomic Update*:

> As part of the fiscal adjustment, direct capital spending by the Central Government (excluding defence capital) fell from about 1.4% of GDP in 1990–91 to 0.7% of GDP in 1997–98, representing 40% of the cut in its deficit. In the States, direct capital spending also fell. . . . Private infrastructure provision may eventually offset some of these investment cutbacks and raise efficiency. However, in many other areas, such as roads, power transmission, urban infrastructure, primary school buildings, and health infrastructure, a strong case exists for more public investment. (1998: 11)

Capital expenditure on 'Development (Social and Economic Services)' also fell as a percentage of total government revenue receipts: from 15.28 per cent in 1990–1 to 9.50 per cent in 1996–7.

Nor is there much evidence to suggest that improvements will soon be forthcoming. A director of Lazard Brothers, writing in the *The Economic Times* on 16 October 1999, noted, as we have done previously (see chapters 3 and 4), that 'it is an accepted fact that growth in GDP is catalysed by investment in the infrastructure sector. The problem remains [he continued] that the government does not have resources to spend on infrastructure.' Notwithstanding eight years of 'reforms', the scale of the government's 'internal debt' is such that: 'Almost 50 per cent of the revenue receipt is eaten away by interest payments alone. India's internal debt to GDP ratio stands at a staggering 55 per cent.' It also needs to be borne in mind, or restated, that whilst government resources are limited, successive governments have refused to make the reform of primary education, for example, a key issue in India, so that, in the words of the editor of the *India Development Report, 1999–2000*, 'roughly 50 million children in the age group of 6–11 are not attending school today. This directly translates to 50 million uneducated citizens of India for decades to come' (Parikh 1999: 6). It further needs to be borne in mind that the estimated 'total annual expenditure required for universal primary education is of the order of Rs 281 billion, i.e. about 2.8 per cent of GDP annually to provide adequate quantity and quality of primary schooling compared to current expenditure of 1.5 per cent on primary education' (p. 7). This is a substantial sum of money, but in terms of current spending forgone it is equivalent to no more than two-thirds of the sum of money which the government forgoes in the form of uncollected taxes from the black economy (see S. Jha 1999: 175).

The violence of reform

The continuing failure of the Indian state to invest in universal primary education could reasonably be described as an act of violence, both against the government's own stated intentions and against those girls and boys who are refused the funds and institutions needed to improve their life chances or choices. This failure, of course, did not begin with the age of economic reforms, but the very visible returns (social, economic, political) which have accrued to many supporters of the reform process – notably those amongst the urban middle classes – have revealed and accentuated the gaps which are now growing between rich and poor in India. It is possible, too, that the anti-state rhetorics of the reform process have been seized upon by some of India's elites, more or less consciously, to weaken those public institutions which are supposed to protect India's weaker communities against the more brutalizing conditions which can obtain in labour markets. The sheer supply of labour in India makes exploitation possible on the basis of absolute surplus value – that is, on the basis of sweated labour rather than on the basis of labour that is combined with new technologies (which is what Marx called exploitation on the basis of relative surplus value).

Jan Breman has long argued along these lines, but the recent work of Barbara Harriss-White offers the most insistent probing of the relationships that might obtain between state power and the patterns of 'accumulative cruelty' which have come increasingly to define relations of capitalist development in India's informal economies (Harriss-White 1997; see also Breman 1996; Balagopal 1992). Harriss-White insists that the recent liberalization of parts of India's high or formal sector economy must be placed in this wider context. In her view, and as we noted at the top of this chapter: 'Calls for the radical privatization of the state ignore the effective radical privatization, informalization and now mafianization that South Asian states have been undergoing for much longer than the era of liberalization in the 1990s' (1997: 19).

The focus of Harriss-White's work is the vast and diverse informal economy in India, or that sector of the economy which provides at least 80 per cent of non-agricultural jobs. She notes that this economy has evolved its own forms of regulation over many years, with contracts typically being enforced on the basis of the spoken word, reputation or the threat of 'goondaism'. She also notes that the growth of the informal economy in Tamil Nadu has been related to patterns of 'state failure'. The inability of the local State to secure funds for its developmental or revenue functions creates a space for private security services or benefit providers. The result, says Harriss-White, is a blurring of the boundary between the state and civil society in rural and urban Tamil Nadu. India's intermediate classes – its rich peasantry and 'lower middle-class' – seek to protect their interests against those of labouring people and the formal sector by colonizing the state with kith and kin, and by expanding the scope of a shadow state. This shadow state

> comes into being because of the formal state and co-exists with it. It is therefore part of the state. Some elements of the shadow state are played simultaneously by real state players – e.g. corrupt lines of tribute, patronage/clientelage. Other shadow state livelihoods are independent of direct state players – e.g. private armies enforcing black or corrupt contracts, intermediaries, technical fixers, gatekeepers and adjudicators of disputes. Hence the real state is bigger than the formal state. (p. 15)

Rob Jenkins would surely recognize this shadow state. After all, his own work is sharply focused on the dirty or backside of democratic politics in India. But Jenkins's refusal to entertain the idea of class interests in a broad liberalization project blinds him to the conclusions which Harriss-White draws from her studies of the local state(s) and the informal economy in Tamil Nadu. Harriss-White insists that: 'As a result of the shadow state and the informal economy, the formal state loses legitimacy. Then state authority will come to reside in the private social status of state agents' (p. 15). She also notes that: 'The norms of the shadow state may become society's norms', and that in a world where ' "an honest man is he who does not know how to live" [as some maintain in the area in which she has done her research]...there are...extreme penalties in not playing according to the shadow state's rules' (p. 15).

What we are seeing now in parts of India is a sustained assault on the idea of the 'servant state'. This idea may always have been fragile in India, as it is in some advanced industrial countries, but it can reasonably be argued that respect for state institutions and functionaries (including Indian Administrative Service officers) has weakened over the past twenty years, and that it has weakened at an alarming rate during the period of economic reform. The idea that liberalization must occur 'of necessity' is being used in some parts of India to weaken the protective and developmental capacities of the very state that is meant to ensure that the poor can access the benefits of sustained economic growth. It seems plausible, then, to agree with Jenkins that the state in India has proved to be more adept in sustaining a process of reform than some critics will acknowledge, while also arguing, with Harriss-White, that the contraction of the 'formal' state at the local level has allowed private capitals to renegotiate their relationships with labour in the 'informal economy' to their obvious advantage. The reforms in India need to be understood in this dialectical context. The reforms are not simply about the renegotiation of India's relationships with the global market-place, nor even are they about the relationships of private capital with the Indian state in the formal economy; the reforms are also about the reworking of the idea of the state itself and of the state's capacity to work on behalf of those who stand outside India's (expanding) social and economic elites. It is in regard to these aspects of 'the reforms', we believe, that the charge of 'partiality' is most apposite, and where it is not unreasonable to describe the changes as being induced (or blocked) by or on behalf of India's contending social and economic elites.

7.5 Conclusions

It would be idle to pretend that a full-fledged process of economic reform in India could not raise the trend rate of growth in the country,[34] or contribute significantly to the reduction of 'mass structural poverty'.[35] By the same token, it would be misleading to suggest that the reforms in India have been enacted entirely at the bidding of the country's proprietary elites, or that they have worked to their exclusive or uncontested advantage. The reforms, as Jenkins reminds us, have sometimes taken on a life of their own, and the dynamic behind them has sometimes come from officials in the central and State governments reacting to changing conditions in the world economy or to new opportunities in the domestic arena. To acknowledge these points, however, is not to concede the three major arguments that we have made in this chapter. These arguments concern the scope and sustainability of the reforms, the partiality of the reforms, and the rhetoric of reformism.

It is unlikely that the process of economic reform in India will be halted in the next few years. The reforms have changed India's relations with its trading partners and erstwhile creditors, and there remain pressures from within the country (including from within the ranks of the BJP), and without, to press ahead with labour reforms,[36] further trade and banking reforms, a privatization programme, and a more 'responsible' fiscal policy (which might yet entail an attack upon water, power and fertilizer subsidies). It is even possible that the incoming (1999) government will make education a priority in fact as well as in rhetoric.[37] But the pace of these reforms remains open to doubt, and not least because the proposed fiscal changes threaten the livelihoods of many of those upon whom governments are forced to rely for political support (and not least, now, in the countryside). In the absence of these budgetary changes the government will be hard pressed to raise the extra funds it considers necessary for social or 'developmental' spending, and it will find that monies drain from the exchequer to pay the interest charges that are mounting on borrowed funds.[38] It is likely, too, as many neo-liberals insist, that continuing high government deficits will produce a measure of inflation at home, and that an overvalued rupee will put further pressures on India's trading and current accounts (much as we saw in the late 1990s).

The process of economic reform is never easy, of course, and it might be argued that India has avoided many of the pitfalls that have dogged attempts at reform in eastern Europe or parts of Latin America. After all, inflation in India was still below 10 per cent at the end of the 1990s (after nearly ten years of 'reform'), and the growth rate of the economy remained respectable at 5–6 per cent per annum. In part, though, these figures reflect the continuing strong performance of the agricultural sector, notwithstanding the fact that this sector has been sidelined in many discussions of reform and may yet be threatened by an assault on the subsidies which have helped to reshape it – in some parts of India – as a vigorous capitalist agriculture. If there is a sense in which the reforms in India have steadfastly refused to acknowledge the strengths of India's past development experience (see section 7.4 above), there is also irony in the fact that a process of economic reform that has been targeted on the 'high' or 'formal' (and 'external') economy in India has been underpinned by the performance of an economic sector which has thus far refused to bend itself significantly to the imperatives of the world market (although this is changing). Here, then, is one aspect of the partiality of the reform process in India, and one reason why the reforms are – as yet – most evident in India's towns and cities.

Another aspect of the partiality of India's reforms concerns class. Not all members of India's proprietary elites have benefited – or benefited equally –

from the reforms, and voices continue to be raised by some industrialists (for example, through the federations of small-scale industry) about the need for continuing protection against foreign goods or competitors. It is significant, however, that these voices are attended to more quickly than the voices of poorer households who worry about rising prices (as witness the three percentage point hike in all non-oil tariffs in September 1997), and it cannot be denied that the broad thrust of the reforms has been to increase the powers of private capital. In the long run, of course, the promise is that the benefits of a higher trend rate of economic growth will trickle down to the poor and poorest, and that government spending will increase (as revenues rise) or will be switched from those activities in which the state should not be engaged (the production of goods and services) to those in which it should play a central role (the regulation of the economy and the building up of social or human capital). In the meantime, however, it is not clear that the long-term trend rate of growth is moving ahead of that established in the mid-1980s, nor is it clear that government will find the funds needed to support those without assets, or to promote their 'access' to the market. The partiality of the reforms, in our view, is confirmed not so much by the controls which India's proprietary elites may or may not exercise over economic policy (*pace* Jenkins), but by the consistency with which the reforms have failed to promote the economic or political interests of those who are excluded from India's 'new' regime of accumulation. In practice, too, as Harriss-White reminds us, the reforms have eroded further those institutions of state which might once have been turned to by the less powerful as a possible source of redress for the 'hidden injuries of class'. Attempts to solve India's looming fiscal crisis by cuts in state spending – and not least in the States, where financial 'indiscipline' is a particular irritant to the World Bank (and other multilateral agencies) – will only promote a hollowing out of the state's capacity at the local level, and its replacement by a 'shadow state' which is run in many places by mafia groups or members of India's intermediate classes. In certain Districts of Bihar it is already the case that 30–40 per cent of development spending (as, for example, on the Employment Assurance Scheme) is creamed off by contractors, and the idea that labourers might take their employers to court for failing to pay the statutory minimum wage is laughable in all but a few Blocks where the labouring poor have been organized by 'Naxalite' groups.[39]

The collapse of the 'idea of the state' in parts of India cannot be laid at the door of the reforms alone – it has been going on for much longer – but the 'idea of reform' has contributed to a new calculus of political (ir)responsibility which threatens to end any semblance of a 'moral' or 'community' order in India's political economy. It is here, perhaps, that the reforms – or the rhetorics of reform – have been most potent. There is little evidence to suggest that the Indian economy is on a new or sustainable growth trajectory in the 1990s: the best that can be said is that conditions in India might have been worse if some measure of stabilization was not attempted in 1991–3.

Nor is there much evidence to suggest that the reform of some parts of India's formal or 'external' economies will be accompanied by reforms in the domestic economy that will threaten the living standards of India's growing middle class. And yet the idea that India is an emerging market, or an economy that is now facing up to a new challenge in the global market-place, is firmly established in the rhetoric of Indian policy makers and their boosters abroad. Here, perhaps, is Manmohan Singh's major achievement, and here too – in the gap between 'the fantasy and the reality of a globalizing India' (as Bagchi puts it: 1994) – we can sense fresh dangers for India and for Indian politics.

8

The Guilty Men? Militant Hinduism and the Politics of Anti-secularism

Social backwardness in the form of a weakly developed sense of civic ties – the bond of responsible citizenship – that would moderate if not replace the divisive primordial loyalties of religion, language and caste, is indeed a very severe handicap. Nehru saw this clearly and articulated it forcefully. What he did not see well was that when the state is made to take on too much out of the ambition and hubris of those who take charge of it, they run the risk of making it totalitarian or seeing it fall flat on its face.

T. N. Madan (1997, ch. 8)

India must liberalise, industrialise and modernise – but it must do so the Indian way. India has to become a light unto itself.

BJP: Humanistic Approach to EconomicDevelopment
– A Swadeshi Alternative

If the 1990s have seen the most thorough-going attempt to restructure and reinvent the Indian economy (and by implication the federal polity),[1] the second of the 'elite revolts' that we described in chapter 6 – the conservative

---

According to the RSS ideologue, Jay Dubashi: 'It was not the Hindu rate of growth that failed India but the Nehru rate of growth, and men like Raj Krishna are as much the guilty men as Nehru himself' (as quoted in Rajagopal 1994: 1659). The late Raj Krishna was the economist who coined the idea of 'the Hindu rate of growth'. It is ironic, perhaps, and somewhat unedifying, that a member of the RSS was willing to name Nehru as a 'guilty man' (as so many did during the celebrations which surrounded fifty years of independent India, and not least because of Nehru's defence of secularism), when a one-time member of the RSS, Nathuram Godse, was guilty of killing the 'father of modern India', Mahatma Gandhi.

revolution of Hindu nationalism[2] – involves the re-imagining of both state and society and places yet further into question the character of democracy in India. These trends are, of course, not unconnected. As we noted in chapter 7, the success of the minority Congress government of the earlier 1990s in negotiating economic reform was aided by the fears of the remainder of the opposition about the BJP and its project of redefining Indian society. These fears led the Janata Dal and its left allies to join with the Congress in a loose coalition to hold the line against the politics of 'anti-secularism'. The cause of secularism has continued to be the most powerful force for uniting opposition to the BJP, although events have shown that it is but a fragile cement against the ambitions of self-seeking politicians.

Part of the new design which the BJP has promised, and part of the reason for the appeal of Hindu nationalism to elites in Indian society, is that *Hindutva* threatens to subdue the plebeian assertiveness (Hansen's phrase) of the political leadership created by India's democratic revolution (see chapters 6 and 9). It also promises that by being fully and truly themselves, rather than attempting to imitate or emulate western values and ways of being, Indians will be able to assert themselves and secure for the country the status and recognition which India should have in a globalizing world. The *Sangh parivar* as a whole is not, as has sometimes been argued, 'anti-modern', but it lays out a different route to modernization from that which was sought by the Constituent Assembly in the 1940s, and then by the Nehruvian state. The BJP as a party of government – somewhat in opposition to the RSS – has not rejected economic liberalization, though it did at one point declare its opposition to 'westernization'; the BJP's 'Swadeshi Alternative' of 1992 suggests that India should become a 'light unto itself'.

In this chapter we examine in more detail the history of Hindu nationalism, the ideological claims that it makes, and the re-imagining of identities and relationships, and of the polity, which it offers. Does it have a peculiar persuasive power? Or is the success of the *Sangh parivar* in defining the terms of Indian politics in the 1990s more a negative triumph that has come about because of the vacuum which has been left by the self-destruction of the Congress, the continuing failure of the left, and the collapse of Nehruvian ideals? (On this, see also our discussion in chapter 6.) We will analyse, too, contemporary debates over secularism in India, and their implications for democracy and a politics which might resist 'militant Hinduism'. It is important, however, that we should first look more closely at the meanings of religion in Indian society. This is a difficult task, for it is necessary to steer a course between Orientalist attitudes (whether held by outsiders or by Indians themselves) which treat the Indian 'Other' as essentially different – mainly by virtue of religion – in what is held to be a supremely spiritual culture, and the no less dangerous kind of reductionism which disregards cultural difference altogether. Such reductionism, by treating religious discourse and practice only as 'ideological smoke screens that hide the real clash of material interests and social classes' (van der Veer 1994: ix), can lead to profound misunderstanding of their significance in the construction of changing social identities.

8.1 Secularism and Religion in Indian Society

The word 'secularism' entered into the English language, Chadwick reminds us, only in 1851, but the process of 'secularization' – referring to 'a growing tendency in mankind to do without religion, or to try to do without religion' (Chadwick 1975: 17, and 91) – has much deeper historical roots. Madan (1997) argues that the idea of 'secularity', as a state of being, or of 'secularism' as ideology, can be traced back to the *philosophes* of the European Enlightenment in the seventeenth and eighteenth centuries, and their self-definition as those who, in 'trampling upon prejudice, tradition, universal consent, authority – in a word, all that enslaves men's minds – dare to think for [themselves]'.[3] Their concern was not, as he says, to 'abolish religion' but rather to put religion in its place by removing appeal to theological authority in explanation. Knowledge is to be founded on reason, not on revelation or on scriptural authority. Religious ideas (those of Protestantism), however, 'contributed to the strengthening of the processes of secularization in the West [and] the latter, in turn, ironically, contributed to the erosion of religious beliefs, practices and authority' (Madan 1997: 13). The development of scientific knowledge further contributed to these processes, which came to be thought of by sociological theorists as essential to what they saw as the universal transformation from 'tradition' to 'modernity'. The idea of the modern state, governed by secular principles, was then greatly influenced by the foundation of the United States and by the American Constitution, which lays down 'non-interference' (the government shall not establish a church) and 'entitlement' (citizens have the right to follow any religion of their choice, or none at all) – ideas which entered into the Constitution of India (see Madan 1997: 23–5). In such a modern state there are – ideally and in theory – citizens imbued with equal rights as individuals, and acknowledging responsibilities to each other and to the state.

Madan, of course, disputes the extent to which such 'responsible citizenship' existed, or exists yet, in the context of Indian society, because of the power of what he refers to as 'primordial loyalties', or what other scholars would refer to as 'ethnic identities', grounded in religion, or language or caste. Madan's argument recalls those of other Indian scholars, concerning the segmented and cellular character of Indian society, to which we referred earlier, and which are summed up in Khilnani's words about there having been 'no [we would say little] reshaping of common beliefs in the society at large' (see chapter 2 above). It is sometimes suggested that these 'loyalties' acquired a peculiar salience in nineteenth- and early twentieth-century India as an outcome of colonial governmentality, and its ways both of classifying and ordering groups of people, and of manipulating differences so as to 'divide and rule'. 'Communities' were reified and discourses about the rights and entitlements of groups, rather than of individuals, became established also within the nationalist movement. It is sometimes held, as well, that what is called 'communalism' – referring usually to conflicts between Hindu and Muslim, and sometimes Sikh 'communities' – was the outcome of elite conflicts, particularly over access to jobs and to opportunities that were opened up by the actions of the colonial state. There is a good deal of agreement, too, amongst anthropologists that the effects of government policies in the colonial period and thereafter, and of economic changes, have been to transform the nature of caste from a relational system, to one in which named groups are thought of as bounded entities – like other kinds of ethnic groups.[4]

All of these arguments are of value, and they call into question the very idea of 'primordial loyalties' – at least if this expression is understood to mean *essential* and inherent attributes of particular groups of people. They show, instead, that people's ideas of themselves as 'Hindu' or 'Muslim' or 'Maratha' or 'Lingayat' – their sense of themselves, or their 'identities', in other words – are changing historical constructions. But none of this means that the strong sense of religious identity which is felt by very many Indians is the result only of nineteenth-century developments, or that it is simply the result of elite manipulations. Of course religion is produced in a field of power, but religious meanings are not to be reduced to political ideology. And the sense of religious community has deep roots in particular historical experiences. According to Peter van der Veer's interpretation of a wealth of recent historical scholarship,[5] Hindu, Muslim and Sikh communities in India have been created by the actions of saints, traders and soldiers. The expansion of *sufi* brotherhoods was, he says, a crucially important aspect of the 'islamization' of South Asia. There were often links between ruling dynasties and the cults surrounding the tombs of particular *sufi* saints, and these gave rise to a sense of regional identity, partly expressed and reinforced in ritual: 'The point is that not only do states play a decisive role in determining the identities of their subjects but religious regimes do the same' (van der Veer 1994: 40). Hindu religious figures – saints and ascetics, who were also often traders or soldiers – were the similar agents of Hindu expansion: 'Hinduism can be seen, very much like Islam, as a not fully-integrated family of ideas and practices spread by ascetics and priestly families over an enormous region inhabited by very different populations. Although there is no church-like organization, there are long-term processes of centralization and homogenization' (p. 46). Such regional identities were amongst what the historian Christopher Bayly has recently described as 'old patriotisms' that came into existence well before British rule was established and long before the Indian nationalist movement emerged (1998). Such identities and the ideas of religious community which they reflected were reworked by social and religious reformers in the colonial period, in ways which we review in the next part of this chapter. They help to explain why it has been that: 'In India the most important imaginings of the nation continue to be religious, not secular – although secular nationalism does (also) exist as an ideological force' (van der Veer 1994: 22).

The sense of religious identity and of religious community, and the ways in which these are reproduced in daily life and in religious practice, is brought out, too, in contemporary ethnographies. The French anthropologist Jackie Assayag, for example, has studied the relations of Muslims and Hindus in part of Karnataka, and describes a Hindu temple complex in which there is also the shrine of a Muslim saint (1995). Here both the beliefs and the practices of Muslims and Hindus are interrelated. They have alternative stories of the relations of the goddess Yellamma and the saint Bar Shah, and Hindus participate in the worship of the saint, Muslims in the worship of the goddess. On the face of it this might seem a remarkable illustration of the religious tolerance or even syncretism which some hold to be characteristic of popular religion in South Asia, but Assayag shows how in practice, in the ways in which they relate to each other in apparently shared rituals, the distinctions between the two communities are retained and affirmed, as they are in their alternative accounts of the relationships between goddess and saint. He concludes: 'In fact, in spite of their permanent contacts and frequent exchanges, daily cooperation and mutual accommodation, the two communities remain in the end very clearly distinguished from each other' (1995: 10, our translation).

This ethnography is significant for two reasons. It shows how (many) people think about their identities through religious ideas and practices.[6] It also casts an interesting light – as we shall explain – upon the ideas of the quite diverse thinkers and activists in India who have been critical of 'secular' thinking. Let us return for a moment to the Constituent Assembly debates. In that first debate, on the Resolution on Aims and Objects, which we briefly described in chapter 2, secularism was not discussed, though given that many speakers referred to the absence of the members of the Assembly from the Muslim League, relations between the members of the two great religious communities were rarely far from speakers' minds. One member, the Reverend J. J. Nichols-Roy, argued specifically – against suggestions which had been made by Churchill and by Lord Simon in the British Parliament – that: 'If the people who are assembled here – whether they be Hindu, Muslim or Christian, or whatever religion they may profess – if they frame a constitution which will be a democratic constitution, which will do justice to everybody, why should that constitution be called a Hindu Raj?'[7] Dr Radhakrishnan, after referring to Ataturk's 'defiant creation of a secular Turkey' further argued that 'the days of religious states are over.'[8] Secularism, on one level, was never seriously in question. It was an essential part of the progressive, modernizing mission of India's developmental state, which – precisely because of the perceptions of the political leadership about the lack of 'civic responsibility' in society – had to be imposed by bureaucratic fiat. Middle-class citizens confronted the masses, who were deemed to remain locked up within their cultural communities, and: 'Secular tolerance was part-and-parcel of the civilizing mission of the modern state vis-à-vis [these] masses who, until they were sufficiently educated, had to remain under the paternalistic tutelage of the state' (Hansen 1999: 54).

It was then a supreme irony that the Nehruvian state should have reneged so comprehensively on the Constitutional commitment to universal primary education, which meant that the westernized ruling elite 'had neither the means nor perhaps the strong urge to consolidate its legitimacy by nurturing relevant symbols of India's incipient statehood' (K. Kumar 1993: 553). But this left a vital space for the activities of Hindu nationalists. As Kumar has shown, they have played, for example, a significant part in the shaping of modern Hindi and in its dissemination, and through the Hindi syllabus have been able to ensure that 'moralizing within a (Hindu) revivalist world view became entrenched in school text-books' (p. 544). Today the organizations of the *Sangh parivar* run more than 20,000 schools in the country. Harsh Sethi makes a telling comparison: 'How many (schools) does the Left (run)? Even in state governments that they control, their record in this field is, to put it mildly, pathetic. Be it textbooks, pedagogy, assuring teacher presence in schools, not to speak of inculcating new and relevant values – one can hardly hold them up as exemplars' (1998: 894).

The deliberations of the Constituent Assembly finally allowed for a particular understanding of the secular state – 'as one that is based on (equal) respect for all religions or non-discrimination on the ground of religion' (Madan 1997: 25) – rather than as entailing a strict separation of state and religion. Even while the Constituent Assembly was meeting, some of the provincial legislatures continued to enact laws for the reform of religious practices, on the lines of earlier legislation.[9] There were, notably perhaps, further bills making it an offence to bar entry to temples on grounds of untouchability – something that was evidently in accordance with both the spirit and the letter of the Constitution which was finally promulgated, but which still represents interference by the state in religious affairs. It was significant that the aim of the legislation was not – in the name of civil rights – to throw open all places of worship to all citizens, and access to many Hindu temples continues to be denied to some categories of citizens (such as Christians). After Independence some of the States (especially in the south) became increasingly involved in managing the affairs of religious institutions. And in accordance, apparently, with the Directive Principle of the Constitution which declared that the state should aim to establish a uniform civil code for all citizens, the reform of Hindu personal laws was undertaken (so as, for example, to legalize divorce and to prohibit polygamy). A few people – amongst them the socialist leader, J. B. Kripalani – drew attention to the fact that this use of state legislation to bring about reforms only in the religion of the majority 'was creating a serious anomaly in the very notion of equal citizenship' (Chatterjee 1997a: 244). The reforming zeal of the political leadership, in its pursuit of the nationalist-modernist project, led it to violate the principal of the separation of state and religion, and made for anomalies which have subsequently been ruthlessly exploited by the Hindu nationalists. Exactly as J. B. Kripalani anticipated, the actions of the Congress government after Independence in reforming Hinduism in the name of civil rights, whilst failing to act in the same way with the other major religions – though this was done in order to reassure non-Hindus – has made it susceptible to the charge of being, in fact, 'communalist' (in Kripalani's words) or only 'pseudo-secular' in the favourite language of the *Sangh parivar*.[10] The state has ostensibly discriminated against the Hindu majority (this was what was at issue in the Shah Bano affair which we discussed in chapter 5) – and as Hansen argues, the secularism and hyper-rationalism of the Nehruvian state proved, on one account, to be empty of real substance (1999, ch. 1).[11]

Both at the time of the drafting of the Constitution and, more recently, there has been, therefore, an attempt to find other principles for the governance of India which take account of religious life in a different way. Common to the positions of a number of thinkers is a kind of reversed Orientalism which aims to create a modern nation around the imagination of this 'supremely spiritual culture' (see Hansen 1996b). They hold that Hinduism, by contrast with the other great religions, is uniquely and distinctively characterized by pluralism and by 'tolerance'. This was Gandhi's view, not least, and it is appealed to by several contemporary writers. We discuss it in some depth in the section 8.3. For the moment, however, we want to draw attention to our second reason for finding Assayag's ethnography so significant: it is that he shows that the long-running coexistence of Hinduism and of Islam has meant that there is mutual adjustment, with both having undergone change. Yet the distinctness of the communities is retained and even emphasized.[12] Coexistence along the lines that Assayag analyses does not amount to the kind of syncretic tolerance proclaimed by some of the 'anti-secularists'.

With this understanding of the religious construction of personal meaning in Indian society[13] and of the anomalies within the Indian version of secularism, we can turn to the history of Hindu nationalism.

8.2   '*Hindutva*' and the History of Hindu Nationalism

From Hindu reformism to Hindu nationalism

Notwithstanding Hindu nationalism's appeal to a primordial and eternal Hindu *rashtra* (nation),[14] the origins of militant Hinduism as a political-cum-ideological project are rooted in the second half of the nineteenth century, and in three processes:[15] the reification of communities through the classifications imposed by colonial governmentality; the acceptance by Indian reformers, if sometimes in reversal, of the ideas of western Orientalist scholars about the essential attributes of Indian civilization; and emulation amongst Hindu groups of discursive modes and organizational forms of the semitic religions. In outline, the Hindu nationalists conceived of the nation in cultural terms, as an organic and homogeneous whole which is threatened by 'foreigners' (notably Muslims and the British). This conception addresses the sense of threat or of loss, and the fear of disorder which people experience in the context of social and political change, by offering to re-establish control through re-establishing the whole that is the nation; and it is at least partly sought to be realized through control of the human body and organizational discipline. Fear is turned outwards, onto the demonized 'Other' which threatens the nation as it has been culturally imagined. Communal violence, seen in this context, is neither irrational nor entirely spontaneous.

The British, as we have argued, contributed to new ways of imagining Hinduism and Islam as communities; and the introduction of separate laws for 'Hindus' and 'Muslims' helped to produce more stable religious identities, as did the introduction of separate electorates for the two 'communities' (see chapter 1). The colonial authorities also provided some of the conditions for organized opposition to British rule in India. The extension of educational opportunities, along with new opportunities for service within the bureaucracies of Empire, encouraged some Indians to reflect on a 'drain of wealth' which kept India subservient to Britain: from this quarter emerged an Indian nationalism which required modern Indians to step in the shoes of their colonial masters and run the country for the general good. A socialist version of Indian nationalism looked to Reason as an antidote to the 'religion' and 'superstition' that prevented Indians from imitating the economic and political successes of Britain and western Europe. In so far as India could define itself in opposition to Great Britain it would be in terms of the injustices of imperial rule. Later on it would invoke the new god of Planning as the embodiment of a hyper-reason which would surpass the empiricism of imperial knowledge.

But the spread of educational opportunities in British India didn't only call forth an Indian – or secular – nationalism. The activities of Christian missionaries, and the categorizing and law-making zeal of India's rulers, also encouraged the emergence of Hindu reform movements like the Brahmo Samaj, and later the Arya Samaj. From this quarter came a very different reading of India's 'present weaknesses and future strengths'. The Arya Samaj was formed in 1875 by a Shaivite ascetic from Gujarat, Swami Dayananda Saraswati, with the aims of purifying and codifying 'Hinduism' in the face of challenges from other organized religions and from a more secularized modernity (see also chapter 1). Hindu revivalism, of course, is not the same thing as Hindu nationalism, and the anti-Brahmanism of some Samajis hardly endeared the sect to north India's political elites; indeed the textualism of the Arya Samaj meant that its appeal rarely extended beyond Punjab, where its 'attack on image worship fell on fertile soil, prepared by centuries of Sikh traditions of imageless devotion' (van der Veer 1994: 66). But while all this is true, the Arya Samaj helped to initiate – along with proponents of a more orthodox or Brahmanical Hindu religion (*Sanatan Dharm*) – the Cow Protection Movement which periodically dominated the politics of north India from about 1880 to 1920. And the Cow Protection Movement 'had nothing to do with reform but much to do with religious nationalism' (p. 66).

The Cow Protection Movement brought together a community of 'Hindus' who were opposed to the 'Muslim' slaughter of *gau mata* (mother cow) and who petitioned the British government to end such butchery. Its significance for an incipient Hindu nationalism is apparent in the way in which it positioned Muslims (and the British) as threats to the stability and natural order of Hindu society, and in its capacity to call to mind a Hindu nation under threat from barbarian influences and practices. The Arya Samaj took a lead in organizing the Cow Protection Movement, and Dayananda used the networks of the Arya Samaj to disseminate an imagery of the cow as the mother of the Hindu nation. Significantly, this imagery drew on Brahmanical conceptions of the cow as the mother of life and the substance of all things.[16] The movement allowed an emergent Hindu nationalism to define a community of Hindus against a community of non-believers (foreigners), and to demand aggressive actions on the part of Hindu males to restore the integrity of Mother India (*Bharat Mata*). Its major achievement was to imagine Hindu India as different from the west or Christianity or Islam, even as it defined *Bharat* in terms that refused the Brahmanical, ascetic or feminized readings of Hinduism that dominated the Orientalist imagination.

Veer Savarkar, the Hindu Mahasabha and the Rashtriya Swayamsevak Sangh

If the Cow Protection Movement was successful in providing a focus for Hindu antipathy or rage, it hardly settled the question of 'Hindu-ness', or of who counted as a Hindu and on what terms. Colonial policies of divide and rule, and the slow extension of the franchise, may have made Hindus more aware of themselves as Hindus *vis-à-vis* Muslims, but these same policies, when combined with new opportunities for education and employment for non-Brahman communities, caused some high-caste groups to fear the assertiveness of the lower castes almost as much as they feared a Muslim-British power bloc. These fears deepened in the late nineteenth and early twentieth centuries, albeit in different ways in different parts of the sub-continent. In Bengal, the anxieties of high-caste Hindus led in the direction of 'paternalist philanthropy and Sanskritizing reform that would uplift or purify the lower castes, an agenda that was now [*c.*1900] coming to be recognized as indispensable for building Hindu or national unity' (S. Sarkar 1996: 286). But matters were different in west and south India, where various low-caste and *dalit* movements refused the Sanskritizing agendas of an incipient and ostensibly inclusive Hindu nationalism. Maharashtra was the home of Jyotirao Phule, 'a *mali* [gardener caste of the *shudra varna*] [who] sought to forge a unity of low and middle castes... using popular religious traditions rigorously avoiding the use of the term or category "Hindu" ' (Omvedt 1990: 727; see also chapter 2, note 6). Phule argued 'that all the non-Brahman castes were the original inhabitants of India, conquered and enslaved by cunning Aryans, whose Brahman heirs continued to use control of political power and religious ideology up through British times (when their control over education allowed them to dominate the bureaucracy) as the means for exploiting the peasantry' (p. 727).

Phule's ideas were reworked and extended by other non-Brahman social reformers across the south, where anti-Brahmanism became politically powerful, as well as by Ambedkar and some *adivasi* leaders in Jharkhand (and see chapter 9). But his ideas were resisted forcefully by the Hindu nationalist leaders who aimed to project an organic conception of the essential unity of Hindu culture and society. These men also came, precisely, from Maharashtra, and had been influenced by Tilak (whom S. Sarkar describes as 'the man who really blazed the trail for Extremism'; 1983: 99): we refer to Savarkar, the ideological father of Hindu nationalism, and Hedgewar and Golwalkar, respectively the founder and the main ideologue of the Rashtriya Swayamsevak Sangh. The institutionalization of Hindu nationalism needs to be seen in this context – recognizing the inspiration of the Maratha war-bands led by Shivaji and his successors against the Mughals (and see chapter 3.1).

The establishment of the Hindu Mahasabha in 1915 brought together mainly high-caste Hindus from different regions and theological traditions, and yet debates continued to rage between Arya Samajists, who advocated the purification of untouchables, and Sanatan Dharm factions who promoted Brahmanical supremacy and paid less regard to missionary work or assimilation.[17] By about 1920, however, the hardliners among the Mahasabha had pushed aside more moderate Hindu leaders like Malaviya and Lal Lajpat Rai, and had set about transforming the Hindu Mahasabha

from a religious and social movement into a political force of Hindu nationalist opposition to the Congress Party and the Muslim League. They advocated hatred of Muslims and groups opposed to their cause of establishing a Hindu nation-state.... In 1932 the Hindu Mahasabha passed a resolution at its annual conference endorsing the formation of the Rashtriya Swayamsevak Sangh (RSS) and encouraged members of provincial Hindu sabhas to support the expansion of the RSS and to assist it in making it a 'strong organization of Hindus'. (McKean 1996: 70, quoting Jones 1981: 460)[18]

The institutionalization of Hindu nationalism led to fresh attempts to define the essence of Hindu culture, and it is here that Savarkar made his particular contribution to militant Hinduism. In the *Essentials of Hindutva* (1922),

Savarkar sets out an account of the formation and qualities ('essentials') of the Hindu nation that remains important in the imagery and iconography of Hindu nationalism. After first defining *Hindutva* as that which 'embraces all the departments of thought and activity of the whole being of our human race', Savarkar defines a Hindu as 'a person who regards this land...from the Indus to the Seas as his fatherland as well as his Holyland' (1949: 110–13). As Varshney points out, this 'definition is territorial (land between the Indus and the Seas), genealogical ("fatherland"), and religious ("holyland"). Hindus, Sikhs, Jains, and Buddhists can be part of this definition, for they meet all three criteria. All these religions were born in India. Christians, Jews, Parsis, and Muslims, however, can meet only two criteria. India is not their "holyland"' (1993: 230–1). But there is rather more to it than this. By defining Hindus as a race which shares a common blood, Savarkar is able to insist on a nation-building project which sees the Hindu identity being forged in a continuing process of violent – and purifying – struggle. This process began with the Aryan invasions and was later continued by the 'clutchings and crushings' which the 'gigantic Octopus of Hindudom' unleashed upon the Muslim Empire (Savarkar, no date, quoted in McKean 1996: 80).

Savarkar's thought and teachings were hardly without contradiction, and they evolved markedly up to and beyond Independence in 1947.[19] On questions relating to Hinduism as a religion, or to caste, Savarkar liked to signal the inclusiveness of Hindu nationalism. He objected to the foreignness of the word Hinduism, and insisted that the *Sanatan Dharm* religion practised by most Hindus was only one of several systems of religious belief that were compatible with *Hindutva*, or the cultural, racial and historical totality of the Hindu nation: Arya Samajis, Sikhs, Jains and Buddhists were all culturally Hindu (after McKean 1996: 82). Savarkar also spoke up for campaigns of conversion, or *shuddhi*, whereby *adivasis*, Untouchables, Christians and even Muslims could publicly embrace Hinduism (the two former groups already being Hindu in terms of 'blood'). But where conversion was refused, there was no possibility, in Savarkar's view, that a Muslim (or Christian) born in India could be at home in a country that was racially and culturally the land of the Hindus. The anti-Muslim theme in his writings grew stronger as Independence approached and as the Partition of India became a real prospect. In a sickening attack on the Muslim League, which invoked the claims of Nazism in Europe, Savarkar warned that 'if we Hindus in India grow stronger in time these Moslem friends of the League will have to play the part of German-Jews' (Savarkar 1949: 65, quoted in McKean 1996: 87).

The threat of Partition also encouraged Savarkar to step up his attacks on the Congress. Gandhi was reviled for meeting Muslim 'aggression' with a politics of non-violence. This gave quite the wrong impression of how the Hindu nation had been forged by struggle and military conquest. As we saw in chapter 1, Gandhi had tried to respond to the militaristic leanings of Savarkar as early as 1908, when he published *Hind Swaraj*, but to no avail.

Savarkar's version of Hindu nationalism carved out a third way between the modernizing (imitative) nationalism of Nehru and the socialists and the romantic nationalism of Gandhi – a nationalism which aimed to revive the pacific glories of an earlier Hindu civilization.

Nationalists in the Hindu Mahasabha joined with Gandhi to counterpose the glories of Hindu civilization to the avarice and immorality of 'the west', but they asserted Kshatriya values in opposition to Gandhi's Brahmanical ideals in seeking to reinvent a golden past by military force: only through strength would freedom come. It was for this reason that Savarkar dismissed Gandhi's opposition to industrialization, and it was for this reason that he urged Hindu nationalists to look upon Rama's triumphant return to Ayodhya from Lanka as the birth of the Hindu nation. As McKean points out, it was in *Essentials of Hindutva* that Savarkar 'proclaimed Rama as the founder of a new political institution, the *chakravartin*, or world conqueror-ruler' (McKean 1996: 80; and see below). This same attitude informed Savarkar's account of the righteous Hindu woman. Savarkar not only celebrated the woman as mother – the person who instils a love of country in her children (and not least in her sons) – but also as a courageous fighter in her own right: as witness the exploits of the Rani of Jhansi, Savarkar's favourite heroine.

Although Savarkar fell out of favour after the assassination of Gandhi in 1948, the militant Hinduism which he espoused was continued by members of the Hindu Mahasabha. The organization which he led as the 'supreme dictator' from 1938–9 contested the general elections of 1952, 1957 and 1962, albeit with little success. In the longer run, the significance of Savarkar lies in his accounts of *Hindutva* and in his attempts to forge an assertive Hindu nation in the face of opposition from the colonial authorities, mainstream and secular nationalists, and various low-caste and tribal movements which resisted the Mahasabha's ideology of assimilation.

Mahasabhaites also played a part in initiating and supporting the activities of the RSS, and here too we see a link – albeit not an unbroken link – between the concerns and teachings of Savarkar and the politics of Hindu nationalist movements in the period since about 1980. Under its first leader, Dr Keshav Baliram Hedgewar, the RSS was successful in spreading its organizational structures and teachings from its base in Maharashtra to many parts of northern India, and not least Punjab. The RSS was organized from the first as a quasi-military brotherhood of young men who wore a distinctive uniform, which came to consist of a white shirt, khaki shorts, black cap, leather belt, socks and shoes. These men were schooled in the Sangh's ideology by a 'corps of provincial organisers (*pracharaks*), who were the most able of the Sangh's full-time workers and [who] had taken vows of continence and abstinence' (Graham 1990: 15). Such vows were consistent with the *brahmacharya* belief that the body of the nation could only be strengthened by proper attention to the strength and purity of the body of the Hindu male, and they meshed with the Sangh's self-image as a disciplined and hierarchical association of volunteers 'dedicated to the improvement of Hindu society and to the eventual creation of a *Hindu rashtra*, or Hindu nation' (p. 7). Under the leadership of Madhav Sadashiv Golwalkar (from 1940) members of each local branch of the RSS (the *shakas*) were required to meet on a daily basis for the purposes of physical exercise and team games, and for a weekly talk on the aims and objectives of the RSS, which are to bring about the ideal of Hindu unity for building a strong Indian nation.[20]

Bruce Graham suggests that the RSS had between 400,000 and 500,000 members in 1947; RSS sources claimed a membership of about 600,000 in early 1948 (Jaffrelot 1996: 75). Following the assassination of Mahatma Gandhi this figure dropped to about 100,000, and in February 1948 Nehru persuaded the Home Ministry to proscribe the RSS and place its leaders under arrest. By July 1949, however, Nehru was facing pressures to lift the ban on the RSS (which he did: Golwalkar had been released from prison in August 1948), and by March 1951 the RSS had recovered its numerical strength after having led agitations around the war with Pakistan in Kashmir (in 1948) and the passage of the Hindu Code Bill. Notwithstanding the poor performance of the Hindu Mahasabha and the Bharatiya Jana Sangh in the first three general elections after Independence, it would be misleading to suggest that Hindu nationalism withered away in the 1950s or 1960s, or that the Jana Sangh or the RSS played no role in laying the foundations of the Hindu nationalist resurgence which shook India in the 1980s. The Jana Sangh won 41 of 288 seats in the Legislative Assembly election in Madhya Pradesh in 1962, and the party returned 35 MPs to the Lok Sabha in 1967 on the basis of 9.4 per cent of the popular vote. Of more significance, perhaps, is the fact that the Jana Sangh, with the RSS, helped to reinvent the languages (or at least the slant) of Hindu nationalism after Partition, and so provided a base upon which the BJP and the VHP were able to build in the 1980s. The Jana Sangh continued to insist, of course, on the geographical and cultural unity of undivided India. Its first election manifesto, which was written and approved in 1951, referred to Bharat Varsha as 'the mother of all Bharatiyas who all have equal rights. Its recent partition, instead of solving any problem, communal or otherwise, has given rise to many new ones. Culturally, economically, politically, as well as internationally, United India is essential' (as quoted in Graham 1990: 49). But the Jana Sangh (and the RSS) also mapped out a new position in respect of secularism and Kashmir, both of which it linked to a Muslim threat to what remained of Bharat Varsha. The Jana Sangh signalled its opposition to a theocratic state – a *Khilafat* – even as it declared that: 'Secularism, as currently interpreted in this country . . . is only a euphemism for the policy of Muslim appeasement. The so-called secular composite nationalism is neither nationalism nor secularism but only a compromise with communalism of those who demand [a] price even for their lip-loyalty to this country' (p. 50, quoting the Jana Sangh Manifesto).

We shall see later how Advani and the BJP reworked this attack on India's 'pseudo-secularism'. Throughout the 1950s, 1960s and 1970s the RSS devoted itself to the task of building up a 'brotherhood in saffron', and it campaigned with the Jana Sangh and the Hindu Mahasabha for a fantastical, essentialized and racialized *Bharat*-India' from which the impurities of a Muslim fifth column would be removed, and within which differences of caste and class would be dissolved amidst the harmony of what Golwalkar liked to call 'race pride'. Notwithstanding its lack of success in the democratic political arenas of modern India, the Jana Sangh mounted an opposition of sorts to the Congress Party on issues including Kashmir (where it opposed 'concessions' to Pakistan or to Kashmiri nationalists, including Article 370), the use of Hindi as a national language (which it largely supported), the Hindu Code Bill (which it opposed in some respects but not in all), the status and legality of Pakistan (which it contested) and economic policy (where it sought to take the part of small independent producers and traders against the state, landlords and big business).

The petty-bourgeois orientation of the Jana Sangh limited its electoral appeal as much as did its fervent anti-secularism or obvious northern bias. In the General Election of 1971 its share of the vote declined to 7.4 per cent (from 9.4 per cent in 1967), and in the wake of the Emergency in 1975–7 the Jana Sangh found itself wrapped up in the Janata Party. When the Janata coalition unravelled in 1979 the political forces of Hindu nationalism were obliged to reinvent themselves once more, and in April 1980 many who had been active in the Jana Sangh and the RSS regrouped as the Bharatiya Janata Party.

The Bharatiya Janata Party and the Vishwa Hindu Parishad

The ideology of the BJP, and several of the political campaigns organized by the BJP-VHP, have certainly reworked old themes, but it is important to recognize the extraordinary dynamism and the ideological inventiveness of the constituent organizations of the *Sangh parivar* in the changing political circumstances of the 1980s and 1990s. The electoral successes of the BJP cannot be understood simply as the culmination of 'decades of disciplined, well-managed organisational and (silent) ideological expansion' (Hansen 1993: 2271) – although these have played a part, as we explained in chapter 6. We need to develop further our understanding of how it was that the *Sangh parivar* was able to exploit new spaces for political action, sometimes unwittingly perhaps, but often with great ingenuity.

The continuities and discontinuities in post-1980 Hindu nationalism emerge very clearly from an account of the *Sangh parivar's* campaigns through this period. These campaigns have consistently sought to exploit what Jaffrelot calls the 'inferiority complex' of the Hindu majority in secular India, most obviously in relation to India's Muslim 'Other', but also in relation to Christianity, the state and various of the world's great powers. It was the VHP which took the lead in many of these campaigns in the 1980s, after coming to prominence in 1981 (as we explained in chapter 5) when it protested against the conversion to Islam of some one thousand members of the Scheduled Castes in Meenakshipuram, Tamil Nadu. This followed on the heels of reports of mass conversions of Hindus in the Gulf States, and they added to fears that Islam was on the march worldwide or that it was armed with enormous sums of money. A secret note prepared for a meeting of a consultative committee of the Ministry of Home Affairs on 14 September 1981 articulated these fears when it reported that:

> Financial aid from Gulf countries to Muslim institutions, mosques and groups has ... been coming in, in many cases not through proper channels. There is enough indication that the zeal which the Jamaat-e-Islami-Hind and other revivalist groups are working in the area to accelerate the conversion of Harijans, is at least partly attributable to the resources these parties have acquired from the Muslim countries and the pan-islamic organisations over the last two or three years.[21]

It is worth noting how even 'official' (secular?) India was unable to accept that the (so-called) *Harijans* of Meenakshipuram were converting to Islam to escape from patterns of social exclusion and hierarchy that confined them to the bottom of the social pile regardless of their ability to acquire some of the trappings of material wealth. Hindu nationalism, of course, maintained a systematic silence on this issue – on this division within the so-called Hindu race – and placed the emphasis squarely on a Muslim threat, or on an international Islamic conspiracy to secure the mass conversions of *Harijans*. In a series of six articles published in the RSS's journal, the *Organiser*, Sita Rama Goel identified Christianity, 'Macaulayism' and Islam as three sources of external threat to Hindu India. He also warned that 'the death of Hindu society is no longer an eventuality impossible to envisage.'[22]

Christophe Jaffrelot is right to argue that '[one] distinguishing feature of the 1980s undoubtedly lay in the way this feeling of vulnerability was discussed and communicated to other Hindus through the appearance of other "threats" such as Sikh separatism, the influx of Bangladeshi immigrants into Assam, the visit of Pope John Paul II, and the government's "pro-Muslim bias" in the "Shah Bano controversy" and the "Rushdie affair" ' (Jaffrelot 1996: 343; and see our discussion in chapter 5). But an examination of the VHP's response to this 'threat' suggests that the challenge wasn't only perceived in religious terms. The conversions at Meenakshipuram presented a threat to the worldview of the *Sangh parivar* because they challenged the integrity and unity of the Hindu 'race', and thus the presumed connections between an essentialized and biologized account of 'being' and culture, on the one hand, and territory on the other. Towards the end of the 1980s the BJP would make determined efforts to adapt its brahmanical worldview and Sanskritic rhetorics to appeal to caste groups other than the high castes of north India. But even then the tensions between *mandir* and Mandal were rarely far below the surface, and in the early 1980s the response of the VHP to the twin threats of Islam and 'unclean' India was the deeply traditional one of presenting Mother India (*Bharat Mata*) as being under threat from external forces or fifth columns. The VHP demanded acts of atonement, purification or sacrifice to restore the glories and unity of Hindudom.

The VHP's campaigns for national unity, or around Ayodhya, from the mid 1980s have been extraordinarily effective, as we argued in chapters 5 and 6. In place of the gradualism that marked the politics of the RSS under Golwalkar, the VHP placed its faith in a more spectacular and public politics in order to create the illusion, as Advani put it, 'that you [we] are likely to come to power'.[23] Great public rituals, part religious procession, part pilgrimage, began, as we noted earlier, with the *Ekatmatayajna* (the 'All-India Sacrifice For Unity') in 1983. Three large and well-organized processions traversed India, mapping out an account of *Bharat*-India which was indebted to Savarkar's ideas about the mythological unity of the country. At their heads were trucks decked out as temple chariots, on which images of gods were carried as in temple rituals. The imagery of the temple chariot was blended with the 'militant symbolism of the war chariot of Arjuna in the Bhagavad Gita', a text which speaks of 'the duty of the warrior to fight when war is inevitable' (van der Veer 1994: 125). Ritual creations of this kind have since then become regular events.[24] In 1984 there was the *janmabhoomi yatra*; in 1989 the *ramshilapuja*; in 1990 the *rath yatra* which was organized by the BJP in protest against Mandal; there were processions in 1995 and 1996 directed at the 'liberation' of temples at Kashi and Mathura; and in September 1995 an *ekatmata yatra* which converged finally on the stupa of Dr Ambedkar and which was supposed, clearly, 'to rally militant dalits and tribal people', and to restore to India the harmony between Hindus, Buddhists and Jains which is said to have existed before the Muslim and the British invasions (Assayag 1998). These carefully orchestrated events – not all equally successful, and some of them failures – have served several symbolic and practical political purposes. Their 'militant cartography', claiming the public space, has been aimed at 'periodically rejuvenating the body of India' and they have become 'the instrument for a xenophobic and revanchist renegotiation of the nation' (pp. 140, 142). They have been successful in drawing in large numbers of people by playing on a few emotive stereotypes – *Bharat*, Rama, Gangamata – through intense use of a variety of media. And: 'Ancient pilgrimage paths were taken so as to stop in a few sacred sites, which the selective memory of the Hindu community transformed into "traumatic places" of humiliation inflicted by Muslim "foreigners"' (p. 141). Through these events politics have been reconfigured on a religious base.

At the heart of the imaginative geography of Hindu nationalism is the city of Ayodhya in eastern Uttar Pradesh. The destruction of the Babri Masjid can be seen, in part, as the culmination of a long campaign by Hindu nationalists to define – or imagine – Hindudom (*Akhand Bharat*) as the territory of a race of Hindus which stretches from the Indus to the Seas. Ayodhya stands at the centre of the west–east axis of this sacred territory. More importantly, Ayodhya is the capital city of Rama, an incarnation of Vishnu which has been made to appear martial by the ideologues of the *Sangh parivar*, and by centring its political campaigns on the site of the Babri Masjid-*Ramjanmabhoomi* the VHP summoned up an avenging and masculine Hinduism. The forces of *Hindutva* would reclaim *Bharat* from the 'two imperialisms' – Muslim and British – which were cankers in the body of Hindudom and which had turned the country away from its true and natural course. As ever, masculinity was a critical trope in the politics of Hindu nationalism.

As we saw in the Cow Protection Movement in the late nineteenth and early twentieth centuries, Hindu nationalism imagines the nation as feminine – *Bharat Mata* – and has aimed to create a modern masculine Hindu culture so that her 'sons' shall be capable of protecting her. In place of the supposedly effete or androgynistic – not to say appeasing – Hinduism of Gandhi, and of the imagination of Orientalist scholarship in the west, the *Sangh parivar* sought to forge a unity between the disciplined bodies of individual Hindu males and the re-made body of the nation. This was the ultimate purpose of the RSS *shakhas* – and as we argued earlier the organizational discipline, and the disciplined behaviour of individual *swayamsevaks*, has marked out the RSS from most other movements and organizations.

Just as the female body of the nation had to be made pure by driving out the foreign bodies of Islam and the British Raj (including 'bodies' like the Taj Mahal and the Victoria Memorial in Calcutta according to some accounts), so too should the male body be made resolute against the sins of the flesh. The campaigns around the Babri Masjid coincided with a renewed interest in wrestling in parts of north India (see Alter 1992). They also coincided with an attack upon degenerate westernism, whether in the form of western attachments to beef or the cinema. According to the VHP ideologue, Shastri: 'As a form of entertainment, cinema is a great enemy of modern society. It is full of obscene, erotic, and indecent images which enter the sub-conscious, lie dormant, and then result in night-emission' (quoted in Alter 1994: 49). Hindu nationalism aims at the sublimation of sexual energy into ideologically purified services to the mother nation.

But while there are strong continuities in the messages of Hindu nationalism as between the 1920s and the 1980s, it is misleading to see the events of the 1980s or 1990s as the simple or logical culmination of the well-worn plans of the *Sangh parivar*. The Ayodhya campaigns of the late 1980s and 1990s were remarkable for their violence and for their re-working of a fairly conventional and deeply territorial iconography of Hindu nationalism. But these campaigns also broke fresh ground in their use of 'mass-mediated images' (Rajagopal 1994: 1659), and these images helped the BJP to exploit the 'opening space' in Indian politics (created, as we argued in chapter 6, by the decline of the Congress) to its massive and unexpected political advantage.[25] In the period from January 1987 to August 1989 the cause of Hindu nationalism was boosted by the decision of the state-owned television network, Dordoorshan, to screen weekly instalments of a serialization of the *Ramayana*. As directed by Ramanand Sagar, and as further developed by Advani and the BJP, the hero of this epic tale, Lord Rama, was presented not as a gentle family man, 'flanked by Sita and Lakshman, with Hanuman at their feet', but as 'a solitary hero ... striking a range of poses as if to suit the varying mood of the consumer: child-like, adult and war-like, benevolent and godly, and so on' (Rajagopal 1994: 1663).[26]

Rajagopal accepts that not all consumers of the Ramayana telecast received the story in the ways that Sagar may have intended, or as it was reinterpreted by the VHP, but he insists that the Sunday screenings of the Ramayana made 'the notion of a great Hindu culture as a libidinal collectivity ... familiar, domesticated and comfortable' (p. 1662). The so-called secular state became the principal vehicle by which the Ayodhya movement was placed before the Indian public. The television version of the Ramayana also used the personal narrative of Rama's discovery of himself and his 'birthplace' to forge 'a broader historical narrative of the failure of post-Independence India – with Rama presented as a national symbol, even the national symbol, of a return to origins, as an attempt at revitalisation, of the renewal of the distinctive energy and spirit of the national project' (p. 1662). As reworked by the *Sangh parivar* in its calendars, pamphlets, Ramayana videos, audiocassettes and the like, this narrative of loss and redemption became a telling critique of a once strong nation of Hindus brought to its knees first by the Muslims (and the British) and more recently by the Congress and allied pseudo-secularists – the people who have lost touch with the essentials of *Hindutva*. The destruction of the Babri Masjid was more than just an assault on a mosque, important though that was: it was also an attack upon the secular principles of the Indian state and a terrifying climax to a politics of revenge and redemption. The Hindus who tore down the Masjid were exhorted by various pamphlets circulating in and around Ayodhya to be 'Angry Hindus' – angry men (and women) who should have the courage to fight back against a Muslim threat which was putting 'India in Danger' *now*. Hindu nationalists represented themselves as the protectors of a nation under threat; a nation which had been fatally weakened from within.

Significantly, amongst the most powerful voices heard at Ayodhya, urging on the destruction of the mosque, and goading Hindu men into violence against Muslims, were those of two women, Sadhvi Rithambara and Uma Bharati. They are to be heard still on widely distributed cassette tapes – 'Rithambara's voice circulates with the ubiquity of a one-rupee coin in north India' (T. Basu et al. 1993: 100). And for a good many observers the most striking and deeply shocking form of women's activism in contemporary India is their vigorous participation in Hindu violence against Muslim families. Amongst many other examples: 'Rural women at Bhagalpur in 1989 or upper middle class Maruti-driving women at Ahmedabad in 1991 have appropriated active roles on the centre of riot scenes' (p. 79); 'In October 1990 in the town of Bijnor in western Uttar Pradesh, Hindu women led a procession through a Muslim neighbourhood with *trishuls* (tridents) in hand, shouting bigoted, inflammatory slogans. In the aftermath of the violence in which several hundred people were killed, these women radiated pride at their actions' (A. Basu 1998: 167).

Why is it that women who are themselves so often the object of violence in patriarchal households in contemporary South Asia, participate in this way in violence which is often directed against other women? There is no simple answer to this question, but we can start to find one through a consideration of the gender ideology of Hindu nationalism. The image of woman in this discourse – as in the discourses of Hinduism – is both that of the Mother, and also that of Durga, the goddess who is a fearsome killer. The ideology of *Hindutva* contrives to combine 'a revitalized moral vision of domestic and sexual norms that promises to restore the comforts of old sociabilities and familial solidarities' with the incorporation of women 'as leaders of anti-Muslim violence [allowing them] a new role in activism that was earlier withheld . . . [so] Older forms of gender ideology are merged with new offers of self-fashioning and relative political equality in the field of anti-Muslim and anti-secular violence' (T. Sarkar 1998: 104).

The great public events which have been created by the *Sangh parivar*, the *yatras*, and finally the destruction of the Babri Masjid, have been associated, as our accounts in earlier chapters have described, with numerous incidents of communal violence, among them the Bombay riots of 1992–3. These incidents have occurred in diverse contexts, involving different factors – including material ones, such as the purposive destruction of property, or struggles for control over turf. They are certainly not 'mindless', and Stanley Tambiah has shown from careful comparative analysis of crowd violence that they regularly include similar features – which 'might form part of a manual of communal violence in South Asia' (1996: 231) – including processions which claim public space, rallies and public speeches, and particular triggering actions (like the slaughter of cows, or playing religious music in an antagonistic way). They reflect and they reproduce existing forms of subjectivity which are based partly on discourses about the 'Other', such as those perfected by Hindu nationalism, but also on the routine experience of religious difference, like that which Assayag describes, and of what Hansen calls the experience of 'back-to-back intimacy', where powerful stereotypes develop in circumstances in which there is only limited social interaction amongst neighbours. These images are reinforced through the power of rumour and by narratives about, as well as in the actual experience of riots. Finally, as Thomas Hansen puts it: 'We (may) regard communal violence as integral to the specific struggle for the constitution of national and ethnic differences within the historically produced political field in

India' (1999: 209). Communal violence is not a separate phenomenon but rather the dark side of nationalism.

A summing up: why should the message of Hindu nationalism have played so well?

The assertion of Hindu nationalism in the last decade, after a century of struggle in which it seemed for so long and to so many – not least to political scientists – to be only a marginal influence, has certainly drawn on the failures of the earlier nationalist elite – those 'tall men' whom we discussed in chapter 3. Kumar's point – it is Kaviraj's too – about the failure of that elite 'to consolidate its legitimacy by nurturing relevant symbols of India's incipient statehood' (cited above) is a powerful one. The symbols of modernity that Nehru articulated, through his progresses to the (literally) concrete achievements of the developmental state – the dams, factories and power stations that he sometimes described as 'temples' of the new India – were not entirely lifeless. But they were meaningful principally to the middle classes who were already active participants in the modernizing mission of the state. The mass of the people were the objects not the authors of modern development, and not much is known about the meaning of the new 'temples' to them. It may be that Kaviraj takes too far his insight about the 'neighbourly incommunication' between the spheres of middle-class and of subaltern discourse (see chapter 2), but a gap there assuredly was. And it was a gap which came to be occupied to a degree by the ideas of Hindu nationalism, partly through its influence on the establishment of Hindi, and on education in the medium of that language, partly through the activities and the influence of the RSS, and latterly through the sheer genius of the use by the VHP of ritual and of modern media. At the same time the constituency for cultural nationalism has grown larger across a wide spectrum of Indian society, from the middle and upper class and mainly upper-caste elites who are fearful of the disorderly realm of democratic politics and of the threats which it poses to their privilege to the frustrated, semi-educated and often unemployed youth of the cities who are offered action and an enemy.

For various reasons – some of them unwitting – the *Sangh parivar* in the 1980s developed what Hansen has called a 'multi-layered and ingenious Hindu nationalist discourse' centred on Rama (1996c: 608), and melded this to an organizational culture which placed a premium on discipline and a cell-like structure at the grass-roots level. We have emphasized the distinctiveness of the BJP as a political party (even if not across the country as a whole). The forces of Hindu nationalism were able to take advantage of the disintegration of the Congress party at the local level, and the failure of the Congress-(I) under Indira and Rajiv Gandhi, to abide by India's secular principles. As a number of commentators have remarked, the *Sangh parivar* was able, too, to exploit a political and economic landscape in the post-Indira period that was characterized by high levels of uncertainty and a fair degree of disenchantment with the projects of modernization and nation-building that had been pursued since 1947. Building on fears of an aggressive Islam without and a 'pampered' Muslim minority within, and a feeling that India's imitation of the west had failed to make it the west's equal or gain the west's respect, the BJP was well placed in the 1990s to argue for a Hindudom that would exchange its modern feet of clay in a globalizing world for the strong anchorage of a mythical Hindu past. In place of 'pseudo-secularism', the BJP began to argue for a 'true secularism' that would offer 'rule by the majority according to ancient Hindu principles. True secularism meant Hindu majoritarianism and the subordination of cultural minorities, not least the Muslims' (p. 608).

But *if* Hindu nationalism succeeded where the older modernizing elite did not, or cared not to, in communicating with those outside its own charmed circle, the deep flaw within it which limits its success in reinventing modern India, is that its organic conception of Hindu society has still not been persuasive to many (most?) of those who have historically been the subjects of caste and class oppression – even though some of them may have participated in its theatre of violence.[27] The message of Hindu nationalism has played well. But whether or not the Hindu nationalism which is still epitomized by the RSS will finally be successful in reinventing modern India as a *Hindu rashtra* is doubtful – for the reasons that we have alluded to here and which we will explore further in the next chapter. The BJP may well be more successful than it has been already, and win wider electoral support both geographically and socially. But this is likely to depend upon conjunctural factors – such as the splits in the opposition which were so apparent in the summer of 1999 before the Thirteenth Lok Sabha elections – and the gap between what it is able to achieve and the goals of the (religious) nationalist movement are likely to be very wide. Its authoritarian tendencies confront the rising tide of Indian democracy and the irreducible pluralism of Indian society.

8.3   The Politics of Secularism and Anti-secularism

The rise to power of the BJP, and even more so the demonstrations of religiosity which have helped to underpin a resurgent Hindu nationalism, have occasioned a profound rethinking of state–society relations within India's intellectual and public policy establishments. Although many intellectuals continue to speak up for India's secular principles (or a version thereof), some others have advanced a critique of Indian secularism which is unquestionably powerful, and which shares with Thomas Blom Hansen the view that the 'secularism and the hyper-rationalism of the Nehruvian state' was a myth – not in the sense in which we have used this word, but in the sense of a 'sham'. It might appear that there is little more point in trying to restore that secularism, when it is shot through with contradictions and anomalies, than there is in trying to go back to 'the Third Way' of building socialism. But just as our criticism of Indian planning does not lead us to accept the economic arguments of neo-liberalism, so we do not accept the conclusions which are drawn by the foremost intellectual critics of Indian 'secularism': T. N. Madan and Partha Chatterjee, to whose work we have already referred, and Ashis Nandy.

These writers – Chatterjee and Nandy explicitly so, but Madan too, by association of ideas – are the most powerful voices amongst those whom Pranab Bardhan has recently described as 'anarcho-communitarian', who aim to call fundamentally into question the whole enterprise of the rationalizing and modernizing state, and who would substitute for it the reconstruction of society on the basis of indigenous communities. In this view the outcome of the struggle against colonialism was a pyrrhic victory, because the nationalist elite took over the rationalizing project of the colonizers and sought to make a reality of it through the scheme of planned, national economic development (see also Inden 1995). This project, supposedly, could not and cannot succeed in the institutional context of Indian society. The result has been that the modernizing project has been imposed on people by the state and constitutes an apparatus of control.[28]

Like Bardhan, we have some sympathy for the criticism of the way in which a small elite 'arrogated to itself the title to speak on behalf of the society in general' (1997: 189). But we too are not persuaded by the conclusions which the 'anarcho-communitarians' draw about an alternative politics for the years ahead. The way ahead, for these thinkers, is through struggle '[a]gainst [the] arrogant, intolerant, self-aggrandising rational subject of modernity...[by]...trying to resurrect the virtues of the fragmentary, the local and the subjugated in order to unmask the will to power that lies at the very heart of modern rationality' (Chatterjee 1993). What this means, in practice, is a turn to the local, and to a concept of 'community' – and to 'religion as faith'. The final chapter of Chatterjee's *The Nation and Its Fragments* (1993) is a passionate restatement of that sense of the loss of 'community' which also drives the work of Weber and Durkheim – and of Marx, too (see Sayer 1991). The problem is, for us as for Bardhan, how to square this ideal with the realities of local power in India and the possibility that the 'traditional community' is actually shot through by inequality and injustice.[29]

The rise of militant Hinduism in the 1980s and 1990s has been vigorously contested by these intellectuals, but not through a defence of secularism. Ashis Nandy has declared emphatically that he is not a secularist: 'In fact, I can be called an anti-secularist' (1990: 73; and 1985). T. N. Madan, though he does not make the same assumptions as Nandy about the inherent tolerance of South Asian religions, has joined him in arguing that secularism is an alien concept in India, and in arguing for a politics of pluralism and toleration that respects the realities of religion as 'faith' and not as 'ideology', and which draws part of its inspiration from Gandhi. Chatterjee's case also relies less than does Nandy's on assumptions about 'inherent tolerance', but he too is opposed to the idea that the state should impose a framework for the cultural rights of minorities from 'outside'. He argues for a 'strategic politics of demanding toleration' which involves a two-fold struggle – 'resist homogenisation from the outside and push for democratisation inside' (1997a [1994]: 261).

For Nandy, militant Hinduism is like secular nationalism in being 'fearful of diversities, intolerant of dissent... and panicky about any self-assertion or search for autonomy by ethnic groups' (Nandy et al. 1995: 19). He is able to lump together secular and religious nationalisms as violent, *dirigiste* projects (or as reactions to these projects) because of the ways in which he conceives of the state and modernity, on the one hand, and religion on the other. In Nandy's view, the nation-state is a power container that is defined by the violence which it is bound to dispense in its quest to govern the margins of the country that it claims to represent and to speak for. In post-colonial India – as in late British India – the lifeworlds of India's 'social majorities' (religious lifeworlds, local lifeworlds, plural lifeworlds) have been dismissed or partially transformed by the discourses of modernization and secularism, with the result that people have either suffered from a loss of dignity or have turned to a false religion – religious fundamentalism – in a tragic effort to take charge of the state in the name of a political project that outdoes the violence of its secular counterpart.

It is here that Nandy makes use of a distinction between 'religion as faith' and 'religion as ideology' which is empirically suspect and (finally) unsustainable. It is also the basis of the alternative which he proposes, both to secular nationalism and to militant Hinduism. Nandy maintains that the true religions of South Asia are religions of faith, meaning 'religion as a way of life', religious ways of being which are inherently open, heterodox and syncretic, whereas the modern state and the Hindu nationalists deal with religion as ideology – 'populations contesting for or protecting non-religious, usually political or socio-economic interests' – which is a perversion of the true nature of religion (1998: 330). The doctrine of secularism is an ideology which promises that the state will maintain an equal distance from all religions, but which in practice seeks to contain or dismiss religious ideas in the name of reason or modernity. It is, then, 'definitionally ethnophobic and frequently ethnocidal' (p. 331); while militant Hinduism is a perversion of religion as faith.

Madan is less willing than Nandy to dismiss secularism for the violence of its will to power, and he concedes that in the west secularism contributed to the enlargement of human freedom. But he does describe secularism as an alien import in South Asia,[30] and he joins with Nandy in suggesting that the adoption of secularism as a state ideology – what he calls the 'dream of a minority which wants to shape the majority in its own image' (Madan 1987: 748) – is at odds with the everyday understandings of India's masses and with the hierarchical traditions of South Asia's own religions. The political lessons that he draws are not always very clear – his concern is, as he says, to analyse not to prescribe. But the implication of his work seems to be that the violent landscapes of modern Indian politics will be mended only by a return to religion as faith; that is, to the open and tolerant worlds of a religion which refuses to be corrupted by the state or by politicians and atheists, whether this be Hinduism, Islam, Buddhism or Sikhism.

Partha Chatterjee's key point is not so much that secularism is an alien ideology in India, but rather that in practice – as we also have argued, drawing substantially on his analysis – the state has failed to keep religion and politics apart, or to keep government at an equal distance from competing faiths. He joins with Madan and Nandy in arguing for a politics of religious toleration, but with a twist that comes from his reading of Foucault and the communitarians. Chatterjee insists that an effective defence of 'minority cultural rights' must take its cue from a politics of difference that empowers minorities to say 'we will not give reasons for not being like you.' In more detail, and with reference to 'the specifics of the Indian situation':

> my approach would not call for any axiomatic approval to a uniform civil code for all citizens. Rather it would start from the historically given reality of separate religion-based personal laws and the intricate involvement of state agencies in the affairs of religious institutions. Here legal citizenship already stands qualified by the legal recognition of religious differences; the 'wall of separation' doctrine cannot be strictly applied either. Given the inapplicability of the neutrality principle, therefore, it becomes necessary to find a criterion by which state involvement, when it occurs in the domain of religion, can appear to the members of a religious group as both legitimate and fair. Toleration...can, it seems to me, supply us with this criterion...What this will mean in institutional terms are processes through which each religious group will publicly seek and obtain from its members consent for its practices insofar as those practices have regulative power over the members. [Hence the dictum we referred to: 'resist homogenization from outside, fight for democracy within'.] (1997a [1994]: 258)

He thus opposes a politics of accommodation from within to a coercive politics of state-directed normalization (the secular ideal) from without, and in this respect, as in the hope that true communities of believers will remove religion as ideology from the realm of democratic politics, Chatterjee's argument bears comparison with those of Nandy and Madan.

A defence of secularism in India

These arguments warrant a more substantial critique than we can offer here, but this is a task which has been taken up by others (most notably, perhaps, by Bhargava 1994, and Vanaik 1997, ch. 4). The most important points in relation to our own arguments are these. The 'anti-secularist' position depends upon a sharp distinction being drawn between the disposition to violence that supposedly marks the linked projects of statism, modernization and secularism on the one hand, and the commitments to toleration and non-violence which are supposedly to be found in South Asian religious traditions. But this distinction is unconvincing. Anti-secularists make their arguments with reference to a caricatured view of the post-colonial state in India, and a conception of religion as faith which is bluntly asserted rather than properly argued through.

For Nandy, the state is seemingly a site of violence and nothing else. He arrives at this conclusion because for him, as for Gandhi, modernization is a deeply violent, dislocating and disenchanting process which turns human beings away from their true selves – and it is the state, of course, which has driven the process of modernization in India. Secularism is read as one moment of a zealous attempt to normalize the Other – and so Nandy writes of it as 'ethnophobic and frequently ethnocidal' (cited above), and as resembling nothing so much as 'the crusading and inquisitorial role of religious ideologies' (1998: 337). In so doing, Nandy fails to convey a sense of the enabling dimensions of state power, with the result that questions of access to the state, or of state capacity, figure only thinly in his politics. Politics, for Nandy, is premised on the need to oppose or dissolve the state, and to this end he is prepared to describe secularism in India as if it was a threat – and only a threat – to the possibility of religious faith. But this is far from being the case. Nehru's India differed from the USSR or Ataturk's Turkey precisely in terms of its regard for religious freedoms, a point that Madan clearly recognizes. Though it seems almost to pain him to say so, Madan writes that: 'It must be admitted...that the pluralistic situation which Nehru and the other framers of the Constitution faced was immensely more complex than anything that Lenin, and far less Ataturk, faced: yet the fact remains that Nehru did not use his undoubted hold over the people as a leader of the freedom movement and his vast authority as head of government to bring communal tendencies under strict control [a policy of atheism born of authoritarianism]' (1987: 757). Madan goes on to suggest that Nehru's reluctance to police India's religions had less to do with his liberalism than with his faith 'about the decline of the hold of religion on the minds of people' (p. 757), but the concession has been made and a lapse into caricature avoided.

But this in turn raises questions about Madan's work and arguments. If Madan accepts that secularism in India has not sought to ride roughshod over religious sensibilities, on what grounds does he seek to put secularism in its place? Madan seems to be arguing that secularism *should* not work in India because it is a foreign ideology and because it fails to chime with the totalizing and hierarchical worldviews of South Asia's own religions, and most obviously Hinduism. But these are curious arguments and they lack conviction. It is not clear why the foreign origins of secularism should make it unsuitable for service in South Asia, particularly where secularism is intended as a guide to state policy and not as a policy for the eradication of religious faith. André Beteille makes the point that the Constitution of

India 'marks a departure from tradition in its stress not only on secularism but also on equality and liberty' (1994: 560). He also writes that:

> It would be peevish to find fault with a constitution or a plan for a new way of life on the ground that it is the work of intellectuals who constitute a minuscule minority. Nor is it reasonable to denigrate a constitution on the ground that many of its basic components have had their origin in other traditions than our own. Surely, the test of an idea or an institution is whether it is able or unable to meet our present needs and not its provenance. (p. 560)

There is also the real danger, in Madan's work, that a Brahmanical view of the 'totalizing' lifeworlds of Hindus is adopted as of right and without critical reflection. Beteille makes the point that 'those who wrote [the] constitution were more representative of it [the Indian population] than the authors of the *Dharmashastras*' (p. 560), but this is not the impression given by Madan. Madan's appeal to the totalizing worldview of Hinduism exaggerates the contrast between the domestic and the alien which he is so keen to draw, and it imposes and unhelpful silence on various challenges to the Brahmanical conception of Hinduism as a hierarchizing totality. It was precisely to avoid the totalizing and hegemonic claims of Brahmanism that Ambedkar opted for a principle of secularism and for a religious worldview (Buddhism) which refused the assimilationist claims of Brahmanical Hinduism.

These moments of silence and refusal point up the most worrying aspect of the politics of anti-secularism: its uncritical attitudes towards religious faith and the presumed virtues of religious communities. In place of a reasoned defence of secularism, anti-secularists make an appeal to a politics of toleration which takes for granted precisely that which it must demonstrate. Secularism, as Bhargava reminds us, 'developed initially in response to situations of inter-religious conflict. In conditions of religious warfare and more generally in the face of irresolvable conflicts the only way to exclude the blind pursuit of ultimate ideals, to expel from public life frenzy and hysteria which they usually generate, and to protect ordinary life, is to embrace political secularism' (1994: 1787).[31] Anti-secularism, in contrast, assumes that violence is unknown to religion as faith (violence comes only from the corruption of faith), and suggests that disputes between religious communities will recede to the extent that these communities are free to police themselves without recourse to a set of rules or procedures laid down by the state.

This argument is complacent. Christopher Bayly has argued that incidents of communal violence were not unknown before the consolidation of British rule in India. His argument calls into question the idea that communalism was a colonial construction pure and simple, an argument that is necessary for the prosecution of a broader and less reliable argument about a golden age of religious harmony in pre-modern India.[32] More seriously, a post-modern refusal to accept 'external' guidelines for political action or negotiation leaves the armoury of anti-secularism bare when it comes to the adjudication of disputes *between* religious and ethnic groups. Chatterjee's defence of the 'right not to give a reason for being different' might empower social groups against the state, but it has little to say about the resolution of disputes between groups with contending worldviews and yet overlapping lifeworlds (say Muslims and Hindus); it also has little to say to those groups within 'a group' who extend a politics of toleration in one direction and yet fail to see it reciprocated (for example, low-caste Hindus who might admit high-caste Hindus to 'their' temples or wells only to find that high-caste Hindus are invoking a right to be different to protect their own privileges). It speaks not at all to the problems of gender relations.

For all its undoubted strengths, a radicalized politics of difference – what we might call an essentialized politics of difference – is only likely to succeed in conditions where there is a low level of interaction between social groups with more than one set of ultimate ideals. In other conditions, and assuming that this so-called golden age cannot be invented anew, it is incumbent on societies to refer conflicts between contending groups to a set of rules or procedures that are widely agreed. These rules are not so much a substitute for a politics of toleration or difference as a grounding for them. If appeals to 'difference' or 'toleration' are to have any purchase they must accept an external principle that seeks to ensure that two or more parties agree to the same criterion for respecting difference. To put it another way, an appeal to difference presupposes an appeal to sameness, if and where that appeal to difference is sought to be reciprocated.

It is in this specific sense that we are prepared to raise the charge of complacency against the protagonists of anti-secularism in India. We accept the force and integrity of several of the arguments made by Nandy, Madan and Chatterjee, and we are certainly not arguing against a politics that recognizes religiosity (rather than just 'respecting' it – this is Madan's point), or toleration, or an expanded conception of difference and democracy. But we are concerned that the anti-state and pro-community logics of the anti-secularist position will prove to be less than robust in organizing a political opposition to the exclusionary projects of militant Hinduism. It is important that a case for toleration is allied to a reasoned case for political secularism.[33] Anti-secularism presents its agendas for change on the basis of a romanticized account of religious faith or community, and in the wake of its ringing denunciations of the state and modernity. It fails to measure up to the task that it sets for itself: the task of opposing the violence that is written into the worldviews of religion as ideology. It also fails to acknowledge the ways in which many poorer groups in India have been empowered by the state or by an ideology of secularism, or, indeed, by secularizing institutions, wittingly or otherwise.[34] In the next chapter we describe some of the political campaigns and ideologies which have sought to advance agendas of popular democracy and to challenge the exclusionary discourses both of economic liberalization and of Hindu nationalism.

9

Transfers of Power? Subaltern Politics, Sites of Empowerment and the Reshaping of India's Democracy

India has seen two transfers of power, one from the British to the Indians and the second from the upper castes/classes to the middle ranks, but not a third transfer: power sharing with the bottom half of society. This will come about, but it will take a long time. Meanwhile, as the bottom cried 'upward' and those above cry 'back', there will be turmoil and some violence as elements within society test both the goals and the institutions of the constitution.

Granville Austin (1993: 119)

We do not want a little place in Brahman alley. We want the rule of the whole country. Change of heart, liberal education will not end our state of exploitation.... To eradicate the injustice against Dalits, they themselves must become rulers. This is the people's democracy.

Dalit Panther 1973, quoted in Omvedt (1996: 334)

Towards the end of his comparative account of dictatorship and democracy in the modern world, Barrington Moore argued that 'if democracy means the opportunity to play a meaningful part as a rational human being in determining one's own fate in life, democracy does not yet exist in the Indian countryside. The Indian peasant has not yet acquired the material and intellectual perquisites for democratic society' (1966: 408). Since the time that Moore was writing in the early 1960s India's 'peasants' have come to play a significant role in India's democratic polity, both in terms of their participation in social movements (like the farmers' movements which we described in chapter 5) and in the elections that must be held at least every five years at national, regional and (under the revived *panchayati Raj* legislation) local levels. Varshney suggests that 'farm pressures in party and non-party politics... increased in the 1980s to the extent that there are virtually no dissenting voices left in party politics arguing against the farmers' demands' (1995: 183). At the same time, however, as he goes on to relate, much of the energy expended by India's farmers in or around the Commission on Agricultural Costs and Prices has come to nought because real power lies with the Finance Ministry, and the politics which matters is the 'inter-bureaucratic politics of the state institutions' concerned with India's rural economy.

In other words, and as Ayasha Jalal argues from a very different perspective, the theatre and spectacle of representative politics in India – regular elections in the world's largest democracy – can obscure a growing concentration of power among political and economic elites which operate away from the front-stage of party politics. Jalal, indeed, maintains that a democratic-authoritarian state in India has ridden roughshod over the developmental aspirations of India's social majorities, and she contends that the Indian state has allowed a commitment to undivided sovereignty to underpin a series of genocidal programmes – or police actions – around the periphery of the so-called nation-state, both on its north-eastern frontiers and in Punjab and Kashmir. The recent work of Paul Brass, too, concerns the ways in which configurations of power in north India are buttressed by the control which local elites exercise over a corrupt police force and an increasingly demoralized bureaucracy. In States like Bihar or Uttar Pradesh the lack of accountability of government at the local level has encouraged subaltern social movements to challenge the authority of the state from without. Naxalism is often mentioned in this regard, and the Chipko *andolan* has been widely acclaimed for its anti-state and anti-development outlook (as we acknowledge in the first part of this chapter).

The work of Jalal and Brass is complemented in a recent account of democracy and the state in India by Niraja Gopal Jayal, which makes the important observation that: 'Despite the clamour of celebration that attends every election ritual, and the tributes paid to the vibrancy and resilience of Indian democracy, there is cause for concern in that intermediaries are crucial to this democracy, not just as brokers of votes, but also to represent the needs of the vulnerable' (1999: 255). Jayal has in mind the ways in which 'Muslim women divorcees did not represent their own cases' in the wake of the Shah Bano affair, or the fact that 'it took a group of middle-class activists to energize the movement against the Sardar Sarovar dam in the Narmada valley' (pp. 255–6). It is not just the case, then, that many women or tribals continue to lack access to education in India, which is the point that animates Barrington Moore's remarks on India's weak democracy; it is also the fact that, as a trip to any Block Office in Bihar will confirm, poorer men and women – and especially women – will be kept waiting for hours or even days to gain access to a government officer responsible for the allocation of pensions or some other benefit. And when the audience is at last secured it is almost always with the help of a *dalal* (broker or contractor) or other intermediary. Many voters are not able to speak directly to 'government'.

But the failings of India's democracy – and the erosion of political institutions, including, most notably, the Congress Party – should not be taken as a sign of the absence of democracy, or of the failure of India's democracy to offer some forms of protection or advancement to the poor. Niraja Jayal recognizes that democracy is not a discrete variable, and she points out that various discourses of resistance (as around the Sardar Sarovar dam) have deepened India's democratic cultures, just as a vigilant press and a 'judiciary receptive to public interest legislation' (p. 238) pushed the state to respond, finally and fitfully, to famine deaths in the Kalahandi District of Orissa in the 1990s.[1] Countries are more or less democratic, and the connections between democracy, empowerment and development are often forged in strange and contradictory ways, and as a result of the unintended consequences of state policy, or even state failure. In the second and third parts of this chapter we chart the uneven and contested ways in which India's 'Backward Communities' have inserted themselves into the political process at local, State and national levels: a process of incorporation that Austin refers to as a second transfer of power in India, and which we believe constitutes a third moment in the reinvention of India in the 1990s (a decade that belonged to Laloo Prasad Yadav in Bihar and Mulayam Singh Yadav in Uttar Pradesh as much as it belonged to Manmohan Singh or Atal Behari Vajpayee). We review the enabling role of government policies in respect of education, agrarian reform, credit provision and reservation (in the breach as well as in the observance), and we consider the ways in which a diverse group of 'Backward' communities has sought to rework long histories of anti-Brahman politics to challenge for power in the country. The achievements of India's Other Backward Classes are more obvious than those of India's Scheduled Communities (*dalits* and *adivasis*), but there are signs that these last-named communities are now beginning to make their numbers count. Even the BJP is having to prosecute its conservative and exclusionary politics by including amongst its representatives some members of the plebian (or *bahujan*) communities from whose wider ranks is emerging a challenge to the 'revolt of the elite' that we described in chapter 8.[2]

It is true, of course, that the rise to power of various Scheduled or Backward Caste parties does not guarantee an improvement in the livelihoods or social standing of the social groups that propelled them into power. Nor should we assume that the politics of the *Sangh parivar* will be tempered by the inclusion amongst its ranks of non-'Forward Caste' members or representatives. Herein lies the force of Paul Brass's critique of the state in India. Politicians of the poor can be coopted or corrupted by the real powers in the land, and we can be returned, very swiftly, to the argument that the poor will be empowered only by community-based or anti-state social movements (or by voluntary groups or NGOs). But while this argument fits neatly with the concerns of the anarcho-communitarians (see our comments in chapter 8), it is glumly one-sided in its understandings of the state and the political process in India *and* in its accounts of community and social movements. In the fourth part of the chapter we argue that it is misleading to suppose that citizens' movements, NGOs and community organizations – for all their evident vibrancy in India – provide an alternative to the state. Our analysis leads us to distinguish between the ways in which democratic government works in different parts of the country according to the balance of class power. We contend that citizens' movements are most effective where they put pressure on the state to take the part of the poor, or to protect the poor from some of the abuses heaped upon them. We also suggest that contemporary concerns about 'corruption' in public life, while they point up a warranted cynicism about the workings of politics or government, also help to define norms and standards for public servants, and – potentially at least – provide for leverage for political activism. The state in India might indeed be increasingly rotten, but it is not accurate to say that ordinary men and women have lost faith, entirely, in the idea of the state, or what Thomas Hansen calls the mythology of the 'sublime' state.

9.1   Democratic Pretensions

The ideal of justice and everyday practices

On 6 August 1991 a group of *dalit* men in Chunduru, Andhra Pradesh, were massacred, it is alleged, by a police party under the leadership of Circle Inspector Saibaba. The massacre followed a period during which local Reddy landowners had organized a boycott of the *dalit* community, and was prompted, it seems, by an incident in a nearby cinema (on 4 July) when a *dalit* student sitting in the chair class had crossed his legs and 'touched an upper caste viewer in the chair ahead' (Samata Sanghatana 1991: 2079). The massacre in Chunduru was hardly an isolated event. Reports produced by the Commissioner for Scheduled Castes and Scheduled Tribes record the number of 'harijan atrocities' on a State-by-State basis, and in Bihar the villages of Belchi (1977), Bishrampur (1978), Pipra (1980), Arwal (1986), Sarathua (1995), Bathanitola (1996), Nanuar (1997), Haibaspur (1997), Lakshmanpur-Bathe (1997) and Shankarbigha (1999) define a gruesome geography of upper-caste or police attacks upon *dalits* and other poor people.[3] The massacres in Bihar took place against a background of continuing caste violence since the Emergency, but they peaked in the late 1970s, when Karpoori Thakur's Janata party was in power, and in the 1990s, when Laloo Prasad Yadav's Janata Dal (or Rashtriya Janata Dal) again moved against the interests of Bihar's Brahman-Bhumihar-Rajput elites. As in Chunduru, upper-caste violence against *dalits* or the labouring poor was in response to lower-caste challenges to established privilege. Such attacks were also meant to reinforce the institution of untouchability. Notwithstanding the passing of the Untouchability Offences Act of 1955, the Chunduru incident revealed that the institution of untouchability is still widely regarded and defended by high-caste Indians, even (and perhaps especially) when *dalits* refuse to accept the restrictions on mobility and behaviour that untouchability imposes.

The broader issue here concerns the gap between the state's official stance against untouchability or 'casteism' and the everyday practices of exploitation and repression that are ignored or even reproduced by officers of the state. Notwithstanding all the fine speeches and Acts which have followed Independence,[4] the state in India has a poor record of empowering its poorest citizens to behave as active agents pursuing their own interests. Land reform acts have been passed and promptly ignored, and the state has often failed to protect those few *dalits* and *adivasis* ('tribals') who have received an education, or acquired a degree, from the most extreme forms of social exclusion. Even the independence of the press can be called into account on this reading of India's democracy. In a footnote to their account of the Chunduru massacre, the Samata Sanghatana report that 'one aged Reddy farmer' was killed in a retaliatory attack by local *dalits* when some upper-caste villagers tried to prevent the (Christian) *dalits* from burying their dead on the outskirts of the village. 'It is interesting to note', they continue, 'that the press, which had spared the reader gory pictures of the murdered *dalits*, decided to splash the picture of the Reddy farmer's body across the front pages' (Samata Sanghatana 1991: 2080).

We will have more to say on the lack of 'positive freedoms' (or lack of development) that continues to plague the lives of many *dalits* and *adivasis*. But what of the negative freedoms that democracy is meant to ensure, such as freedom from false arrest or freedom from torture? While Jalal acknowledges 'an expanding sphere of democratic politics' in India after the Emergency, she maintains that 'state authority in India [is] resting more and more on the non-elected institutions of the state, the civil bureaucracy, the police and the military' (1995: 169). Jalal has in mind, not least, the powers of the central state to police the borders of India to ensure the territorial integrity of the 'nation-state'. In the absence of effective government programmes to ensure the equitable development of the country's space-economy – to ensure *support* for the national project – New Delhi in the 1980s and 1990s resorted to coercion to maintain India's fabled unity in diversity (see also chapter 5).

But the violence of the state 'project' is also reproduced within the country, both in Centre–State relations, and in the everyday lives of the urban and rural poor. In a disturbing account of the relations between civil society, the state, law and order and the police, Paul Brass describes a Hobbesian state of war in rural India, wherein 'Villagers...do not discern a society based on abstract law and prevailing order' (1997: 273; and see our discussion in chapter 5). This state of war has several dimensions. In part, it is a war between a village and its external world: a state of war 'where marauding bands of robbers may descend upon the villages in the night, and where the villagers must provide for their own security' (p. 273). But it is also a war between certain sections of village society and the police, just as it was in the massacres at Chunduru or Arwal. Brass argues that: 'We come still closer to the "Hobbesian" world when we consider the perceptions of the police as marauders, equivalent to *dacoits*, not their protectors, but rather an additional, more powerful, and more dangerous band of robbers than those for whom robbery is a vocation' (p. 274). More pointedly, Brass notes that while the police are at the centre of the war in the north Indian countryside, village elites or local politicians are not concerned to bring the police under the control of a neutral state; they aim, rather, 'to bring the police under their own control: to oversee their recruitment, their posting, and their behaviour, to insure that they act on one's behalf and not on behalf of one's enemies' (p. 274).

This is precisely what happened in Chunduru and it rings true for large parts of India. We have known for some time that the dominant castes in rural India have sought to press-gang 'their' *dalits* into voting as part of a vote bank (and not least in elections prior to 1977), but it is only recently that scholars have provided us with an ethnography of the state itself.[5] The translation of India's formal democracy into a substantive democracy depends on the capacity and willingness of state officials to engage with civil society according to the rational and disinterested norms that are built into the Constitution of India. Sudipta Kaviraj suggests this engagement is beset by all sorts of translation problems between India's upper and lower orders. This is undoubtedly the case, but the translation problems are made worse by concerted acts of sabotage or violence by local elites who are concerned to frustrate the developmental ambitions of the state (ambitions which they understand only too well). It is for this reason that local power brokers will go to great lengths to remove honest government officers from their posts, either by effecting their transfer or by bringing false charges against them. And it is for this reason, too, that well-off farming families will pay considerable sums of money to have one of their members placed in the lower ranks of the police (see, for example, Jeffrey 1999). Where these links are forged by criminal households or gangs it is reasonable to speak of the lumpenization of politics. In large parts of north India the state presents itself to poor men and women not as a patron or guardian, but in the guise of a brutalizing police force and a corrupt administration. The state then becomes something to be resisted or at least avoided, and not something that is turned to for justice or as a source of empowerment.

Resisting state violence

Numerous political movements have emerged to contest the 'democratic-authoritarian' state in India, or to challenge those 'designs for the transformation of India into a great and powerful industrial-military state' (P. Brass 1997: 11). In Jharkhand, for example, *advisasi* groups and other people's movements were active in the 1990s in contesting plans for the eviction of tribal families from around the Netarhat firing range, or to make way for dams along the Koel-Karo river system. These movements challenged the more established politics of the Jharkhand Mukti Morcha or the Jharkhand Coordination Committee, both of which remain committed to the idea of seizing (state) power across the territory of Jharkhand.[6] Jharkhandi politicans have also been challenged in Palamau and Hazaribagh Districts by the Naxalite movements that are moving southwards from central Bihar. Although the Naxalite movement began in West Bengal in 1967, its main areas of strength are the central Districts of Bihar and parts of Andhra Pradesh and Orissa. In Bihar, Naxalite groups including Liberation and the Maoist Coordination Centre (MCC) have been active in organizing Scheduled Caste groups like the Musahars (Bhuiyas) in agricultural labour organizations, and in contesting the power of established politician-contractor groupings. According to Bela Bhatia:

> The [Naxalite] movement [in central Bihar] has succeeded in restoring confidence among the *dalits* of the region, drawing attention to their plight, demanding that they be treated with basic human dignity. Among the principal achievements of the movement are an increase in agricultural wages, the end to extreme forms of social oppression – such as the sexual exploitation of *dalit* women – and, in many villages, the confiscation and distribution of ceiling land as well as of *gairmajurwa* (village common) land under the illegal occupation of the upper classes. (1998: 30)

Naxalite groups are also engaged in an armed struggle with the private armies of upper-caste landlords, the most notorious of which is the Ranvir Sena. The price of labour in the 'flaming fields' of Bhojpur, Gaya and Jahanabad Districts is determined by the balance of forces between the armies of the upper castes (usually with police support) and the armies of the labouring poor.[7] In this Hobbesian world the empowerment of the poor and poorest is often in defiance of the state and its officers. Empowerment means resistance, just as it did in Chunduru. After the massacre at Chunduru not one of the culprits was 'punished by the courts. [Instead] the main accused, Chenchu Ramaiah, was killed by the People's War' (Samata Sanghatana 1991: 2081).

   Not all resistance to state power is as violent as it is in central Bihar, and nor is state violence always as naked as it is there. Environmental activists in India have focused on state violence in a different sense. Protestors along the Narmada river valley, or in Uttarakhand, have used the democratic spaces of India to contest the violence of the state's accumulation process. The environmental movement has developed a powerful critique of the modernization process in South Asia which has centred on the state's ideology of development. Ramachandra Guha suggests that India's programmes of planned industrial development have plagued the country with 'a gross caricature of European capitalism, reproducing and intensifying its worst features without holding out the promise of a better tomorrow' (1989: 195). Because India lacks the colonial resource frontier that was available to the major European powers, it is forced to exploit its own resource base to meet the needs of its city-based or elite populations: the one-sixth of the Indian population whom Gadgil and Guha describe as 'have-all' *omnivores* (1995: 3–4). Large dams along the Narmada which aim to produce cheap power or irrigation for richer farmers in Gujarat and Maharashtra are just one manifestation of the connections between economic and political power, on the one hand, and environmental destruction on the other. The pollution of India's rivers and groundwater supplies by chemical fertilizers and pesticides, the replacement of fruit trees by eucalyptus in the name of commercial or scientific forestry, even the disaster at Bhopal, can all be read as evidence of the violence of a state-directed process of development which treats the environment as a commodity.[8] The upshot, Gadgil and Guha conclude, is that development in India serves the interest of the country's social minority (the *omnivores*), even as it shrinks the life-chances of the country's social majorities: the *ecosystem people* (the 50 per cent of the population who depend on 'nature') and the *ecological refugees* (the remaining one-third of the population).

But, again, people fight back. Guha joins with Vandana Shiva in acclaiming the Chipko struggles in Uttarakhand for seeking 'a way of life more harmoniously adjusted with natural processes' (Guha 1989: 196). He sees the Chipko movement as one in a long line of social movements that have sought to defend the moral economy of the peasantry in Uttarakhand against 'the tentacles of the commercial economy and the centralizing state' (p. 196). Shiva, for her part, is more inclined to see the Chipko struggle as a feminist movement in which women are seeking to restore village forest management regimes which are based upon the feminine life principle (*prakriti*: see Shiva 1989). In both accounts there is a presumption that the Chipko struggles are anti-state and anti-development. The Chipko andolan is coded as a social or people's movement which refuses leaders (although Guha highlights the roles of Chandi Prasad Bhatt and Sunderlal Bahuguna), and which refuses the temptation to turn itself into an organized political party that should run for power in Lucknow or New Delhi. Chipko activists are lauded for their defence of a 'natural economy' which would aim to meet local needs with local resources, including the practical and intellectual resources of local people. Guha argues that the Chipko movement, like other environmental movements, is an imaginative response to a centralizing and unsustainable process of mal-development. Its anti-state bias is a sign of strength and not of weakness. It is precisely because the state's project of development is so profoundly undemocratic in its aims and actions that an effective environmental politics in India must operate outside the state and in opposition to the false promises of development. Guha concludes that: 'Far from being the dying wail of a class about to drop down the trapdoor of history, the call of Chipko represents one of the most innovative responses to the ecological and cultural crisis of modern society. It is a message we may neglect only at our own peril' (1989: 196).

Natural economies?

The scale of India's environmental crisis is well documented, and Gadgil and Guha are right to link the crisis to patterns of resource use rather than to brute demographic pressures. Effective forest cover is down to 15 per cent in India, as against the 30 per cent which is thought to be necessary to guard against soil erosion, local climate change and what threatens to be an irreversible loss of biodiversity.[9] The decline of India's Village or Protected Forests has implications, too, for the working lives of female firewood collectors, as several studies have shown.[10] It is not uncommon for women in Uttarakhand to spend an average of four hours a day in firewood collection activities. Meanwhile, water conflicts are common in the Delhi region, as well as in parts of south India, and Delhi is not alone among India's major cities in suffering from high levels of urban air pollution. Gadgil and Guha suggest that India's '[o]mnivores have subverted democratic processes on a variety of scales and in a variety of ways' (1995: 38). The post-colonial state has made use of the draconian powers of the Land Acquisition Act of 1894 to disregard the interests of India's ecosystem people, and has consistently demonstrated its commitment to an instrumental – even high modernist – account of external nature. The task of defending India's environment has fallen to those groups who are prepared to oppose the worst excesses of the country's commitment to rapid 'development'.

And yet it is no slight on the work of India's environmental activists to suggest that the very powerful critique of India's environmental policies that has been pressed by Gadgil and Guha is weakened by its romantic accounts of 'community' or a 'natural economy'.[11] Haripriya Rangan disputes the view that villagers in north-west India are bluntly opposed to development, or that they want a blanket ban on tree felling or road building in the Uttarakhand. Activists who have migrated from the Chipko movement to the Uttarakhand/(Uttaranchal) movement are demanding statehood as a means of effecting and controlling development in the hill regions: 'Lack of development coupled with inefficient administration, they assert, is the cause of high unemployment and increasing marginalization of hills regions in the state of Uttar Pradesh' (Rangan 1996: 205; see also Mawdsley 1997).

This point can be generalized. While state violence against poor people in India is deep-rooted, and takes many forms, it is misleading to suppose that people are always empowered in opposition to the state, or that they fail to seek power within or from state structures. The rise of India's Backward Castes gives the lie to this supposition, and so too does the enhanced power of some *dalit* and *adivasi* groups. Whether and how women have been empowered to challenge the patriarchal structures which govern their access to resources and political power is more difficult to say. Some women have been empowered by state-sponsored education and welfare schemes, but the government's record in terms of the protection of women from male violence is wretched, and in most of India's Districts women's access to property is still poorly defined (as Bina Agarwal has shown so powerfully: 1994) and even under threat (as common property resources shrink), and their election to power in various *panchayats* has only rarely threatened the *de facto* power which male relatives exercise over the political process.[12]

9.2 The Law of the Fishes

The Scheduled Castes and Tribes

Amongst those at the bottom of the social pile in India – women and men both – are members of the Scheduled Castes, who, as Mendelsohn and Vicziany report: 'Increasingly . . . look like a particularly downtrodden proletariat, sometimes lumpenproletariat' (1998: 9). The same description might also be offered of many of India's Scheduled Tribal or *adivasi* communities, and particularly those groups which have lost their land to various development projects that have been declared to be in 'the national interest'. But if conditions continue to be grim for many SC and ST households, it would be reasonable to argue, in addition, that some progress has been registered by these communities since Independence in the linked spheres of politics and the 'public arena'. Mendelsohn and Vicziany use the word 'Untouchable' in preference to *dalit*, or *Harijan*, or Depressed/Scheduled Caste – 'the word "Untouchable" is highly evocative of a condition which we see as one of the more pernicious forms of subordination to be encountered anywhere' (p. 5) – but they do so in the knowledge that the most extreme forms of 'untouchability' are dying out (notwithstanding the incident at Chunduru), or are being actively contested by Untouchable groups.

There is a danger, of course, in some recent writings on 'caste', that 'untouchability' is simply conjured out of existence, the victim of a discourse which maintains that 'caste did not exist prior to British rule, but rather that the British exaggerated out of all proportion the importance and unchangeability of caste within Indian society' (p. 17, and see our remarks on the production of religious meanings in chapter 8). This is plainly not the case, and nor is it plausible to argue that the Untouchables do not resist the ideology which defines their condition. There is plenty of evidence which suggests that India's *dalit* communities have not internalized a brahmanical conception of purity and pollution,[13] and there is abundant evidence, too, that upper-caste Indians are continuing to rework and deploy longstanding ideas about the polluting – and supposedly inhuman – qualities of India's

Untouchables (see S. Bayly 1999, ch. 8). Many untouchables continue to be shunned in 'private situations or spaces', if not in public spaces, and Mendelsohn and Vicziany make the important point that for many SC women: 'Untouchability was always a curse, never a protection...the Untouchable woman was never so degraded or ritually polluted as to be sexually unapproachable' (1998: 11). Any improvements in the position of India's Scheduled Communities need to be seen against this violent and depressing background. But there have been improvements, and at least some of these developments have taken shape within a tradition of *'empowerment from without'* that is, very largely, a product of the post-Independence period. The Constitution of India makes explicit provision for the reservation of jobs for SCs and STs, as well as of educational places and seats in political assemblies. Alongside these provisions, the government has allied a more general commitment to the economic uplift of the SCs and STs by means of the franchise, secular education, and laws that aim to 'abolish' untouchability and other forms of discrimination.

Empowerment from without: state actions and the politics of 'apparent failure'

We have already challenged the idea that these provisions have had a major and direct effect upon the lives or livelihoods of India's Scheduled Communities (see our discussion in chapter 6). But this is not to say that they have had a negligible impact, or that they haven't changed the terms of engagement between India's Scheduled and non-Scheduled Communities. In her classic account of 'development through political change' in Medak District, Andhra Pradesh, Marguerite Robinson considered the terms of these engagements in Mallannapalle *gram panchayat* from the late 1950s until the mid-1980s. Robinson noted how the economic and political powers of four (once)-dominant and related Reddy families were diluted in the 1960s and 1970s as disputes among the (male) household heads left them unable to resist a 'creeping revolution' in village, Block and District politics. This revolution was prompted in part by the introduction of new agricultural technologies and an associated improvement in the position of agricultural labour (much as we described in chapters 3–5). But it was also inspired by new educational and communications opportunities in Medak District, and by a growing appreciation amongst voters and politicians that 'numbers count', and that each community was in a position to drive its own bargain with a political suitor. As Robinson puts it:

> Improvements in communication (buses, television, etc.) have resulted in publicity about higher wage rates found elsewhere; this information has strengthened the resolve of Mallannapalle labourers to demand similar wages for themselves. In addition, Mallannapalle voters now expect their candidates to provide direct employment opportunities, as well as the indirect ones which

arise from the greater productivity of village land. The latter, in turn, is caused, at least partly, by increased access to institutional credit...here is India's revolution. (1988: 259)[14]

Perhaps the most intriguing part of Robinson's argument, however, concerns the indirect effects of government policies for the uplift of the poor, both in terms of their success and their *apparent failure*. Robinson notes that: 'What landlords most fear is a population without fear.... Credit for productive activities among the rural poor, *despite all the difficulties of implementation*, has played an essential role in this regard' (p. 259, our emphasis). Although land reform remains largely fictive in this part of India, the fear of land ceilings legislation has discouraged some 'landlords' from lending money: as one respondent told Robinson, 'why should I lend money when I can't take land on mortgage as collateral'. In addition, while many bureaucrats are in the pockets of local elites, not all of them are. Lower level bureaucrats live in fear of being reported to their superiors for misdeeds or for bribery, and this fear can override local pressures to disregard the poor. It is possible that Robinson is being generous to the government when she writes that: 'The economic gains of the new agricultural technology did not, in general, "trickle down" to the poor; where the latter have benefited it has usually been because of direct government action' (p. 265). But Robinson makes an important point when she reports that:

> government credit programmes have begun to reach the poor directly – by circumventing the elites, rather than by utilizing their 'good offices'. *De facto*, this often means that the poor have increased their opportunities to bribe officials directly. This may not look much of a revolution from the outside, but the twenty-rupee bribe to a government official which is collected from twenty poor farmers rather than being paid by one landlord, signals a profound change in rural credit relations (and in other aspects of the social structure). (p. 11)

Robinson is not, of course, arguing that power has been transferred to the *Harijans* of Mallannapalle (except in relative terms), and she recognizes that *Harijan* ownership of land in Mallannapalle is high by all-India standards. Even so, it is interesting – and significant – that Robinson concludes her study by emphasizing the connections between the provincial state, politics and progress in post-Independence India. Robinson accepts that the bureaucracy in India 'seems to have retrogressed over the past few decades' (p. 273), and not least in terms of its probity, but in her view: 'The centre, and where feasible the state governments, should play an increasingly active role – not only in directing resources and messages, but also by neutralizing, co-opting and bypassing the elites and by identifying, guiding, and monitoring the intended receivers' (pp. 272–3).[15]

Empowerment from within: the politics of India's 'Depressed Classes'

In a sense, of course, this belief in the progressive powers of the state and the democratic process is precisely what has driven *dalit* and *adivasi* politics over the past 100 years, and certainly up to the time of those movements which have sought power over the state rather than compensation from the state. Here is the strategy of '*empowerment from within*'.

According to Suresh, '[t]here were stirrings of protest against untouchability and social oppression as far back as the mid-nineteenth century' (1996: 358), and we can understand the Dalit Movement in contemporary India – in part, at least – in terms of its engagements with these former stirrings. We have previously described Mahatma Jotirao Phule as the first great low-caste leader in modern times (see chapters 2 and 8), and Phule's critique of the 'brahmanical tyranny and conspiracy' which reduced India's *shudras, adi-shudras* and women to a state of servility and misery was taken up by various reform movements in the late nineteenth century (including the Namashudra movement in Bengal, the Adi-Dharma movement in Punjab, and the Pulaya Mahasabha in Kerala), and later on by *dalit* political movements under the leadership of men like M. C. Rajah in Madras (the Depressed Classes Federation), Ayyankali in Travancore and Dr B. R. Ambedkar in Maharashtra (after Suresh 1996: 359).

Ambedkar, of course, was the towering leader of the *dalit* community in the twentieth century, and his debates with Gandhi define many of the issues that remain at the heart of the Dalit Movement. Like Phule, he maintained that: 'Untouchability is not a religious system but an economic system which is worse than slavery... [it] is a gold mine to the Hindus' (1945: 196–7). This system had to be broken down by a process of political struggle that would unite the original non-Aryan inhabitants of India (the *dalits, adi-shudras* and *adivasis*) against their Aryan exploiters, and which would seek independence from the British as a precondition for the liberation of India's 'non-Brahman' populations. Ambedkar sought to expose the double standards of those – like many in the INC – who fought against the British, but not against discrimination at home (in terms of the entry of the Backward Classes into the public services),[16] and he looked to a more enlightened state for the means of redress which would restore these communities to their non-agricultural glories. In the classic rhetorics of Ambedkarism, some traces of which continue to be felt in the Dalit Movement, the politics of reason would restore the non-Brahmans to their rightful place in the public sphere, as persons with administrative talents.

Ambedkar supported a system of reservations for all non-Brahmans, but in the years after Independence he found it necessary to argue for reserved seats, and a Double Member Constituency System, specifically for the Scheduled Castes.[17] Ambedkar recognized, as Gandhi did not, that the reservation of seats for *dalit* politicians would not by itself guarantee that these politicians would represent the interests of India's Depressed Classes. In a Single Member Constituency system, such as India has now, a large number of seats might indeed be reserved for Scheduled Caste MPs or MLAs. But these politicians generally earn their tickets from the major political parties, and as such they might be expected to tow the party line. They also court votes from all the electors in a given constituency, whether they are members of a Scheduled Community or not. Under a Double Member Constituency System two representatives are returned to the Parliament or the Legislative Assembly. One seat is 'contested by anyone irrespective of caste or community'. The other seat is 'contested only by candidates belonging to SCs/STs who would be elected by an electorate exclusively consisting of SCs/STs in the constituency' (Suresh 1996: 379). Under this system there is some pressure on SC and ST politicians to respond directly and on a regular basis to the concerns of the SC/ST electorate.[18]

Ambedkar was successful in ensuring that Double Member Constituencies were provided for in the Constitution (the provision lasted until 1959), and he worked alongside Nehru in the Constituent Assembly to define more closely a system of compensatory discrimination in the field of employment.[19] In 1951, however, Nehru's failure to introduce land reforms that would benefit the SCs, or to prioritize an Untouchability Offences Act, caused Ambedkar to resign his post as Law Minister. Such an Act was passed in 1955, but Ambedkar had by then lost faith in caste Hindus and Hinduism. He had taken Gandhi to task in the 1930s for using the Harijan Sevak Sangh to draw 'the claws of the opposition of the Untouchables which he knows is the only force which will disrupt the caste system and will establish a true democracy in India' (Ambedkar; quoted in Dube 1998: 83). Mr Gandhi, he said, was 'a Tory by birth as well as by faith . . . His main object, as every self-respecting Untouchable knows, is to make India safe for Hindus and Hinduism' (p. 83). In October 1956 Ambedkar acted on this belief and converted to Buddhism, along with about 6 million fellow *dalits* (mainly from the Mahar community). Within a year he was dead, and the Dalit Movement which he had done so much to shape and lead was in disarray. Ambedkar's legacy to his supporters was not so much a generation of leaders to follow him, but a new political organization, the Republican Party of India (RPI), which was 'formed in 1957 on the basis of an open letter to the people written by Ambedkar and posthumously published' (Suresh 1996: 367).

The Republican Party enjoyed some success in parts of Uttar Pradesh, but it was unable to stop the Congress Party strengthening its hold on the SC vote in the 1960s and 1970s. Members of India's Scheduled Communities voted disproportionately for the Congress in national and State elections through this period (save, perhaps, in Jharkhand). High-caste politicians were not slow, either, to exploit various schisms within the *dalit* community, and not least between Buddhist and Christian SCs on the one hand, and Hindu SCs on the other, a tactic that is continued today the *Sangh parivar*.

Dalit *politics*

But the idea of a *dalit* politics didn't wither away, and in 1972 the Dalit Panthers were formed in Maharashtra with the aim of carving out new spaces of empowerment for India's *dalit* communities. The Panthers enjoyed some success in the urban areas of Maharashtra, but soon ran up against the problems which have always faced *dalit* groups and leaders: whether to ally with poorer caste Hindu groups, and if so how and on what terms; whether to include Hindu *dalits* alongside non-Hindu *dalits*; and whether to seek redress from the state or power over the state. The rhetoric of the Dalit Panthers suggested that they were not searching for 'a little place in Brahman alley. . . [but for] a people's democracy' (see the quotation at the head of the chapter). In practice, though, the Panthers were beset by bitter leadership disputes, and they failed to work out a strategy for achieving or using power. In so far as questions of empowerment were thought through, the Panther faction led by Raja Dhale preferred to emphasize questions of cultural revolution over those of socio-economic transformation. This reflected a debt to Ambedkar and a willingness to respect his anti-communist line. But it also reflected a line of thought that can be traced back to Phule, and which was encouraged in the early 1970s by the emergence of black power movements in the USA. The Dalit Panthers took their place in a long line of movements which refused a brahmanical interpretation of *dalit* social worlds.[20]

The cultural legacy of the Panthers continues to be felt in Maharashtra and Karnataka, but it was not until the 1990s that a mainly *dalit* party challenged seriously for power at the State level in India, and then in Uttar Pradesh. The man responsible for this turnaround was Kanshi Ram, a Chamar from Punjab who first made waves as a *dalit* activist in Poona, where he formed organizations in the 1960s to advance the interests of Scheduled and Backward Caste workers in reserved jobs.[21] Most of the members of these organizations came from the Mahar Buddhist community, and it was partly to widen his base of support that Kanshi Ram helped to set up the All India Backward and Minority Employees' Federation (BAMCEF) in 1973. Kanshi Ram spent the next several years spoking out from Poona or Delhi to towns in Punjab, Haryana, Madhya Pradesh and Uttar Pradesh. BAMCEF's motto of 'Educate, Organize and Agitate' was taken from Ambedkar, and it was Ambedkar's life and works that BAMCEF sought to connect to issues of caste violence and poverty in north and west India. Before long, however, Kanshi Ram was seeking a new vehicle for his *dalit* agendas, and in 1984, after experimenting briefly with the Dalit Soshit Samaj Sangharsh Samiti (a political counterpart to BAMCEF), he formed the Bahujan Samaj Party (BSP) as a fully-fledged political party with a base in Maharashtra and in the Hindi heartland.

The ideological base of the BSP is not sophisticated. Its main proposition is that 'Indian society is characterized by the self-interested rule of 10 per

cent over the other 90 per cent (the *bahujan samaj* or common people)'
(Mendelsohn and Vicziany 1998: 223). But Kanshi Ram proved to be an
able political organizer, and in the second half of the 1980s the BSP worked
tirelessly in Uttar Pradesh (especially in the east and with the Chamars) to
build a bank of supporters that would deliver the party to power. The BSP
first made a name for itself in Uttar Pradesh politics in 1985 when a female
Chamar from Delhi, Mayawati, stood for the Lok Sabha seat of Bijnor in a
by-election. Mayawati lost out to Ram Meira Kumar, the daughter of
Jagjivan Ram, himself for many years the leading Untouchable in the Congress movement or party. In later years, however, it was Mayawati's star
which rose, and by the early 1990s the BSP was well placed to exploit the
decline of the Congress Party in Uttar Pradesh. Kanshi Ram won a seat in
the Lok Sabha in a by-election in 1992, and in 'the four State Assembly and
Parliamentary (Lok Sabha) polls for Uttar Pradesh between 1989 and 1991
the Bahujana Samaj Party's share of the vote varied only marginally between
8.7 and 9.4 per cent' (p. 225). This share of the vote translated into a paltry
12 (out of 425) seats in the State Assembly in 1991, but it demonstrated the
hold which the BSP now exerted on the Chamar vote in UP (with the
exception of a few western Districts). Given that power was Kanshi Ram's
only goal by this time, it came as little surprise that the BSP chased the
Muslim vote through the 1990s (and post-Ayodhya), or that it was prepared
to form governments in Lucknow in 1993–5 with the Samajwadi Party (a
vehicle mainly for the Backward Castes: see section 9.3) and in 1996–7 with
the BJP. Rather more surprising, perhaps, and certainly to UP's elites, was
the fact that Mayawati (with Kanshi Ram in the background) came to power
in June 1995 as the Chief Minister of Uttar Pradesh.

It would be idle to pretend that Mayawati's tenure as the Chief Minister of
Uttar Pradesh coincided with an improvement in the living standards of the
State's labouring poor, or even of the Chamars. Her Chief Ministerships
were short-lived, and were prone to the same sorts of petty politics and
fears of 'floor-crossing' that had dogged politics in UP for many years.
Worse still, the BSP had no agendas for government that were worth the
name. Its focus was on the assumption of power and not the use of power
for particular purposes. But there is a sense in which all of this misses the
point. What is remarkable about the Mayawati years is that they
happened at all, and that they might happen again. The Chamars of Uttar
Pradesh are now voting for themselves and not for those who hold
economic power over them. They have been freed to vote in this way by
the same changes that Robinson describes in Mallannapalle: access to education and reserved jobs, and changes in local land, labour and credit
markets.

Many of these changes were instigated by the Government. For all its
failings, the government has helped to attenuate ' "the law of the fishes",
according to which the bigger fish swallows the smaller ones' (Kautilya,
Arthasatra; quoted in Robinson 1988: vi). But only in part: the Chamars of

UP have also been empowered by the simple existence of the BSP, and by at least some of its actions during its short stints in office. The BSP may not have transferred much land to the *dalit* landless of UP, or even improved agricultural wages, but Kanshi Ram and Mayawati did replace some high-caste senior civil servants in UP with their low-caste, Muslim or *dalit* supporters. Mayawati also ordered her government to build a Pariwartan Chowk – or Revolution Square – in Lucknow, and to bedeck the Chowk with 'huge statues of the great figures of anti-Brahman activism: Phule, Periyar, Ambedkar, Shahu Maharaj' (Mendelsohn and Vicziany 1998: 230). As it turned out, the Chowk was not completed before Mayawati was removed from office, but the point was made. People are not em-powered by land or wages alone, which is perhaps how the Left has under-stood power and poverty in India; the victims of discrimination can also be empowered by a heightened sense of their worth or honour (*izzat*), and this is where the BSP made a difference. Mendelsohn and Vizciany wisely conclude that while:

> Kanshi Ram and Mayawati have their faults...they do represent a more aggressive attack on the order of social orthodoxy than has previously been seen from participants in the mainstream of Indian electoral politics. Kanshi Ram has shown that a person of Dalit origins can lead a party that wins seats at the ballot box and is not afraid to form a Government that puts the interests of the most subordinated Indians at its very centre. Throughout India it will now be more difficult to ignore the interests of Dalits. (p. 233)[22]

9.3   Demanding Jobs and Power

Not everyone accepts that Mayawati's governments did put the interests of the most subordinated Indians at the centre of its plans, or at least not straightforwardly. Siddharth Dube calls to mind the split between the left and cultural wings of the Dalit Panther movement when he writes that:

> The failure of both the Bahujan Samaj and the Samajwadi parties to represent the interests of the poor, who are the primary backers of both parties, is rooted in the fact that the parties are led by the small elite of the scheduled and middle castes that has developed since Independence. While the middle-class elite developed largely as a result of benefiting from land reform, the scheduled caste elite grew out of the affirmative-action programmes in higher education and in government jobs.... The Bahujan Samaj, in particular, began essentially as a pressure group to improve the position of scheduled caste officers in the bureaucracy. Since then, the agendas of both the Samajwadi and the Bahujan Samaj parties have been dominated by the effort to raise the numbers of, respectively, the middle castes and the scheduled castes in colleges, specialized education and the bureaucracy. (1998: 206)

Dube further points out that the growth of government jobs or educational places in Uttar Pradesh has failed to keep pace with the number of Scheduled Caste men and women applying for these jobs and places, and one of his principal respondents in the UP village of Baba ka Gaon, Hansraj, complains that: 'Today one can't get government jobs on merit, without corruption, as was possible in my father's time' (p. 144). Hansraj continues: 'Bribing is the only way to pass the exam and to get a job, there's no attention to merit. To get a good grade in the exam you have to give Rs 50,000 to someone, or even Rs 75,000 or Rs 100,000. . . . But where will I get Rs 100,000 from, when my family is barely surviving' (p. 144). His brother Shrinath agrees with him, and adds that: 'many people pay bribes to get certificates that show they are scheduled-caste when they are not' (p. 129).

Reservations

This assessment of the reservations system rings true for many Districts across north India, and probably not only for north India. The number of reserved jobs on offer is indeed miserly when compared to the scale of the unemployment problem amongst the SC and ST populations, and most of the jobs which are on offer are in Classes III and IV of Central and State government services or the public sector. But none of this means that the reservations system has 'failed' the poor, as Dube perhaps implies, or that a majority of India's Backward Castes (including the Scheduled Castes and Tribes) would like to see an end to the system, as opposed to its extension or reform. The main protagonist of Dube's book, Ram Dass, reports that higher and middle-caste villagers in Baba ka Gaon – men like the new *pradhan*, Ram Saran Maurya – 'will discriminate against the scheduled castes even if we are now vegetarians' (p. 211). But he goes on to say that, 'to my knowledge, there are very few people amongst the middle castes who are not poor. So in my understanding they should get reservations. In the social environment here, middle castes and scheduled castes are almost the same. There is sometimes only a very slight difference' (pp. 211–12).

Ram Dass and his friends remind us that the reservations issue is about power as much as it is about employment, even where the two are closely linked. And whilst these men *are* scornful about the BSP's lack of attention to land reform issues (they have time only for the Communists), they refuse to define their poverty in material terms alone. Ram Dass and Shrinath (and Hansraj) want respect and opportunity, as Dube fully recognizes, and they look upon a system of economic and political 'compensation' as one key but imperfect means for securing these goods. The economic standing of Ram Dass's family has improved slowly since Independence. The family has a small amount of land, and stints of employment in Bombay have given Ram Dass some leeway in his dealings with his Thakur neighbours (even though the family remains in debt). But Ram Dass recognizes that his grandchildren are unlikely to see India's political democracy translated into an economic democracy unless and until the Scheduled Castes join with the middle castes to seize power from the upper castes. This is why Ram Dass likes Mayawati and Kanshi Ram, and this is why he wants the reservations system to be extended to the middle castes: to make both groups the enemies of the upper castes.

Ram Dass's comments point to a new way of looking at the reservations issue, at least in north India. The Government of India provides some data on the workings of the reserved jobs system, in terms of quotas filled and court cases filed, and a small number of academic studies have reported on the capture of key government jobs by members of the 'creamy' layers of the Scheduled or Other Backward Caste communities. Kanchan Chandra, however, has broken fresh ground in her studies of the *political* consequences of reserving jobs and educational places in Punjab and Uttar Pradesh. She agrees that the main beneficiaries of the various systems of reservation for SCs in both States have come from the small SC middle class to which Dube refers. But if the emergence of this middle class of government officers and clerks has been one consequence of the reservation system, Chandra notes that the 'radicalization of the clerks' was prompted rather more by the social discrimination which the holders of reserved posts continued to face at work and within the Congress Party. Chandra argues that a new middle class of SCs took over the leadership of the BSP because of the 'representational blockage' which they faced in the District Committees of the Congress Party (2000).[23]

Aside from the findings of a few academic studies the main reason for supposing that the reservations system has helped to empower India's poorest social groups is to be found in the consistent and continuing opposition of the country's upper castes to an effective system of reservations. But this is more than just a question of the 'Mandalization' of politics. The case for reservations has been pressed in different ways in different parts of India over the past seventy or so years, and it makes sense to consider the history of the reservations issue in terms of a geography of non-Brahman (or Backward Caste) politics that has swung slowly from south India to north India.

The Backward Castes and Classes

Lower-caste groups first came to power in the southern parts of India. The non-Brahman movement that was based in the Madras and Bombay Presidencies encouraged the Justice Party in Madras, in the years leading up to 1921, to rally 'the Shudras and the ati-Shudras to challenge and resist the dominance of the Brahmans and higher castes' (Suresh 1996: 365). This alliance did not survive the Justice Party's accession to office – when 'the untouchables were gradually pushed out of the Justice Party' (Irschick 1969: 188) – but the success of anti-Brahman politics in south India can also be measured by the rise to power of the DMK in Tamil Nadu in the 1960s, and of the Communist Party of India in Kerala in 1957.

It was in south India, too, that the report of the (first) Backward Classes Commission had some repercussions. The Commission was established in January 1953 under the Chairmanship of Kaka Kalelkar, an erstwhile disciple of Gandhi. In the report which it submitted on 30 March 1955, the Backward Classes Commission identified 2,399 Backward Castes or communities in India, and recommended that 70 per cent of seats in all technical and professional institutions should be reserved for qualified students belonging to the Backward Classes (including the Scheduled Castes and Tribes). This figure reflected the estimated weight of the Backward Classes in the population of India. The Commission also urged that women should be treated as a backward class, and that vacancies in Class I government services should be reserved at the level of 25 per cent, as against 40 per cent for vacancies in Classes II and III.

These recommendations – and not least the intended quota for women – proved too much for the Government of India, as indeed they proved too much for Kaka Kalelkar himself and the three members of his Commission who submitted notes of dissent.[24] Nehru's government refused to act on the report's recommendations, at least in regard to Central Government jobs, and chose instead, in August 1961, to invite the States 'to draw up their own lists of backward classes and fix their own quotas of reservation'. The nettle was grasped in south India rather more so than in north India, as might be expected. Varshney reports that: 'In Southern Indian states, over and above the scheduled caste quota, close to 50 per cent of the state government jobs has been reserved for OBCs in the state of Karnataka since the 1960s; in Tamil Nadu, OBC reservation was 31% to begin with [and] increased to over 50 per cent later; in Kerala, the OBCs have had a quota [that] has been 40 per cent; and in Andhra Pradesh, 25 per cent' (1998: 24).[25]

In North India, the power of the upper castes was sufficient to delay these reforms for the best part of thirty years. In Central Government, too, the argument continued to be made that reservations would benefit only an elite amongst the Backward Classes, or that the quality of government service would decline if staffing decisions were taken mainly on 'non-merit' grounds. Varshney dismisses this last claim when he remarks that, 'it is widely recognized that the Southern states are governed better than the North Indian states like Bihar and UP. Large-scale affirmative action in bureaucratic recruitment does not appear to have undermined governance in the South' (p. 25). But regional differences matter, as Varshney would also acknowledge. The political struggle against 'Brahmanism' had not been won in north India in the 1960s and 1970s, and when the question of reservations for the Other Backward Classes did push itself to the centre stage of politics, as it did in Bihar in 1978, or in Gujarat in 1980, the upper castes responded with violence or by playing the communal card.

By this time, though, the battle was engaged. The riots that broke out in Bihar in March 1978 were prompted by the decision of the State government to increase the quota for OBCs from 24 to 26 per cent. In Gujarat, the upper castes were enraged by the decision of the State government to provide a 5 per cent quota for the OBCs in medical colleges. In 1980 the upper castes in Gujarat enjoyed some success in knocking back the government's small efforts on behalf of the OBCs. By the mid-1980s, however, the Congress Party in Gujarat needed to court the OBC vote, and it promised to act on some aspects of the Rane Committee report if it was returned to power in the 1985 State Assembly elections. The Rane Committee had been appointed in 1981 and its report of that year had proposed a 28 per cent quota for OBCs in Gujarat – a recommendation that the Congress Party had refused to act on before its pre-election promise in 1985. Once again riots broke out in Ahmedabad, and once again the government was required to back down from some of its promises (see Mitra 1987).

Increased competition among India's political parties in the late 1980s and 1990s led to a new wave of rhetoric which seemed to favour reserved jobs for the OBCs, and even to some action. The decline of the Congress Party coincided with a new era in which numbers mattered, and where politicians had to respond to the demands of India's 'social majorities' in a way that they had not had to previously. The breakthrough came in 1990, during the period of the National Front government of V. P. Singh. Singh's decision to act upon at least some of the recommendations of the Mandal Commission Report was taken for political reasons, of course: his government accepted Mandal's recommendation that 27 per cent of posts in central government services or the public sector should be reserved for 'socially and education-ally backward classes', yet it largely ignored the Commission's recommenda-tions in respect of improved education for children or for vocational training schemes. But the effect of V. P. Singh's order was critical nonetheless, and notwithstanding the fact that opposition to his announcement helped bring down the National Front government in November 1990 (opposition that included widespread and organized rioting in Delhi).

The real significance of V. P. Singh's announcement on 7 August 1990 was that it changed the terms of political debate in India. As we explained in chapter 6, the Congress Party was placed on the back foot, and the BJP was faced with a dramatic challenge to its attempt to forge a single Hindu nation, undivided by caste. In the short run, the BJP was encouraged to stoke up communal tensions to disguise the threat that V. P. Singh was posing to the Sangh parivar's most enduring constituency, the upper castes. In the longer run, however, the BJP was forced to accept that the terms of the political game in India had been changed, and it was moved to field candidates from the Backward Castes in its search for power in the country at large. In the States, meanwhile, the Mandal-Singh 'decision' further encouraged those political parties which had emerged in the 1980s to press the claims of the Backward Castes, or at least some sections of them. In Haryana and Uttar Pradesh the running was made by the Samajwadi Party, led by Mulayam Singh Yadav. The Samajwadi Party came to power in Uttar Pradesh in November 1993 as part of a coalition government with the Bahujan Samaj

Party (see section 9.2). The party was formed as a breakaway faction from within Singh's Janata Dal, and its main support base has been amongst the Backward – or middle status – Castes, and most especially the Yadavs. In the 1993 State Assembly elections in Uttar Pradesh, the Samajwadi Party took 25.8 per cent of the vote and won 109 seats, which put it second to the BJP (then recently removed from power by the Centre and the choice of 33.3 per cent of the electors (177 seats)). The government of Mulayam Singh lasted until June 1995, when it was brought down by Kanshi Ram and Mayawati. BSP leaders charged Mulayam Singh with turning a blind eye to Yadav attacks on Scheduled Caste men and women in UP, and with putting pressure on some Kurmi members of the BSP to cross the floor of the Legislative Assembly to join the Samajwadi Party.

The unity of the Scheduled Castes and Backward Castes has been just as hard to maintain in Bihar, where the Janata Dal and Rashtriya Janata Dal governments of Laloo Prasad Yadav and his wife, Rabri Devi, dominated politics in the 1990s. Although Laloo Yadav was successful in this period in building a political alliance against the State's 'Forward Castes', the main beneficiaries of his regime were the Yadavs and (at first) the Kurmis, two caste groupings which benefited from the land reforms of the 1950s and 1960s and which are very much in the creamy layer of the Other Backward Classes. Laloo Yadav's Bihar became legendary, of course, for its cronyism and misrule, as well as for an extreme privatization of the State. These developments led some commentators to despair about the nature of politics in India, or about the consequences of 'ill-bred' or 'ill-educated' people coming to power in the State Assemblies. But social elites have long warned about the 'poisonous' effects of democracy on the lower orders (and vice versa), and the abject failings of the (Rashtriya) Janata Dal in Bihar should not lead us to conclude that Laloo Yadav is without his supporters there, or that his cronies have not sought to perfect a political game – the ransacking of the state – that has long been practised by the State's Forward Castes.[26] If Bihar holds a lesson for India it is not about the failings of democracy but about the failings of government.

This distinction needs to be kept firmly in mind. The rise to power of governments like those of Mulayam Singh Yadav or Laloo Prasad Yadav signals a profound shift in the nature of India's democratic politics – what Yogendra Yadav has called 'a second democratic upsurge' (and see our discussion in chapter 6).[27] Numbers matter now in a way that they did not in the 1950s or 1960s, and the evidence from north India suggests that Backward Caste and (some) Scheduled Caste groups are using their caste identities as a way of taking power over the state/State. This instrumental use of caste markers has encouraged Subrata Mitra to argue – like Edmund Leach, long ago (1960) – that caste consciousness is undermining 'the ideological basis of the *varna* scheme' (Mitra 1994: 64). And with power comes empowerment, at least to a degree. Across north India, the majority communities who make up the Backward Classes are at last beginning to get a taste of power; they are acquiring a sense that government might be made to do their will, or that the police and the courts might be encouraged to think twice before dismissing their petitions or pleas for protection.

But this sense of power – or empowerment – is fragile, and the use of power has not often translated into government policies that are pro-poor in a more traditional or economic sense. In part, this has to do with the powers of India's elites to fight back: to demand that the state is taken out of 'the economy' (at least when it comes to the redistribution of wealth), or to frustrate the will of an elected government through a continuing control of local bureaucrats, the police, or other gatekeepers. Rather more so, however, it has to do with a failure of governance. Critics of strong government in India, as elsewhere, have enjoyed a good innings over the past twenty years. The post-left has argued that much of the bloodshed in the world today springs from the high modernist ambitions of government, or from the capacity of the 'nation-state' to monopolize the means of violence. The right, for its part, has taken government to task for its inefficiency, or for its inability to provide people with what they want. But while both of these arguments have a certain force, they are inattentive to the enabling powers of government in divided societies. The problems facing Bihar today spring not from a surfeit of government, but from a lack of effective governance. Evidence from other parts of the country, including from Bihar's eastern neighbour, West Bengal, suggests both that government can 'make a difference', and that good (or better) government is most likely to emerge where civil society is 'activist' in orientation and where political parties are forced to compete to represent the interests of the poor or poorest. There is little evidence to suggest that the poor do not want 'good government', even if or when their first thought is to keep 'government' at a distance.

9.4 Government Makes a Difference: Indian Democracy at Work

We argued in chapter 2 that democracy – 'government by the people' – may be understood as an ideal, which is approached more or less closely according to the balance of class power in a society and the nature of the state system. And India's States, all of which have formally democratic political systems, differ significantly in terms of the substance of their democracies – according to the balance of class power. The detailed evidence which is presented in the series of studies of 'dominance and state power' in the major States, directed by Frankel and Rao (1989, 1990), supplemented by that from more recent studies (such as those collected together by Hansen and Jaffrelot 1998), shows that State regimes are distinguished from one another by variations in the nature and extent of the political participation of lower castes/classes, as well as by differences in their party systems.[28] On the whole a political system with reasonably stable and well-institutionalized parties, which compete for the votes of poorer and of lower-class people, is more likely – we suggest – to be responsive to their needs and aspirations, and to open up spaces of empowerment in an ongoing process of historical change. In the current conjuncture, different regimes may be distinguished as follows:[29]

A(i) States in which upper-caste/class dominance has persisted and Congress remained strong in the context of a stable two-party system ('traditional dominance' rather than politics of accommodation *vis-à-vis* lower classes)
Madhya Pradesh
(?Orissa)
Rajasthan

A(ii) States in which upper-caste/class dominance has been effectively challenged by middle castes/classes, and Congress support has collapsed in the context of fractured and unstable party competition (both 'dominance' and the politics of accommodation have broken down)
Bihar
Uttar Pradesh

B States with middle-caste/class dominated regimes, where the Congress has been effectively challenged but has not collapsed (the politics of accommodation *vis-à-vis* lower-class interests have continued to work effectively, most effectively in Maharashtra and Karnataka, least effectively in Gujarat)
Andhra Pradesh
Gujarat
Karnataka
Maharashtra
(?Punjab)

C States in which lower castes/classes are more strongly represented in political regimes
Kerala
Tamil Nadu
West Bengal

This pattern of difference is not simply 'given', but is rather the outcome of long-running historical processes and political struggles. It is also important to recognize that the challenges made by some lower-caste/class groups will be resisted, and in some cases – as in Maharashtra perhaps (see Lele 1989) – might be neutralized for a while. Nevertheless, there is evidence to show that those States in which the lower castes/classes are more strongly represented politically have been among the most successful in reducing poverty. The work of Datt and Ravallion (1998), comparing the performance of the major States in reducing poverty, shows the influence of initial conditions, in terms of agricultural infrastructure and of levels of education and of health, which were substantially the inheritance of colonial rule; and subsequently of rates of growth of farm yield, which also reflect long-run economic dynamics. Divergences of different States from what would be predicted on the basis of these conditions can be explained by their politics, and the balance of class power (see J. Harriss 1999). Thus, for example, Andhra Pradesh, with its by now relatively well-institutionalized competition between Congress and the Telugu Desam, and the contest between these parties for the votes of poorer people, has done much better in reducing poverty than Karnataka, where party competition is more fragmented and clientelist politics remains strong. Maharashtra, too, where until recently at least Congress 'machine' politics – in which there is selective accommodation of groups of poorer people – has endured, has done less well than might have been expected in reducing poverty. The States in which the lower castes/classes are more strongly represented politically are also those in which there is evidence of stronger and more extensive organization in civil society.[30]

The opening up of sites of empowerment by the state, through a dialectical process of interaction between governmental and societal organizations, is most in evidence in Kerala, which has become celebrated for 'public action' as a result, in particular, of the writings of Jean Drèze and Amartya Sen.[31] Kerala has been successful in reducing poverty and in raising standards of 'human development' in spite of its relative poverty, and comparatively poor rates of agricultural growth, partly because of the efficiency and effectiveness of service provision. One of the conditions of this success is the existence of public action, which gives poorer people 'voice' to bring pressure upon state agencies (see Nag 1989). This in turn cannot be understood except in a context in which power-holders at the 'centre' – in this case in the State – have supported popular struggles against local power-holders.[32] Elsewhere those who are powerful locally are still often able to crush the voice of the subalterns.

There is some comparable evidence from West Bengal – though Nag's research suggested that 'public action' is much less effective there than in Kerala, and the standard of provision of public health and education services in the State is still not especially good. But it is striking that in a rigorous comparative examination of evidence concerning experiments with decentralized government from around the world, Crook and Sverrisson should have found that for West Bengal's system of *panchayats* alone is there a convincing case for saying that decentralization – which is being strongly touted by development agencies as a key means of making government more responsive to poorer people – really has benefited poorer people. Karnataka, the other Indian State where *panchayati Raj* has been in operation for some time, 'showed little evidence of having been particularly responsive to "vulnerable groups", the poor or the marginalised' (Crook and Manor 1998: 301). Crook and Sverrisson argue that: 'It is highly significant that the most successful cases (of decentralisation) were the ones [like West Bengal, *a fortiori*] where...government not only had an ideological commitment to pro-poor policies, but was prepared to engage actively with local politics... to challenge local elite resistance if necessary and to ensure implementation of policies' (1999: 41). As Glyn Williams observed in research that he conducted in three villages in Birbhum District in 1992–3: 'For many richer villagers, the CPM has been all too effective in its development objectives of producing a radicalised rural poor and a democratised local government' (1997: 2109).

Left-of-centre regimes

There has been a lively debate about the performance of the CPI(M)-led Left Front government in West Bengal (much more so than for the case of Kerala). Atul Kohli and G. K. Lieten have concluded that it has been successful in pushing out the frontiers of progressive possibility within the constraints of India's federal structure (Kohli 1987; Lieten 1992); Ross Mallick has been caustic in his criticisms of the regime for its excessive reformism and a bias against the Scheduled Castes and agricultural labour (1990; 1992). One of us (Harriss 1993), Ben Rogaly (1998) and John Eche-verri-Gent (1993) have staked out more nuanced positions. Echeverri-Gent is quite sympathetic to Kohli's position, and acknowledges: 'The party's relative success in dislodging traditional landed elites'. But he argues that Kohli fails to stress 'that democratic competition is essential in maintaining party commitment and discipline over the longer run' and he fears (as does Rogaly) that: 'The declining competitiveness of politics in West Bengal suggests that there may be a reduction in responsiveness to the rural poor' (these quotations, 1993: 168–9).

The record of the Left Front is certainly not above criticism, but the balance of the argument seems to be broadly in support of Kohli's general case, which was that there is room for manoeuvre – for politics and policies which are sympathetic to the needs and aspirations of poorer people – even in the context of a democratic capitalist polity in India which has a regime, at the Centre (as we, too, have argued) which is 'incapable of imposing authority (and) typically provides economic incentives to propertied groups to buttress its own political support' (1987: 8).

Kohli's strong conclusion, from comparison of the performances of state regimes in West Bengal, Uttar Pradesh and Karnataka, was that 'a tightly organised ideological party can penetrate the rural society without being coopted by the propertied groups' whereas, conversely 'multi-class regimes with loose organisation and diffuse ideology are not successful at reformist intervention' (1987: 224). This last statement referred particularly to the Janata government of Uttar Pradesh. In Karnataka 'Coherent leadership and populist ideology [in the time of Devraj Urs's Chief Ministership in the 1970s] facilitated a modicum of reform. The organisational base, however, was weak and the propertied classes penetrated the ruling groups. The reformist thrust thus remained limited' (p. 228). In other words it is most likely that empowerment of poorer people will be accomplished by well-organized left-of-centre regimes, like the one which has held power in West Bengal now since 1977, and which has the following critical characteristics (according to Kohli): (a) coherent leadership; (b) ideological and organizational commitment to exclude propertied interests from direct participation in the process of governance; (c) a pragmatic attitude toward facilitating a non-threatening as well as a predictable political atmosphere for the propertied entrepreneurial classes; and (d) an organizational arrangement that is simultaneously centralized and decentralized, so that the regime is both 'in touch' with local society whilst not being subjected to local power holders. These regime attributes, Kohli argues, 'make the institutional penetration of society possible, while facilitating a degree of regime autonomy from the propertied classes' (1987: 11).

Such left-of-centre regimes, or the kind of institutionalized populism which has been characteristic of Tamil Nadu and latterly of Andhra Pradesh – and which appears to have delivered some of the same results – are not a 'policy choice', of course. But the lessons of Kerala and of West Bengal are that poorer people can be empowered at the local level where they are supported from the 'centre', in their struggles with local power-holders. Community-based organizations, NGOs and social movements can powerfully assist in the development of the political capabilities – involving organizational capacity and a strong sense of dignity and self-worth – of poor people. But they are not a substitute for programmatic political parties. Echeverri-Gent sums up the general argument very well:

> Political parties, NGOs and social movements stand in complementary if often antagonistic relationships. While parties are indispensable for aggregating diverse social interests in electoral systems, NGOs and social movements can play an important role in enabling the poor to articulate and act on their interests. They can empower the poor to curb political parties' tendency to allow partisan interests to reduce their popular responsiveness. Promoting political competition among programmatic political parties and a vibrant NGO and social movement sector may be the best way to surmount the paradox of participation [which is that if public participation is to make the state responsive to the needs of the poor, their interests must be equitably represented, but as long as the poor remain poor, their position in the process of interest representation is disadvantaged]. (1993: 172/169)

Glyn Williams's field research in West Bengal adds weight to this argument. Most of the villagers that Williams spoke to displayed a 'healthy cynicism' about the CPM's bias to its own supporters, but he contends that the 'state-sponsored patronage networks' created by the CPM's reforms have, nonetheless, had a significant 'effect on village power relations' (1997: 2106–7). Partly as a result of the CPM's mass action campaigns, and partly because the Left Front government has used the quota system to improve the class and gender balance of the *panchayats*, the *panchayats* were able to ensure that 'a fairly low incidence of benefits [from development programmes] were passed on to richer households' (p. 2107).[33] The access of lower-caste individuals to positions of political office gave them control over development funds and 'the potential to wield power and influence within the village equal to that of the most substantial local landowners' (p. 2107). Representatives of the lower castes were returned to power if they proved effective in securing resources for their *dol* (a group of several allied households), or their *Gram Panchayat*, from higher levels within the state system. They would also be judged as 'good politicians' if they used the government machine to help poorer supporters of the CPM assert themselves against their employers. As one disgruntled General Caste employer and business owner told Williams: 'The relationship with casual labourers is not good – casual workers are always clever – they try to get away without working for their money. You need to supervise them all the time. Any vegetables I grow will be stolen by *chhotolok* [Scheduled Caste] women, and if I complain the party [CPM] will stick up for them' (p. 2109).

9.5 Conclusions

West Bengal is not a 'model' for the rest of the country. If there are lessons to be learned from West Bengal – or from Kerala or Tamil Nadu or even Andhra Pradesh – they are difficult lessons about party building, governance and ideological commitment. But the findings of scholars about West Bengal should also make us think twice before dismissing the state as a site of empowerment of poor people in India. The cultural turn in development studies is raising interesting questions about the claims to power which are written into various doctrines of development, no doubt, but there is a danger in 'post-development' studies that the state is seen as the embodiment of modernity in a disabling way: the state is a source of power, and power is always deployed as an instrument of repressive governmentality. In this account of social power, poorer people win access to 'true development' only when they escape from the violent clutches of the state, or when they turn their back on state-inspired (mal)development. Kaviraj edges toward this formulation in the distinction that he makes between the discourses of the upper and the lower orders in India: a discourse of imposed development is opposed to a counter-hegemonic discourse of autonomous development which seeks to build on local traditions and understandings. But we believe that this is to define *empowerment* in too restricted a fashion.[34] The state in India is not the colossus that some of its critics like to imagine.

Kaviraj knows this as well as anyone, but it is worth reminding ourselves that the connections between state power and democratic development in India are highly contingent and are the result of political struggles at a variety of spatial scales. In central Bihar, the state has allied itself with landlord armies and is a principal oppressor of rural labour. The state has demonstrated little regard for human or civil rights in Bhojpur or Bhagalpur, and it is little wonder that the 'lower orders' have sought to empower themselves against the state by joining people's movements or engaging in an armed struggle. In neighbouring West Bengal, by contrast, as in Kerala or even Tamil Nadu, the state has made significant efforts to take the part of the poor since the late 1970s. The gap between the state's rhetorics of development and actual government practices is less noticeable in these States than it is elsewhere in India. In West Bengal a disciplined and well-organized political party has developed a pro-poor bias in its development policies, and has made consistent efforts to empower the poor and to retrain government officers (although this might be changing as the CPM becomes established as a party of government). The advantages of the Left Front's model of development have already been outlined, but not the least of these advantages is a record of achievement across the State of West Bengal. If and when states commit themselves to a model of democratic development, they can reach out to their supplicants or petitioners in a way that is not open to non-governmental organizations, however virtuous and hardworking these organizations might be. Difference is not always a blessing. When it comes to the provision of basic education or health care, or even participatory institutions, a state which is committed to coverage on a universal basis has several advantages.

West Bengal and Kerala aside, it is not unreasonable to suggest that most people in India have been empowered by the state indirectly rather than directly, where they have been empowered at all. This judgement is a little harsh, because literacy and life-expectancy rates in India attest to a fair measure of government support for education and health care, at least for males in the non-Scheduled communities, and in comparison with rates of provision before 1947. But it captures at least some part of Marguerite Robinson's account of politics and development in Medak District, Andhra Pradesh, and it speaks to those forms of empowerment that have come about as a result of the green revolution and the ending of the one-party system in India. Even in Uttar Pradesh, then, or at least in its western Districts, there are signs of growing affluence and self-confidence among the rural poor. In his account of 'postcolonial developments' in Alipur village, western UP, Akhil Gupta describes:

> Growing economic opportunities that enabled lower castes not to rely as heavily on agricultural labor in the village...[These opportunities], together with the rhetoric of social equality and the dependence of the upper castes on the electoral support of the lower castes, led to a phenomenal transformation in the confidence with which lower-caste people dealt with erstwhile landlords and other socially superior groups. Younger, lower-caste men, still primarily wage laborers, publicly criticized upper-caste people, something that their fathers would not have dreamed of doing. Lower-caste people also...criticized

state officials for not implementing government development programs properly. (1998: 17)[35]

Gupta's work in UP also reminds us, finally, that the difficult and sometimes dangerous struggles that are being waged in India for power as well as for development, are very often being made in recognition both of the state's failings and with regard to a conception of how the state ought to behave. His reports of villagers asking government officials to implement programmes 'properly' are at one with a body of work which is beginning to emerge on the anthropology of the state in India, and which points in two key directions. To begin with, and this returns us to a long tradition of writing on the Indian state, it reminds us that the state is not just at the service of the country's proprietary elites. The state in India consists of various institutions, and its officers are not uncommonly bound by their own rules of service and the cultural norms which go with them. We believe that it is an exaggeration to suggest that the state in India is 'a self-determining third actor', as the Rudolphs have maintained, but the integrity displayed by the Srikrishna Commission, for example, which enquired into the Mumbai riots, and which exposed the bias against Muslims and the brutality of the police, does begin to indicate, as Thomas Hansen has argued, the manner in which an appeal to the idea of the state – what he calls the 'sublime' state – can be used to critique and even to reform the actual practices of government (or those of the 'profane' state: Hansen 1998b). And secondly, more broadly, we are reminded that this same distinction (between the 'sublime' and the 'profane', between the actual and imagined workings of the state or the state-idea) informs the understandings of the state – or of *sarkar* (government) – which are displayed daily by men and women who complain about corruption or the misdeeds of government officers. Jonathan Parry's work in and around the steel plant at Bhilai in Madhya Pradesh leads him to conclude that, 'the widening experience of corruption [which] is an almost inevitable corollary of the expanded reach of the state [is also]... testimony to an internalisation of its norms and values... Corruption has seemed to get worse not [only] because it has, but also because it subverts a set of values to which people are increasingly committed' (1999b: 30).[36]

To put it one last way, the evident failings of the state in India, or even the willingness of politicians from the lower castes to behave corruptly (recall the remarks of Pranab Bardhan, which we reported in chapter 6.4), do not in themselves provide evidence of a more general state of incommunication between the upper and lower orders. We believe that it is not only the case that a 'lower discourse... assert[s] itself and mak[es] itself heard precisely through the opportunities created by the upper one' (Kaviraj 1991: 94), but also that the discourse of the 'lower orders' continues to demand empowerment with reference to 'the universalistic and impersonal values associated with modern bureaucracy' (Parry 1999a: 2). This appeal to the rather austere ideals of the Nehruvian era, moreover, is in opposition, very often, to the less inclusive accounts of the state idea which are being prosecuted by the proponents of economic liberalization and militant Hinduism. The 'revolts of the elites' that we described in chapters 6–8 are being contested, in no small part, by means of discourses that these elites once claimed for themselves.

Conclusion

The history of independent India can be seen ... as the history of a state [a modernizing, developmental state] ... and as the adventure of a political idea: democracy.

Sunil Khilnani (1997: 4–5)

More than half a century after the invention of India as the would-be 'Light of Asia' the mood in the country is unsettled. While the fiftieth birthday celebrations engendered a good deal of publicity abroad – and a fair amount of nostalgia in the United Kingdom – the parades in New Delhi failed to draw the expected multitudes, and the political commentators employed by Dordoorshan, Star TV and the BBC to discuss the legacies of the Nehru–Gandhi dynasty were, for the most part, disparaging of the progress that the country had made since the time of its 'tryst with destiny'. The dominant refrain was that India had missed the boat, or that its years of state-sponsored development had amounted to 'an opportunity lost'. Even Pakistan was said to have made more progress as an emerging economy.

This pessimism was relieved in part by the nuclear tests at Pokhran in 1998. But if the bombs encouraged a brief swelling of national pride, the failure of the BJP government to secure its independence from Jayalalitha reinforced the view that the central state in India had been fatally weakened, and that the personal ambitions of regionalist politicians were holding the country to ransom. Seen from this perspective, the idea of India mapped out by an earlier nationalist elite was in disarray. In the eyes of some observers, too, the rise to power of the BJP seemed to confirm that: 'The idea of political equality ha[d] engendered the menace of a tyranny of the religious majority, a threat traumatically manifested in 1992 by the destruction of the Babri Masjid at Ayodhya by militant Hindu activists' (Khilnani 1997: 10).

The adventures of a political idea (democracy), to paraphrase Khilnani, had finally opened the door to a political ideology or institution which contested many of the modernizing ambitions of the early post-colonial state. The success of the BJP and its allies in the 1999 general elections seemed to underline the strength of this challenge.

It is worth noting that this conclusion, which is not fully endorsed by Khilnani,[1] is of a hue different from that reached by Francine Frankel at the end of her survey of *India's Political Economy, 1947–1977* (1978). Writing at the end of the 1970s, Frankel blamed India's slow and uneven rates of economic growth since Independence on the country's accommodationist politics and the failure of the state to effect radical land reforms. What she did not critique, and in this respect she was not exceptional – Pranab Bardhan adopted a similar line in his *Political Economy of Development in India* (1984) – was the hubris of the state's plans for development or modernization, or the idea that a strong state would be necessary to effect structural transformation and to secure the relief of poverty. In the 1990s, by contrast, and in keeping with recent critiques of high modernism or *dirigisme*, the authority of the state – in the sense of its claims to govern – was challenged more vigorously, and with this challenge has come a greater willingness to critique the mythologies of governance that were mapped out for India in the late 1940s and early 1950s.

This challenge to the authority of the state has drawn inspiration from different sources. For neoliberals like Bhagwati and Srinivasan, the main failing of the 'state idea' in India has related to the government's presumption, until about 1991, that it could direct the market, or even take its place. In this discourse, economic planning is objected to not so much because of the claims to Reason which it advances (which is Ronald Inden's point: see chapter 2), but rather because the simplifications of economic planning cannot hope to capture (by design) or displace the decentralized workings of an efficient economy. Neoliberals, then, object not to the idea of development (as modernization) – in this respect they share certain assumptions with Frankel and Bardhan – but rather to the suggestion that the state should be made the central actor in the organization and direction of that development.

A more radical stance on the state is taken by those critics whose work is informed by post-structuralism. From this quarter has come the charge that the state in India has failed its citizens since 1947 because successive governments have sought to impose a model of development upon the people which is neither widely understood nor especially desired. This charge has been developed in an illiberal guise by some members of the *Sangh parivar*, who have argued in favour of a '*swadeshi* liberalism' which would feign to secure India's integration into the world economy without posing a threat to its assumed cultural distinctiveness or even 'oneness'. A more sophisticated, and assuredly very different version of this critique has been essayed by Sudipta Kaviraj and Partha Chatterjee, and has focused rather more on the gaps in understanding – the conflicts over intelligibility – which they believe have surrounded, and finally eroded, the attempts made by successive governments to impose 'development' from without. Seen from this perspective, the disappointments of India's experiments with planned development were caused not only by '[a] reliance on the bureaucracy to translate the plans of the intellectuals, to fulfil a cultic role as bearers of Reason's flame to the society' (Khilnani 1997: 88), but also, and rather more so, by the unwillingness of ordinary men and women in India to see anything special, and far less anything sacred, in the new temples of industrial modernity which the government set before them as markers of their own futures. This critique has been added to by those who object to the normalizing ambitions of the Indian state, or to its secular pretensions, and by those critics who want India to develop a more genuinely participatory and decentralized federal democracy, and who object, in varying degrees, to what might be described as the 'centralizing and authoritarian' ambitions of successive Indian governments, including those of Jawaharlal Nehru.

There is a good deal to be said for these critiques of the state, if not for that of the *Sangh parivar*. It seems clear to us – as it has seemed clear to Bhagwati, Varshney and Kaviraj in contrasting ways – that Nehru's ambitions for a secular Republic of India, within which a government of Reason would promote development within a framework of deepening democracy, were defeated as early as the late 1950s, and not least because India's proprietary elites made use of the country's electoral systems (notably at the State level) to repel New Delhi's attempts, such as they were, to deliver land to the tiller or to build a commanding industrial sector. The lack of a bourgeois revolution in India, combined with an electoral system which promoted, from the 1960s, the 'ruralization' of Parliament (and especially the Lok Sabha), pushed the Centre to promote development or modernization by means of an expensive and technocratic 'passive revolution' which substituted the conceits of planning not just for 'the market' but also for a concerted attack upon the economic and political privileges of India's richer farmers, monopoly industrial bourgeoisie and leading civil servants.

This passive revolution in turn ensured that the state in India would arrogate to itself an increasing number of powers – sometimes in the name of 'development', but also in the names of 'reason' and the imperatives of 'nation-building' (the 'national interest') – such that democracy itself was weakened (most notably at the time of the Emergency), or turned into a pale shadow of what it had once promised to become. And when at last the Backward Castes partly were pulled or partly pushed themselves into the political landscapes of India, in the 1980s and 1990s, it was, seemingly, to promote a sectionalist or even regionalist agenda that was radically at odds with the Nehruvian design for India, and which, by virtue of its demands upon the state's coffers, further undermined the accumulation project which had been mapped out by Nehru and Mahalanobis.

It is hardly surprising, then, that we should have highlighted the contradictions of 'democratic development' in India, although we have sought to argue that these were latent in the first designs for the post-colonial state. Atul Kohli, while being more charitable to Nehru, has suggested that these contradictions emanate from the discontent generated in a democracy which has proved incapable of promoting sustained economic growth or the reduction of poverty; the Rudolphs, for their part, write of the rise of 'demand politics' in India after the death of Nehru, and join with Kohli in highlighting the 'deinstitutionalization' of the Congress Party and with it the capacity of a political elite to manage the economy and civil society. And Sunil Khilnani, in his considered account of *The Idea of India* (1997), has argued that it is true *both* that the democratic idea has quite profoundly changed the ways in which Indians think about themselves, and that democracy in practice has (often, we would say) come to mean, simply, 'elections'.[2] On one side of the coin the common people have more voice than they used to, and traditional authority has been weakened; on the other side there is evidence of a growing concentration of power among political and economic elites. On one side of the coin India appears to have a vibrant civil society, with what may be the most active and diverse 'NGO sector' anywhere in the world, civil rights organizations, vigorous women's movements, and farmers' movements and movements of 'indigenous peoples' (as 'tribal' groups are described outside India) which are – for instance – carrying on a struggle against biotechnology multinationals which extends into Europe and the United States, and which have succeeded in bringing about a questioning of some of its policies at the highest levels in the World Bank.[3] On the other side there is abundant evidence of the crude violence of the state in India, which is regularly reported in news magazines such as *Frontline* or *Sunday*, as well as by Amnesty International. Recent research sponsored by the World Bank at 468 sites in 23 developing countries has shown that oppressive policing is very widely identified by poor people as amongst their most pressing problems. This surely applies in India too.

India, as one of us argued earlier, is 'an awkward case' (Harriss 1998), both because the country has sought to promote development without putting into place a developmental state, and in the sense that – more controversially – the sort of 'generalized morality'[4] which some consider to be the basis of economic growth in the west might be lacking in a society that dances to a different beat: a society where nationhood is more often imagined in religious than in secular terms, Nehru notwithstanding, and where the cellularity of civil society constrains the development of a national economy and a commitment to economic or social policies which might favour 'Indians as Indians' (as opposed to as 'Yadavs' or 'Lingayats' or 'Tamils'). The pluralism of Indian society, which Nehru acknowledged at the time of States reorganization in the 1950s, is giving rise increasingly to political movements which aim to challenge the integrity of the 'nation-state', or which, more certainly, will promote greater antagonisms between

States, or between New Delhi and the regions, not least around the distribution of public money and the capture of private capitals. Whereas it appeared to many of the 'tall men' of the 1950s that a new India could be invented which would combine socialism and secularism in a federal, democratic Republic, it now appears to many of India's critics that the compulsions of democratic politics, and the inherent pluralism of Indian society, have at once survived the erosion of socialism and secularism as political ideals, and threaten India either with an absurd over-politicization of public life – Sunil Khilnani suggests that: 'In a fundamental sense, India does not "have" politics but is actually constituted by politics' (1997: 9) – or with a profoundly undemocratic backlash wherein various of India's elites seek to impose their own very different and sternly contested visions of order and modernity upon the truculent masses.

This last point, of course, is one that we argued in part III. We are not claiming that India *will* soon be faced with a Bonapartist regime – although we do not discount this possibility – but we have sought to maintain that the politics of the 1990s needs to be understood 'from above' as much as 'from below'. If there is design in the current conjuncture, it comes largely from India's business communities and middle classes, and from the ranks of the Hindu nationalists, each of whom is continuing to stage what we have called a 'revolt of the elites'. To make this argument, however, and to note, as we have, that these revolts are sharply contested, is also to signal where our accounts of the reinvention of India differ from those of other commentators.

Our commitment is to a tradition of scholarship which is centrally concerned with class and the dynamics of capital accumulation. Our accounts of India's contested modernities, and understanding of why it was that India was unable to effect a successful programme of planned economic development, rely heavily on the Gramscian idea of a 'passive revolution'. This is not meant to conjure up a notion of stasis, however, and we sought to describe, in chapters 4 and 5, some very remarkable developments in the Indian economy through the 1970s and 1980s; developments which changed the balance of power that Bardhan described in his account of the political economy of development in India. At the heart of these developments was the so-called green revolution, which secured, in just a few regions of India at first, but more widely through the 1980s and 1990s, a transition to agrarian capitalism and with it a new assertiveness on the part of India's rural elites. This assertiveness, crucially, was directed not so much towards a defence of existing landholding structures (although that surely continued), but rather more so towards a 'new farmers' politics' which aimed to improve the terms under which India's rural elites were integrated into the country's fast extending circuits of commodity capitalism. Notwithstanding the fact that the Nehru-Mahalanobis model of planned industrial development ran out of steam in the mid-1960s, the same governments which were responsible for this model and for many of its failings were also responsible, if not always wittingly, for supporting a private sector in the countryside long before liberalization became the fashion.

The green revolution, to be sure, has not been the success that some of its boosters claimed that it would be (whether in terms of output growth, equity or sustainability), but it probably was successful, as Lipton and Longhurst have argued, in helping to guard India against famines or a more generalized rural poverty, and it did contribute to the emergence of a sizeable middle class in rural India. And this middle class, we would maintain, parts of which now have strong interests in 'urban India', was largely successful in the 1990s in making sure that the economic liberalization which was pushed for by some of India's urban elites did not extend with any vigour into the Indian countryside. Whether this situation can continue is a moot point; our point, simply, is that the uneven and partial nature of liberalization in India can be explained in part by the changing structures of class power across the Indian space-economy. More generally, the project of liberalization itself, while it has not corresponded directly to a singular class interest, has demonstrated once again the importance of class forces in determining patterns of accumulation in India. The structural adjustment which India is presently experiencing is at once driven by a revolt of the elites, and is constrained by the failure of some fractions of industrial capital to set an agenda for reform that would significantly erode the subsidies made over to the middle classes.

To write in these terms, of course, is to invite the complaint that we analyse economic developments in crudely Marxian terms. Chapter 7, we believe, gives the lie to any such charge. In any case, we have also been concerned throughout this book with questions of intentionality and the unintended effects of social action. Part of our argument in respect of the Indian economy is that state spending in support of private agriculture helped to curb the incidence of rural poverty through the 1980s. The government had not sought to support agriculture in this manner in the 1950s, but the contradictions of the Nehru-Mahalanobis model, together with the evident power of richer farmers in the regions, ensured that the state would seek to promote a version of agrarian capitalism from the late 1960s. By the same token, government support for heavy engineering complexes, or steel plants, helped to ensure the growth of regional bourgeoisies in India, and this fuelled an assault upon the very powers of the Centre which were required to push through the dream of industrial modernity that was favoured by Nehru and some of his colleagues.

But this is to treat of intentionality rather thinly. Our more important argument has concerned the wider legacies of the Nehru years, and the mythologies of governance that marked out the invention of independent India. It is true, of course, that the Nehruvian dream of India was contested from the start. It is also true that Nehru's plans for India were never fully shared or even understood by the mass of the Indian population, and that the commands of New Delhi were very often cast in different terms by bureaucrats or politicians located in India's States, Districts or Blocks.

Recent work on the anthropology of the Indian state has begun to reveal the huge gaps in understanding and performance that surround many government programmes for employment provision, for example, or for the 'development of women and children in rural areas'.[5] In this respect it is adding to an earlier literature on 'vernacular' and 'official' understandings of the place of religion in the political life of the Republic. Most Indians have not abandoned their faith, or their community identities, in the way that Nehru expected they would do following the advent of mass education and universal suffrage. But while all this is true, it would be a mistake to suppose that the different lifeworlds described by Kaviraj are opposed in all respects, or that they stand in relation to each other like oil and water. The failure of the Nehruvian dream of modernity might be explained, in part, in terms of the failure of successive governments in India to invest in the educational systems which Nehru thought would bring Reason to India's towns and villages.[6] Moreover, the failure of the Nehruvian design for India – and we agree that it was a failure in large part – should not be taken as evidence that all parts of that project failed in equal measure, or that its legacies have yet been fully worked out. The greater involvement of the 'Backward Castes' in India's political life in the 1980s can be attributed in part to the reservations system (see chapter 9) and to the importance of 'numbers' in a representative democracy. But this involvement, as with the slower empowerment of India's Scheduled Communities, can also be attributed – as it is, for example, by Marguerite Robinson – to the existence of government-funded education and credit schemes (however badly they work in their own terms), or to the effects of land reforms legislation (in the breach as well as in the observance) or a state-sponsored green revolution.

Like Beteille, we believe that there has been a slow but insistent secularization of Indian life since Independence (through schools, universities, hospitals and the mass media, for example), *and* that this secularization has impinged on public debates surrounding the secular principle in India (there was a significant backlash against the destruction of the Babri Masjid in 1992), or around the responsibilities which the state must shoulder in respect of environmental pollution, say, or the freedom of the press, or even famine relief. This is not, of course, to suggest that the state has dealt with these issues in the manner of a rational-legal or Weberian state-apparatus. It is rather to suggest that some of the pressures which are brought to bear upon the state by 'ordinary' people – such as demands for labour laws to be implemented, or demands for the disciplining of corrupt officials – take the form of protests which make reference to an idea of the state which is not so very different from that imagined by the 'tall and inspiring men' of the 1950s. The legacy of the Nehru years is more durable than some commentators have allowed, and the working out of this legacy (not least in terms of the development of secular institutions and the political enfranchisement of the lower orders) continues to inform the contested reinvention of India nearly forty years after his death. The 'elite revolts' that we described in chapters 7 and 8 might indeed threaten the foundations of the Nehruvian vision of India, but these revolts are being constrained by the lower orders and by their willingness to make demands which articulate the claims both of difference and of universalism.

It is this fractured modernity which, finally, inspired our remarks on the changing nature of politics in India, and on the possibilities for empowerment which might exist within India's democratic polity. We recognize, of course, that India's democracy is damaged in all sorts of ways (most democracies are), and it has been a major part of our argument that India's 'social majorities' are still very often the victims of the violence which emanates from the state or from the social elites which have largely had command of the state. We have no truck, then, with the triumphalism that informs Francis Fukayama's account of 'The end of history' (1989), in which he proposes that the 'victory' of liberal democracy and of its stable-mate, market capitalism may constitute the end-point of man's ideological evolution and the final form of government. At the same time, however, we are drawn only in part to the claims of post-development, or to Manuel Castells's suggestion that the class-based politics which were consolidated in the period of 'high industrialization', when people's sense of their own identities was supplied most significantly by what they did, are being replaced increasingly by the politics of issue-based social movements, and by mobilizations based on ethnicity which lack – or refuse – coherent programmes of social change (Castells 1997).

It is possible that late capitalism has disappointed the progressive ambitions of modernity in the west, as it has in part in India. But in India class-based politics continues to remain important, and the state continues to be the focus of social movements as it is of organized political parties. Precisely because 'ordinary' men and women understand so well the importance of the state in India, the history of independent India continues to be written around the state and the 'state idea'. Where change has come, it has come mainly in terms of the ambitions and organization of the state or in respect of new accounts of the 'state idea'. When India was invented as a post-colonial country, in the late 1940s and 1950s, the state sought to arrogate to itself the capacity to define a singular modernity for a singular nation-state. Since that time, the pretensions of a modernizing elite have been challenged by India's farmers, as by its religious nationalists, and the commands of New Delhi have been rebuffed by two generations of regionalist parties and politicians. India has been reinvented and continues to be reinvented. But these reinventions still have regard for the structure and power of the state, and for good reason.

We agree with Paul Brass that the defining struggle in Indian politics today is that between the centralizing instincts of the BJP and the Hindu nationalists (notwithstanding their nods towards decentralization) and 'the counterveiling forces of mobilization of the lower half of north Indian society and the forces of caste mobilization in general' (Brass 1997: 281).

But whereas Brass is inclined to celebrate 'the particular interests, needs, and claims of [subaltern] groups in society defined within their regional and local contexts' (p. 281), and of the States against the Centre, we are inclined to focus as well on the possibility that the state might yet be made to do the bidding of India's lower orders. Both at the Centre and in the States there is much to play for. It is significant, furthermore, that the poor are becoming ever more involved in India's politics, and that they are pushing hard for a greater share of state resources. India's social majorities are seeking greater control, too, over the government structures which still, for the most part, define and regulate access to the 'processes of development'. That they are doing so is testament both to the failures of the post-colonial state in India, and, less wittingly perhaps, and more slowly for sure, to the more positive legacies of Nehru's dream of modernity. Notwithstanding the threats posed to them by India's business elites and religious nationalists, the deepening of democracy in India offers India's 'social majorities' their best hope for taking some control over the economic and political structures which govern their lives and which might yet be made to work for their empowerment. As ironic as it might seem to some critics, their attempts to reinvent India still have regard for the invention of India that was proposed in the Constituent Assembly.

Notes

Preface

1 Mark Nicholson, 'What a difference a year can make', *Financial Times* (London), 26 October 1998.
2 It is also known that only pressure from the United States government dissuaded the Narasimha Rao government from going ahead with nuclear tests earlier in the 1990s: see Abraham (1998). See also Mishra (1998).
3 This way of thinking owes a lot, of course, to Benedict Anderson's *Imagined Communities* (Anderson 1983).
4 The idea of 'intermediate classes' is derived from the work of Michael Kalecki (1972). See also the discussion of the application of Kalecki's ideas in the India context by K. N. Raj (1973); and the exposition by Barbara Harriss-White (1999). The defining characteristic of these classes is that there is no contradiction between capital and labour.

1 The Light of Asia? India in 1947

1 Attlee (British Prime Minister, 1945–51) made this remark in a speech on 15 March 1946. Interestingly, Churchill wrote to Nehru in February 1955 as follows: 'I hope you will think of the phrase "The Light of Asia". It seems to me that you might be able to do what no other human being could in giving India the lead, at least in the realm of thought, throughout Asia, with the freedom and dignity of the individual as the ideal rather than the Communist Party drill book' (quoted in Gopal 1989: 284). When Sir Edwin Arnold wrote his famous book-length poem 'The Light of Asia' in 1885, his subject was, of course, 'that noble hero and reformer, Prince Gautama of India, the founder of Buddhism' (Arnold 1996: vii).

2   This term has been applied, by outsiders, to a group of historians associated with Cambridge University, some of whom at one point developed a Namierite analysis of Indian nationalism. It is a labelling which historians such as Christopher Bayly and David Washbrook reject.

3   By 15 August 1947 Mountbatten had persuaded 562 Princely States to sign a Treaty of Accession; Nehru was left to deal with Kashmir, Hyderabad and Janagarh. It was Sardar Patel, however, who was largely responsible for managing the integration of these States into what became, in 1950, the Republic of India (see our discussion in chapter 3).

4   After D. Arnold (1988a: 44). A. K. Sen (1981, ch. 6) provides a valuable discussion of the Great Bengal Famine.

5   The word collaboration might be more accurate and would call to mind one of the major works of 'Cambridge School' Indian historiography – Anil Seal's account of *The Emergence of Indian Nationalism: Competition and Collaboration in the Later Nineteenth Century* (Seal 1968).

6   The eighteenth century was once described as a period of secular decline in India, but more recent historiography suggests that Europeans were attracted to India by the relative vibrancy of economic and trading life in the region: see C. Bayly (1988; 1990) and Richards (1993). See also our remarks in chapter 2.3.

7   It is not until the 1850s, however, that we can speak of the British ruling 'India'.

8   It was from about this time, too, that the British sought to map India, or to fix the territories of 'British India' by means of the Great Trigonometrical Survey (GTS): see Matthew Edney's outstanding account of the GTS (Edney 1997).

9   Hettne (1978) provides a good account of the political economy of indirect rule in Mysore in the period 1881–1947.

10 See S. Bose (1993); see also James Boyce's forceful analysis of the agrarian impasse in Bengal (Boyce 1987).

11 On the Kol revolt, see J. Jha (1964); on the Bhils, see Hardiman (1987).

12 Many nationalists complained, or came to complain, of a lack of effective tariff policies for the protection and promotion of Indian industry. See Naoroji (1962 [1901]).

13 The persistent peasant revolts which shook the Deccan in the 1870s – following the collapse of the cotton boom – ensured that there were similar Acts in western and central India; on the latter, see Baker (1993: 153).

14 For a general discussion, see the collection of essays edited by Peter Robb (1995). See also Dewey (1993) for an account of 'the mind of the Indian civil service'.

15 Geraldine Forbes offers an interesting commentary on the long struggle for women's franchise. She notes that the Southgate Franchise Committee, which toured India in 1918, advised against an extension of the franchise to women on the ground that it would be 'premature'. 'Lord Southborough decided Indian women did not want the vote and even if they did, social customs would impede its implementation' (Forbes 1996: 95). Some women did gain the vote in the Provinces in the 1920s (beginning with Bombay and Madras in 1921 and following continuing agitations), but the Women's Indian Association felt 'betrayed' when the India Act of 1935 'fixed the ratio of [female to male] voters at 1:5' (p. 112); by this time some women's organizations, and several female legislators, were pushing for a universal franchise.

16 The centralization of power also encouraged a strong sense of subnationalist identity, which is evident still and to which we will return in later chapters.

17 We discuss this further in chapter 2.3. On the 'invention' of caste, see Dirks (1992), and compare with Quigley (1993) and Fuller (1996). The hardening of caste identities was encouraged rather more by the Census of 1911, and the creation of reserved electorates as part of the Morley-Minto reforms.

18 Kulke and Rothermund note that the 'case for separate electorates for Muslims' was 'brilliantly argued' by Risley, 'and finally convinced Morley – or at least silenced his opposition – so that this fateful construction became the leading principle of the constitutional reform of 1909' (Kulke and Rothermund 1986: 272). H. H. Risley was the British Home Secretary at the time.

19 Meghnad Desai (personal communication) reminds us that Gandhi lent heavily on Ambedkar to get his way (he embarked on a fast); he also suggests that the Pact 'forever consigned the Dalits to be exploited by caste Hindus!' Ambedkar called the fast 'a political stunt', a 'vile and wicked act' – quoted in Parekh (1997: 18).

20 For more detail on Jinnah and the Muslim League, see Jalal (1985) and Ahmed (1997).

21 Taken from data assembled by Myrdal (1968).

22 These data from Byres and Nolan (1976: 12, table 2). The cropping index is an expression of the total sown area in relation to the cultivable area as a whole, so that an index of 94 shows that there was land which could have been cultivated which was not sown, and one of 130 shows that 30% of the cultivated land was sown (cultivated) twice.

23 See, for example, Reidinger (1974).

24 See Tomlinson's development of this argument (1988: 133–5).

25 The findings, made by Papanek, are discussed by Lipton with Longhurst (1989) in an analysis of the impact of the 'green revolution' on livelihoods.

26 See Heston's commentary on the debate about living standards in the colonial period (Heston 1982). The poverty estimates referred to are those of Dandekar and Rath (1971), as discussed by Chaudhuri (1979: 203).

27 Saith's table of 'Benchmark Estimates of Poverty Incidence in Rural Asia' gives for 1965: India 53%, Bangladesh (East Pakistan) 83%, Indonesia 47%, South Korea 36%, Malaysia 59%, Nepal 67%, Pakistan (West) 43% and Philippines 56% (Saith 1995).

28 The estimate for 1947 is taken from the United Nations Statistical Yearbook for that year. According to the World Bank's *World Development Report* (1997a) India's population in mid-1995 is estimated to have been 929.4 million. In 1947 India is estimated to have had about 14.5% of the population of the world; by the mid-1990s this had increased to almost 16.5%. According to the Census of India, 14% of the population was urban in 1941; according to World Bank data the urban population of India in 1995 was 27% of the total.

29 The rate of growth of India's population increased to about 2.0% per annum in the 1950s, and then to an even higher rate. It stood at 2.1% per annum in 1980–90, and was reckoned to have fallen back to about 1.8% by the mid-1990s (World Bank 1997a). Life expectancy for men was 26.9 years and for women 26.6 years in the decade 1921–31. By 1951–61 life expectancy had risen to 41.2 years (averaged across both sexes); and in mid-1995 it was 62 years. The infant mortality rate for 1945 was 150.9 per 1,000 live births; it was 116 in 1980 and it

was estimated to have fallen to 68 by 1995. On the problem of the adverse sex ratio in India, see Dreze and Sen (1995, ch. 7). On female infanticide in Tamil Nadu, see Chunkath and Athreya (1997).

30   The phrase 'step-in-your-shoes-nationalism' is after Maddison (1971: 71).

31   On the Mundari rebellion, see Adas (1979) and K. S. Singh (1983).

32   It should be noted that the INC had few Muslim members to begin with, not least because many Muslims had been advised by Sir Syed Ahmed Khan to demonstrate their loyalty to the British after their leading role in the events of 1857. We owe this point to Meghnad Desai.

33   Naoroji's account of *Poverty and Un-British Rule in India* was first published in 1901, although the work for it was mainly carried out in the 1870s. See also Dutt's two-volume *Economic History of India* (1950 [first published in 1904]).

34   And not just the Raj: the Indian Army was also deployed in East Africa, Aden and East Asia.

35   Of course, Gandhi himself objected strongly to the Naoroji-Dutt line that India should use its missing funds to make a better fist of industrialization. In *Hind Swaraj*, Gandhi writes as follows: 'When I read Mr Dutt's *Economic History of India*, I wept; and, as I think of it again, my heart sickens. It is machinery that has impoverished India' (Gandhi 1997 [1908]: 107).

36   On the economics of Empire, particularly in its final years, see Tomlinson (1978). Dominion status was foreseen but ran foul of the interests of some 'native states'. See also, on the transfer of power, Potter (1996, ch. 3).

37   This point is well made by Parekh (1997).

38   We owe this point to the excellent Introduction provided by Anthony Parel to the 1997 *Cambridge Texts in Modern Politics* edition of *Hind Swaraj*. 'It is difficult to estimate the extent of Savarkar's role in the formulation of the philosophy of *Hind Swaraj*: D. Keer, the biographer of both Gandhi and Savarkar, goes so far as to claim that it was written in response to Savarkar. This is clearly an exaggeration, but there is definitely some truth in it. However that may be, during the later decades the ideological gap between the two only widened. Savarkar, who in his London days was a supporter of Hindu-Muslim unity, later changed his attitude towards the Muslims and propounded the intensely anti-Muslim ideology of *Hindutva*. Not surprisingly, it was one of Savarkar's militant supporters who turned out to be Gandhi's assassin' (Parel in Gandhi 1997: xxvii–xxviii).

39   The Mahasabha dates back to 1907 in Punjab, but was established on an all-India basis in 1915; V. D. Savarkar was its President from 1937 to 1944. For the most part the Indian National Congress kept its distance from the Mahasabha, but it did consider a merger shortly before Gandhi's death: see Jaffrelot (1996).

2   'Sovereign, Democratic, Federal, Socialist, Secular': The Invention of Modern India

1   This quotation, and the quotation at the head of the chapter, come from speeches made before the Constituent Assembly: Constituent Assembly Debates [CAD] I; CAD II, 3, 316.

2 Twenty-seven years after the promulgation of the Constitution of India, during the period of Emergency Rule, the liberties referred to in its Preamble were significantly abrogated, and the conventions of parliamentary government were suspended, drawing on emergency powers which were a legacy of the colonial government of India. It was in this moment of modern India's history that the words of the Preamble were changed under the Constitution (Forty-Second Amendment) Act of 1976, to introduce the terms 'Socialist' and 'Secular' into the definition of the Republic, and the word 'integrity' after 'unity' (to give 'unity and integrity of the nation' – reflecting the constant preoccupation of the political elite).

3 New lists of Scheduled Castes and Tribes were issued in 1950 under Articles 341 and 342 of the Constitution. Article 46 states that: 'The State shall promote with special care the educational and economic interests of the weaker sections of the people, and, in particular, of the Scheduled Castes and Scheduled Tribes, and shall protect them from social injustice and all forms of exploitation.' We will discuss the state's provisions for the 'uplift' of the Scheduled Communities in chapter 9.

4 The Communist Party of India was founded in 1925. The Congress Socialist Party was founded in 1934 and was pushed out of the Congress in 1948 by Patel.

5 'The Congress High Command became adept at contriving unity for agitational purposes. The oligarchic style of decision-making was continued after it came to power' (Sudarshan 1994: 62). Gandhi wanted the Congress to become a campaigning oppositional group after Independence – the conscience of the nation, perhaps – but it was not to be.

6 Such elitism led to fears among some thinkers from outside the charmed circle of the mainly high caste, English-speaking professional elite. Already, in the 1870s in Maharashtra, a Non-Brahman leader, Mahatma Jotirao Phule, had founded an organization, the Satyashodhak Samaj, which in 1889 published a paper proclaiming, 'We do not want the National Congress because it does not represent the interests of the people' (in O'Hanlon 1985: 284). Polly O'Hanlon continues this line of thought: 'The Congress represented a spectre that had haunted non-Brahman thinkers since the 1870s: a political body, dominated by Brahmans and the urban-educated, that was capable of winning for itself an institutionalised position as a mediator between the British government and the larger masses of Indian society. Such a development would not only deprive of an effective political voice groups who felt their own interests diverged sharply from those represented in the leadership of the Congress. In the longer term it would mean that the effects of freedom from British rule would not be to emancipate the lower classes' (p. 284). See also our discussion in chapter 9.

7 On the continuities between the colonial and post-colonial state, see Washbrook (1997).

8 According to Herring: 'The Karachi platform [of the Congress] of 1931 was clearly socialist: "land to the tiller and power to the people"; in the 1930s the socialist wing of the movement gained enormously' (1998: 8).

9 The big business class was not only small, it was often disunited. 'The groups formed around the family business empires of the Tatas and Birlas took different stances, based on different visions of how to get along with the new state. The Tatas initiated the Forum for Free Enterprise (the "Bombay Group") which eventually formed the nucleus of an oppositional political party – Swatantra (Freedom) – to contest the premises of socialist development. The Birlas backed

the accommodationist policies of the rival national business organisation (FICCI)' (Herring 1998: 13).

10   For an excellent review of development thinking since about 1945, see Streeten (1997); see also Leys (1995). Desai makes the important point that the Nehru-Mahalanobis model of a 'machine goods'-oriented approach to 'socialism' owed as much to Feldman and Stalin as to two-sector models of the economy (Desai 1998).

11   The Directive Principles of State Policy, unlike the Fundamental Rights of the Constitution, are not justiciable.

12   Not that vote-banks are unknown in some western democracies: the UK is an exception and not a rule in this regard.

13   'The president of India may declare a state of emergency under any one of three or more circumstances [including]: Under Article 352 of the constitution, where there is a threat to the security of the country as a result of war or external aggression... or internal disturbance [sic] (as in 1975)' (Thakur 1995: 112).

14   'No government at the centre – or at the state level – can get away without extreme political damage if it fails to take early action against famines. The presence of active opposition parties and a relatively free news distribution system provide the political triggering mechanism that the Famine Codes in their original form lacked' (A. K. Sen 1989: 775).

15   We offer some brief comments on the workings of *panchayati Raj* in chapter 9. There have been no such elections in Bihar since 1977.

16   Raja Chelliah recently described 'the overwhelming economic power wielded by the Centre' (1998: 346).

17   Jalal notes that, in India, 'Pragmatism triumphed over principle. The notion of a federalism based on divided sovereignty was rejected out of hand' (Jalal 1995: 162).

18   Nehru's thoughts on socialism and secularism can be found in several of the chapters of his autobiography (Nehru 1962). See also Akbar (1988) and Wolpert (1996).

19   Nandy (1998); Inden (1990); Madan (1987). Related – and yet rather different – arguments have also been made by Sudipa Kaviraj and Partha Chatterjee, and we shall consider their arguments at length in parts II and III of this book.

20   On the essentialism of much 'anti-essentialism', see Nanda (1991). Our comments here mirror those of Sugata Bose and Ayesha Jalal: 'A sharply defined fault-line between tradition and modernity as well as Indian and European modernity makes it impossible to take full account of the contestations that animated the creative efforts to fashion a vibrant culture and politics of anti-colonial modernity.... A difference-seeking distortion has crept into studies, such as those of Partha Chatterjee, which privilege a particular strand of "our" modernity as *the* tradition of social and historical thinking on modernism and nationalism' (1998: 112; emphasis in the original). It should also be acknowledged that India's major encounter with the west/modernity was with a country which carried on with many irrational and 'unmodern' (if not anti-modern) social practices: the 'peculiarities of the English' are as important as those of the Indians in any account of modernity in South Asia. (We owe this point to Meghnad Desai.)

21   Where 'high modernism' is understood according to the outline account provided by James Scott; namely, as a form of state-initiated 'large-scale social

engineering' in which 'high modernist ideology [or a 'self-confidence about scientific and technical progress' (1998: 4)] provides the desire, the authoritarian state provides the determination to act on that desire, and an incapacitated civil society provides the leveled social terrain on which to build' (1998: 5).

22   On capabilities and commodities, see A. K. Sen (1985). For a review, see Gasper (1997). See also the annual *Human Development Reports*, since 1990, of the United Nations Development Programme, which develop some of these insights in terms of the measurement of development.

23   The work of Krishna Bharadwaj, in particular, modifies and amplifies Moore's argument on this point. While 'parasitic landlords' – extracting large amounts of surplus from tenant cultivators, and not investing at all in agricultural production – are part of the story she tells, her analysis rather demonstrates the significance of what she calls 'the compulsive involvement in the market of the mass of small farmers' (and which we discuss in chapter 3). Bharadwaj's analysis helps to explain both the low productivity of Indian agriculture and the vulnerability of the mass of rural people. See Bharadwaj (1974; 1985).

24   This famous quotation comes from an article that Marx wrote for the *New York Herald Tribune* in 1853.

25   See Washbrook's (1976) discussion of the governance of the Madras Presidency. Beck (1972) describes a form of social organization in part of south India which was based on territorial units beyond the village, and which was weakened, if not destroyed, by colonial rule.

3   The 'Tall Men' and 'Third Way': Nehru, Patel and the Building of Modern India

1   Kothari writes that: 'Gandhi's death was followed by a coalition of two men, Nehru and Patel. It was in many ways a strange coalition. In their ideological positions, personalities, basic attitudes and political appeal, the two men had differed all along...Although both needed each other in these critical years, were mutually deferent and very discreet, and tried to avoid a showdown, the differences were so fundamental and the issues so pressing...that the conflict had to be resolved before long' (1970: 168). See also Austin's comments on their relationship in the Constituent Assembly (Austin 1966: 315).

2   We are using 'the Nehru years' mainly as a shorthand for the period from 1947 to 1964, but it could reasonably be argued that the years when Nehru was in command ran from 1951 (after the death of Patel) until 1959, when Charan Singh frustrated Nehru's agrarian programmes, or 1962 (the border war with China).

3   For studies of Indian bureaucracy, see David Potter's major study of *India's Political Administrators* (2nd edn 1996); and also Heginbotham (1975), Mook (1974), Potter (1994), Taub (1969) and Mooij (1999). For a careful review of the politics of bureaucratic transfers and their implications, see Wade (1985).

4   These events, and their significance, are discussed by Frankel (1978, ch. 2).

5   Omvedt has briefly traced the history of this tradition, which she opposes to that of Indian communism. This 'derived from the radical nationalism symbolised by Tilak, defined itself against the "anti-industrial peasantism" of Gandhi and

ignored Phule and similar low-caste traditions' (1993: 15). She adds: 'With the aid of communists . . . by the end of the 1930s, in spite of all the mass turmoil and the efforts at autonomous organising by nonbrahmins and dalits, the Congress had increased its hegemony over popular upsurges. And the Congress [like the CPI, too] remained under the control of the upper-caste elite' (p. 21).

6   Nehru noted at the time that: 'The Congress has now attracted into its fold thousands who are not eager for achieving swaraj or to join the fight, but are merely seeking personal gains' (in Gopal 1976: 393).

7   Frankel notes that: 'The AICC's attempt in 1949 to curb the practice of bogus enrollment by amending the Congress constitution to eliminate the four-anna fee for primary membership backfired. The new provision actually encouraged even more massive abuses' (1978: 73).

8   The Congress had a well-developed organizational structure from an early stage, with a hierarchy of units from village and taluka-levels, through district and provincial committees, to its All-India committees, with members of the committees at each level being elected by the lower units.

9   A sophisticated exemplar and a classic of the genre is Adrian Mayer's *Caste and Kinship in Central India* (1960). Another, which follows Weber's classic analysis of the different dimensions of power, is Andre Beteille's *Caste, Class and Power* (1965).

10   Frankel and Rao define the concept of 'dominance' in this context. 'The term "dominance" is used to refer to the exercise of authority in society by groups who achieved politico-economic superiority, and claimed legitimacy for their commands in terms of superior ritual status, or through alliances with those who controlled status distribution' (1989: 2). The concept of the 'dominant caste' is one of the many important contributions to Indian social anthropology made by the late M. N. Srinivas (1959).

11   The new generation of leaders has often been typified by Kamaraj, who displaced Rajagopalachari as Chief Minister in Madras in 1953, and who had little English and was ignorant of Hindi (as by Harrison 1960: 90). He was also an outstanding political strategist!

12   The late W. H. Morris-Jones, cited here and elsewhere in this chapter, made a number of important contributions to Indian political studies. See his *Government and Politics of India* (1971) and *Politics Mainly Indian* (1978).

13   Nehru's optimism about the lower levels of the bureaucracy was reflected in his interviews with Karanjia: 'You have a lot to say about cadres and our failure to create them. I am not for a moment thinking about a party like the Congress or any other party sending people to push on or organise them. *But the real cadres are being built at the village level all the time.* They are not party cadres in that sense: they are village level workers, agriculturalists, peasants – that type, who we give proper training' (Karanjia 1960: 72; emphasis in the original). Yet the reports of the Planning Commission's evaluations had already shown how these sorts of official 'cadres' were easily suborned by the local landholding notables (Hanson (1966) discusses these reports). See also Dube's analysis of village-level development in this period (1958).

14   What we have described as the 'language issue' had several elements: should Hindi become the official national language? what should be the role of English? what should be the status and the relationships to each other and to the political units of the Indian Union of the fourteen or fifteen major languages

spoken in the country, and the thirty or more languages with upwards of a million speakers? A compromise was hammered out in the Constituent Assembly which made Hindi the official language of the country, while postponing the implementation of this decision for fifteen years; it retained English as the official language of the Union and for inter-provincial communication, and recognized the major regional languages as 'national languages'. On the fears which accompanied the linguistic reorganization of States in the 1950s, see Brass (1990: ch. 5). For a positive assessment of the reforms, see King (1997 and in note 17 below).

15 On this, see Hawthorn (1982); and the work of L. I. and S. H. Rudolph on *The Modernity of Tradition* (1967).

16 M. G. Ramachandran, founder of the All India Anna DMK, and later Chief Minister of Tamil Nadu, film star and populist politician extraordinary, might well be described as a pulp fiction hero (see Pandian 1997).

17 This is also the judgment of history, at least according to Robert King. King concludes his preface to his recent book on *Nehru and the Language Politics of India* with the following strong statement. 'It is my considered opinion that if the first prime minister of India had been a linguistic naïf rather than a linguistic sophisticate like Nehru, then we should have today not a unified India with a strong government at the centre but an India weakly divided along linguistic and cultural lines into two or three semi-autonomous regions. The unity of India would be as a faded dream' (King 1997: xvi).

18 There is a confessed Whiggishness in our historiography, writing as we do after the success of the Bharatiya Janata Party in the 1998 and 1999 general elections, the BJP being the current avatar of what was originally the Jana Sangh. To those writing on Indian politics in the later 1980s neither the RSS nor even the Jana Sangh/BJP seemed as important as they do to us writing ten years later. Brass (1990) has two references to the RSS; and Kohli (1990a) has only one. Indeed, it is rather remarkable that Kohli's valuable and astute analysis of trends in Indian politics should not have given more weight to Hindu nationalism. Both Vanaik (1990), especially, and the Rudolphs (1987) were more perceptive. It is perhaps not so surprising, however, that political scientists should have regarded the Hindu nationalists as being not so important, given the way that they had been marginalized after the early 1950s, and also the centrality of the Congress in mainstream political science studies of India up to the time they were writing. Yet Howard Erdman, in his study of the Swatantra Party published in 1967 had recognized 'the substantial, if often latent or untapped or disorganised reservoirs of right-wing strength in India' (1967: 260), and specifically criticized political commentators for their tendency to disregard this strength. Even now some commentators allow their hostility to right-wing and Hindu nationalist positions to stand in the way of substantial critical analysis.

19 The history of the relationships of the Jana Sangh and the RSS is analysed in scrupulous detail by Jaffrelot (1996, chs 2–5).

20 A selection of Nehru's speeches at India's irrigation and power projects was put together by C. V. Sharma (1989) for the Central Board of Irrigation and Power. Some of these are cited by Arundhati Roy in her scathing attack on India's 'big dam' projects, and not least the Narmada valley dams (1999).

21 In a huge literature, see World Bank (1993), and Wade (1990).

22   Leftwich (1994) offers a more extended discussion of the features of 'developmental states'.

23   The question arises as to why the Taiwanese regime, or those in the People's Republic of China, or South Korea, or Japan should have had these capacities, and India not. There is agreement amongst several writers that (in Wade's formulation of the argument): 'a shared sense of the vulnerability of the nation has helped to concentrate the rulers' minds on performance-enhancing measures as a means of their own survival. Policies are seen as having been dictated by "the politics of survival" ' (Castells 1998: 267). Yet in India, too, there have been deep anxieties about the integrity and the security of the nation. Perhaps the vital difference with India is that the regimes which were responsible for the economic success of the 'East Asian Tigers' were born out of armed struggle (or crushing military defeat in the case of Japan), and that they were then ruled in the context of US military power (which shored up the regimes in Japan, Taiwan and South Korea, and continually threatened the PRC). In India, in contrast, 'There were always dissonant chords that undermined the purposive commitment to state control of economic growth that characterised the East Asian nations' (Herring 1998: 10).

24   This argument has often been put in the pages of *The Economist* (see, for example, the supplement on India of 22 February 1997).

25   See Lewis (1954). On the Lewis model, see also Toye (1987).

26   This was the title, for example, of an influential book edited by Paul Streeten and Michael Lipton (1968).

27   Nehru summed up his own position in his interview with Karanjia in 1960: 'I confess I am not satisfied with the rate of progress made (in agriculture)... It is basically a problem of moving the masses fast enough and changing the accumulated inertia of centuries into action and, in our case, doing all this within the democratic framework... once we start moving, as we are doing through the village community projects and now cooperative farming and village panchayats – that is, giving more and more power to the cooperatives and the panchayats, the pace will become quicker and the steps more confident' (Karanjia 1960: 47–8).

28   This term was suggested by Michael Lipton in his contribution to the volume on *The Crisis of Indian Planning* (Streeten and Lipton 1968); it was elaborated in his later monograph, *Why Poor People Stay Poor* (1977). He, and the American economist John Mellor, in his book *The New Economics of Growth* (1976), both criticized the Nehru-Mahalanobis model for its neglect of agriculture, and advocated an agriculture-led strategy for economic growth based on arguments about the efficiency of small-scale agriculture and the potential in the growth-stimulating linkages forwards and backwards from agriculture. They both focused more on the demand side of the economy than did the Nehru-Mahalanobis model.

29   The idea of compulsive – or compulsory, perhaps – involvement in the market is especially associated with Krishna Bharadwaj (1974).

30   We believe this phrase was the invention of Goran Djurfeldt and Staffan Lindberg in their book, *Behind Poverty* (1975).

31   The significance of this development was pointed up by Paul Brass, who noted the importance of the opposition of the bulk of the middle peasantry, especially in the north, as providing a persistent basis of support for opposition parties (1982: 258).

4   Jealous Populism, Crises and Instability: Indira's India

1   The distinction which we make here between 'state-as-organization' and the 'state-idea' is taken from Philip Abrams (1988).

2   These arguments, in regard to the introduction of the New Agricultural Strategy by C. Subramaniam, are thoroughly critiqued by Ashutosh Varshney (1995, ch. 3).

3   See on this the sensible discussion in Chaudhuri (1979: 198–202).

4   Hari Sharma warned that India's countryside was like a water melon: green on the outside, but red inside (1973). Francine Frankel also analysed these developments in her valuable and not untypical book from this time, *India's Green Revolution: Economic Gains and Political Costs* (1971). Those who followed her, however, like one of us, already found within a very few years reason to doubt the possibilities for radical agrarian mobilization outside a few particular pockets of the Indian countryside (J. Harriss 1977a and 1980), and to question her interpretations of some of her observations (J. Harriss 1977b). See also Bouton (1985).

5   Annual plans took the place of the Fourth Five Year Plan in the period from 1966 to 1969.

6   The move away from the US was prompted in part by Lyndon Johnson's allegedly dismissive treatment of Mrs Gandhi when she visited Washington in 1966 (although Frankel reports that Indira was 'warmly welcomed by President Johnson' (Frankel 1978: 297)); Johnson also blocked a promised World Bank aid package to India even after the country agreed to the devaluation of the rupee in 1966.

7   The text of Mrs Gandhi's letter was published in *The Statesman*, 12 November 1969 (Frankel 1978: 427). On the story of the split and the background to it, and especially the activities and the ideas of the Congress Forum for Socialist Action, see Frankel (1978, ch. 10). See also Nayar (1971).

8   The 'R' in 'Congress-(R)' stands for 'Requisition' – which comes from a meeting in November 1969 'requisitioned' by Mrs Gandhi against the authority of the Congress President, Nijilingappa. The 'O' in 'Congress-(O)' means 'Organization'.

9   On the decline of 'traditional authority' see also Mendelsohn (1993). It is also an important theme in Kohli's analysis of political change in the 1980s (1990a).

10   Kochanek (1976) and Manor (e.g. 1983) were early expositors of this argument. More recently it has been developed by Kohli (1988; 1990a). See also Manor (1988), P. Brass (1990) and Rudolph and Rudolph (1987).

11   In general elections at the national level these have been, successively, the 'Indira wave' (1971), the 'Janata wave', expressing protest at what happened during the Emergency (1977), another 'Indira wave', reflecting disillusionment with the Janata government (1980), the 'Sympathy wave' which swept Rajiv Gandhi to power after the assassination of his mother in October 1984, and then the wave of support for V. P. Singh and the National Front, and against the perceived corruption of the Rajiv Congress, in 1989.

12   The DMK – Dravida Munnetra Karagham – with its roots in the Dravidian Movement of the pre-Independence period, won power in what was then the State of Madras in the 1967 elections. The party split in 1972, not long after the

death of its founder, C. N. Annadurai, when the film star and politician M. G. Ramachandran led the breakaway All-India Anna DMK, claiming the mantle of the founder. The AIADMK found a more or less ready-made network of local organizations in the well-established MGR fan-clubs which existed throughout the State, but it depended on loyalty to the 'Talaivar' (leader). The DMK depends much more on its organizational roots (see also Kohli 1990a: 187). The political traditions and vehicles of Hindu nationalism and social democracy-communism are discussed in chapters 8 and 9 respectively.

13   The consequences are vividly described by Paul Brass in his account of national power and local politics in Uttar Pradesh over a twenty-year period. He showed that by the early 1980s, by contrast with the situation that had obtained in the 1960s, 'national power lacks a firm institutional base independent of government' (1984: 115), though local structures of power remained important, 'wave factors' or Mrs Gandhi's attempts to nationalize issues notwithstanding.

14   See Kohli (1990a: 308) for the same summary of positions.

15   There was a wide consensus on these reasons for the downturn in industrial growth after the mid-1960s. See Bagchi (1975), Patnaik (1972; 1979), Patnaik and Rao (1977) and Rubin (1985).

16   The provisions of this Act were almost immediately undermined. See the later editorial comments of the *Economic and Political Weekly* for 8 May 1982 and 30 May 1987.

17   'Intensification' refers to a pattern of increasing agricultural production by making more intensive use of the land, rather than through the 'extensive' means of bringing more land into cultivation. In the first fifteen years after Independence, India's agricultural output grew as much as a result of the extension of the agricultural frontier as from intensification (see also chapter 3). Thereafter increased output resulted almost entirely from the latter cause.

18   Just what a gamble it was is shown in the fact that agricultural output actually declined in the first years of the supposed 'green revolution'. So convinced were the planners that output must be increasing – or such were the political compulsions under which they were operating – that an expert committee decided that the statistical returns must be wrong and that output figures should be increased before publication. See Boyce (1987) for a lucid discussion of agricultural production statistics and fallacies in post-green revolution India.

19   See, for example, chapters in Farmer (1977) referring to a semi-arid region in northern Tamil Nadu; see also J. Harriss (1993) on the belated green revolution of the 1980s in West Bengal.

20   On the economic activities of this class in India in the recent past, see Harriss-White (1996), Upadhyay (1988), Rutten (1995) and Jeffrey (1999).

21   All these points have been exhaustively analysed and discussed. See Byres (1981), Farmer (1977) and J. Harriss (1987a); and in a wider context Griffin (1974). On the adoption of new technology by smaller producers, albeit after some time lag, and for a more positive, 'revisionist' analysis of the green revolution than those offered by Griffin, Byres or Frankel, see Lipton with Longhurst (1989).

22   This helpful phrase comes from Staffan Lindberg (1995).

23   Amongst other writers on the political economy of India perhaps the only ones to emphasize this point in the way that we have sought to are Vanaik (1990) and Varshney (1995).

24 For a more elaborate critique of the Rudolphs' position, see Byres (1988); see also J. Harriss (1992). The idea of 'partial proletarianization' is discussed by Byres (1981) and by Harriss (1992). For a recent ethnography which demonstrates the point we are making about the polarization of agrarian class structures – *contra* the yeoman farmer/bullock capitalist fantasy – see Lerche (1995).

25 As noted in chapter 3, and as derived from Bharadwaj (1974; 1985) and Bhaduri (1983).

26 See the following articles for various critical remarks on the Mellor-Lipton line on agricultural growth and rural-urban growth linkages: Basant (1987), Harriss and Harriss (1984), J. Harriss (1991), Islam (1987), Saith (1986, 1995), Vaidyanathan (1986), Walker and Ryan (1990).

27 This is the argument of Lipton with Longhurst (1989), in particular, although it is broadly supported by some other writings on Indian poverty. (Lipton and Longhurst remind us that famines might well have stalked India in the absence of a green revolution.) For a short review, see J. Harriss (1992). S. Bhalla (1987) shows that some of the positive impacts of the green revolution, in terms of employment and labour productivity, were already fading in the 'high' green revolution areas of northwest India by the mid-1980s. This argument takes no account of the environmental effects of the green revolution or of its longer-run consequences (on which see Shiva 1991 for an emotive account).

28 At the time it was very widely believed that the green revolution was responsible for increased pauperization. See Pearse (1980).

29 This was the title of an important book, which influenced development policies internationally, produced jointly by the World Bank and the Institute of Development Studies at the University of Sussex, and published in 1975 (Chenery et al.).

30 The Rudolphs associate the Janata with the formulation of a fourth strategy for agriculture, which they characterize in terms of 'Rural Employment and Increased Investment in Agriculture', and see as an attempt to implement the kind of agriculture-first development policy proposed in Mellor's *New Economics of Growth* (1976) (Rudolph and Rudolph 1987: 329).

31 The Constitutional Amendments passed by Indira Gandhi's governments were reversed by Janata. See Frankel (1978), and Rudolph and Rudolph (1987, ch. 3).

5 Drifting Towards Catastrophe:
The Powerlessness of the Congress-(I)

1 The idea that India's 'growing crisis of governability' was caused by the close connections between 'democracy and discontent' is explored further in Kohli 1990a. We agree that India became more democratic in the 1980s, in the sense that more people were able and minded to take part in the political process, parliamentary or otherwise. It is important to insist, however, that this democratization of the public sphere went hand in hand with a corruption of at least some of the democratic principles and institutions that were announced in, or set up in accord with, the Constitution of the Republic of India. See also our discussion in chapter 9.

2   This quotation comes from an essay that Chatterjee wrote on the eve of the 1984 general election. The argument that is summarized in the statement we have quoted here can be traced through several of Chatterjee's essays: see his *A Possible India: Essays in Political Criticism* (1997a [1977]).

3   Weiner's generalization was not necessarily accepted by other political scientists. Manor, for example, noted that it probably did not hold for the south (Manor 1984: 164–5). Note, too, that Weiner's use of the term 'middle peasant' here is idiosyncratic, and that he seems to be talking about those whom we have described rather as constituting the rich peasantry.

4   The quotation from Chatterjee makes it clear that he does not think of the Congress Party as an instrument of class rule for a single class; the Congress party was an instrument for holding together a coalition of landed and urban elites in order to rule India.

5   One of us recalls a conversation in Delhi in December 1989 with an old friend who was by then one of the most senior members of the Indian Administrative Service. In his time as a Collector in the 1950s and early 1960s, he said, there was no question of his pre-eminence in his District, whereas now, he thought, the District Superintendant of Police must often count for much more. For a discussion of the 'tariffs' that are often paid to gain a position in the police force, in this case in western Uttar Pradesh, see Jeffrey (1999).

6   The weak-strong state formulation is developed by Rudolph and Rudolph (1987).

7   These events are described in detail by the Rudolphs (1987, ch 5).

8   The charts prepared by Butler, Lahiri and Roy (1997: 150–1) are a useful guide to the bewildering history of India's political parties.

9   This analysis derives from the work of Roderick Church (1984).

10   These patterns are analysed in detail in the various studies of State politics in the two-volume work edited by Frankel and Rao, *Dominance and State Power in Modern India* (1989 and 1990).

11   'The disintegration of the Janata Party was virtually complete by 1984 when its components contested as four separate national parties: Indian Congress (Socialist), Bharatiya Janata Party, Lok Dal and the Janata Party.... The Congress faced a disunited opposition everywhere except in a few states either where strong state parties had emerged (as in Andhra Pradesh where N. T. Rama Rao's Telugu Desam swept the polls) or where the opposition had organized itself into a local coalition (as in Kerala)' (Butler, Lahiri and Roy 1997: 152).

12   Partha Chatterjee, even in December 1984, was much less sanguine about the prospects for change, and foresaw the continuing crisis of the political system (Chatterjee 1997a [1984]). See also note 2 above.

13   Kohli has analysed the events of the Rajiv period in some detail: see Kohli 1988; 1990a, chs 11 and 12; and 1994. The Rudolphs give a detailed account of Rajiv's failure to reform his party (1987: 148ff). Weiner's '*Mid-Term Assessment*' (1987) was characteristically shrewd, and concluded: 'For a brief historical moment there was an opportunity for significant change. That moment appears to have passed.'

14   Chatterjee wrote at this time, too, of the 'considerable hiatus between the economic dreams of the present rulers and the political compulsions of ruling the country' (1997a [1985–6]: 110). The project of economic liberalization

conflicted with what most Congress members believed to be necessary to keep their constituents quiet.

15   The allegation that illegal commissions were paid by the Government of India – in March 1986 – to the Swedish firm, Bofors, for the purchase of 410 155 mm howitzers. This allegation was also bound up with claims that the Indian Army had not wanted the contract to be awarded to the Swedish firm, and with the allegation that Rajiv Gandhi benefited personally from illegal commissions or kickbacks.

16   See Atul Kohli's forceful development of this argument (1990a, ch. 13).

17   According to Planning Commission data, the annual percentage rate of growth of industrial production in India was 7.3% during the First Plan period (1951–6), 6.6% during the Second Plan period (1956–61), and 9.0% in the Third Plan period (1961–6). Following the work of Rakshit (1982), economists are sceptical of the claim that 'real savings and hence investment rates are...as high as a proportion of GNP as the estimated 22–3 per cent estimates at current prices.' Nevertheless, as Bhagwati goes on to say: 'real gross fixed capital formation as a proportion of GDP...increased by more than 70 per cent during the period 1950–80, on a very conservative basis' (1993: 42–3).

18   For a generally excellent account of the growth of a 'subsidy Raj' through the 1970s and 1980s, see Mundle and Govinda Rao (1991). What is largely missing from this account of India's public finance, however, is an analysis of the massive growth of police and defence-related expenditure in India during this period.

19   During the Emergency (1975–7), as Chatterjee noted, the Congress leadership in New Delhi had moved 'to clip the wings of the new rich peasant body. That the Emergency regime collapsed because of the combined opposition of practically the entire rural population in northern India, from landlords down to poor peasants, was not in small part due to these moves to curtail the power of the dominant rural classes. This is an important part of the history of the rise to power of the Janata party' (1997a[1978]: 68–9).

20   As Talbot reminds us, 'Technically the state's formal accession to India provided for the extension of India's jurisdiction over Jammu and Kashmir only in matters of defense, foreign affairs, and communications. In fact, New Delhi's influence went considerably further' (1991: 131), and therein lies one source of the more recent 'troubles'. See also Navlakha (1996).

21   After Guhan (1985: tables 8 and 9).

22   Toye (1981) remains a useful primer on India's fiscal federalism.

23   The economic underpinnings of the crisis in Punjab are usefully explored in an essay by Bhushan (1984). See also, and more generally, Chadda (1997).

24   On conceptions of identity and territory among some Sikhs, see Pettigrew (1984) and Mahmood (1996); McLeod (1989) is also valuable.

25   The Anandpur Sahib Resolution of 1973 was later radicalized by Sikh nationalist leaders including Bhindranwale and Harchand Singh Longowal. Longowal would split from Bhindranwale in 1984.

26   This figure after McGirk (1996).

27   Interestingly, the MP for Faizabad at this time, Vinay Katiyar, was the chief of the newly formed (July 1984) Bajrang Dal. As Ashis Nandy and his colleagues point out: 'The name of the Dal invokes the imagery of the army of monkey warriors in the Ramayana, led by their king Hanuman, also known as Bajrang.

As the functionaries of the Dal never fail to remind one, Hanuman was the most devoted and obedient of all disciples of Lord Ram and fought on the side of the Lord against the demon-king Ravan, to ensure the triumph of good over evil' (Nandy et al. 1995: 95).

28 The figures given in and to the official Mishra Commission inquiry into the killings; the first figure comes from the Delhi administration and the second from the Citizens' Justice Commission.

29 For an excellent account of 'the colors of violence' which have come to surround the hardening of Hindu and Muslim identities in India, see Kakar (1996). See also M. Hasan (1996), and, on the Shah Bano controversy, Engineer (1987).

6   'Elite Revolts': Reforming and Reinventing India in the 1990s

1 On this incident, see the account given by Sisson (1990).

2 Jayati Ghosh shows the deep roots of the liberalization debate in India (1998).

3 The shifts in middle-class values and attitudes are the subject of Pavan Varma's book, *The Great Indian Middle Class*, in which he argues that the principled, sometimes priggish, high-mindedness of the middle class in the Nehru period tended to give way to the unprincipled pursuit of narrow self-interest thereafter. 'For all the achievements of the Indian state in the last fifty years', he writes, 'there is for its middle and elite classes, a crippling ideological barrenness which threatens to convert India into a vastly unethical and insensitive aggregation of wants' (1998: xii).

4 This quotation from *The Economic Times*, 14 January 2000.

5 These links are 'significant but problematic' because the BJP owes much of its success to the organizational strength of the cadre-based RSS, and to the popular mobilizations over Ayodhya driven by the VHP, but: 'The political elements in the BJP must look at [the] extremist agenda [of these organizations] with some discomfort, as this would completely disrupt the social fabric of everyday life in India' (Kaviraj 1997: 15). The tensions between the 'compulsions of office' and the agenda of *Hindutva* were already evident within a matter of a few weeks of the BJP's resumption of office in October 1999. The question of whether or not the construction of a Ram temple at Ayodhya was still on the agenda of the BJP became an embarrassment to Prime Minister Vajpayee, as he sought to manage the contending demands of both coalition partners in the National Democratic Alliance and the other constituents of the *Sangh parivar*. See *Frontline*, 25 December 1999.

6 Our argument here does not discount the possibility of the involvement of BJP leaders in some of the notorious scams of the 1990s. Hansen and Jaffrelot note that while 'the BJP benefited from the image of integrity and even asceticism cultivated by some of its cadres and inherited from the RSS . . . this asset may be dwindling because of the coming in of new members and the party's tendency to fall in line with the general trend of more leaders and candidates with criminal records: in 1993–5, out of the 126 MLAs of UP charged of a criminal case . . . 49 belonged to the BJP' (1998: 20).

7 We are grateful to Barbara Harriss-White for prompting here. D. L. Sheth, in a recent article, reports on survey results which show that the self-definition of the

'middle class' includes the following four characteristics: (1) ten years of schooling or more; (2) ownership of at least three of these four assets: motor vehicle, television set, electric pumpset, non-agricultural land; (3) residence in a pucca (brick built) house; (4) white-collar occupation (Sheth 1999).

8   Adrian Mayer writes of the village in Madhya Pradesh which he has studied over nearly forty years that 'there are a few *uttam* (lower caste) households who have especially benefited from the new economic opportunities. As farmers they have prospered under government policies of subsidising inputs and of floor prices for crops as well as the absence of agricultural income tax, and to this they have added the incomes(s) from professional jobs in government service and/or in industry or commerce. Such households now boast colour television, fans (and by now an air cooler), perhaps a tractor, motor cycle and/or jeep, and modern furniture, clothes and so forth. In this they are starting to resemble the "ruppy" of more advanced regions such as Haryana and Maharashtra [who are said to be mainly from middle-ranking castes rather than from the traditional landowners of the upper castes]' (1996: 54).

9   These figures are taken from Dubey (1992).

10 This statement, made by Raja Chelliah, then Director of the National Institute of Public Finance and Policy, is quoted by Dubey, who also gives the numerical estimates we have cited here (1992: 143–8).

11 Both Thomas Hansen's (1996a) careful account for Maharashtra, and Zoya Hasan's (1998) for UP, situate the rise of the BJP in these States in the context of growing dissatisfaction with the Congress.

12 This is indicated in polling data reproduced by Dubey (1992: 161) which shows that while 22.9% of 'middle-class voters' polled in 1988 (or 1989, Dubey is ambiguous as to the date) intended to vote for the National Front, this proportion had fallen to 4.5% by late 1990.

13 The Chief Minister involved here was Jayalalitha, at the head of the AIDMK government of the State. As Fuller notes, the training of temple priests to recite Sanskrit is something which was absolute anathema to traditional Dravidian nationalists. But, as he goes on to observe, 'Writers on Hindu nationalism, observing its strength in northern and western India, have tended to underestimate it elsewhere, whereas at least in Tamilnadu it has actually had a major impact' (1998: 19). Another writer has also described 'the end of the Dravidian era in Tamil Nadu' (Pinto 1999).

14 Compare also Z. Hasan, writing with specific reference to Uttar Pradesh: the main appeal of the BJP, she says, 'was to the insecurities of the upper castes who were willing to switch support after the decline of Congress dominance to the BJP' (1998: 223). Her analysis of the increasing influence of the BJP in UP lays particular emphasis on the idea of a 'filling of the vacuum' created by the failure of the Congress, and of the state itself.

15 Bayly refers, for example, to the claims of Jat cultivators to be protecting themselves against 'unvirtuous' Harijan-Chamars (1999: 349ff). The conflictual dynamics of rural labour markets in which – according to some writers – rich peasants may seek to re-establish forms of labour bondage against the assertiveness of labourers, some of whom have become somewhat better off, are the subject of studies in a special issue of the *Journal of Peasant Studies* (Byres et al. 1999). *Frontline* has commented more starkly that the 'politics of hate may actually be popular among key sectors of the Indian polity, notably the profes-

sional middle classes and the trading bourgeoisie in northern India' (12 February 1999, p. 17).

16 See Praful Bidwai's article 'Marginalising Kalyan Singh – It's Goodbye to Social Engineering', *Times of India*, 26 November 1999.

17 The contrast between north and south is significant. Social movements of Backward Classes were successful in the south, even before the end of the colonial period, in taking power from the upper castes (who were, anyway, much less numerous there than in the 'Hindi heartland': see Frankel (1989) and see also our discussion in chapter 9). These political mobilizations in the south help to explain the generally higher level of social development (or 'human development', according to current jargon) there than in most of the north of the country.

18 See Jaffrelot's discussion of the significance of the results of the 1991 elections (1996: 443–8); and also Manor (1992). By the end of the 1990s, however – as we explain – it could no longer be claimed that the BJP was just a party of the Hindi heartland.

19 Chris Fuller notes that there was a marked change, too, in Hindu attitudes towards Muslims in Tamil Nadu after the demolition at Ayodhya: 'Even in 1991, when I had interviewed Minakshi temple priests about the Ayodhya campaign, there was lukewarm support for Hindu nationalists and no serious antipathy towards Muslims, whereas three years later attitudes had altered a lot. Thus in 1994–5, numerous priests recited the standard litany of complaint that Muslims were violent and fanatical, were polygamous and had too many children, were favoured by the pseudo-secular state, and so on' (1999: 27).

20 These issues are touched upon by Bhatty (1996).

21 In Coimbatore, as earlier in Bombay (Mumbai), both communal bias in the police force and struggles amongst the mafia of the bazaar played an important part in these events. See *Frontline*, 7–20 March 1998.

22 In spite of the outcome of the 1999 general election, for reasons that we outline later in this chapter, we still consider the forward march of the BJP to be 'uncertain'.

23 Hansen is here quoting from the BJP's *Humanistic Approach to Economic Development (A Swadeshi Alternative)*. Hansen's account of '*Hindutva and Capitalism*' (1998b) shows the discrepancies and contradictions to which this policy position has given rise, as Hindu nationalists have sought to show how economic liberalization in internal affairs can be combined with a protectionist posture towards the world market (see also chapter 7 below).

24 Laloo Yadav's power in Bihar was thereafter challenged by public interest lawyers who sought to expose his role in the 'fodder scam'. One of his main antagonists, Ravi Shankar, is now a leading light in the BJP in both State and national circles.

25 The returns to office of both Digvijay Singh, the Congress Chief Minister of Madhya Pradesh, and of Chandrababu Naidu, leader of the regional party, the Telugu Desam, founded by his father-in-law N. T. Rama Rao, were remarkable because they went so much against the long-standing tendency in Indian politics for incumbents to be voted out at the next election. This tendency has been associated with the reliance by politicians on populist promises to the electorate which cannot, however, be delivered. Both Digvijay Singh and (latterly) Chandrababu Naidu eschewed such promises, and seemed to have won the confidence

of voters on account of their vision and competence. Thus they seemed to some observers to be the harbingers of a new political style.

26 See Abraham (1998) for an interesting historical account; see also Corbridge (1999). On the post-bomb conflicts between India and Pakistan, particularly in the Kargil region, see Bidwai and Vanaik (1999).

27 These are the arguments of N. Ram, Editor of *Frontline*, 21 May 1999. See also World Bank (1998: xiii): 'foreign institutional investors withdrew more than $400 million from [India's] stock markets in May and June 1998' following India's nuclear tests and the G7's retaliatory sanctions.

28 From an article by the historian K. N. Pannikar in *Frontline*, 12 February 1999. See also the detailed inventory which appears in the same issue.

29 It has to be said that, in contrast with its performance earlier in the year, the BJP government succeeded in managing hostility by some within the *Sangh parivar* to the visit of the Pope to India in November 1999, so that the visit passed off without incident. The extent to which the BJP really had moved more to the centre-ground of Indian politics by the beginning of the year 2000 remained uncertain, in spite of the statement of intent in the 'Chennai declaration' which is referred to in this chapter.

30 The argument about 'fuzzy' boundaries and the development of an 'informal state' is that of Barbara Harriss-White (1997), but similar points are made in the work of Akhil Gupta (1995) and of Thomas Hansen (1998b). See also the discussion by Fuller and Harriss (2000) and our discussion in chapter 7.4.

31 There clearly is evidence for this proposition, but we are wary of the sweep of Bardhan's generalization, and his apparent suggestion that lower-caste leaders understand only the politics of 'corruption' (see our discussion in chapter 9.5).

7 The Dialectics of Reform: The State and Economic Liberalization

1 In one sense, of course, informal economies are always 'unregulated'. What we are calling attention to here is a weakening of the moral codes and legal frameworks which are meant to 'regulate' the basic employment conditions of workers in the informal sector, as elsewhere; hence 'deregulation' in a broader sense.

2 The NSSO method of poverty estimation uses State-specific poverty lines and a more robust measure of price inflation (or price deflator).

3 Heston (1990) rightly comments that nutrition-income measures of poverty are not the only indicators of poverty in use: the World Bank (1989a) has tried to count the 'poor' and the 'ultra-poor', while others have moved towards entitlements or self-definition accounts of poverty and empowerment (see A. K. Sen 1983 and Jodha 1988 respectively).

4 An estimated 80% of funds came from the Centre for most such programmes.

5 The Maharashtrian scheme has been widely commended: for a critical but not unsympathetic overview, see I. Singh (1990: 265–70); see also Echeverri-Gent (1988; 1993) and Reynolds and Sunder (1977). The Chief Minister's Nutritious Noon Meal Programme in Tamil Nadu, to give it its full name, was criticized at first for putting untenable pressures on the State's financial resources: for a

discussion, see B. Harriss (1984). Some of its beneficial impacts became clear in subsequent years: on a possible link between the Noon Meal scheme and the increased attendance of children (especially boys) in rural schools, see Ramachandran (1990: 247). See also I. Singh (1990).

6 On the IRDP, especially, see Dreze (1990) and Swaminathan (1990); for a useful comparison of rural credit and employment schemes, see Kabeer and Murthy (1996).

7 Montek Ahluwalia declared that: 'A growth rate of 5 per cent is now definitely sustainable and could even be bettered if the considerable unused potential built up from past investment in the economy is effectively exploited. There is considerable scope for reaping such benefits both in agriculture and in industry, with present levels of the rate of investment or modest improvements therein. The policy initiatives being taken in the industrial sector will help to bring about this outcome' (1988: 359, based on a conference paper delivered in 1986). The World Bank began its review of the Indian economy at the end of the 1980s in similar fashion, and claimed to detect clear signs of liberalization and policy transition: 'The last two years have seen a good growth performance: GDP grew at an average rate of about 5%, so the Seventh Plan is off to a commendable start. The 1980s to date are showing that growth of at least 5% a year is achievable. Investment is being sustained at nearly 25% of GDP. A consistent 92–94% of this investment is being financed by domestic savings, which have been growing' (World Bank 1989b: 1).

8 The Open General License category was introduced in fiscal year 1978–9 and encouraged the free importation of items used for domestic production, save for those items that were specifically banned or restricted. On this and other policy changes in the late 1970s and early 1980s, see Harriss (1987b), Joshi and Little (1995) and Wolf (1982).

9 Deepak Lal was thus being harsh but not untruthful when he declared, in an essay first published in 1988, that 'the translation of [Rajiv's] good intentions was at best hesitant, and largely window dressing' (Lal 1999: 35; and compare Patel 1987). A possible exception to this judgement is the autos industry, which was significantly restructured in India in the 1980s: for an account of the Hero–Honda tie-up and other joint ventures, see Karlekar (1999).

10 In fairness, it should be pointed out that while direct taxes 'were reduced on both individuals and corporations [in 1985]...direct tax revenue collections *rose* by 24 per cent in [1985/6]' (Lal 1999: 35, quoting the Government's *Economic Survey 1985–6*, p. 4; emphasis in the original).

11 Our description of India's first steps toward new industrial and trade policies is indebted to Khatkhate (1992: 57–9), and it is Khatkhate who refers to average nominal tariff rates in India of 117%, 'which compares unfavorably with countries like Indonesia and the Philippines where the average nominal tariff rates are in the region of 50–60 per cent' (p. 59).

12 The agricultural sector has been affected by changes in India's trade policy regime, but not always in a predictable or symmetrical manner: quantitative restrictions on agricultural imports into India were removed more quickly than were restrictions on agricultural exports (Nayyar and Sen 1994: 64). The agricultural sector was also challenged by various of the Dunkel Draft proposals which emerged as part of the Uruguay Round of Multilateral Trade Negotiations in the early 1990s. With the exception of Shetkari Sanghatana, most farmers' movements in India

objected to the Dunkel text on Trade-Related aspects of Intellectual Property Rights, and the prospect (or possibility) of Indian farmers being forced to buy patented high-yielding seeds from agribusiness companies. The phasing out of India's expensive fertilizer subsidy (roughly 0.6% of GDP in the mid-1990s) was recommended by the Hanumantha Rao committee.

13   The Chelliah Committee's interim report on tax reforms was delivered to the Government of India in December 1991; the Narasimhan Committee Report on financial sector reform was also delivered in 1991.

14   This sum is still dwarfed, of course, perhaps by as much as twenty-fold, by the investment sums flowing into China.

15   For Sachs's views, see Sachs (1994) and Bajpai and Sachs (1996; 1997). Padma Desai's views are neatly related in a story that Bhagwati tells at Sachs's expense: 'The last time when technocratic full-speed ahead advice to a reforming government backfired badly was when shock therapy for macro-stabilization was prescribed for Russia, with a backlash that gave Russia much political turmoil and little economic progress while returning Jeffrey Sachs unceremoniously to begin a life again at Harvard. I am reminded of his famous line: "You cannot cross a chasm in two leaps", to which Padma Desai...replied: "You cannot cross it on one leap either unless you are Indiana Jones; so you drop a bridge instead" ' (Bhagwati 1998: 37).

16   For a less optimistic account of the reforming instincts of some State-level politicians, see Weiner (1999).

17   A particular target for Jenkins is the World Bank and its overdrawn contrasts between the 'new democracies and their authoritarian predecessors' (Jenkins 1997: 5; and compare with World Bank 1992 and 1994). For more general writings on democratic regimes and the politics of reform, see Haggard and Webb (1994), Haggard and Kaufmann (1995) and Przeworski (1991).

18   In a paper first presented at Harvard University in December 1996, Varshney argued that a minority Congress government was able to push through various 'reforms that touch, directly or primarily elite politics' (for example, devaluation or liberalization of the trade regime: Varshney 1996: 25). The Congress was able to do this by exploiting the Janata Dal's opposition in the early 1990s to the BJP and Hindu nationalism. The Rao-Singh regime was less successful, however, or so Varshney argues, in effecting reforms that would have negative or uncertain consequences in the sphere of 'mass politics' (including the reform of India's labour laws or a credible programme of privatization).

19   The reference is to a comment on page 34 of Jenkins's doctoral dissertation; a version of this dissertation was published as a monograph in 1999 (Jenkins 1999).

20   Varshney also refers to the possibility that the reforms in India might be expanded by government attempts to create 'larger political spaces for big moves by stealth' (1996: 35), but he has in mind a government that would exploit further the politics of identity (see note 18), or which would convince ordinary men and women that 'deeper and quicker reforms [might be] positively linked to mass welfare' (p. 35).

21   The Bank also called for 'a realignment of government toward basic human development and truly public infrastructure, with greater reliance on the private sector in other areas' (1998: xiii). We take up this point later in the text.

22   I. G. Patel made the same point in 1992. Patel accepted that 'we have under-estimated the role of markets, incentives and private initiative and relied excess-ively on the state in the sphere of investment and production.' At the same time, he maintained that: 'If the present crisis is the greatest we have faced since independence, it is for no underlying economic factor which is more adverse now than what we have had to contend with in the past several decades. It is because successive governments in the 1980s chose to abdicate their respons-ibility to the nation for the sake of short-term partisan political gains and indeed out of sheer political cynicism' (1992: 43).

23   The possibility of deindustrialization is discussed by P. Sarkar (1991), Nambiar and Tadas (1994) and the EPW Research Foundation (1994). The idea that foreign companies will crowd out Indian companies is reviewed by Chandrase-khar (1996), and is largely dismissed by Majumdar (1996).

24   It is clear that some neoliberals do worry, however, about the failure of the reforms in India significantly to improve the competitiveness of Indian goods and services in the global market-place. India's share of world export markets did not increase in the 1990s, the reforms notwithstanding.

25   The literature on the so-called East Asia miracle is vast, and we have referred to it already in chapter 4. Key texts would include Amsden (1989), Wade (1990) and the World Bank (1993). For a more recent review, see Akyuz, Chang and Kozul-Wright (1998).

26   On inclusionary and exclusionary regimes of accumulation, see Lipietz (1987). On the Mexican peso crisis of 1995, see Griffith-Jones (1996); on the crisis in South-East Asia, see Thurow (1998). On the possible effects on and lessons for India (and China) of the 'Asian meltdown', see Bhalla and Nachane (1998).

27   'The cutting of development expenditure appears to us to be a little beyond what appears prudent; growth later may be compromised by this, so the govern-ment needs to examine this question carefully' (Bhagwati and Srinivasan 1993: ii).

28   Some among the poor were also helped by the continued workings of the Public Distribution System, even if – as Jan Mooij surmises in a fine account of food policy and the Indian state – foodgrain prices tend to be at a higher level in areas where procurement takes place than they would have been otherwise, and even though 'richer households may profit more on average than poorer households' (Mooij 1999: 223).

29   For more on these cuts, and on the negative impacts of reform upon rural equity and poverty, see the careful and judicious paper by S. P. Gupta (1995). See also Suryanarayana (1996) who considers – and dismisses – the argument that increases in rural and urban poverty in India post 1991 should be blamed on 'natural or climatic causes'. (For a different view, see Tendulkar and Jain 1995.) For more on liberalization in the agricultural sector, see G. S. Bhalla (1994).

30   Craig Jeffrey has argued this point, after Pierre Bourdieu, in his doctoral dissertation (1999).

31   Bhagwati refers to the need for government and NGOs to work together on an anti-poverty agenda that would begin with efficiency and growth, but which would embrace indirect (employment creation) and direct (social capital) anti-poverty strategies (Bhagwati 1998: 39). The 'orthodox' position is that increased

government spending on the capital account should be funded by cuts in current expenditures and the divestment of state assets (see Joshi 1998). One objection to this agenda is that it dismisses too bluntly the growth-enhancing effects of the 'hidden' subsidies on power or irrigation; another is that it discounts the benefits to the poor of some government spending (notwithstanding its clear bias, in practice, to the middle classes: see also note 28).

32 In the public sector (central government), the power of some members of the middle class was evident in their ability to secure pay awards in 1998–9 that were substantially in excess of those recommended by the Pay Commission: the World Bank refers to raises worth '0.6% of GDP more than budgeted, including arrears' (1998: 6). In addition, the pay award was 'not accompanied by any measures to increase efficiency and the Pay Commission's proposals to reduce staff by 30% over 10 years and eliminate unfilled positions were rejected as part of the final wage settlement' (p. 6).

33 All these figures calculated from World Bank data (1998: tables A4.2–A4.4). It should also be pointed out that considerable funds have been spent, since 1993, on the District Primary Education Programme, with results that have not as yet been properly assessed. Funding for the DPEP comes mainly from the World Bank (IDA) and the European Union. Large-scale external funding for primary education in India was a new development in the 1990s – see Varghese (1999: 131); see also World Bank (1997c).

34 Jeffrey Sachs has suggested that the reforms may have 'raised India's growth potential... to around 5–6 per cent per year' (1994: 1).

35 Deepak Lal distinguishes between mass structural poverty, destitution and conjunctural poverty. While 'income transfers are the only way to tackle private destitution and conjunctural poverty' (1999: 149 – he has in mind private transfers), 'mass structural poverty can only be alleviated within one generation by sustained and rapid economic growth' (p. 148).

36 Most obviously from the World Bank, but also from some in the Confederation of Indian Industry.

37 We are not sanguine about this possibility, but we should acknowledge that there are pressures on the BJP-led government to take a more expansive view of the 'national interest'. It is possible, too, that some of the more 'go-ahead' State governments will put pressure on New Delhi to release funds for their own educational or 'social investment' projects.

38 'The government today has to borrow close to Rs 90,000 crores to finance its interest payment obligations. India is... headed for an internal debt trap if things are allowed to drift any further' (a Director of Lazard Brothers writing in *The Economic Times*, 16 October 1999).

39 These figures drawn from Corbridge et al. (2000).

8 The Guilty Men? Militant Hinduism and the Politics of Anti-secularism

1 As we sought to show in chapters 6 and 7 the 're-imagining' of the Indian economy that has gone on has been more profound, in some respects, than the actual re-structuring that has taken place. In part, this is the point that economic reform has legitimated very different values and attitudes amongst the middle

and upper classes from those which existed amongst earlier generations (see Varma 1998).

2   The idea of the rise of Hindu nationalism as a conservative revolution is the theme of Thomas Blom Hansen's book *The Saffron Wave* (1999).

3   This definition comes from Diderot's *Encyclopaedia* of 1751.

4   These processes have been described as the 'substantialization' of caste, following parts of the argument of Louis Dumont (1970). See Barnett (1975), Fuller (1996) and J. Harriss (1982, ch. 6).

5   See van der Veer (1994), especially chapter 2, from which our account here is derived.

6   Another fascinating perspective on religion in Indian society today appears in Vidal's essay 'When the Gods Drink Milk', which is a study of the widespread 'miracle' of September 1995 when it appeared that stone and metal images of gods drank milk from spoons. Vidal's analysis leads him to emphasize 'how many people today – especially in urban areas – combine, in their daily lives in India, attitudes and opinions testifying to their religious devotion as well as an open pragmatism and rationalism' (1998: 168).

7   This was in the session on 18 December 1946.

8   Session of 20 January 1947.

9   The points which follow have been made by a number of the authors in the recent literature. Our account follows Chatterjee (1997a, ch. 14).

10 Hansen suggests another interpretation, asking whether there is not an assumption implicit in the legislation that Hindus are the core-citizens of the 'state-community' (1999: 53).

11 This is not the only account that can be offered of the state's discrimination against some Hindu practices or institutions. We have some sympathy for the philosopher Brian Barry's argument that states must necessarily 'discriminate' against those in power (in the field of institutionalized religion as elsewhere) in order to empower other groups – those without power, the marginalized – to participate more fully in society (including in religious affairs): 'The point is that a secular state is not necessarily one that maximizes the freedom of religious organizations' (Barry 1998: 4). On this reading, too, the failure of the state in the Shah Bano case was not that it 'discriminated' against the Hindu majority (except in a secondary sense), but that it discriminated against its own secular principles. We shall have more to say about the politics of secularism and anti-secularism in section 8.3.

12 Achin Vanaik, similarly, notes that: 'This was a world neither of sharp polarities and divisions, nor of cultural synthesis or social merger' (1997: 136) and remarks that 'folk Hinduism did not meaningfully synthesise with folk Islam' (p. 136).

13 Thinking in terms of religious constructions of personal meanings implies the rejection of the distinction which is sought to be made by some 'anti-secularists' between religion as 'faith' and as 'ideology': see our discussion in section 8.3.

14 Or, perhaps more accurately for most ordinary people, a Hindu *desh* (country). Veronique Benei, in a study of 'teaching nationalism in Maharashtra schools', argues that: 'Still a haunting question remains ... is it the state, the nation, the nation-state, that is actually being sung into existence [in the anthems and hymns that children sing in school]? None of these, it seems. Indeed, at least as I was able to observe it in this part of Maharashtra [Kolhapur], it is, rather, the

"country" (*desh*). Only in such composed words as "rashtriya geete" is the word commonly translated as "nation" actually used ... [and] ... Most of the expressions, phrases, songs and discourses about India are only about "desh", i.e "country". Patriotism and nationalism are being transmitted through the idiom of "desh", and not that of "rashtra" or "rajya" ... the idea of the nation-state is here utterly downplayed at the benefit of the more powerfully emotionally-binding one of "country" ' (1999: 16–17). Similarly, in Tamil Nadu, it seems likely that the emotive word in use amongst those influenced by and supportive of Hindu nationalism is 'nadu' (Chris Fuller, personal communication).

15   This follows Hansen (1996b; and 1999, ch. 2).

16   This imagery calls into question the anti-Brahmanical ideology of the Arya Samaj, at least in part. Many Brahmanical claims or images were internalized in the discourse of high-caste Samajists. In addition, as van der Veer points out, the 'dark goddess, or Durga, who rides a tiger, were often invoked in [cow protection meetings] ... The iconography of Hindu nationalism makes abundant use of the two images of the mother: the nurturing cow and the dangerous Durga on her tiger' (1994: 89; and see also our remarks on gender and Hindu nationalism later in this section).

17   On the relations between the Hindu Mahasabha and the Indian National Congress, see Gordon (1975).

18   The RSS was formed in 1925. For a generally excellent account of its organization and activities, see Andersen and Damle (1987).

19   McKean (1996) provides a good account of Savarkar's thought; see also the biography by Keer (1966).

20   The RSS *shaka* has been described in this way by Krishna Kumar: 'an open-air evening class for socializing male adolescents into a quasi-military brotherhood' (1993: 545).

21   The note was leaked to the press in 1982 and published by *The Statesman* in New Delhi on 16 November 1982: see Jaffrelot (1996: 341).

22   *Organiser*, Independence Day Special, 1981: 7, cited in Jaffrelot (1996: 343). Macaulayism is a point of reference for 'western' education.

23   Interview with Advani in *The Economic Times*, 10 August 1993.

24   What follows here does not claim to be a complete listing.

25   See also the collection of essays edited by Babb and Wadley (1995).

26   On the iconography of Ram-Rama, see Kapur (1993) and Pinney (1997); see also Freitag (1980).

27   As Sumantra Bose puts it: 'while Hindutva ideologues claim that theirs is a "catch-all" term encompassing a pan-Indian identity, it is in reality more of a "cover-up" construct for various types of social conflict and cleavage, based on class, caste, regional and ethnic differences, that have become especially salient in the 1980s and 1990s' (1997: 139). We have also chosen to italicize the word 'if' in order to underline our unease with some parts of the argument that has been developed recently by Kumar or Kaviraj, or indeed Chatterjee and (rather less so) Khilnani. In the next chapter we will argue that a process of secularization – if not an ideology of secularism – has deepened sufficiently in India to call into question those accounts of Indian politics which draw a sharp distinction between the secular-modern-'English' worlds of a closed elite (the charmed circle) and the religious-vernacular lifeworlds of the mass of 'ordinary' Indians. See also note 34.

28   The argument is paralleled, for example, in James Ferguson's analysis of development in Lesotho, in his book *The Anti-Politics Machine* (1990), which shows both how development planning in that country has depended upon its being constructed as a particular kind of object, and then how projects which fail dismally in terms of their stated objectives succeed wonderfully well in relation to political power. A less satisfactory version of the same argument is Escobar's *Encountering Development* (1995).

29   There are continuities between the ideas of the 'anarcho-communitarians' and the 'new traditionalist' discourse of Indian environmentalism, which also conveniently assumes away 'any consideration of inequity and injustice within the "traditional community"' (Sinha, Gururani and Greenberg 1997).

30   Madan describes secularism as a gift of a resolutely Protestant Christianity. For a lively critique of Madan on *Secular Myths and Locked Minds*, see A. Shah (1998). See also the classic account by Smith (1963).

31   We might also note that the 'secularism-versus-communalism' binary has mainly had relevance in north India. In south India, as Dharma Kumar reminds us, '"communal" refers to *caste* divisions; thus the famous Communal Government Order of 1921 prescribes caste-wise reservations in government employment' (1994: 1803; emphasis in the original). We have sought to argue throughout this chapter that the politics of militant Hinduism cannot be understood except in relation to caste and class tensions within the so-called Hindu community.

32   Bayly also challenges the idea that syncretic practices must prevent the outbreak of communal riots: Bayly (1985); and compare with Thapar (1989).

33   Bhargava draws an instructive comparison between 'ethical secularism', or a system of values where 'the believer gives up everything of significance' (1994: 1787), and political secularism. 'Political secularism demands only that everyone – believers and non-believers – give up a little bit of what is of exclusive importance in order to sustain that which is generally valuable. If everyone is assured that politics will not be invaded by one particular ultimate ideal, then all are likely to restrict the scope of their respective ideas' (p. 1787). His conclusions are mirrored by those of Amartya Sen in his review of 'secularism and its discontents': 'the abandonment of secularism [a demand for symmetric political treatment of different religious communities]...would make things far more wintry than they currently are' [1996: 42–3]). For a perspective on the rights of religious minorities that draws on Sen, but which reaches different conclusions, see Chandhoke (1999).

34   Beteille makes the important point that secularization in post-Independence India has been promoted by 'external material forces and factors' (1994: 561), including the market, bureaucratization and new communications networks; it has also entered people's lifeworlds through schools and universities and through doctors' surgeries and hospitals. To the extent that it has also been promoted by the state directly, secularization has been encouraged by the myth of secularism and by ideas of equality and participation in relation to public-sector employment and democratic politics. The hyper-rationalism of the Nehruvian state may have been a myth or a sham, as Hansen maintains (see earlier), but that a measure of secularization has occurred in India in part because of Nehru's design for the country is not in doubt. (See also Bharucha 1994, and Bilgrami 1994.)

9   Transfers of Power? Subaltern Politics, Sites of Empowerment and the Reshaping of India's Democracy

1   Varshney makes the same point about the variegated nature of democracy: 'If inequality, despite democratic institutions, comes in the way of a free expression of political preferences, such inequality makes a polity *less* democratic, but it does not make it *un*democratic. So long as contestation and participation are available, democracy is a *continuous* variable (expressed as "more" or "less"), not a *discrete* variable (expressed as "yes" or "no"). Variations in degree and dichotomies should be clearly distinguished' (1998: 19; emphasis in the original). For a more general discussion, see Haynes (1997). On the crisis in Kalahandi, see Currie (1993) and Sainath (1996); on the Narmada struggles, see Baviskar (1995) and Drèze, Samson and Singh (1997).

2   Although the Bahujan Samaj Party in Uttar Pradesh is mainly a party of the Scheduled Castes, or *dalits*, the *bahujan samaj* are generally understood to be the 'common people'.

3   The massacres in Bihar are discussed in Mendelsohn and Vicziany (1998) and Bhatia (1997). The massacres at Belchi, Bishrampur and Pipra, it should be noted, were organized by *kurmi* landlords (that is, by a caste grouping that would not be considered 'upper caste' at this time). For an account of the breakdown of the brahmanical social order in Bihar, see Frankel (1989).

4   Rohinton Mistry picks up this point in his novel, *A Fine Balance*. 'The speeches were crammed with promises of every shape and size: promises of new schools, clean water, and health care; promises of land for landless peasants, through redistribution and stricter enforcement of the Land Ceiling Act; promises of powerful laws to punish any discrimination against, and harassment of, backward castes by upper castes; promises to abolish child labour, sati, dowry system, child marriage. "There must be a lot of duplication of our country's laws," said Dukhi. "Every time there are elections, they talk of passing the same ones they passed twenty years ago. Someone should remind them they need to apply the laws" ' (1996: 143)

5   We think, in particular, of Breman's work on the government labour officer (1985b), Gupta's work on the 'staging' and performative aspects of government (1995), Wade's work on corruption and canal irrigation (1982) and Hansen's work on the police in Mumbai (Hansen 1998b), all of which concern the social practices and perceptions of state officials who mediate between the elite and subaltern worlds described by Kaviraj, and Chatterjee: see also Fuller and Harriss (2000) and Srivastava (1998).

6   On various aspects of the struggles in Jharkhand, see Corbridge (1988; 1993), Das (1992), Devalle (1992), Munda (1988) and Parajuli (1996).

7   It was a CPI (M-L) document from 1986 which referred to the flaming fields of Bihar: see V. Mishra (1986). On agrarian radicalism in Bihar, see the important paper by Walter Hauser (1993).

8   A serious and provocative account of the Bhopal outrage can be found in V. Das (1995); on India's eucalyptus craze, see Saxena (1994).

9   See the discussion in Agarwal (1986); see also Blaikie (1985) and Rangan (1997).

10   See, for example: Agarwal (1994; 1998) and Saxena, Prasad and Joshi (1995).

11   For a development of this argument, see Corbridge and Jewitt (1997); see also Baumann (1996) and Sinha, Gurarani and Greenberg (1997). More generally, see Jackson (1993) and Nanda (1991).

12   For an outstanding account of changing gender relations in rural Haryana before and after Independence, see Chowdhury (1994).

13   Michael Moffatt's arguments concerning the replication of brahmanical ideology amongst Untouchables have been strenuously challenged by Deliege and are reviewed by Mosse (see Moffatt 1975; Deliege 1992; Mosse 1994). Nor do women always abide by male stereotypes of womanly behaviour or female sexuality: see the detailed accounts of the latter in Raheja and Gold (1994).

14   There is an important point to be made here about the changing role of politicians in rural India. Politicans are judged increasingly by their electors – most of whom are now organizing 'horizontally' in caste or other associations, and not 'vertically' at one end of a patron–client relationship – in terms of their ability to act as 'brokers' who connect particular social groups, or even localities, to the state and its resources. For an interesting account of these connections, in the context of the 1999 general election in Hajipur Constituency, north Bihar, see Ranjan (1999).

15   Robinson is sceptical of the claims of political decentralization. Her point here, concerning the importance of the role of the 'Centre', anticipates one of the important conclusions of Crook and Sverrisson's comparative study of decentralization experiments (1999), which we discuss later in this chapter. Rather like Ambedkar, Robinson is inclined to see India's villages as 'dens of ignorance, narrow-mindedness and communalism' (Ambedkar in the Constituent Assembly Debates, quoted in Galanter 1991: 3). We are more sanguine than she is about the potential of decentralization, though under particular political conditions which we discuss in section 9.4.

16   In regard to this issue, Ambedkar asked 'whether it is not open to the Backward Classes to allege against the Brahmans and allied classes all that was alleged by the late Mr Gokhale on behalf of the Indian people against the foreign agency' (quoted in Omvedt 1996: 340–1).

17   Dipanker Gupta (1997) contrasts the moral universalism of Ambedkar with the exceptionalist view of caste that permeates the report of the Mandal Commission (a view that Gandhi also feared). The chief vehicles for Ambedkar's (changing) politics in the 1930s and 1940s were the Independent Labour Party (1936–42) and the Scheduled Caste Federation.

18   We know rather little about the performance of Scheduled Caste MPs or MLAs in the Lok Sabha or in various State Assemblies. See Narayana (1978 and 1986) for two early reviews of the social background of Scheduled Caste MPs and their performance in various Lok Sabha debates. The picture that Narayana paints is less than encouraging.

19   A system that was pointed towards by legislation in 1935 and 1943. For an overview of the debate on 'affirmative action' (or compensatory discrimination) in India, see D. Kumar (1992); see also Baxi (1990) and Mahajan (1998).

20   On the Dalit Panthers, see Gokhale-Turner (1979); and Gokhale (1993). For a more general discussion of 'dalit politics' and the politics of caste, see Kothari (1994), Mahar (1972), Omvedt (1994) and Zelliott (1972, 1992).

21 Kanshi Ram himself benefited from a reserved job when he worked for the Survey of India in the 1950s. Ram was born in 1934 to a community of Chamars who had converted to Sikhism.

22 A similar story might be told of the leader of the Backward Classes in Bihar, Laloo Prasad Yadav. Notwithstanding his very public – and publicly recognized – failings, Laloo Yadav won the support and affection of many of Bihar's poorer communities, at least from 1990 to 1995, precisely because he spoke in their language, and because he advanced their claims for respect and empowerment (rather more, as it turned out, than their claims for development in a more conventional sense). Mr Yadav told one of us, in an interview in December 1999, that he was not interested in providing development for the poor in Bihar. Development, he said, was a 'foreign and polluting' ideology; what people needed was the respect and 'honour' that was due 'to all human beings'.

23 Two further studies offering 'two cheers' for reservations are Parry (1999a) and Corbridge (2000).

24 An excerpt from Kalelkar's letter to the President of India has recently been reprinted in Mahajan (1998). The position of women in independent India did not concern the Congress Party greatly in the 1950s or 1960s, notwithstanding the roles played by many women in the nationalist movement. It is true, of course, that Nehru's government passed The Hindu Code (as separate Acts) in 1955 and 1956, 'rewrote for Hindus the laws of marriage and divorce, adoption and inheritance', and added women to the electoral roll on the same basis as men (Forbes 1996: 223), but Geraldine Forbes is right to maintain that the government's smug satisfaction with its modernizing policies (for women and for men) was not shaken much before the publication of a Government of India-commissioned report on the status of women, *Toward Equality*, in 1974. A diverse and very active women's movement in India has helped to change this situation since the mid-1970s (Calman 1992 and R. Kumar 1993 offer excellent reviews), but, in parts of north India especially, the dependence of poorer women on urban-based women activists or on local male intermediaries is still very apparent. The obscene sex ratios which obtain in parts of north India also highlight the grim realities of life for many females: on this, see Miller (1981) for the start of a trail which leads through to Drèze and Sen (1995, ch. 7).

25 Varshney also writes of politics in north and south India as follows: 'In this century, the South has experienced caste-based politics much more intensely than the other regions of India. If a Hindu-Muslim cleavage has been a "master narrative" of politics in North India for much of the 20th century, caste divisions have had the same status in Southern India' (Varshney 1998: 2)

26 For an interesting account of the 'poisoning of the minds of the lower orders', see Don Herzog's (1998) study of the birth of conservatism in England as an anguished response to democracy and the French Revolution.

27 Yadav suggests that a first democratic upsurge in independent India occurred in the mid-1960s, after the death of Nehru and with the beginnings of the end of the Congress 'one-party system': see Yadav (1996). Yadav also points out that the poor are now more likely to vote than the rich, and villagers more so than town-dwellers. As Varshney points out: 'Unless we assume short-sightedness, the subaltern seem to think that democracy is working for them, a view not shared by the traditional elite, at least to the same degree' (1998: 27). On the transfor-

mation of authority in rural India, see Mendelsohn (1993); on transformations in Centre–State relations, see Sathyamurthy (1989; 1996).

28 This analysis, and the categorization of caste/class groups on which it depends, was inspired by Church's essay on 'The Pattern of State Politics' to which we referred in chapter 5. The categorization of caste/class groups is briefly laid out in that chapter.

29 The detailed workings of the argument on which this typology of state regimes is based are given in J. Harriss 1999.

30 Some evidence in support of this claim comes from the strategic decision in the mid-1990s of ActionAid India, an influential NGO, to relocate its work away from the southern and western states to north India, in view of the lower levels of NGO activity there (personal communication from ActionAid India staff to John Harriss in 1994).

31 See Drèze and Sen (1989; 1995) and Gita Sen (1992). Note that Drèze and Sen do not equate 'public action' with 'state action'. As they say 'It is important to see the public as an agent and not merely as a passive patient' (1989: 19).

32 See Ronald Herring's studies of Kerala (1983; 1998). See also Isaac et al. (1998).

33 In the 1993 *panchayat* elections in West Bengal, 'one third of all seats were reserved for women, and seats were reserved for Scheduled Caste and Scheduled Tribe members to reflect the size of these groups in the local population' (Williams 1997: 2105). Set against this, it is important to note that Amrita Basu, in a rich ethnography of women's activism in parts of West Bengal and Maharashtra, found that the CPM had enjoyed only modest success in mobilizing women, and, indeed, had allowed the dominance of the (predominantly male) *bhadrolok* in the party to discourage some local activists from addressing gender issues. Basu accepted, nonetheless, that 'wage rates in West Bengal [Midnapur] are higher and women more apt to receive nearly equal wages with men . . . than in Dhulia district [Maharashtra: home to the Shramik Sanghatana]. Moreover, the CPI(M) had been far more effective than the Shramrik Sanghatana in protecting the rural poor from repression by "communal organizations" in complicity with the police' (1992: 236).

34 On the poverty of post-developmentalism, see Corbridge (1998).

35 We should acknowledge that Gupta is reluctant to draw the conclusion that villagers in Alipur have bought into the state's model of development since Independence. Jeffrey and Lerche (1999) are less hesitant than is Gupta to discuss, and sometimes to acknowledge, the role of the state – and of political appeals to the idea of the state – as an occasional site of empowerment for poorer people dealing with the reproduction of class advantage in Uttar Pradesh. It should be noted, however, and this is consistent with Gupta's argument and our broader argument in this chapter, that the state in UP is still most often called upon – or mobilized – by local elites to *consolidate* the bases of their class power. The fact that the poor are making increasing demands around the idea of the state, or of how it should behave, does not, of course, mean that they have yet won power over the state, either in political terms (although this is changing) or with regard to control over state agencies and the bureaucracy. (For more on western UP, see Jeffery and Jeffery 1997.)

36 Parry also writes as follows: 'The Hindi words *brashtachar* and *ghus* cover roughly the same ground as our English categories "corruption" and "bribe". Neither is morally neutral, and we can immediately dismiss the cultural relativist

fantasy that it is merely ethnocentric to employ terms like "bribery" and "corruption" to talk about payments which contemporary Indians regard as legitimate perquisites of office. On the whole they do not – especially when the office is somebody else's and it is they who are providing the perks' (1999b: 2).

Conclusion

1 Khilnani is also sensitive, as are we, to the pressures that are brought to bear on India's religious nationalists by the country's long traditions of 'centrist politics'. In this regard, it is significant, perhaps, that the *New York Times* (NYT) should have described the victory of the BJP-led coalition in the 13th Lok Sabha elections as a victory for 'a centrist coalition of 24 parties that appears likely to offer India its most durable government in several years' (8 October 1999). Whether the BJP has indeed mutated from the party which was the 'ugly, anti-Muslim face of Hindu revivalism', as the NYT also claimed, remains to be seen. We are less sanguine than the NYT, that in 'exchange for its allies' support' the BJP will indeed keep its promise not to 'pursue the agenda that has raised the heckles of Muslims and secularists alike' (8 October 1999). We do note, however, that the BJP did not significantly increase its number of seats in the Lok Sabha in the 1999 elections.

2 Khilnani writes that: 'The democratic idea has penetrated the Indian political imagination and has begun to erode the authority of the social order and of a paternalist state. Democracy as a manner of seeing and acting upon the world is changing the relations of Indian to themselves' (1997: 17). He also suggests that: 'the meaning of democracy has been menacingly narrowed to signify only elections.... [They] are the sole bridge between state and society' (p. 58). See also the fine – if depressing – account of the 1999 elections in Allahabad by Pankaj Mishra (1999).

3 The campaigns against the Narmada developments in the 1980s helped to bring about some changes in the World Bank: see, for example, Caulfield (1996). Campaigns especially against Monsanto were widely reported in the British press in 1999; see, for example, the *Guardian*, 17 February 1999.

4 The phrase is most often associated with Platteau (1994).

5 Alpa Shah (1999) concludes her report on the workings of the state in Bero Block, Ranchi District, Bihar by noting that the DWCRA (development of women and children in rural areas) programmes which she had been studying for six months had 'in fact' been 'replaced' several months previously by New Delhi.

6 There is a real sense in which India is not 'modern' enough, at least from the point of view of those who are routinely denied decent health care or a reasonable education. This point continues to be argued by Jean Drèze and Amartya Sen, amongst others. It is also worth noting that 'development' or even 'modernization' has not failed India in quite the manner that some post-structuralists (or anarcho-communitarians) maintain. Real wages for the rural poor increased in many Districts in the 1980s in the wake of the green revolution, and average life expectancies for men and women (combined) increased from 41.2 years in the mid-1950s to 62 years in 1995 (see also chapter 1, note 29).

References

Abraham, I. 1998: *The Making of the Indian Atomic Bomb: Science, Secrecy and the Postcolonial State*. London: Zed Books.

Abrams, P. 1988: Notes on the difficulty of studying the state. *Journal of Historical Sociology*, 1(1), 58–89.

Adams, J. 1990: Breaking away: India's economy vaults into the 1990s. In M. Bouton and P. Oldenburg (eds), *India Briefing, 1990*, Boulder: Westview and The Asia Society, 77–100.

Adas, M. 1979: *Prophets of Rebellion: Millenarian Protest Movements Against the European Colonial Order*. Cambridge: Cambridge University Press.

Agarwal, B. 1986: *Cold Hearths and Barren Slopes: The Woodfuel Crisis in the Third World*. London: Zed Books.

——— 1994: *A Field of One's Own: Gender and Land Rights in South Asia*. Cambridge: Cambridge University Press.

——— 1998: Environmental management, equity and ecofeminism: debating India's experience. *Journal of Peasant Studies*, 25, 55–95.

Ahluwalia, I. J. 1985: *Industrial Growth in India: Stagnation Since the Mid-1960s*. Delhi: Oxford University Press.

Ahluwalia, M. S. 1988: India's economic performance, policies and prospects. In R. Lucas and G. Papanek (eds), *The Indian Economy: Recent Developments and Future Prospects*, Delhi: Oxford University Press, 345–60.

Ahmed, A. 1997: *Jinnah, Pakistan and Islamic Identity: The Search for Saladin*. London: Routledge.

Akbar, M. 1988: *Nehru*. London: Viking.

Akyuz, Y., Chang, H.-J. and Kozul-Wright, R. 1998: New perspectives on East Asian development. *Journal of Development Studies*, 34 (6), 4–36.

Aloysius, G. 1997: *Nationalism Without a Nation in India*. Delhi: Oxford University Press.

Alter, J. 1992: *The Wrestler's Body: Identity and Ideology in North India*. Berkeley: University of California Press.

——— 1994: Celibacy, sexuality, and the transformation of gender into nationalism in north India. *Journal of Asian Studies*, 53, 45–66.

Alternative Survey Group (ASG) 1997: *Alternative Economic Survey 1996–97*. New Delhi: Delhi Science Forum.

Ambedkar, B. R. 1945: What Congress and Gandhi have done to the Untouchables. In Vasant Moon (ed.), *Dr Babasaheb Ambedkar: Writings and Speeches, I*, Bombay: Government of Maharashtra.

Amsden, A. 1979: Taiwan's economic history: a case of étatism and a challenge to dependency theory. *Modern China*, 5, 341–80.

—— 1989: *Asia's Next Giant: South Korea and Late Industrialization*. Oxford: Oxford University Press.

Andersen, W. 1982: India in 1981. *Asian Survey*, 22, 16–31.

—— and Damle, S. 1987: *The Brotherhood in Saffron: The Rashtriya Swayamsevak Sangh and Hindu Revivalism*. New Delhi: Vistaar Publications.

Anderson, B. 1983: *Imagined Communities: Reflections on the Origin and Spread of Nationalism*. London: Verso.

Arnold, D. 1988a: *Famine*. Oxford: Blackwell.

—— 1988b: The Congress and the police. In M. Shepperdson and C. Simmons (eds), *The Indian National Congress and the Political Economy of India, 1885–1985*, Aldershot: Avebury, 208–30.

Arnold, E. 1996: *The Light of Asia*. New Delhi: D. R. Chopra.

Assayag, J. 1995: *Au Confluent de deux rivières: Musulmans et Hindous dan le sud de l'Inde*. Paris: Ecole Française d'Extrème Orient.

—— 1998: Ritual action or political reaction? The invention of Hindu nationalist processions in India during the 1980s. *South Asia Research*, 18, 125–48.

Austin, G. 1966: *The Constitution of India: Cornerstone of a Nation*. Oxford: Oxford University Press.

—— 1993: The constitution, society, and law. In P. Oldenburg (ed.), *India Briefing 1993*, Boulder: Westview and The Asia Society, 103–29.

Babb, L. and Wadley, S. (eds) 1995: *Media and the Transformation of Religion in South Asia*. Philadelphia: University of Pennsylvania Press.

Bagchi, A. 1975: Some characteristics of industrial growth in India. *Economic and Political Weekly*, 10, 157–64.

—— 1994: Globalising India: the fantasy and the reality. *Social Scientist*, 22, 18–27.

Bailey, F. G. 1963: Politics and society in contemporary Orissa. In C. H. Philips (ed.), *Politics and Society in India*, London: Allen and Unwin, 97–114.

Bajpai, N. and Sachs, J. 1996: India's economic reforms: some lessons from East Asia. Harvard Institute for International Development: Development Discussion Paper no. 532a.

—— 1997: Fiscal policy in India's economic reforms. Harvard Institute for International Development: Development Discussion Paper no. 557.

Baker, D. 1993: *Colonialism in an Indian Hinterland: The Central Provinces 1820–1920*. Delhi: Oxford University Press.

Balagopal, K. 1992: Economic liberalism and decline of democracy: case of Andhra Pradesh. *Economic and Political Weekly*, 27, 1958–62.

Balasubramanyam, V. 1984: *The Economy of India*. London: Weidenfeld and Nicolson.

Bardhan, P. 1984: *The Political Economy of Development in India*. Oxford: Blackwell.

—— 1988: Dominant proprietary classes and India's democracy. In A. Kohli (ed.), *India's Democracy*, Princeton: Princeton University Press, 214–24.

Bardhan, P. 1997: The state against society: the great divide in Indian social science discourse. In S. Bose and A. Jalal (eds), *Nationalism, Democracy and Development: State and Politics in India*, Delhi: Oxford University Press, 184–95.
—— 1998: *The Political Economy of Development in India*, 2nd edn. Delhi, Oxford University Press.
Barnett, S. A. 1975: Approaches to changes in caste ideology in South India. In B. Stein (ed.), *Essays on South India*, Honololu: University of Hawaii Press.
Barry, B. 1998: Secularism in India: ideal or illusion? *The Book Review*, 22 (6), 3–4.
Barthes, R. 1972: *Mythologies*. London: Jonathan Cape.
Basant, R. 1987: Agricultural technology and employment in India: a survey of recent research. *Economic and Political Weekly*, 22, 1297–308 and 1348–64.
Basu, A. 1992: *Two Faces of Protest: Contrasting Modes of Women's Activism*. Berkeley: University of California Press.
—— 1998: Hindu women's activism in India and the questions it raises. In P. Jeffrey and A. Basu (eds), *Appropriating Gender: Women's Activism and Politicized Religion in South Asia*. London: Routledge, 167–84.
Basu, T., Datta, P., Sarkar, T., Sarkar, S. and Sen, S. 1993: *Khaki Shorts, Saffron Flags*. New Delhi: Orient Longman.
Bates, R. 1981: *Markets and States in Tropical Africa: The Political Basis of Agricultural Policies*. Berkeley: University of California Press.
Baumann, P. 1996: Decentralising forest management in India. Unpublished Ph.D. Dissertation: University of Cambridge.
Baviskar, A. 1995: *In the Belly of the River: Tribal Conflicts Over Development in the Narmada Valley*. Delhi: Oxford University Press.
Baxi, U. 1990: *Political Justice, Legislative Reservation for Scheduled Castes, and Social Change*. Madras: University of Madras.
Bayly, C. 1985: The pre-history of 'communalism': religious conflict in India, 1700–1860. *Modern Asian Studies*, 19, 177–203.
—— 1988: *Indian Society and the Making of the British Empire*. Cambridge: Cambridge University Press.
—— 1990: Beating the boundaries: South Asian history, *c.*1700–1850. In S. Bose (ed.), *South Asia and World Capitalism*, Delhi: Oxford University Press.
—— 1998: *The Origins of Nationalism in South Asia: Patriotism and Ethical Government in the Making of Modern India*. Oxford: Oxford University Press.
Bayly, S. 1999: *Caste, Society and Politics in India from the Eighteenth Century to the Modern Age*. Cambridge: Cambridge University Press.
Beck, B. 1972: *Peasant Society in Konku: A Study of Right and Left Sub-Castes in South India*. Vancouver: University of British Columbia Press.
Benei, V. 1999: Nation, region and state: teaching nationalism in Maharashtra schools. Mimeo: Department of Anthropology, London School of Economics. (Forthcoming, 2000, in V. Benei and C. Fuller (eds), *The Everyday State: Anthropological Perspectives on the State and Society in Modern India*, Delhi: Social Science Publishers and London: Zed Books.)
Bentall, J. and Corbridge, S. 1996: Urban–rural relations, demand politics and the 'new agrarianism' in north-west India: the Bharatiya Kisan Union. *Transactions of the Institute of British Geographers*, 21, 25–48.
Beteille, A. 1965: *Caste, Class and Power: Changing Patterns of Stratification in a Tanjore Village*. Berkeley: University of California Press.
—— 1994: Secularism and intellectuals. *Economic and Political Weekly*, 29, 559–66.

Bhaduri, A. 1983: *The Economic Structure of Backward Agriculture*. London: Academic Press.

—— and Nayyar, D. 1996: *The Intelligent Person's Guide to Liberalization*. New Delhi: Penguin.

Bhagwati, J. 1993: *India in Transition: Freeing the Economy*. Oxford: Clarendon Press.

—— 1998: The design of Indian development. In I. J. Ahluwalia and I. M. D. Little (eds), *India's Economic Reforms and Development: Essays for Manmohan Singh*, Delhi: Oxford University Press, 23–39.

—— and Desai, P. 1970: *India: Planning for Industrialization*. London: Oxford University Press.

—— and Srinivasan, T. 1975: *Foreign Trade Regimes and Economic Development: India*. New York: Columbia University Press and NBER.

—— and Srinivasan, T. 1984: Indian development strategy: some comments. *Economic and Political Weekly*, 19, 2006–8.

—— and Srinivasan, T. 1993: *India's Economic Reforms*. Government of India: Ministry of Finance Press.

Bhalla, A. and Nachane, D. 1998: Asian meltdown: ramifications for India and China. Sidney Sussex College, Cambridge: Sino-Indian Liberalization Project, Discussion Paper no. 4.

Bhalla, G. S. (ed.) 1994: *Economic Liberalization and Indian Agriculture*. New Delhi: Institute for Studies in Industrial Development.

Bhalla, S. 1987: Trends in employment in Indian agriculture, land and asset distribution. *Indian Journal of Agricultural Economics*, 42, 537–60.

Bharadwaj, K. 1974: *Production Conditions in Indian Agriculture*. London: Cambridge University Press.

—— 1985: A view on commercialisation in Indian agriculture and the development of capitalism. *Journal of Peasant Studies*, 12, 7–25.

Bhargava, R. 1994: Giving secularism its due. *Economic and Political Weekly*, 29, 1784–91.

Bharucha, R. 1994: In the name of the secular: cultural interactions and interventions. *Economic and Political Weekly*, 29, 2925–9.

Bhatia, B. 1997: Massacre on the banks of the Son. *Economic and Political Weekly*, 32, 3242–5.

—— 1998: Rethinking revolution in Bihar, *Seminar*, 464, 27–31.

Bhatty, Z. 1996: Social stratification among Muslims in India. In M. Srinivas (ed.), *Caste: Its Twentieth Century Avatar*. Delhi: Penguin, 244–62.

Bhushan, B. 1984: The origins of the rebellion in Punjab. *Capital and Class*, 24, 5–13.

Bidwai, P. and Vanaik, A. 1999: *South Asia on a Short Fuse: Nuclear Politics and the Future of Global Disarmament*. Delhi: Oxford University Press.

Bilgrami, A. 1994: Two concepts of secularism: reason, modernity and archimedean ideal. *Economic and Political Weekly*, 29, 1749–61.

Blaikie, P. 1985: *The Political Economy of Soil Erosion*. London: Methuen.

Bose, Sugata 1993: *Peasant Labour and Colonial Capital: Rural Bengal Since 1770*. Cambridge: Cambridge University Press.

—— and Jalal, A. 1998: *Modern South Asia: History, Culture, Political Economy*. London: Routledge.

Bose, Sumantra 1997: 'Hindu nationalism' and the crisis of the Indian state. In Sugata Bose and A. Jalal (eds), *Nationalism, Democracy and Development: State and Politics in India*, Delhi: Oxford University Press, 104–64.

Bouton, M. 1985: *Agrarian Radicalism in South India*. Princeton: Princeton University Press.

Boyce, J. 1987: *Agrarian Impasse in Bengal: Institutional Constraints to Technological Change*. Oxford: Oxford University Press.

Brass, P. 1982: Pluralism, regionalism, and decentralizing tendencies in contemporary Indian politics. In A. Wilson and D. Dalton (eds), *The States of South Asia: Problems of National Integration*, London: Hurst, 223–64.

—— 1984: National power and local politics in India: a twenty year perspective. *Modern Asian Studies*, 18, 89–118.

—— 1990: *The Politics of India Since Independence*. Cambridge: Cambridge University Press.

—— 1994: *The Politics of India Since Independence*, 2nd edn. Cambridge: Cambridge University Press.

—— 1997: *Theft of an Idol: Text and Context in the Representation of Collective Violence*. Princeton: Princeton University Press.

Brass, T. (ed.) 1995: *New Farmers' Movements in India*. London: Frank Cass.

Breman, J. 1974: *Patronage and Exploitation: Changing Agrarian Relations in South Gujarat, India*. Berkeley: University of California Press.

—— 1985a: *Of Peasants, Migrants and Paupers: Rural Labour Circulation and Capitalist Production in West India*. Delhi: Oxford University Press.

—— 1985b: 'I am the government labour officer'. State protection for the rural proletariat of South Gujarat. *Economic and Political Weekly*, 20, 1043–55.

—— 1996: *Footloose Labour: Working in India's Informal Economy*. Cambridge: Cambridge University Press.

Butler, D., Lahiri, A., and Roy, P. (eds) 1997: *India Decides: Elections, 1952–1995*. New Delhi: Living Media Limited.

Byres, T. 1974: Land reform, industrialisation and the marketed surplus in India: an essay on the power of 'rural bias'. In D. Lehmann (ed.), *Agrarian Reform and Agrarian Reformism: Studies of Peru, Chile, China and India*, London: Faber and Faber, 221–61.

—— 1981: The new technology, class formation, and class action in the Indian countryside. *Journal of Peasant Studies*, 8, 405–54.

—— 1988: A Chicago view of the Indian state: an oriental grin without an oriental cat and political economy without classes. *Journal of Commonwealth and Comparative Politics*, 26, 246–69.

—— and Nolan, P. 1976: *Inequality: India and China Compared, 1950–1970. (Patterns of Inequality – Unit 25–29: Part 2)*. Milton Keynes: The Open University.

—— Kapadia, K. and Lerche, J. (eds) 1999: *Rural Labour Relations in India*. London: Frank Cass.

Calman, L. 1992: *Toward Empowerment: Women and Movement Politics in India*. Boulder: Westview.

Castells, M. 1997: *The Rise of the Network Society*. Oxford: Blackwell.

—— 1998: *End of Millennium*. Oxford: Blackwell.

Caulfield, C. 1996: *Masters of Illusion: The World Bank and the Poverty of Nations*. London: Macmillan.

Chadda, M. 1997: *Ethnicity, Security and Separatism in India*. Delhi: Oxford University Press.

Chadwick, O. 1975: *The Secularization of the European Mind in the Nineteenth Century*. Cambridge: Cambridge University Press.

Chakravarty, S. 1987: *Development Planning: The Indian Experience*. Delhi: Oxford University Press.

Chandhoke, N. 1999: *Beyond Secularism: The Rights of Religious Minorities*. Delhi: Oxford University Press.

Chandra, K. 2000: The transformation of ethnic politics in India: the decline of the Congress and the rise of the Bahujan Samaj Party in Hoshiapur. *Journal of Asian Studies*, 59 (1), 39–61.

Chandrasekhar, C. 1996: Explaining post-reform industrial growth. *Economic and Political Weekly*, 31, 2537–45.

Chatterjee, P. 1977 [1997]: Nineteen seventy seven. Written in 1977 and first published in P. Chatterjee, *A Possible World: Essays in Political Criticism*, Delhi: Oxford University Press, 58–66.

—— 1978 [1997]: Caran sim-er rájniti prasange. *Anik*, 15, 104–8. Reprinted in P. Chatterjee, *A Possible World: Essays in Political Criticism*, Delhi: Oxford University Press.

—— 1984 [1997]: The writing on the wall. *Frontier*, 22 December, 5–7. Reprinted 1997 in P. Chatterjee, *A Possible World: Essays in Political Criticism*, Delhi: Oxford University Press.

—— 1985–6 [1997] Rajiv's regime. *Frontier*, 2 March 1985–20 December 1996 (various issues). Reprinted 1997 in P. Chatterjee, *A Possible World: Essays in Political Criticism*, Delhi: Oxford University Press.

—— 1986: *Nationalist Thought and the Colonial World: A Derivative Discourse*. London: Zed Books.

—— 1989 [1997] The National Front and after. *Frontier*, 23 December. Reprinted 1997 in P. Chatterjee, *A Possible World: Essays in Political Criticism*, Delhi: Oxford University Press.

—— 1993: *The Nation and Its Fragments: Colonial and Postcolonial Histories*. Princeton: Princeton University Press.

—— 1994 [1997]: Secularism and toleration. *Economic and Political Weekly*, 29, 1768–77. Reprinted 1997 in P. Chatterjee, *A Possible World: Essays in Political Criticism*, Delhi: Oxford University Press.

—— 1997a: *A Possible World: Essays in Political Criticism*. Delhi: Oxford University Press.

—— (ed.) 1997b: *State and Politics in India*. Delhi: Oxford University Press.

Chaudhuri, P. 1979: *The Indian Economy: Poverty and Development*. New Delhi: Vikas.

—— 1988: The origins of modern India's development strategy. In M. Shepperdson and C. Simmons (eds), *The Indian National Congress and the Political Economy of India, 1885–1985*, Aldershot: Avebury, 272–81.

Chelliah, R. 1998: Liberalization, economic reforms and Centre-State relations. In I. J. Ahluwalia and I. M. D. Little (eds), *India's Economic Reforms and Development*, Delhi: Oxford University Press, 344–74.

Chenery, H., Ahluwalia, M., Bell, C., Duloy, J. and Jolly, R. 1975: *Redistribution With Growth*. London: Oxford University Press and the World Bank.

Chossudovsky, M. 1993: India under IMF rule. *Economic and Political Weekly*, 28, 385–7.

Chowdhury, P. 1994: *The Veiled Women: Shifting Gender Equations in Rural Haryana, 1880–1990*. Delhi: Oxford University Press.

Chunkanth, S. and Athreya, V. 1997: Female infanticide in Tamil Nadu: some evidence. *Economic and Political Weekly*, 32, WS22–8.

Church, R. 1984: The patterns of State politics in Indira Gandhi's India. In J. Wood (ed.), *State Politics in Contemporary India*, Boulder: Westview.

Cohn, B. 1996: *Colonialism and Its Forms of Knowledge: The British in India*. Princeton: Princeton University Press.

Committee on the Status of Women in India 1974: *Toward Equality*. New Delhi: Government of India, Ministry of Education and Social Welfare.

Corbridge, S. 1988: The ideology of tribal economy and society: politics in the Jharkhand, 1950–1980. *Modern Asian Studies*, 22, 1–41.

—— 1993: Ousting Singbonga: the struggle for India's Jharkhand. In P. Robb (ed.), *Dalit Movements and the Meanings of Labour*, Delhi: Oxford University Press, 121–50.

—— 1995: Federalism, Hindu nationalism and mythologies of governance in modern India. In G. Smith (ed.), *Federalism: The Multiethnic Challenge*, Harlow: Longman, 99–122.

—— 1998: 'Beneath the pavement only soil': the poverty of post-development. *Journal of Development Studies*, 34, 138–48.

—— 1999: 'The militarisation of all Hindudom'?: The Bharatiya Janata Party, the bomb, and the political spaces of Hindu nationalism. *Economy and Society*, 28, 222–55.

—— 2000: Competing inequalities: the Scheduled Tribes and the reservations system in India's Jharkhand. *Journal of Asian Studies*, 59 (1), 62–85.

—— and Jewitt, S. 1997: From forest struggles to forest citizens? Joint forest management in the unquiet woods of India's Jharkhand. *Environment and Planning A*, 29, 2145–64.

—— Williams, G., Srivastava, M. and Veron, R. 2000: State Performance and Spaces of Empowerment in Bihar and West Bengal, India. ESRC Research Project: Working Paper 1.

Crook, R. and Manor, J. 1998: *Democratisation and Decentralisation in South Asia and West Africa: Participation, Accountability and Performance in Comparative Perspective*. Cambridge: Cambridge University Press.

—— and Sverisson, A. 1999: To what extent can decentralised forms of government enhance the development of pro-poor policies and improve poverty-alleviation outcomes? Mimeo: Institute of Development Studies, University of Sussex (and forthcoming in P. Houtzager, M. Moore and J. Putzel (eds), *Politics and Poverty*, London: Routledge).

Currie, B. 1993: Food crisis, administrative action and public response: some general implications from the Kalahandi issue. Unpublished Ph.D. Dissertation, University of Hull.

Dandekar, V. and Rath, N. 1971: Poverty in India – Dimensions and Trends. *Economic and Political Weekly*, 6, 25–48 and 106–46.

Das, A. 1992: *The Republic of Bihar*. New Delhi: Penguin.

Das, S. 1994: The Indian National Congress and the dynamics of nation-building: aspects of continuity and change. In T. Sathyamurthy (ed.), *State and Nation in the Context of Social Change*, vol. 1; Delhi: Oxford University Press, 274–97.

Das, V. 1995: *Critical Events*. Delhi: Oxford University Press.

Das Gupta, J. 1981: Review of recent developments: India. *Asian Survey*, 2 (February), xx–xx.

Datt, G. and Ravallion, M. 1998: Why have some Indian States done better than others at reducing rural poverty? *Economica*, 65, 17–38.

Deliège, R. 1992: Replication and consensus: untouchability, caste and ideology in India. *Man*, 27, 155–73.

Desai, M. 1998: Development perspectives: was there an alternative to Mahalanobis? In I. J. Ahluwalia and I. M. D. Little (eds), *India's Economic Reforms and Development: Essays for Manmohan Singh*, Delhi: Oxford University Press, 40–7.

Devalle, S. 1992: *Discourses of Ethnicity: Culture and Protest in Jharkhand*. New Delhi: Sage.

Dewey, C. 1993: *Anglo-Indian Attitudes: The Mind of the Indian Civil Service*. London: The Hambledon Press.

Dirks, N. 1987: *The Hollow Crown: Ethnohistory of an Indian Kingdom*. Cambridge: Cambridge University Press.

——1992: Castes of mind. *Representations*, 37, 56–78.

Djurfeldt, G. and Lindberg, S. 1975: *Behind Poverty: The Social Formation in a Tamil Village*. London: Curzon Press.

Dreze, J. 1990: Poverty in India and the IRDP illusion. *Economic and Political Weekly*, 25, A95–104.

——and Sen, A. K. 1989: *Hunger and Public Action*. Oxford: Oxford University Press.

——and Sen, A. K. 1995: *India: Economic Development and Social Opportunity*. Oxford: Clarendon Press.

——Samson, M. and Singh, S. (eds) 1997: *The Dam and the Nation: Displacement and Resettlement in the Narmada Valley*. Delhi: Oxford University Press.

Dube, S. C. 1958: *India's Changing Villages: Human Factors in Community Development*. London: Routledge and Kegan Paul.

Dube, S. 1998: *In the Land of Poverty: Memoirs of an Indian Family, 1947–1997*. London: Zed Books.

Dubey, S. 1992: The middle class. In L. Gordon and P. Oldenburg (eds), *India Briefing 1992*, Boulder: Westview and The Asia Society, 137–64.

Dumont, L. 1970: *Homo Hierarchicus*. London: Paladin.

Dutt, R. C. 1950 [1904]: *The Economic History of India* (2 vols). London: Gollancz.

Echeverri-Gent, J. 1988: Guaranteed employment in an Indian State. *Asian Survey*, 28, 1294–310.

——1993: *The State and the Poor: Public Policy and Political Development in India and the United States*. Berkeley: University of California Press.

Edney, M. 1997: *Mapping an Empire: The Geographical Construction of British India, 1765–1843*. Chicago: University of Chicago Press.

Engineer, A. 1987: *The Shah Bano Controversy*. Delhi: Ajanta.

EPW Research Foundation 1994: What has gone wrong with the reforms? *Economic and Political Weekly*, 29, 1049–53.

Erdman, H. 1967: *The Swatantra Party and Indian Conservatism*. Cambridge: Cambridge University Press.

Escobar, A. 1995: *Encountering Development: The Making and Unmaking of the Third World*. Princeton: Princeton University Press.

Etienne, G. 1968: *Studies in Indian Agriculture: The Art of the Possible*. Berkeley: University of California Press.

Farmer, B. H. (ed.) 1977: *Green Revolution? Technology and Change in Rice Growing Areas of Tamil Nadu and Sri Lanka*. London: Macmillan.

Ferguson, J. 1990: *The Anti-Politics Machine: Development, Depoliticisation and Bureaucratic Power in the Third World*. Cambridge: Cambridge University Press.

Forbes, G. 1996: *Women in Modern India*. Cambridge: Cambridge University Press.

Frankel, F. 1971: *India's Green Revolution: Economic Gains and Political Costs*. Princeton: Princeton University Press.

——1978: *India's Political Economy, 1947–1977: The Gradual Revolution*. Princeton: Princeton University Press.

——1989: Caste, land and dominance in Bihar: breakdown of the Brahminical social order. In F. Frankel and M. Rao (eds), *Dominance and State Power in Modern India: Decline of a Social Order*, vol. 1, Delhi: Oxford University Press, 46–132.

——and Rao, M. (eds) 1989: *Dominance and State Power in Modern India: Decline of a Social Order*, vol. 1. Delhi: Oxford University Press.

——and Rao, M. (eds) 1990: *Dominance and State Power in Modern India: Decline of a Social Order*, vol. 2. Delhi: Oxford University Press.

Freitag, S. 1980: Sacred symbol as mobilization ideology: the north Indian search for a 'Hindu community'. *Comparative Studies in Society and History*, 22, 597–625.

Fukuyama, F. 1989: The end of history. *The National Interest*, 16, 3–16.

Fuller, C. (ed.) 1996: *Caste Today*. Delhi: Oxford University Press.

——1998: Religion, politics and the crisis of the state in south India. Mimeo: Department of Anthropology, London School of Economics.

——1999: The Minaksi temple priests and the state in Tamilnadu. Mimeo: Department of Anthropology, London School of Economics.

——and Harriss, J. 2000: Introduction: For an anthropology of the Indian state. In V. Benei and C. Fuller, (eds), *The Everyday State: Anthropological Perspectives on the State and Society in Modern India*, Delhi: Social Science Publishers and London: Zed Books.

Gadgil, M. and Guha, R. 1995: *Ecology and Equity: The Use and Abuse of Nature in Contemporary India*. London: Routledge.

Galanter, M. 1991: *Competing Equalities: Law and the Backward Classes in India*, 2nd edn. Delhi: Oxford University Press.

Gandhi, M. K. 1997 [1908] *Hind Swaraj and Other Essays* (edited and introduced by A. Parel). Cambridge: Cambridge University Press.

Gasper, D. 1997: Sen's capability approach and Nussbaum's capabilities ethics. *Journal of International Development*, 9, 281–302.

Ghosh, J. 1998: Liberalization debates. In T. Byres (ed.), *The Indian Economy: Major Debates Since Independence*, Delhi: Oxford University Press, 295–334.

Gokhale, J. 1993: *From Concessions to Confrontation: The Politics of an Indian Untouchable Community*. Bombay: Popular Prakashan.

Gokhale-Turner, J. 1979: The Dalit Panthers and the radicalisation of the Untouchables. *Journal of Commonwealth and Comparative Studies*, 17, 77–93.

Gopal, S. 1984: *Jawaharlal Nehru: A Biography* (3 vols). London: Cape.

——1989: *Jawaharlal Nehru: A Biography*. Delhi: Oxford University Press.

Gordon, R. 1975: The Hindu Mahasabha and the Indian National Congress, 1915 to 1926. *Modern Asian Studies*, 9: 145–203.

Government of India 1969: *The Causes of the Present Agrarian Tension*. Ministry of Home Affairs Press.

Graham, B. 1990: *Hindu Nationalism and Indian Politics: The Origins and Development of the Bharatiya Jana Sangh*. Cambridge: Cambridge University Press.

Griffin, K. 1974: *The Political Economy of Agrarian Change*. London: Macmillan.

Griffith-Jones, S. 1996: The Mexican peso crisis. University of Sussex: IDS Discussion Paper no. 354.

Guha, R. 1989: *The Unquiet Woods: Ecological Change and Peasant Resistance in the Himalaya.* Delhi: Oxford University Press.

Guhan, S. 1980: Rural poverty: policy and play acting. *Economic and Political Weekly*, 15 (47), 1975–82.

—— 1995: Centre and States in the reform process. In R. Cassen and V. Joshi (eds), *India: The Future of Economic Reform*, Delhi: Oxford University Press, 71–111.

Gupta, A. 1995: Blurred boundaries: the discourse of corruption, the culture of politics and the imagined state. *American Ethnologist*, 22, 375–402.

—— 1998: *Postcolonial Developments: Agriculture In the Making of Modern India.* Durham, North Carolina: Duke University Press.

Gupta, D. 1997: Positive discrimination and the question of fraternity: contrasting Ambedkar and Mandal on reservations. *Economic and Political Weekly*, 32 (31), 1971–8.

Gupta, S. 1995: Economic reform and its impact on poor. *Economic and Political Weekly*, 30, 1295–313.

Haggard, S. and Kaufmann, R. 1995: *Political Economy of Democratic Transitions.* Princeton: Princeton University Press.

—— and Webb, S. (eds) 1994: *Voting for Reform: Democracy, Political Liberalization and Economic Adjustment.* Oxford: Oxford University Press and World Bank.

Hansen, T. B. 1993: RSS and the popularization of Hindutva. *Economic and Political Weekly*, 28, 2270–3.

—— 1996a: The vernacularisation of Hindutva: the BJP and Shiv Sena in rural Maharashtra. *Contributions to Indian Sociology*, NS 30, 177–214.

—— 1996b: Recuperating masculinity: Hindu nationalism, violence and the exorcism of the Muslim 'other'. *Critique of Anthropology*, 16, 137–72.

—— 1996c: Globalisation and nationalist imaginations: Hindutva's promise of equality through difference. *Economic and Political Weekly*, 31, 603–16.

—— 1998a: The BJP and the politics of Hindutva in Maharashtra. In T. B. Hansen and C. Jaffrelot (eds), *The BJP and the Compulsions of Politics in India*, Delhi: Oxford University Press.

—— 1998b: Governance and state mythologies in Mumbai. Mimeo: Department of Geography, Roskilde University, Denmark. (Forthcoming, 2000, in V. Benei and C. Fuller, (eds), *The Everyday State: Anthropological Perspectives on the State and Society in Modern India*, New Delhi: Social Science Publishers and London: Zed Books.)

—— 1999: *The Saffron Wave: Democracy and Hindu Nationalism in Modern India.* Princeton: Princeton University Press.

—— and Jaffrelot, C. (eds) 1998: *The BJP and the Compulsions of Politics in India.* Delhi: Oxford University Press.

Hanson, A. 1966: *The Process of Planning: A Study of India's Five Year Plans, 1950–1964.* London: Oxford University Press.

Hardgrave, R. 1984: *India Under Pressure.* Boulder: Westview.

Hardiman, D. 1987: *The Coming of the Devi: Adivasi Assertion in Western India.* Delhi: Oxford University Press.

Harrison, S. 1960: *India: The Most Dangerous Decades.* Princeton: Princeton University Press.

Harriss, B. 1984: *State and Market.* Delhi: Concept.

Harriss, B. and Harriss, J. 1984: 'Generative' and 'parasitic' urbanism? Some observations from the recent history of a South Indian market town. *Journal of Development Studies*, 20, 82–101.

Harriss, J. 1977a: The limitations of HYV technology in North Arcot District: the view from the village. In B. H. Farmer (ed.), *Green Revolution?*, London: Macmillan, 124–42.

—— 1977b: Bias in perception of agrarian change in India. In B. H. Farmer (ed.), *Green Revolution?* London: Macmillan, 30–7.

—— 1980: Contemporary Marxist analysis of the agrarian question in India. Discussion Paper, Madras Institute of Development Studies.

—— 1982: *Capitalism and Peasant Farming: Agrarian Structure and Ideology in Northern Tamil Nadu.* Bombay: Oxford University Press.

—— 1987a: Capitalism and peasant production: the Green Revolution in India. In T. Shanin (ed.), *Peasants and Peasant Societies*, 2nd edn, Oxford: Blackwell, 227–46.

—— 1987b: The state in retreat? Why has India experienced such half-hearted liberalisation in the 1980s? *IDS Bulletin*, 18, 31–8.

—— 1989: Indian industrialization and the state. In H. Alavi and J. Harriss (eds), *Sociology of Developing Societies: South Asia*, London: Macmillan, 70–90.

—— 1991: The Green Revolution in North Arcot: economic trends, household mobility, and the politics of an 'awkward class'. In P. Hazell and C. Ramasamy (eds), *The Green Revolution Reconsidered: The Impact of High-Yielding Varieties in South India*, Baltimore: Johns Hopkins University Press, 57–84.

—— 1992: Does the 'depressor' still work? Agrarian structure and development in India: a review of evidence and argument. *Journal of Peasant Studies*, 19, 189–227.

—— 1993: What is happening in rural West Bengal? Agrarian reform, growth and redistribution. *Economic and Political Weekly*, 28, 1237–47.

—— 1998: Development studies and the development of India: an awkward case? *Oxford Development Studies*, 26, 287–309.

—— 1999: How much difference does politics make? Regime differences across Indian States and rural poverty reduction. Mimeo: Development Studies Institute, London School of Economics. (Forthcoming in P. Houtzager, M. Moore and J. Putzel (eds), *Politics and Poverty*, London: Routledge.)

Harriss-White, B. 1996: *A Political Economy of Agrarian Markets in South India: Masters of the Countryside.* New Delhi: Sage.

—— 1997: The state and informal economic order in South Asia. Mimeo: Queen Elizabeth House, Oxford.

—— 1999: How India works: the character of the local economy. Cambridge University Commonwealth Lectures (unpublished).

Hart, H. (1976): Indira Gandhi: determined not to be hurt. In H. Hart (ed.), *Indira Gandhi's India*, Boulder: Westview, 241–74.

Hasan, M. 1996: The changing position of Muslims and the political future of secularism in India. In T. Sathyamurthy (ed.), *Social Change and Political Discourse in India*, vol. 3, *Region, Religion, Caste, Gender and Culture in Contemporary India*, Delhi: Oxford University Press, 200–28.

Hasan, Z. 1998: *Quest for Power: Oppositional Movements and Post-Congress Politics in Uttar Pradesh.* Delhi: Oxford University Press.

Hauser, W. 1993: Violence, agrarian radicalism and electoral politics: reflections on the Indian People's Front. *Journal of Peasant Studies*, 21, 85–126.

Hawthorn, G. 1982: Caste and politics in India since 1947. In D. MacGilvray (ed.), *Caste Ideology and Interaction*, Cambridge: Cambridge University Press, 204–20.

——1991: 'Waiting for a text?' Comparing Third World politics. In J. Manor (ed.), *Rethinking Third World Politics*, Harlow: Longman, 24–50.

Haynes, J. 1997: *Democracy and Civil Society in the Third World*. Cambridge: Polity.

Heginbotham, S. 1975: *Cultures in Conflict: The Four Faces of Indian Bureaucracy*. New York: Columbia University Press.

Herring, R. 1983: *Land to the Tiller: The Political Economy of Agrarian Reform in South Asia*. New Haven: Yale University Press.

——1998: Embedded particularism: India's failed developmental state. In M. Woo-Cumings (ed.), *The Developmental State in Historical Perspective*, Ithaca: Cornell University Press.

Herzog, D. 1998: *Poisoning the Minds of the Lower Orders*. Princeton: Princeton University Press.

Heston, A. 1982: National income. In D. Kumar and M. Desai (eds), *The Cambridge Economic History of India*, vol. 2, Cambridge: Cambridge University Press, 376–462.

——1990: Poverty in India: some recent policies. In M. Bouton and P. Oldenburg (eds), *India Briefing, 1990*, Boulder: Westview and The Asia Society, 101–28.

Hettne, B. 1978: *The Political Economy of Indirect Rule: Mysore, 1881–1947*. London: Curzon Press.

Inden, R. 1990: *Imagining India*. Oxford: Blackwell.

——1995: Embodying God: from imperial progresses to national progress in India. *Economy and Society*, 24, 245–78.

Irschick, E. 1969: *Politics and Social Conflict in South India: The Non-Brahman Movement and Tamil Separatism, 1916–29*. Berkeley: University of California Press.

Isaac, T., Francke, R. and Raghavan, P. 1998: *Democracy at Work in an Indian Industrial Cooperative: The Story of Kerala Dinesh Beedi*. Ithaca: Cornell University Press.

Islam, R. (ed.) 1987: *Rural Industrialization and Employment in Asia*. New Delhi: ILO-ARTEP.

Jackson, C. 1993: 'Women/nature or gender/history: a critique of ecofeminist development. *Journal of Peasant Studies*, 20, 212–26.

Jaffrelot, C. 1996: *The Hindu Nationalist Movement and Indian Politics: 1925 to the 1990s*. New Delhi: Viking.

——1998: The Sangh Parivar between Sanskritization and social engineering. In T. B. Hansen and C. Jaffrelot, (eds), *The BJP and the Compulsions of Politics in India*, Delhi: Oxford University Press.

Jalal, A. 1985: *The Sole Spokesman: Jinnah, the Muslim League and the Demand for Pakistan*. Cambridge: Cambridge University Press.

——1995: *Democracy and Authoritarianism in South Asia: A Comparative and Historical Perspective*. Cambridge: Cambridge University Press.

Jayal, N. 1999: *Democracy and the State: Welfare, Secularism and Development in Contemporary India*. Delhi: Oxford University Press.

Jeffery, R. and Jeffery, P. 1997: *Population, Gender and Politics: Demographic Change in Rural North India*. Cambridge: Cambridge University Press.

Jeffrey, C. 1998: Soft states and hard bargains: money, class and power in northwest India. Paper presented in the Panel on 'UP 2000' at the 15th European Conference of Modern Asian Studies, Prague. Mimeo: Department of Geography, University of Cambridge.

—— 1999: *Reproducing Difference: The Investment Decisions of Richer Jat Farmers in Meerut District, Uttar Pradesh, India*. Unpublished Ph.D. dissertation: University of Cambridge.

—— and Lerche, J. 1999: Stating the difference: state, discourses and class reproduction in Uttar Pradesh, India. Mimeo: Edinburgh University and London University (SOAS). (Forthcoming, 2000, in V. Benei and C. Fuller (eds), *The Everyday State: Anthropological Perspectives on the State and Society in Modern India*, Delhi: Social Science Publishers and London: Zed Books.)

Jenkins, R. 1997: *Democratic Adjustment: Explaining the Political Sustainability of Economic Reform in India*. Unpublished D.Phil. dissertation: University of Sussex.

—— 1999: *Democratic Politics and Economic Reform in India*. Cambridge: Cambridge University Press.

Jha, J. 1964: *The Kol Insurrection of Chota Nagpur*. Calcutta: Thacker, Spink, and Co.

Jha, S. 1999: Tax evasion, amnesty schemes, and black income: theory, evidence, and issues. In K. Parikh (ed.), *India Development Report 1999–2000*, Delhi: Oxford University Press, 165–76.

Jodha, N. 1988: Poverty debate in India: a minority view. *Economic and Political Weekly*, 23, 2421–8.

Jones, K. 1981: Politicized Hinduism: the ideology and program of the Hindu Mahasabha. In R. Baird (ed.), *Religion in Modern India*, New Delhi: Manohar, 447–80.

Joshi, V. 1998: Fiscal stabilization and economic reform in India. In I. J. Ahluwalia and I. M. D. Little (eds), *India's Economic Reforms and Development: Essays for Manmohan Singh*, Delhi: Oxford University Press, 147–68.

—— and Little, I. M. D. 1994: *India: Macroeconomics and Political Economy, 1964–1991*. Washington DC: The World Bank.

—— and Little, I. M. D. 1995: Macroeconomic stabilization in India, 1991–1993 and beyond. In R. Cassen and V. Joshi (eds), *India: The Future of Economic Reform*, Delhi: Oxford University Press, 31–51.

Kabeer, N. and Murthy, R. 1996: Compensating for institutional exclusion: lessons from Indian government and non-government credit interventions for the poor. University of Sussex: IDS Discussion Paper no. 356.

Kakar, S. 1996: *The Colors of Violence: Cultural Identities, Religion, and Conflict*. Chicago: University of Chicago Press.

Kalecki, M. 1972: Social and economic aspects of 'intermediate regimes'. In M. Kalecki, *Selected Essays on the Economic Growth of Socialist and Mixed Regimes*, Cambridge: Cambridge University Press.

Kalelkar, K. 1998 [1955]: Backwardness, caste and the question of reservations. In G. Mahajan (ed.), *Democracy, Difference and Social Justice*, Delhi: Oxford University Press, 451–62.

Kapur, A. 1993: Deity to crusader: the changing iconography of Ram. In G. Pandey (ed.), *Hindus and Others: The Question of Identity in India Today*, Delhi: Oxford University Press.

Karanjia, R. 1960: *The Mind of Mr Nehru*, London: Allen and Unwin.

Karlekar, I. 1999: *The Political Economy of Liberalization in India: The Autos Sector.* Unpublished Ph.D. dissertation: University of Cambridge.

Kaviraj, S. 1984: On the crisis of political institutions in India. *Contributions to Indian Sociology*, 18, 223–43.

—— 1988 [1997]: A critique of the passive revolution. *Economic and Political Weekly*, 23, 45–7; and in P. Chatterjee (ed.), *State and Politics in India*, Delhi: Oxford University Press.

—— 1991: On state, society and discourse in India. In J. Manor (ed.), *Rethinking Third World Politics*, Harlow: Longman, 72–99.

—— 1994: On the construction of colonial power: structure, discourse, hegemony. In D. Engels and S. Marks (eds), *Contesting Colonial Hegemony: State and Society in Africa*, London: Curzon Press.

—— 1997: The general elections in India', *Government and Opposition*, 32, 3–24.

Keer, D. 1966: *Veer Savarkar*, Bombay: Popular Prakashan.

Khatkhate, D. 1992: India on an economic reform trajectory. In L. Gordon and P. Oldenburg (eds), *India Briefing, 1992*, Boulder: Westview and The Asia Society, 47–70.

Khilnani, S. 1997: *The Idea of India*. London: Hamish Hamilton.

King, R. 1997: *Nehru and the Language Politics of India*. Delhi: Oxford University Press.

Kochanek, S. 1968: *The Congress Party of India*. Princeton: Princeton University Press.

—— 1974: *Business and Politics in India*. Berkeley: University of California Press.

—— 1976: Mrs Gandhi's pyramid: the new Congress. In H. Hart (ed.), *Indira Gandhi's India*, Boulder: Westview, 100–16.

Kohli, A. 1987: *The State and Poverty in India: The Political Economy of Reform.* Cambridge: Cambridge University Press.

—— 1988: State–society relations in India's changing democracy. In A. Kohli (ed.), *India's Democracy*, Princeton: Princeton University Press, 305–18.

—— 1990a: *Democracy and Discontent: India's Growing Crisis of Governability*. Cambridge: Cambridge University Press.

—— 1990b: From elite activism to democratic consolidation: the rise of reform communism in West Bengal. In F. Frankel and M. Rao (eds), *Dominance and State Power in Modern India: Decline of a Social Order*, vol. II, Delhi: Oxford University Press, 367–415.

Kothari, R. 1964: The Congress 'System' in India. *Asian Survey*, 1161–73.

—— 1970: *Politics in India*. Delhi: Orient Longman.

—— 1988: *State Against Democracy: In Search of Humane Governance*. Delhi: Ajanta.

—— 1994: Rise of the Dalits and the renewed debate on caste. *Economic and Political Weekly*, 29, 1589–94.

Kulke, H. and Rothermund, D. 1986: *A History of India*. London: Croom Helm.

Kumar, D. 1992: The affirmative action debate in India. *Asian Survey*, 32, 290–302.

—— 1994: Left secularists and communalism. *Economic and Political Weekly*, 29, 1803–9.

Kumar, K. 1993: Hindu revivalism and education in north-central India. In M. Marty and R. Appleby (eds), *Fundamentalisms and Society*, Chicago: University of Chicago Press.

Kumar, R. 1993: *The History of Doing*. New Delhi: Kali for Women.

Lal, D. 1976: Agricultural growth, real wages and the rural poor in India. *Economic and Political Weekly*, 11, A47–61.

—— 1999: *Unfinished Business: The Indian Economy in the 1990s*. Delhi: Oxford University Press.

Leach, E. (ed.) 1960: *Aspects of Caste in India and Beyond*. Cambridge: Cambridge University Press.

Leftwich, A. 1994: Governance, the state and the politics of development. *Development and Change*, 25, 363–86.

Lele, J. 1984: One-party dominance in Maharashtra: resilience and change. In J. Wood (ed.), *State Politics in Contemporary India: Crisis or Continuity?*, Boulder: Westview Press, 169–96.

—— 1989: Caste, class and dominance: political mobilization in Maharashtra. In F. Frankel and M. Rao (eds), *Dominance and State Power in Modern India: Decline of a Social Order*, vol. II, Delhi: Oxford University Press, 115–211.

Lerche, J. 1995: Is bonded labour a bound category? Reconceptualising agrarian conflict in India. *Journal of Peasant Studies*, 22, 484–515.

Lewis, W. A. 1954: Economic development with unlimited supplies of labour. *Manchester School*, 22, 139–91.

Leys, C. 1995: *The Rise and Fall of Development Theory*. Oxford: James Currey.

Lieten, G. 1992: *Continuity and Change in Rural West Bengal*. New Delhi: Sage.

Lindberg, S. (1995) New farmers' movements in India as structural response and collective identity formation: the case of the Shetkari Sanghata and the BKU. In T. Brass (ed.), *New Farmers' Movements in India*, London: Frank Cass, 95–125.

Lipietz, A. 1987: *Mirages and Miracles: The Crises of Global Fordism*. London: Verso.

Lipton, M. 1977: *Why Poor People Stay Poor: A Study of Urban Bias in World Development*. London: Temple Smith.

—— with Longhurst, R. 1989: *New Seeds and Poor People*. London: Unwin Hyman.

McGirk, T. 1996: Sikhs query the deadly price of peace. *Independent*, 13 December.

McKean, L. 1996: *Divine Enterprise: Gurus and the Hindu Nationalist Movement*. Chicago: University of Chicago Press.

McLeod, W. 1989: *The Sikhs: History, Religion and Society*. New York: Columbia University Press.

Madan, T. N. 1987: Secularism in its place. *Journal of Asian Studies*, 46, 747–59.

—— 1997: *Modern Myths, Locked Minds: Secularism and Fundamentalism in India*. New Delhi: Oxford University Press.

Maddison, A. 1971: *Class Structure and Economic Growth: India and Pakistan Since the Moghuls*. London: George Allen and Unwin.

Mahajan, G. (ed.) 1998: *Democracy, Difference and Social Justice*. Delhi: Oxford University Press.

Mahar, J. M. (ed.) 1972: *The Untouchables in Contemporary India*. Tucson: University of Arizona Press.

Mahmood, C. 1996: *Fighting for Faith and Nation: Dialogues With Sikh Militants*. Philadelphia: University of Pennsylvania Press.

Majumdar, S. 1996: Fall and rise of productivity in Indian industry: has economic liberalisation had an impact? *Economic and Political Weekly*, 31, M46–53.

Mallick, R. 1990: Limits to radical intervention: agricultural taxation in West Bengal. *Development and Change*, 21, 147–64.

—— 1992: Agrarian reform in West Bengal: the end of an illusion. *World Development*, 20, 735–50.

Manor, J. 1982: The dynamics of political integration. In A. Wilson and D. Dalton (eds.), *The States of South Asia: Problems of National Integration*, London: Hurst, 89–110.

—— 1983: Anomie in Indian politics. *Economic and Political Weekly*, 18, 725–34.

—— 1984: Blurring the lines between parties and social bases: Gundu Rao and the emergence of a Janata government in Karnataka. In J. Wood (ed.), *State Politics in Contemporary India: Crisis or Continuity?*, Boulder: Westview Press, 139–68.

—— 1988: Parties and the party system. In A. Kohli (ed.), *India's Democracy: An Analysis of Changing State–Society Relations*, Princeton: Princeton University Press, 62–98.

—— 1992: The BJP in the South: 1991 general elections. *Economic and Political Weekly*, 27, 1267–78.

Mawdsley, E. 1997: Non-secessionist regionalism in India: the Uttarakhand separate State movement. *Environment and Planning A*, 29, 2217–36.

Mayer, A. 1960: *Caste and Kinship in Central India*. Berkeley: University of California Press.

—— 1996: Caste in an Indian village: change and continuity, 1954–1992. In C. Fuller (ed.), *Caste Today*, Delhi: Oxford University Press, 32–64.

Mellor, J. 1976: *The New Economics of Growth*. Ithaca: Cornell University Press.

Mendelsohn, O. 1993: The transformation of authority in rural India. *Modern Asian Studies*, 27, 805–42.

—— and Vicziany, M. 1998: *The Untouchables: Subordination, Poverty and the State in Modern India*. Cambridge: Cambridge University Press.

Metcalf, T. 1995: *Ideologies of the Raj*. Cambridge: Cambridge University Press.

Miller, B. 1981: *The Endangered Sex*. Ithaca: Cornell University Press.

Mishra, P. 1998: A new, nuclear, India? *New York Review of Books*, 25 June, 55–64.

—— 1999: The other India. *New York Review of Books*, 16 December, 91–100.

Mishra, V. 1986 *Report From the Flaming Fields of Bihar: A CPI (ML) Document*. Calcutta: Prabodh Bhattarcharya.

Mistry, R. 1996: *A Fine Balance*. London: Faber.

Mitra, S. 1987: The perils of promoting equality: the latent significance of the anti-reservations movement in India. *Journal of Commonwealth and Comparative Politics*, 25, 292–312.

—— 1994: Caste, democracy and the politics of community formation in India. In M. Searle-Chatterjee and U. Sharma (eds), *Contextualising Caste: Post-Dumontian Approaches*, Oxford: Blackwell.

Moffatt, M. 1975: Untouchability and the caste system: a Tamil case study. *Contributions to Indian Sociology*, new series 9, 111–22.

Mooij, J. 1999: *Food Policy and the Indian State: The Public Distribution System in South India*. Delhi: Oxford University Press.

Mook, B. 1974: Value and action in Indian bureaucracy. University of Sussex: IDS Discussion Paper 65.

Moore, Barrington Jr, 1966: *Social Origins of Dictatorship and Democracy: Lord and Peasant in the Making of the Modern World*. Boston: Beacon Press.

Morris, M. D. 1982: The growth of large-scale industry to 1947. In D. Kumar and M. Desai (eds), *The Cambridge Economic History of India*, vol. 2, Cambridge: Cambridge University Press, 553–676.

Morris-Jones, W. M. 1971: *Government and Politics of India*, 3rd edn. London: Hutchinson.

—— 1978: *Politics Mainly Indian*. Delhi: Orient Longman.

Mosse, D. 1994: Idioms of subordination and styles of protest among Christian and Hindu Harijan castes in Tamil Nadu. *Contributions to Indian Sociology*, new series 28, 67–106.

Munda, R. D. 1988: The Jharkhand movement: retrospect and prospect. *Social Change*, 18, 28–42.

Mundle, S. and Govinda Rao, M. 1991: The volume and composition of government subsidies in India, 1987–88. *Economic and Political Weekly*, 26, 1157–72.

Myrdal, G. 1968: *Asian Drama: An Inquiry into the Poverty of Nations*. New York: Twentieth Century Fund.

Nadkarni, M. V. 1987: *Farmers' Movements in India*. Delhi: Allied.

Nag, M. 1989: Political awareness as a factor in accessibility of health services: a case study of rural Kerala and West Bengal. *Economic and Political Weekly*, 24, 417–26.

Nambiar, R. and Tadas, G. 1994: Is trade deindustrialising India? *Economic and Political Weekly*, 29, 2741–6.

Nanda, M. 1991: Is modern science a Western patriarchal myth? A critique of populist orthodoxy. *South Asia Bulletin*, 11, 32–61.

Nandy, A. 1985: An anti-secularist manifesto. *Seminar*, 314, 14–24.

—— 1990: The politics of secularism and the recovery of religious tolerance. In V. Das (ed.), *Mirrors of Violence*, Delhi: Oxford University Press, 69–93.

—— 1998: *Exiled At Home*. Delhi: Oxford University Press.

—— Trivedy, S., Mayaram, S. and Yagnik, A. 1995: *Creating a Nationality: The Ramjanmabhumi Movement and Fear of the Self*. Delhi: Oxford University Press.

Naoroji, D. 1962 [1901]: *Poverty and Un-British Rule in India*. New Delhi: Government of India, Ministry of Information and Broadcasting.

Narain, I. 1986: India in 1985: triumph of democracy. *Asian Survey*, 26, 253–69.

Narayana, G. 1978: Social background of Scheduled Caste Lok Sabha members. *Economic and Political Weekly*, 13, 1603–8.

—— 1986: Rule making for Scheduled Castes: analysis of Lok Sabha debates, 1962–71. *Economic and Political Weekly*, 21, 433–40.

Navlakha, G. 1996: Invoking Union: Kashmir and the official nationalism of 'Bharat'. In T. Sathyamurthy (ed.), *Social Change and Political Discourse in India*, vol. 3, Region, Religion, Caste, Gender and Culture in Contemporary India, Delhi: Oxford University Press, 64–106.

Nayar, K. 1971: *India: The Critical Years*. Delhi: Vikas.

Nayyar, D. and Sen, A. 1994: International trade and the agricultural sector in India. In G. S. Bhalla (ed.), *Economic Liberalization and Indian Agriculture*, New Delhi: Institute for Studies in Industrial Development, 61–102.

Nayyar, R. 1991: *Rural Poverty in India: An Analysis of Inter-State Differences*. Delhi: Oxford University Press.

Nehru, J. 1962 [1936]: *An Autobiography*. Bombay: Allied.

O'Hanlon, R. 1985: *Caste, Conflict and Ideology: Mahatma Jotirao Phule and Low Caste Protest in Nineteenth-Century Western India*. Cambridge: Cambridge University Press.

Omvedt, G. 1990: Hinduism and politics. *Economic and Political Weekly*, 25, 723–9.

—— 1993: *Reinventing Revolution: New Social Movements and the Socialist Tradition*. Armonk, NY: M. E. Sharpe.

—— 1994: *Dalits and the Democratic Revolution: Dr. Ambedkar and the Dalit Movement in Colonial India*. New Delhi: Sage.

—— 1996: The anti-caste movement and the discourse of power. In T. Sathyamurthy (ed.), *Social Change and Political Discourse in India*, vol. 3, *Region, Religion, Caste, Gender and Culture in Contemporary India*, Delhi: Oxford University Press, 334–54.

—— 1997: In search of the Indian nation [review of Aloysius, *Nationalism Without a Nation in India*]. *Economic and Political Weekly*, 32, 31, 1996–8.

Pandey, G. 1982: Peasant revolt and Indian nationalism: the peasant movements in Awadh, 1919–1922. In R. Guha (ed.), *Subaltern Studies I: Writings on South Asian History and Society*, Delhi: Oxford University Press, 143–97.

Pandian, M. 1997: Culture and subaltern consciousness: an aspect of the MGR phenomenon. In P. Chatterjee (ed.), *State and Politics in India*, Delhi: Oxford University Press, 367–89.

Panini, M. 1999: Trends in cultural globalization: from agriculture to agribusiness in Karnataka. *Economic and Political Weekly*, 24, 2168–73.

Parajuli, P. 1996: Ecological ethnicity in the making: developmentalist hegemonies and emergent identities in India. *Identities*, 3, 15–59.

Parekh, B. 1997: *Gandhi*. Oxford: Oxford University Press.

Parikh, K. 1999: Overview. In K. Parikh (ed.), *India Development Report 1999–2000*, Delhi: Oxford University Press, 1–24.

Parry, J. 1996: No mother or father like it: the Bhilai steel plant in central India. Mimeo: Department of Anthropology, London School of Economics.

—— 1999a: Two cheers for reservation: the Satnamis and the steel plant. In R. Guha and J. Parry (eds), *Institutions and Inequalities: Essays in Honour of Andre Beteille*, Delhi: Oxford University Press, 128–69.

—— 1999b: Brashtachar in Bhilai: a case-study concerning the moral evaluation of corruption in a central Indian steel town. Mimeo: Department of Anthropology, London School of Economics.

Patel, I. G. 1987: On taking India into the twenty-first century. *Modern Asian Studies*, 21, 209–31.

—— 1992: New economic policies: a historical perspective. *Economic and Political Weekly*, 27, 41–6.

Patnaik, P. 1972: Imperialism and the growth of Indian capitalism. In R. Owen and R. Sutcliffe (eds), *Theories of Imperialism*, London: Longman, 210–29.

Patnaik, P. 1979: Industrial development in India since Independence. *Social Scientist*, 7 (11), 83, 3–19.

—— and Rao, S. 1977: 1975–6: beginning of the end of stagnation? *Social Scientist*, 5, 120–38.

Pearse, A. 1980: *Seeds of Plenty, Seeds of Want*. London: Oxford University Press.

Pettigrew, J. 1984: Take not arms against thy sovereign. *South Asia Research*, 9, 102–23.

Pinney, C. 1997: The nation (un)pictured? Chromolithography and 'popular' politics in India, 1878–1995. *Critical Inquiry*, 23, 834–67.

Pinto, A. 1999: The end of Dravidianism in Tamil Nadu. *Economic and Political Weekly*, 31, 24.

Platteau, J.-P. 1994: Behind the market stage where real societies exist. *Journal of Development Studies*, 30, 533–77, 753–817.

Potter, D. 1994: The Prime Minister and the bureaucracy. In J. Manor (ed.), *Nehru to the Nineties*, London: Hurst, 74–93.

—— 1996: *India's Political Administrators*, 2nd edn. Delhi: Oxford University Press.

Przeworski, A. 1991: *Democracy and the Market*. Cambridge: Cambridge University Press.

Quigley, D. 1993: *The Interpretation of Caste*. Oxford: Clarendon Press.

Radhakrishnan, P. 1996: Mandal Commission Report: A sociological critique. In M. Srinivas (ed.), *Caste: Its Twentieth-Century Avatar*, Delhi: Penguin, 110–34.

Raheja, G. G. 1988: India: caste, kingship and dominance reconsidered. *Annual Review of Anthropology*, 17, 497–522.

—— and Gold, A. 1994: *Listen to the Heron's Words: Reimagining Gender and Kinship in North India*. Berkeley: University of California Press.

Raj, K. N. 1973: The politics and economics of 'intermediate regimes'. *Economic and Political Weekly*, 8, 1189–98.

Rajagopal, A. 1994: Ram Janmabhoomi, consumer identity and image-based politics. *Economic and Political Weekly*, 29, 1659–68.

Rakshit, M. 1982: Income, saving and capital formation in India. *Economic and Political Weekly*, 17, 561–72.

Ramachandran, V. 1990: *Wage Labour and Unfreedom in Agriculture: An Indian Case Study*. Oxford: Clarendon Press.

Rangan, H. 1996: From Chipko to Uttaranchal: development, environment and social protest in the Garhwal Himalayas, India. In R. Peet and M. Watts (eds), *Liberation Ecologies: Environment, Development, Social Movements*, London: Routledge, 205–26.

—— 1997: Indian environmentalism and the question of the state: problems and prospects for sustainable development. *Environment and Planning A*, 29, 2129–43.

Ranjan, V. 1999: The price of democracy: helicopters, onions and the 1999 general election in rural north Bihar. Mimeo: available from Corbridge at University of Cambridge.

Rao, C. H. 1975: *Technological Change and Distribution of Gains in Indian Agriculture*. Delhi: Macmillan.

Reidinger, R. 1974: Institutional rationing of canal water in northern India: conflict between traditional patterns and modern needs. *Economic Development and Cultural Change*, 23, 79–104.

Reynolds, N. and Sunder, P. 1977: Maharashtra's employment guarantee scheme: a program to emulate? *Economic and Political Weekly*, 22, 1149–58.

Richards, J. 1993: *The Mughal Empire*. Cambridge: Cambridge University Press.

Robb, P. (ed.) 1995: *The Concept of Race in South Asia*. Delhi: Oxford University Press.

Robinson, M. 1988: *Local Politics: The Law of the Fishes – Development Through Political Change in Medak District, Andhra Pradesh (South India)*. Delhi: Oxford University Press.

Rogaly, B. 1998: Containing conflict and reaping votes: management of rural labour relations in West Bengal. *Economic and Political Weekly*, 33, 42–3.

Roy, A. 1999: *The Cost of Living*. New York: The Modern Library.

Rubin, B. 1985: Economic liberalisation and the Indian state. *Third World Quarterly*, 7, 942–57.

Rudolph, L. and Rudolph, S. H. 1967: *The Modernity of Tradition*. Chicago: University of Chicago Press.

——and Rudolph, S. H. 1987: *In Pursuit of Lakshmi: The Political Economy of the Indian State*. Chicago: University of Chicago Press.

Rueschemeyer, D., Stephens, E. H. and Stephens, J. D. 1992: *Capitalist Development and Democracy*. Cambridge: Polity.

Rushdie, S. 1991: *Imaginary Homelands*. Cambridge: Granta.

Rutten, M. 1995: *Farms and Factories: Social Profile of Large Farmers and Rural Industrialists in West India*. Delhi: Oxford University Press.

Saberwal, S. 1996: *The Roots of Crisis: Interpreting Contemporary Indian Society*. Delhi: Oxford University Press.

Sachs, J. 1994: *India's Unfinished Reform Agenda*. Mimeo: text of a talk given at the India International Centre, New Delhi, 23 August.

Sainath, P. 1996: *Everybody Loves a Good Drought*. New Delhi: Penguin.

Saith, A. 1986: Contrasting experiences in rural industrialization: Are East Asian successes transferable? Asian Employment Programme Working Paper, New Delhi: ILO-ARTEP.

——1991: Asian rural industrialization: context, features, strategies. In J. Breman and S. Mundle (eds), *Rural Transformation in Asia*, Delhi: Oxford University Press, 458–89.

——1995: *Reflections on South Asian Prospects in East Asian Perspective*. Issues in Development Discussion Paper no. 7, Development and Technical Cooperation Department, Geneva: International Labour Office.

Samata Sanghatana 1991: Upper caste violence: study of Chunduru carnage. *Economic and Political Weekly*, 26, 2079–84.

Sarkar, P. 1991: IMF/World Bank stabilisation programmes: a critical assessment. *Economic and Political Weekly*, 5 October: 2307–10.

Sarkar, S. 1983: *Modern India, 1885–1947*. Delhi: Macmillan.

——1996: Indian nationalism and the politics of Hindutva. In D. Ludden (ed.), *Contesting the Nation: Religion, Community, and the Politics of Democracy in India*, Philadelphia: University of Pennsylvania Press, 270–93.

Sarkar, T. 1998: Women, community and nation: a historical trajectory for Hindu identity politics. In P. Jeffrey and A. Basu (eds), *Appropriating Gender: Women's Activism and Politicized Religion in South Asia*, London: Routledge, 89–104.

Sathyamurthy T. 1989: Impact of Centre–State relations on Indian politics: an interpretative reckoning, 1947–87. *Economic and Political Weekly*, 23 September, 2133–47.

——(ed.) 1996: *Social Change and Political Discourse in India*, vol. 3, *Region, Religion, Caste, Gender and Culture in Contemporary India*. Delhi: Oxford University Press.

Savarkar, V. 1922: *Essentials of Hindutva*. Madras: B. G. Paul.

——1949: *Hindu Rashtra Darshan: A Collection of Presidential Speeches Delivered from the Hindu Mahasabha Platform, 1938–1941*. Bombay: Khare.

Saxena, N. C. 1994: *India's Eucalyptus Craze: The God That Failed*. New Delhi: Sage.

Saxena, S., Prasad, R. and Joshi, V. 1995: Time allocation and fuel usage in three villages of the Garhwal Himalayas, India. *Mountain Research and Development*, 15, 57–67.

Sayer, D. 1991: *Capitalism and Modernity: An Excursus on Marx and Weber*. London: Routledge.

Scott, J. C. 1998: *Seeing Like a State: How Certain Schemes to Improve the Human Condition Have Failed*. New Haven: Yale University Press.

Seal, A. 1968: *The Emergence of Indian Nationalism: Competition and Collaboration in the Later Nineteenth Century*. Cambridge: Cambridge University Press.

Selbourne, D. 1977: *An Eye to India*. Harmondsworth: Penguin.

Sen, A. 1996: Economic reforms, employment and poverty: trends and options. *Economic and Political Weekly*, 31, 2459–77.

Sen, A. K. 1981: *Poverty and Famines: An Essay on Entitlement and Deprivation*. Oxford: Clarendon Press.

—— 1983: Poor, relatively speaking. *Oxford Economic Papers*, 35, 153–69.

—— 1985: *Commodities and Capabilities*. Amsterdam: North Holland.

—— 1989: Food and freedom. *World Development*, 17, 769–81.

—— 1996 Secularism and its discontents. In K. Basu and S. Subrahmanyam (eds.), *Unravelling the Nation: Sectarian Conflict and India's Secular Identity*, New Delhi: Penguin, 11–43.

Sen, G. 1992: Social needs and public accountability: the case of Kerala. In M. Wuyts et al. (eds), *Development Policy and Public Action*, Oxford: Oxford University Press with the Open University, 253–78.

Sethi, H. 1998: Contesting communalism [a review of Vanaik 1997]. *Economic and Political Weekly*, 33, 16, 894–5.

Shah, A. 1998: *Secularism in Contemporary India: An Investigation into a Locked Mind Representing a Modern Myth*. Unpublished M.Sc. Dissertation, Department of Anthropology, London School of Economics.

—— 1999: Gendered designers of the Indian state: policies, bureaucrats and the Development of Women and Children in Rural Areas. Mimeo: Department of Anthropology, London School of Economics.

Shah, A. M. 1996a: The judicial and sociological view of Other Backward Classes. In M. Srinivas (ed.), *Caste: Its Twentieth Century Avatar*, Delhi: Penguin, 174–94.

—— 1996b: Job reservation and efficiency. In M. Srinivas (ed.), *Caste: Its Twentieth Century Avatar*, Delhi: Penguin, 195–202.

Sharma, C. V. (ed.) 1989: *Modern Temples of India: Selected Speeches of Jawaharlal Nehru on Irrigation and Power*. New Delhi: Government of India (Central Board of Irrigation and Power).

Sharma, H. 1973: The Green Revolution in India: prelude to a red one? In K. Gough and H. Sharma (eds), *Imperialism and Revolution in South Asia*, New York: Monthly Review Press, 21–42.

Sheth, D. 1999: Caste and class: social reality and political representations. In V. A. Pai Panandikar and A. Nandy (eds), *Contemporary India*, Delhi: Tata McGraw-Hill, 337–63.

Shetty, S. L. 1978: Structural retrogression in the Indian economy. *Economic and Political Weekly*, 13, Annual Number 185–244.

Shiva, V. 1989: *Staying Alive: Women, Ecology and Survival in India*. New Delhi: Kali for Women.

—— 1991: *The Violence of the Green Revolution*. London: Zed Books.

Singh, I. 1990: *The Great Ascent: The Rural Poor in South Asia*. Baltimore: Johns Hopkins University Press/World Bank.

Singh, K. S. 1983: *Birsa Munda and his Movement, 1874–1901*. Delhi: Oxford University Press.

Sinha, S., Gururani, S. and Greenberg, B. 1997: The 'new traditionalist' discourse of Indian environmentalism. *Journal of Peasant Studies*, 24, 65–99.

Sisson, R. 1990: India in 1989: a year of elections in a culture of change. *Asian Survey*, 30, 111–25.

Sivaramayya, B. 1996: The Mandal judgement: a brief description and critique. In M. Srinivas (ed.), *Caste: Its Twentieth Century Avatar*, Delhi: Penguin, 221–43.

Smith, P. 1963: *India as a Secular State*. Princeton: Princeton University Press.

Spear, P. 1994: *Delhi: Its Monuments and History* (updated and annotated by N. Gupta and L. Sykes). Delhi: Oxford University Press.

Srinivas, M. N. 1959: The dominant caste in Rampura. *American Anthropologist*, 61, 1–16.

Srinivasan, T. N. 1991: Reform of industrial and trade policies. *Economic and Political Weekly*, 26, 2143–5.

Srivastava, M. 1998: Promoting adult literacy in India through state-society synergy: a comparative study of mass literacy campaigns in Kerala and Bihar. Unpublished project paper: submitted to Graduate School of Cornell University.

Streeten, P. 1997: *Thinking About Development*. Cambridge: Cambridge University Press.

—— and Lipton, M. (eds) 1968: *The Crisis of Indian Planning: Economic Planning in the 1960s*. London: Oxford University Press, with the Royal Institute of International Affairs.

Sudarshan, R. 1994: The political consequences of constitutional discourse. In T. Sathyamurthy (ed.), *Social Change and Political Discourse in India*, vol. I, *State and Nation in the Context of Social Change*, Delhi: Oxford University Press, 55–86.

Suresh, V. 1996: The Dalit movement in India. In T. Sathyamurthy (ed.), *Social Change and Political Discourse in India*, vol. III, *Region, Religion, Caste, Gender and Culture in Contemporary India*, Delhi: Oxford University Press, 355–87.

Suryanarayana, M. 1996: Economic reforms, nature and poverty. *Economic and Political Weekly*, 31, 617–24.

Swaminathan, M. 1990: Village level implementation of IRDP: comparison of West Bengal and Tamil Nadu. *Economic and Political Weekly*, 25, A17–27.

Talbot, P. 1991: Kashmir's agony. In P. Oldenburg (ed.), *India Briefing 1991*, Boulder: Westview and The Asia Society, 123–42.

Tambiah, S. 1990: Reflections on communal violence in South Asia. *Journal of Asian Studies*, 49, 741–60.

—— 1996: *Levelling Crowds: Ethnonationalist Conflicts and Collective Violence in South Asia*. Berkeley: University of California Press.

Taub, R. 1969: *Bureaucrats Under Stress: Administrators and Administration in an Indian State*. Berkeley: University of California Press.

Tendulkar, S. and Jain, L. 1995: Economic reforms and poverty. *Economic and Political Weekly*, 30, 1373–6.

Thakur, R. 1995: *The Government and Politics of India*. London: Macmillan.

Thapar, R. 1989: Imagined religious communities? Ancient history and the modern search for a Hindu identity. *Modern Asian Studies*, 23, 209–31.

Thorner, D. 1956: *The Agrarian Prospect in India*. New Delhi: Allied.

Thorner, D. 1964: *Agricultural Cooperatives in India: A Field Report.* London: Asia Publishing House.

—— and Thorner, A. 1962: *Land and Labour in India.* Bombay: Asia Publishing House.

Thurow, L. 1998: Asia: the collapse and the cure. *New York Review of Books,* 5 February, 22–6.

Tomlinson, B. R. 1978: *The Political Economy of the Raj, 1914–1947.* London: Macmillan.

Tomlinson, B. R. 1988: The historical roots of Indian poverty: issues in the economic and social history of modern South Asia. *Modern Asian Studies,* 22, 123–40.

Toye, J. 1981: *Public Expenditure and Indian Development Policy, 1960–1970.* Cambridge: Cambridge University Press.

—— 1987: *Dilemmas of Development: Reflections on the Counter-Revolution in Development Theory and Policy.* Oxford: Blackwell.

Upadhyay, C. 1988: *From Kulak to Capitalist: The Emergence of a New Business Community in Coastal Andhra Pradesh, India.* Unpublished Ph.D. thesis, Yale University.

Vaidyanathan, A. 1986: Labour use in rural India: a study of spatial and temporal variation. *Economic and Political Weekly,* 21, A130–46.

—— 1988: *India's Agricultural Development in a Regional Perspective.* Madras: Sangam Books.

Vanaik, A. 1990: *The Painful Transition: Bourgeois Democracy in India.* London: Verso.

—— 1997: *The Furies of Hindu Communalism.* London: Verso.

Varghese, N. V. 1999: Mass education. In the Alternative Survey Group's *Alternative Economic Survey, 1991–98,* Delhi: Rainbow Publishers, 130–2.

Varma, P. 1998: *The Great Indian Middle Class.* Delhi: Viking.

Varshney, A. 1993: Battling a past, forging a future? Ayodhya and beyond. In P. Oldenburg (ed.), *India Briefing 1993,* Boulder: Westview and The Asia Society, 9–42.

—— 1995: *Democracy, Development and the Countryside: Urban–Rural Struggles in India.* Cambridge: Cambridge University Press.

—— 1996: Mass politics or elite politics? India's economic reforms in comparative perspective. Mimeo: Department of Government, Harvard University.

—— 1998: Is India becoming more democratic? Mimeo: Department of Political Science, Columbia University.

van der Veer, P. 1994 *Religious Nationalisms: Hindus and Muslims in India.* Berkeley: University of California Press.

Vidal, D. 1998: When the gods drink milk! Empiricism and belief in contemporary Hinduism. *South Asia Research,* 18, 149–71.

Wade, R. 1982: The system of administrative and political corruption: canal irrigation in South India. *Journal of Development Studies,* 18, 287–328.

—— 1985: The market for public office: why the Indian state is not better at development. *World Development,* 13, 467–97.

—— 1990: *Governing the Market: Economic Theory and the Role of Government in East Asian Industrialization.* Princeton: Princeton University Press.

Walker, T. and Ryan, J. 1990: *Village and Household Economies in India's Semi-Arid Tropics.* Baltimore: Johns Hopkins University Press.

Wariavwalla, B. 1989: India in 1988: drift, disarray, or pattern? *Asian Survey,* 29, 189–98.

Washbrook, D. 1976: *The Emergence of Provincial Politics: The Madras Presidency, 1880–1920*. Cambridge: Cambridge University Press.
—— 1981: Law, state and society in colonial India. *Modern Asian Studies*, 15, 649–721.
—— 1988: Progress and problems: South Asian economic and social history, *c*.1720–1860. *Modern Asian Studies*, 22, 57–96.
—— 1989: Caste, class and dominance in modern Tamilnadu: Non-Brahmanism, Dravidianism and Tamil Nationalism. In F. Frankel and M. Rao (eds), *Dominance and State Power in Modern India: Decline of a Social Order*, vol. 1, Delhi: Oxford University Press, 204–64.
—— 1997: The rhetoric of democracy and development in late-colonial India. In S. Bose and A. Jalal (eds), *Nationalism, Democracy and Development: State and Politics in India*, Delhi: Oxford University Press, 36–49.
Weber, M. 1958: *The Religion of India* (translated by H. Gerth and D. Martindale). Glencoe, Illinois: Free Press.
Weiner, M. 1967: *Party Building in a New Nation: The Indian National Congress*. Chicago: University of Chicago Press.
—— 1982: Congress restored: continuities and discontinuities in Indian politics. *Asian Survey*, 22, 339–55.
—— 1987: Rajiv Gandhi: a mid-term assessment. In M. Bouton (ed.), *India Briefing, 1987*, Boulder: Westview, 1–23.
—— 1989: *The Indian Paradox: Essays in Indian Politics*. New Delhi: Sage.
—— 1999: The regionalization of Indian politics and its implications for economic reforms. In J. Sachs, A. Varshney and N. Bajpai (eds), *India in the Era of Economic Reforms*, Oxford: Oxford University Press, 261–95.
Williams, G. 1997: State, discourse, and development in India: the case of West Bengal's Panchayati Raj. *Environment and Planning A*, 29, 2099–112.
Wolf, M. 1982: *India's Exports*. Oxford: Oxford University Press.
Wolpert, S. 1996: *Nehru: A Tryst With Destiny*. Oxford: Oxford University Press.
Wood, J. R. 1984: Congress restored? The 'KHAM' strategy and Congress-(I) recruitment in Gujarat. In J. R. Wood (ed.), *State Politics in Contemporary India: Crisis or Continuity?*, Boulder: Westview, 197–227.
World Bank 1989a: *India: Poverty, Employment and Social Services*. Washington DC: The World Bank.
—— 1989b: *India: An Industrializing Economy in Transition*. Washington DC: The World Bank.
—— 1992: *Governance and Development*. Washington DC: The World Bank.
—— 1993: *The East Asian Miracle: Economic Growth and Public Policy*. Washington DC: The World Bank.
—— 1994: *Governance: The World Bank's Experience*. Washington DC: The World Bank.
—— 1997a: *World Development Report, 1997*. Oxford: Oxford University Press and the World Bank.
—— 1997b: *India 1997 Economic Update: Sustaining Rapid Growth*. World Bank: South Asia Region, Report No. 16506-IN, 30 May.
—— 1997c: *Primary Education in India*. Washington DC: The World Bank, and New Delhi: Allied Publishers Limited.
—— 1998: *India: 1998 Macroeconomic Update*. Washington DC: The World Bank.

Yadav, Y. 1996: Reconfiguration in Indian politics: State assembly elections 1993–95. *Economic and Political Weekly*, 31, 2–3.

—— and Kumar, S. 1999: Interpreting the mandate. *Frontline*, 5 November.

Zelliott, E. 1972: Gandhi and Ambedkar: a study in leadership. In M. Mahar (ed.), *The Untouchables in Contemporary India*, Tucson: University of Arizona Press.

—— 1992: *From Untouchable to Dalit: Essays on the Ambedkar Movement*. Delhi: Manohar.

Index